the

Romanticism, Economics and the Question of 'Culture'

PHILIP CONNELL

OXFORD
UNIVERSITY PRESS

OXFORD
UNIVERSITY PRESS

Great Clarendon Street, Oxford OX2 6DP

Oxford University Press is a department of the University of Oxford.
It furthers the University's objective of excellence in research, scholarship,
and education by publishing worldwide in

Oxford New York

Auckland Cape Town Dar es Salaam Hong Kong Karachi
Kuala Lumpur Madrid Melbourne Mexico City Nairobi
New Delhi Shanghai Taipei Toronto

With offices in
Argentina Austria Brazil Chile Czech Republic France Greece
Guatemala Hungary Italy Japan South Korea Poland Portugal
Singapore Switzerland Thailand Turkey Ukraine Vietnam

Oxford is a registered trade mark of Oxford University Press
in the UK and in certain other countries

Published in the United States
by Oxford University Press Inc., New York

First published 2001
First published in paperback 2005

British Library Cataloguing in Publication Data
Data available

Library of Congress Cataloging in Publication Data
Data available

ISBN 0–19–818505–7
ISBN 0–19–928205–6 (Pbk.)

1 3 5 7 9 10 8 6 4 2

Typeset by Best-set Typesetter Ltd, Hong Kong
Printed in Great Britain
on acid-free paper by
Biddles Ltd.,
King's Lynn, Norfolk

for Sophia

Preface and Acknowledgements

This book seeks to reassess the political context of British Romanticism. This is, of course, hardly a novel ambition and, in one way or another, has informed a great deal of recent critical writing on early nineteenth-century literature. The principal justification for my own engagement with this subject lies in the fact that, however sophisticated and self-interrogating literary scholars have proved themselves in questioning the historical constructions of a 'Romantic ideology', the same kinds of sceptical self-awareness have seldom been extended to their use of such concepts as 'laissez-faire', 'political economy', and 'bourgeois ideology'. Equally, however, historians of this period have usually proved quite reluctant to apply their own, more nuanced interpretations of these categories to our received understanding of canonical literary history. This has placed some important limitations on the literary historiography of the early nineteenth century, precisely because the historical identity of Romanticism itself has so often been defined in opposition to a normative understanding of liberal ideology, identified above all with the reductive, calculating rationality of utilitarianism and economic science.

The present study offers a new approach to the political identifications of both the Lake school and the Hunt circle, together with an argument for the broader significance of economic discourse within the cultural history of this period. Whereas political economy has often been regarded as a philistine and intellectually myopic science, I have sought to demonstrate its intersection with contemporary discussions of 'polite' literature and a pedagogic ideal of moral and intellectual 'culture'. And while Romantic writers such as Wordsworth and Shelley have typically been identified with an unambiguous hostility to industrial society and its intellectual apologists, I have tried to explore the far more compromised and accommodatory aspects of their relationships with political economy, utilitarianism, and the 'spirit of commerce'. To this end, the book draws on a range of primary sources and secondary scholarship, in an attempt to integrate the practices and preoccupations of literary criticism with those of political and intellectual history. This has at times meant adopting a few compromised and accommodatory positions of my own. Perhaps most obviously, my use of the term 'Romanticism' remains vulnerable to the perennial charge of historical anachronism. I have chosen to retain it, in the first place, as a means of further integrating canonical literary texts with the political and economic discourse of this period, but also as a foil for my attempts to call into question some of the uses of Romanticism as a category of nineteenth-century literary and intellectual history. Particularly in its conclusion, my argument bears directly on the issue of nineteenth- and twentieth-century canon formation, and this has inevitably dictated the focus and range of some of the earlier chapters.

It should already be clear that my approach is somewhat interdisciplinary in its inspiration and aims, and I hope that it will address the concerns of both historians and literary scholars in roughly equal measure. Whether or not it succeeds in this respect, I could not have sustained an ambition of this kind without the encouragement of colleagues and friends from both these disciplines (and others), many of whom have been kind enough to read and comment upon various sections of my argument. While any remaining errors or infelicities are of course my own responsibility, I should like to express my particular gratitude to John Beer, Sally Bushell, Marilyn Butler, Stefan Collini, Sophia Connell, David Craig, Simon Harrison, Boyd Hilton, Simon Jarvis, John Kerrigan, the late Tony Tanner, Gareth Stedman Jones, and Donald Winch. David Craig and Donald Winch have been particularly generous, over a sustained period, both in reading and criticizing my work on this subject, and in allowing me the opportunity to benefit from their own current research.

The book began as a doctoral dissertation undertaken at the University of Cambridge. Ralph Pite offered much-needed support and advice in the early stages of my research, and Nigel Leask, who guided the thesis to its conclusion, has been an invaluable and unfailing source of criticism and encouragement for several years. My research owes much to the assistance of the rare books staff of the Cambridge University and British Libraries; its preparation for publication has been aided by the attentions of Sophie Goldsworthy, Matthew Hollis, and Hilary Walford at Oxford University Press; while Anthea Connell fielded my art-historical enquiries concerning the cover illustration. Finally, I should like to thank the Master and Fellows of St John's College, Cambridge, for electing me to the Research Fellowship during which I not only wrote much of this book but also, more importantly, discovered its dedicatee.

Part of Chapter 1 has already appeared in print, and it is reproduced here with the permission of the editors of *Essays in Criticism*.

P.J.C.

Selwyn College
Cambridge
October 2000

Contents

Avaunt this œconomic rage!
What would it bring?—an iron age,
When Fact with heartless search explored
Shall be Imagination's Lord,
And sway with absolute controul
The god-like Functions of the Soul.
Not *thus* can Knowledge elevate
Our Nature from her fallen state.
With sober Reason Faith unites
To vindicate the ideal rights
Of Human-kind—the true agreeing
Of objects with internal seeing,
Of effort with the end of Being.

William Wordsworth, 'To the Utilitarians'
(comp. 1833)

But the age of chivalry is gone.—That of sophisters, oeconomists, and calculators, has succeeded; and the glory of Europe is extinguished for ever.

Edmund Burke, *Reflections on the Revolution in France* (1790)

Metaphysics, sir; metaphysics. Logic and moral philosophy. There we are at home. The Athenians only sought the way, and we have found it; and to all this we have added political economy, the science of the sciences.

Thomas Love Peacock, *Crotchet Castle* (1831)

LITTERATURE Occupation des oisifs
ECONOMIE POLITIQUE Science sans entrailles
LIVRE Quel qu'il soit, toujours trop long

Gustave Flaubert, *Dictionnaire des idées reçues*
(comp. *c.*1850)

Introduction: The Condition of England

> It would be scarcely possible for a man of Mr Southey's talents and acquirements to write two volumes so large as those before us, which should be wholly destitute of information and amusement. Yet we do not remember to have read with so little satisfaction any equal quantity of matter, written by any man of real abilities.

While it would surely be little consolation to Mr Southey, critical judgements are rarely so elegantly unforgiving as this. It stands at the head of an article in the *Edinburgh Review* for January 1830, and introduces a discussion of Robert Southey's *Colloquies on the Progress and Prospects of Society*, an extended prose jeremiad on the nation's ills which, it must be admitted, has never made for particularly entertaining reading.[1] Nevertheless, the issues at stake in its critical reception by the *Edinburgh* went far beyond the book's supposed literary deficiencies. For all its prolix eccentricity, the *Colloquies* made a timely, provocative, and influential contribution to public political debate during that volatile period in British constitutional history which saw the passage of Catholic Emancipation and the first Reform Act. Drawing a series of rather unfavourable historical comparisons between contemporary England and the period of the Reformation, Southey's book expressed equal measures of nostalgic regret at the passing of 'traditional' feudal society, and melancholy anxiety at the slow but insidious rise of a commercial economy, the 'manufacturing system', and the popular political agitation which, the author maintained, these developments had brought in their wake. The *Edinburgh Review*, as the leading Whig periodical of the time, a cautious enthusiast for the benefits of commercial society, and a long-standing supporter of moderate

[1] 'Southey's Colloquies on Society', *Edinburgh Review*, 50 (Jan. 1830), 528; Robert Southey, *Sir Thomas More: or, Colloquies on the Progress and Prospects of Society*, 2 vols. (1829).

constitutional reform, could hardly allow this profoundly conservative political disquisition to pass its critical notice unscathed.

Southey's ill-disguised sense of his own importance had landed him in trouble with reviewers and satirists before, and matters were not helped in the case of the *Colloquies* by his decision to frame the book's pronouncements on the perilous state of contemporary society in a series of dialogues with the ghost of Sir Thomas More, whom Southey imagined paying spectral social calls at his Lakeland home to warn the author of impending national crisis. The *Edinburgh* could not resist pointing out the more ludicrous and self-aggrandizing aspects of this conceit; but its raillery was marked by an underlying seriousness and urgency of intent. The *Colloquies* had already gained prominent, favourable notices in the two most important Tory journals, the *Quarterly Review* and *Blackwood's Edinburgh Magazine*, confirming Southey's position as one of the most respected conservative social critics of the day. It should come as no surprise, then, that the measured, Ciceronian temper of the review's opening sentences quickly takes on a more openly abrasive inflection. 'We have', its author continued,

> for some time past, observed with great regret the strange infatuation which leads the Poet-laureate to abandon those departments of literature in which he might excel, and to lecture the public on sciences of which he has still the very alphabet to learn. He has now, we think, done his worst. The subject which he has at last undertaken to treat is one which demands all the highest intellectual and moral qualities of a philosophical statesman,—an understanding at once comprehensive and acute,—a heart at once upright and charitable. Mr Southey brings to the task two faculties which were never, we believe, vouchsafed in measure so copious to any human being,—the faculty of believing without a reason, and the faculty of hating without a provocation.

Southey's failings as a 'philosophical statesman' thus went far beyond mere ignorance. Indeed, far from recognizing his deficiencies in the social 'sciences', he appeared to have dispensed with them altogether in favour of a rather more creative approach to the study of politics. 'Government', complained the *Edinburgh*, 'is to Mr Southey one of the fine arts'.

> He judges of a theory or a public measure, of a religion, a political party, a peace or a war, as men judge of a picture or a statue, by the effect produced

on his imagination. A chain of associations is to him what a chain of reasoning is to other men; and what he calls his opinions, are in fact merely his tastes.[2]

The review goes on to attack Southey's political conservatism, his religious intolerance, and his reductive, polarized view of British social conditions. But above all, it pursues this initial, overriding objection: the poet laureate's shamelessly aestheticized evaluation of the 'progress and prospects of society', and his abject failure to consider that a more rational and reliable approach to his subject matter might have resulted from a closer familiarity with the sciences of social and economic analysis.

The review's author, the journalist and aspiring politician Thomas Babington Macaulay, was ultimately destined for considerably greater celebrity than the unfortunate victim of his critical attentions. Yet Macaulay was still a relatively obscure figure in literary and political society at this time; certainly compared to Southey, who had held the laureateship since 1813 and who, in addition to his political writing, enjoyed a prominent, if turbulent reputation as a poet, historian, biographer, and lapsed republican radical. The young Macaulay, however, was not a complete stranger to controversy himself. He had already humbled the leading utilitarian political philosopher, James Mill, in a review of such severity that years later, at the height of his fame, he chose to suppress it from his collected essays out of respect for the memory of his victim.[3] The same courtesy was never extended to Southey (perhaps because he neglected to produce an intellectual heir of the stature and influence of John Stuart Mill). As a result, Macaulay's Victorian readers were able to appreciate his devastating attack on the *Colloquies*' portentous, reactionary analysis of British society as an important early response to what, by the mid-nineteenth century, could be described as the 'condition of England' question.

The enduring currency of this latter phrase, which is still very much part of our inherited vocabulary for describing nineteenth-century politics and culture, has on occasion tended to encourage a somewhat oversimplified view of the issues at stake. The very idea of a 'condition of England debate', as it is often expressed, can easily suggest a

2 'Southey's Colloquies', *Edinburgh Review*, 50 (Jan. 1830), 528.

3 Thomas Babington Macaulay, *Critical and Historical Essays, Contributed to the Edinburgh Review*, 3 vols. (1843), i, p. viii.

rather formalized public exchange, which left onlookers in no doubt as to who was doing the proposing, and who the opposing, and in which, in the best spirit of Victorian intellectual etiquette, both sides were agreed on the wording of the motion and the appropriate voting procedure. Such polemical punctilio was hardly characteristic of the vitriolic, politically charged atmosphere of early nineteenth-century reviewing in which Macaulay's essay was originally composed. Perhaps more importantly, however, the idea of a condition of England debate, and the adversarial figure of speech upon which it relies, is also commonly invoked as a kind of shorthand for a whole series of dialectical antagonisms—utilitarian and Romantic, science and feeling, the 'march of mind' and nostalgic medievalism, the cash nexus and moral economy—that have traditionally been understood to encapsulate some of the central preoccupations of nineteenth-century social criticism.

The explanatory potential of binary oppositions such as these provides a useful resource for political and cultural historians seeking to discover broad structural coherence in often heterogeneous subject matter. Indeed, the imposition of such conceptual taxonomies upon the ideological contours of early nineteenth-century British history might seem particularly appropriate given the apparent willingness of many contemporary observers to describe the intellectual character of the age in much the same terms. 'The spirit of philosophy in England, like that of religion, is still rootedly sectarian,' wrote John Stuart Mill in 1840. 'Conservative thinkers and Liberals, transcendentalists and admirers of Hobbes and Locke, regard each other as out of the pale of philosophical intercourse; look upon each other's speculations as vitiated by an original taint, which makes all study of them, except for purposes of attack, useless if not mischievous.'[4]

Macaulay's review of the *Colloquies* might seem to exemplify just this kind of bipartisan ideological intolerance. 'Here is wisdom,' the review witheringly remarks of Southey's political opinions: 'Here are the principles on which nations are to be governed. Rose-bushes and poor-rates, rather than steam-engines and independence. Mortality and cottages with weather-stains, rather than health and long life with edifices which time cannot mellow.'[5] Although intended in part as a parody of

[4] [John Stuart Mill], 'Coleridge', *London and Westminster Review*, 33 (Mar. 1840), 261.

[5] [Thomas Babington Macaulay], 'Southey's Colloquies', *Edinburgh Review*, 50 (Jan. 1830), 540.

Southey's naively impressionistic view of British social conditions, these succinct, boldly sketched antitheses remain highly suggestive. Employing, to opposite ends, the same method of allusive antithesis that Augustus Pugin would later exploit in his *Contrasts* (1836), Macaulay's comments effectively politicize the changing visual environment of nineteenth-century Britain, drawing together architecture, landscape, and social reform to evoke a far wider set of cultural and political antinomies—including, not least, those more abstract philosophical prejudices alluded to by Mill.[6]

The sustaining force of Macaulay's criticisms derives from the suggestion that his differences with Southey extended far beyond political opinion, to fundamental questions of method, and even sensibility. This was not simply a case of the poet laureate's idiosyncrasies as a political and social critic. Macaulay was concerned to address a much broader issue, centring upon the value of certain, broadly 'scientific' forms of socio-economic analysis, and their relation to an alternative strain of social criticism, which aligned itself in opposition to the new sciences of society, and which has subsequently come to be identified, above all, with the literary milieu of British Romanticism. In the most general terms, this opposition feeds directly into a much broader, and still operative, conception of 'Victorian thought and sensibility', sceptically adumbrated by Stefan Collini as resting upon

> a familiar dichotomy . . . between, on the one hand, the temper of rational science, leaning to positivism, receptive to Utilitarianism and political economy, and most commonly issuing in some kind of Liberal or reforming politics; and, on the other hand, the temper of essentially Romantic cultural critique, uneasy with modernity, suspicious of the reductive tendencies of science, hostile to the soulless reasonings of political economy, a temper whose political expression, where not straightforwardly Tory, veered, by an intelligible affinity, from a Carlylean authoritarianism to a Ruskinian or Morrisian Socialism.[7]

At the root of this influential view of Victorian culture, the basic terms of which were clearly already available in Macaulay's 1830

[6] Augustus Welby Pugin, *Contrasts; or, a Parallel Between the Noble Edifices of the Fourteenth and Fifteenth Centuries, and Similar Buildings of the Present Day; Shewing the Present Decay of Taste* (1836).

[7] Stefan Collini, *Public Moralists: Political Thought and Intellectual Life in Britain 1850–1930* (Oxford, 1991), 185–6.

review, lies a series of long-standing, and often belligerent disagreements over the nature and function of political economy, the most influential—and controversial—science of society in nineteenth-century Britain.

To an extent that literary and cultural historians of the Romantic era have tended to forget, political economy was *the* dominant mode of social analysis in this period. Looking back from the late 1870s, Walter Bagehot wrote that 'Political Economy was, indeed, the favourite subject in England from about 1810 to about 1840, and this to an extent which the present generation can scarcely comprehend'. Contemporary reactions certainly bear out this claim, often from rather unexpected quarters. 'But my best Canto, save one on Astronomy, / Will turn upon "Political Economy",' declared Byron at the conclusion of *Don Juan*, Canto XII (1823). '*That* is your present theme for popularity.' Although he never made good on this promise (not through lack of nerve, one suspects), Byron's judgement is confirmed by Henry Addington's remark, in 1826, that 'We hear nothing on all sides at dinners, parties, in church and at the theatre, but discussions of political economy and the distresses of the times.'[8] University chairs in the subject were established in Oxford, London, and Cambridge around this time, consolidating its respectability as an academic discipline. But political economy also had a significant presence in Parliament, in political journalism and pamphleteering, in the programmes of working-class education at the new 'mechanics' institutes', in the popular morality tracts of Harriet Martineau and Jane Marcet, and in the radical economic theories of Thomas Hodgskin, William Thompson, and John Francis Bray. It found supporters and exponents amongst Tories and Whigs, Anglicans and atheists, aristocrats and artisans. Yet the question of political economy's 'popularity' needs to be approached carefully, not just because it took so many different forms, but also because what inspired interest and discussion was often not so much the theoretical and empirical problems occupying contemporary economists themselves, as the political and social questions with which the discipline found itself linked, and the issue of its intrinsic value as a means to their solution.

[8] Walter Bagehot, *Economic Studies*, ed. Richard Holt Hutton (1880), 154; George Gordon, Lord Byron, *Complete Poetical Works*, ed. Jerome McGann, 7 vols. (Oxford, 1980–93), v. 521; Henry Addington to Charles Vaughan (2 Mar. 1826), quoted in Boyd Hilton, *The Age of Atonement: The Influence of Evangelicalism on Social and Economic Thought 1785–1865*, 2nd edn. (Oxford, 1991), 36.

The remarkable prominence of political economy during this period can be adequately explained only by reference to a variety of different causes, including not just the 'distresses of the times' mentioned by Addington, but also public policy debates over such issues as monetary convertibility, poor law reform, protectionism, and the peculiarities of the wartime economy.[9] On these issues, as on others, economic discourse played a crucial role in redefining the boundaries of political argument in an often reactionary post-revolutionary era. The opinions of contemporary economists gained an additional significance as a result of the growth of manufacturing and the 'machinery question', even if many of their fundamental assumptions continued to be derived from pre-industrial conditions.[10] But political economy also exercised a profound influence upon a whole range of issues surrounding what might be described as the cultural consequences of economic modernity, including the changing role of literature, education, and learning in a commercialized and industrializing society. Indeed, it is one of the claims of this book that our inherited sense of the incompatibility between literary sensibility and economic science has obscured the extent to which early nineteenth-century political economy, and the debate on its legitimacy, scope, and function, played a formative role in the emergence of the idea of 'culture' itself, as a humanistic or spiritual resource resistant to the intellectual enervation produced by modern, commercial societies.

It was precisely because these issues proved so divisive that the 'political economy question' quickly became linked to an increasingly intractable opposition between 'scientific' and 'literary' responses to social and economic change. This development is signalled particularly clearly in Macaulay's review, through the coruscating *reductio ad absurdum* with which he denies the sufficiency of the aesthetic as a mode of judgement appropriate to political and social questions:

> Mr Southey has found a way, he tells us, in which the effects of manufactures and agriculture may be compared. And what is this way? To stand on a hill, to look at a cottage and a manufactory, and to see which is prettier.

[9] Ibid. 37–8.

[10] Maxine Berg, *The Machinery Question and the Making of Political Economy 1815–1848* (Cambridge, 1980), 2–3; Donald Winch, *Riches and Poverty: An Intellectual History of Political Economy in Britain, 1750–1834* (Cambridge, 1996), 5–6.

Does Mr Southey think that the body of the English peasantry live, or ever lived, in substantial and ornamented cottages, with box-hedges, flower-gardens, bee-hives, and orchards? If not, what is his parallel worth? We despise those *filosofastri*, who think that they serve the cause of science by depreciating literature and the fine arts. But if any thing could excuse their narrowness of mind, it would be such a book as this. It is not strange that, when one enthusiast makes the picturesque the test of political good, another should feel inclined to proscribe altogether the pleasures of taste and imagination.[11]

The issues raised at this point prefigure what we often think of as a central area of contention within Victorian social criticism, a debate that was, perhaps, less concerned with the 'condition of England' itself than with the means by which that 'condition' might legitimately be identified and assessed. But Macaulay's remarks also imply that the leading terms of that later dispute were already beginning to achieve some currency. Moving, with a certain degree of equanimity, from Southey's 'picturesque' politics to the objectionable attitudes of philistine '*filosofastri*', the review alludes to a contemporary controversy—with which the reader is assumed to have some familiarity—concerning the relative merits of an 'aesthetic', affective evaluation of the public good, and the hard-headed, 'scientific' spirit of economic analysis and social reform.

The terms of this distinction become clearer in Macaulay's response to Southey's discussion of the 'manufacturing system' and, in particular, 'political economy'. Opposing hard fact to imaginative whimsy, the review accuses Southey of wilful ignorance, not just of actual social conditions in the new industrial towns, but also of the empirical and analytical tools by means of which such conditions might be more accurately determined and explained. Southey is taken to task for his failure to consult the parliamentary returns on poor relief levels and the demographic statistics on mortality rates but also, and above all, for his gross misunderstanding of the scientific 'laws' governing the nation's economy.[12] As we shall see, Southey himself considered economic science as a symptom of the corrupt, immoral tendency of contemporary society, and the product of a 'rank, noxious, putrescent and pestilential' philosophy.[13] For Macaulay, however, it was the most telling mark of Southey's

[11] [Macaulay], 'Southey's Colloquies', 540.
[12] Ibid. 539.
[13] Southey, *Colloquies*, ii. 262.

retreat into blinkered, nostalgic aestheticism that he was so wilfully ignorant of the true principles of economic science. Much of the review is given over to exposing the economic fallacies underlying the *Colloquies*' discussions of paper money, national debt, taxation, and public expenditure. Macaulay thereby suggested not just that Southey was unqualified to make judgements on such issues, but that his prejudice against the scientific principles of political economy had blinded him to its obvious value in formulating and applying a progressive, ameliorative legislative programme.

In spite of the exuberantly *ad hominem* attacks that enliven much of the review, Macaulay's arguments also had a much broader application to what he himself clearly regarded as some of the most fundamental issues governing contemporary political and literary life. Indeed, many of his remarks may well have been directed not just at the author of the *Colloquies*, but also at a young Scottish journalist called Thomas Carlyle, whose essay on 'Signs of the Times' had appeared in the *Edinburgh* the previous year. Carlyle had been keen to review the *Colloquies* himself but, unlike Macaulay, he shared something of Southey's dismay at the insidious ascendancy of a barren, materialistic spirit of socio-economic investigation.[14] 'Signs of the Times' is a fine example of Carlyle's strikingly original, and already well-formed prose style, which draws together idealist philosophy and the rhetoric of Calvinist and millenarian Christianity to forge a powerful and influential indictment of the contemporary 'Age of Machinery'.[15] Many of the themes of Carlyle's later social criticism were already in place in this essay, which defended a 'dynamic', spiritual form of human thought and experience against the calculating, empirical, and utilitarian spirit of the age. It was on the basis of this distinction that Carlyle would go on to address the 'condition of England' question (which he was, of course, the first to describe as such), and to popularize the heroic 'man of letters' as a kind of literary counterbalance to the corruptions of 'mechanistic' thought.[16] But the contemporary significance of 'Signs of the Times' rested firmly upon Carlyle's gifts for intellectual synthesis and rhetorical flair. For all its flamboyant stylistic originality,

[14] Wendell V. Harris, 'Interpretive Historicism: "Signs of the Times" and *Culture and Anarchy* in their Contexts', *Nineteenth-Century Literature*, 44 (1990), 445.

[15] [Thomas Carlyle], 'Signs of the Times', *Edinburgh Review*, 49 (June 1829), 438–59.

[16] Thomas Carlyle, *Past and Present* (1843), 1; id., *On Heroes, Hero-Worship, & the Heroic in History. Six Lectures* (1841).

the essay was heavily indebted both to German philosophical idealism, and to the English Lake poets' earlier attacks upon political economy and individualist ethics, including those of Southey himself.[17] Indeed, to the extent that 'Signs of the Times' draws on Southey's *Colloquies* as one of its subtexts, Macaulay's review of the latter can, in turn, be seen as an implicit response to Carlyle's 'spiritual' critique of reductive, mechanistic forms of social and economic analysis. In defending the value of political economy against Southey's reliance upon 'taste and feeling', Macaulay was also discreetly, but firmly, rebutting Carlyle's recent attempt to align the *Edinburgh Review* with the picturesque politicians of the Lake school.

In the year following Macaulay's review, Thomas Love Peacock published the jovially irreverent novel of ideas *Crotchet Castle*. His earlier gothic pastiche *Nightmare Abbey* (1818) had satirized the spirit of morbid introspection and foggy philosophizing which, in the persons of Shelley, Byron, and Coleridge, descended upon English literary culture in the years following Waterloo. In 1831, with the Shelley circle long dispersed and Coleridge terminally quiescent, Peacock turned his attention to the debate on the nature and value of political economy. *Crotchet Castle* gives a prominent place to a witty burlesque on this new 'science of the sciences' in the character of 'Mr Mac Quedy', Peacock's sobriquet for John Ramsay McCulloch, the recently appointed Professor of Political Economy at the new London University.[18] A humourless and pedantic Scotsman, Mac Quedy embodies many of the characteristics that were coming to be habitually identified with political economy by its detractors in the world of polite literature and belles-lettres. Peacock was by no means as damning in his implied criticism as some of his contemporaries, yet the picture he offers is representative enough. The intellectual hubris and reductive materialism supposedly associated with economic science are summed up in Mac Quedy's assertion that 'Nothing is so easy as to lay down the outlines of perfect society. There wants nothing but money to set it going.' The economist is scornful of a certain nostalgic view of the national past that he considers hopelessly romanticized, and is a supporter of the 'Steam Intellect Society', an association for popular scientific education modelled by Peacock on Henry Brougham's Society for the Diffusion of Useful

[17] On Carlyle's debt to Southey, see David Eastwood, 'Robert Southey and the Intellectual Origins of Romantic Conservatism', *English Historical Review*, 104 (1989), 315.

[18] [Thomas Love Peacock], *Crotchet Castle* (1831), 30.

Knowledge. Yet for all his utopian meliorism, Mac Quedy possesses a narrowly Benthamite view of psychological motivation, and seems completely lacking in distress or indignation when contemplating the widespread poverty that his system purports to 'explain' according to immutable scientific laws.[19]

In intellectual terms, Mac Quedy's polar opposite in the novel is Mr Skionar, the 'transcendental poet' whose nebulous philosophical pronouncements on Mac Quedy's opinions were themselves intended by Peacock as a thinly veiled parody of Coleridge's more recondite criticisms of political economy and the 'mechanical' systems of thought from which he considered it to derive. 'Your philosophy', Skionar pompously informs Mac Quedy in a typically overblown effusion of intellect, 'is too literal for our imperfect vision. We cannot look directly into the nature of things; we can only catch glimpses of the mighty shadow in the camera obscura of transcendental intelligence.' The novel's characters expostulate back and forth in a series of mock philosophical dialogues, in which their intellectual incompatibilities often appear so comically extreme as to preclude even that degree of mutual comprehension which might allow them to recognize their differences.[20]

Peacock ultimately appears not so much to have been taking sides as attempting to depict, through the lens of fictional satire, a rapidly widening fault line within British intellectual life. Like Carlyle, albeit rather more even-handedly, he was responding to an important new set of distinctions within political and literary discourse, centred in the first instance upon the confrontational claims of moral imagination and economic science, but broadening into a more fundamental opposition between literature, aesthetics, and feeling, on the one hand; and science, utility, and reason, on the other. During the late 1820s these antitheses became peculiarly intransigent, resulting in an influential rhetoric of ideological and attitudinal disjunction—or 'two cultures', as it has sometimes been described—that would form an enduring element of British intellectual life until well into the twentieth century (and perhaps beyond).[21] But, while political economy, utilitarianism, and the 'march of mind' would henceforth find themselves, more often than not,

[19] Ibid. 99–100.

[20] Ibid. 48–9; Marilyn Butler, *Peacock Displayed: A Satirist in his Context* (1969).

[21] Cf. Stefan Collini, 'Introduction' to C. P. Snow, *The Two Cultures* (Cambridge, 1993), pp. x–xi; Wolf Lepenies, *Die Drei Kulturen* (1985), trans. R. J. Hollingdale as *Between Literature and Science: The Rise of Sociology* (Cambridge, 1988).

in profound and enduring tension with the claims of literature, tradition, and the Romantic 'culture of feelings', the origins of these antagonisms, in the post-revolutionary era of the early nineteenth century, are both more equivocal, and more complex, than Macaulay, Peacock, and Carlyle might have led us to expect.

CHAPTER ONE

'A deeper nature': Malthus, Poetry, and Political Economy

The year 1798 has traditionally enjoyed a certain prominence in the canons of both English literature and economic thought. In each case, however, the justification for such distinction can no longer be considered entirely self-evident. For historians of political economy, 1798 is notable, above all, as the year in which Thomas Robert Malthus's *Essay on the Principle of Population* first appeared. There is no doubt of the tremendous influence of this work, nor of the enduring notoriety it quickly achieved. But Malthus's 'population principle'—the claim that population growth will always tend to outstrip the means of subsistence—was, as the author himself conceded, heavily indebted to the earlier demographic speculations of Hume, Smith, and Wallace. The significance of the 1798 edition of the *Essay on Population* for the development of 'classical' economic theory was, in most other respects, relatively minor. Arguments for the first *Essay*'s originality and importance as a contribution to economic analysis have therefore tended to rest upon its claims to methodological novelty and, more specifically, Malthus's supposed synthesis of eighteenth-century political economy with the experimental rigour of Newtonian natural science.[1] More recently, however, the idea that Malthus's *Essay* marked a significant step towards a positivist, secular science of economics has become rather more contentious, as a result of historical research suggesting that the book was one of the earliest, and most important examples of an intellectual alliance between Christianity and political economy which was to play a crucial role in moderating the ideological tensions

[1] See James Bonar, *Malthus and his Work* (1885), 2nd edn. (1924), 38–43; and, latterly, Gertrude Himmelfarb, *The Idea of Poverty: England in the Early Industrial Age* (1984), 101; Deborah A. Redman, *The Rise of Political Economy as a Science: Methodology and the Classical Economists* (Cambridge, Mass., 1997), 271–2.

of Britain's *ancien régime* during the early years of the nineteenth century.[2] This persuasive new assessment of the *Essay on Population* as Anglican political polemic has also helped to reaffirm Malthus's moderate, reformist Whiggism, in the face of the widespread, and remarkably persistent misconception of the *Essay*'s politics as either straightforwardly reactionary or, at the very least, so morally deracinated as to render its author a callously unreflective apologist of existing social inequality.[3]

A similarly revisionist attitude is now an established component of the critical discussion surrounding the most celebrated literary publication of 1798, the *Lyrical Ballads* of Wordsworth and Coleridge. Long considered the *terminus ad quem* of eighteenth-century literary neoclassicism and the originary moment of English Romanticism, Wordsworth's self-consciously 'experimental' verse, which he later identified with the 'real language of men', has also typically been understood to reflect an essentially democratic aesthetic, coordinate with the radical humanitarianism of his poetry. William Hazlitt was one of the earliest and most influential proponents of this view that Wordsworth's poetry 'partakes of, and is carried along with, the revolutionary movement of our age'.[4] Yet, as with Malthus's *Essay*, there have for some time been quite serious doubts about the extent to which the *Lyrical Ballads* can be described as in any sense a 'revolutionary' text. The ballad revival, magazine poetry, sentimentalism, and that late-eighteenth-century strain of poetic subjectivism sometimes termed 'preromanticism' can all be cited in qualification of the collection's claims to represent a watershed in English literary sensibilities.[5] In turn, the politically radical credentials of the *Lyrical Ballads* have become rather more questionable, and while the issue inevitably remains subject to

[2] D. L. LeMahieu, 'Malthus and the Theology of Scarcity', *Journal of the History of Ideas*, 40 (1979), 467–74; J. M. Pullen, 'Malthus's Theological Ideas and their Influence on his Principle of Population', *History of Political Economy*, 13 (1981), 39–54; Edmund M. Santurri, 'Theodicy and Social Policy in Malthus's Thought', *Journal of the History of Ideas*, 63 (1982), 315–30; A. M. C. Waterman, *Revolution, Economics and Religion: Christian Political Economy, 1798–1833* (Cambridge, 1991).

[3] On Malthus's politics, see Winch, *Riches and Poverty*, 253–5.

[4] Wordsworth, *Prose Works*, ed. W. J. B. Owen and Jane Worthington Smyser, 3 vols. (Oxford, 1974), i. 116–18; [William Hazlitt], *The Spirit of the Age: or Contemporary Portraits*, 2nd edn. (1825), 233.

[5] See Heather Glen, *Vision and Disenchantment: Blake's* Songs *and Wordsworth's* Lyrical Ballads (Cambridge, 1983); Mary Jacobus, *Tradition and Experiment in Wordsworth's* Lyrical Ballads *(1798)* (Oxford, 1976); Robert Mayo, 'The Contemporaneity of the *Lyrical Ballads*', *Publications of the Modern Language Association of America*, 69 (1954), 486–522.

debate, literary historians have shown an increased tendency to stress the counter-revolutionary, or at least incipiently apostatic attitudes and influences latent in Wordsworth's verse of the late 1790s.

It should, then, no longer be possible to regard the political instincts of these two writers, at least during this critical period, as quite so divergent as has often been assumed. Nevertheless, their broader situation within nineteenth-century political and literary history continues to be informed by the presumption that, in terms of their intellectual formation, ideological orientation, and perhaps even moral sensibilities, Malthus and Wordsworth were fundamentally inimical to one another. Particularly within literary historiography, attitudes to the original circumstances and significance of the Malthusian controversy have often been conditioned by the idea of an antagonistic encounter between English Romanticism and the new sciences of nineteenth-century society, of which Malthusian economics, together with Benthamite utilitarianism, are commonly held to have been the principal representatives. The tradition of Romantic anti-economism in British social criticism began with the response to Malthus's *Essay* on the part of the 'Lake school' of poets, comprising Wordsworth, Coleridge, and Southey. That response, we tend to assume, was urgent, uncompromising, and sustained; a 'prolonged campaign of abuse', in Donald Winch's words.[6] To suggest, as one recent critic has, that 'Wordsworth and Malthus responded in similar ways to the same cultural moment' might therefore seem, at least at first glance, to betray either a wilful insensitivity to the conventions of British cultural history, or (which often amounts to the same thing) a significant lapse of literary critical tact.[7] Yet, as Winch himself has done much to demonstrate, because the original grounds of the Lake school's reaction to Malthus have been overshadowed by their subsequent denunciations of 'political economy' more generally, the precise character of their original response to the *Essay on Population* has often been taken for granted.[8] The more nuanced aspects

[6] Winch, *Riches and Poverty*, 288.

[7] Marilyn Gaull, 'Malthus on the Road to Excess', in Richard Cronin (ed.), *1798: The Year of the* Lyrical Ballads (Basingstoke, 1998), 94. See also Frances Ferguson, *Solitude and the Sublime: Romanticism and the Aesthetics of Individuation* (New York, 1992), 114–28; Thomas Pfau, *Wordsworth's Profession: Form, Class, and the Logic of Early Romantic Cultural Production* (Stanford, Calif., 1997), 341–62.

[8] In addition to chs. 11 and 12 of his *Riches and Poverty*, see also Donald Winch, 'Mr Gradgrind and Jerusalem', in Stefan Collini *et al.* (eds.), *Economy, Polity, and Society: British Intellectual History 1750–1950* (Cambridge, 2000), 243–66.

of the *Essay*'s initial reception that have already come to light demonstrate the complexity of the Lake poets' original encounter with the 'dismal science', as well as indicating something of the broader pattern of criticism and tacit engagement that was to characterize the subsequent relationship between political economy and Lake school literary conservatism.

Nevertheless, an adequately contextualized account of the early years of the Malthusian controversy has taken a surprisingly long time to emerge. This is not just because of a traditional predisposition to treat the debate sparked by the *Essay on Population* as a kind of intellectual backdrop for the 1834 Poor Law.[9] It can also be traced to the nineteenth-century legacy of Lake school anti-economism, which, in a more obviously judgemental but similarly anachronistic fashion, did much to inspire that influential view of Malthus's *Essay* as a cruel harbinger of the Victorian workhouse system, and little else besides. As a result, a less prejudiced understanding of the *Essay*'s place within contemporary social and political argument during the French revolutionary wars will require some further reappraisal of the original encounter between Malthus's anti-utopian polemic and the small circle of writers who were later to become its most trenchant critics.

WORDSWORTH AMONG THE ECONOMISTS: THE CASE OF 'THE OLD CUMBERLAND BEGGAR'

In the late summer of 1798, the Wordsworths and Coleridge travelled to London, *en route* for Yarmouth and a boat to Germany. The two poets took the opportunity to visit their London publisher, Joseph Johnson, to whom Wordsworth had recently (and unsuccessfully) attempted to transfer responsibility for their forthcoming *Lyrical Ballads*, after growing dissatisfied with the Bristol bookseller Joseph Cottle. Before they left town, Johnson provided Coleridge with a copy of Malthus's *Essay*, which he himself had published that June. Although this first edition of the *Essay* appeared anonymously, it is extremely likely that Coleridge soon discovered the name of its author—a name which, moreover, he would probably have recognized. Malthus was a fellow

[9] More recent research on the New Poor Law is surveyed in David Eastwood, 'Rethinking the Debates on the Poor Law in Early Nineteenth-Century England', *Utilitas*, 6 (1994), 97–116; Peter Mandler, 'The Making of the New Poor Law Redivivus', *Past and Present*, 117 (1987), 131–57.

Cantabrigian, had been taught by Coleridge's tutor William Frend, and was a non-residing fellow of Jesus College, the scene of Coleridge's own, briefer, and rather less successful academic career. In London, Malthus was a *habitué* of the same liberal dissenting circles around Johnson and the Aikin family with which Coleridge also enjoyed contacts.[10] William Frend, for one, was aware of Malthus's authorship of the *Essay* soon after its publication, and if Johnson himself did not apprise Coleridge of the book's author when handing over the *Essay*, it seems extremely unlikely that he would not soon have discovered it through another of their mutual friends and acquaintances, in either Cambridge or London. The poets may even have heard, and to varying degrees approved, of Malthus's educational background in Gilbert Wakefield's dissenting academy at Warrington, his heterodox theological opinions, and his friendship with the more liberal members of the Jesus College fellowship such as William Otter.[11] The intellectual character of the *Essay* clearly marked it out as a distinctive, if somewhat unorthodox product of Cambridge latitudinarian theology, an association that may also have been suggested by Johnson's Cambridge connections with unitarian writers such as Wakefield, and of course Coleridge himself.

The *Essay*'s full title, which announced that the volume contained critical 'remarks' on the perfectibilist philosophies of William Godwin and the Marquis de Condorcet, further recommended the book to the attention of both poets. With Coleridge's encouragement, Wordsworth was at this time engaged in planning and composing an epic poem, provisionally entitled *The Recluse or views of Nature, Man, and Society*. The *Recluse* project was to haunt Wordsworth's entire literary career, but, in its inception, the poem can best be understood as the imaginative expression of his growing disillusionment with Godwin's theory of rational benevolence, and the naturalized expression of Coleridge's alternative, pantheistic philosophy of the 'One Life'.[12] Coleridge himself had

[10] Gerald P. Tyson, *Joseph Johnson: A Liberal Publisher* (Iowa City, 1979), 171–4; Patricia James, *Population Malthus: His Life and Times* (1979), 81–2; Winch, *Riches and Poverty*, 339.

[11] Frida Knight, *University Rebel: The Life of William Frend (1757–1841)* (1971), 303; Ben Ross Schneider, *Wordsworth's Cambridge Education* (Cambridge, 1957), 145–6; John Gascoigne, *Cambridge in the Age of Enlightenment: Science, Religion and Politics from the Restoration to the French Revolution* (Cambridge, 1989), 227; James, *Population Malthus*, 19–55.

[12] Dorothy and William Wordsworth, *Letters*, ed. Ernest de Selincourt, 2nd edn., rev. and ed. Chester L. Shaver *et al.* (Oxford, 1967–88), i. 214 (11 Mar. 1798). Stephen Gill, *William Wordsworth: A Life* (Oxford, 1989), 143–4; Nicola Trott, 'The Coleridge Circle

been planning 'a book of Morals in answer to Godwin', a treatise which, he anticipated, would also demonstrate 'the defects of all the systems of morality before & since Christ'. This typically immodest proposal was, however, quickly subsumed in his equally ambitious hopes for *The Recluse* and its author, the 'Giant Wordsworth'.[13] The latter's fragmentary *Essay on Morals*, composed in Germany in late 1798, certainly suggests that Wordsworth was taking his new vocation as philosopher-poet seriously. The *Essay on Morals* addresses 'such books as Mr Godwyn's [and] Mr. Paley's', dismissing their works as excessively reliant upon the faculty of 'reason', and recommending instead a language that will 'melt into our affections' so as to secure right action through the associative force of habitual feeling. Although brief and suggestive, the *Essay on Morals* clearly gestures towards the sublimation of moral philosophy in a poetic rendering of human suffering capable of a truly affective moral education, and it seems to have been in these terms that Wordsworth conceived his projected synthesis of poetry and philosophy in *The Recluse*.[14]

Given all these circumstances, it would certainly be surprising if Malthus's own, independent critique of Godwinian rational benevolence did not attract Wordsworth's close attention.[15] But a concern with the shortcomings of Godwin's *Political Justice* was by no means the only intellectual preoccupation that Wordsworth and Malthus shared in common during this period. For in addition to its direct and extensive attacks upon Godwin and Condorcet, the *Essay on Population* also included a discussion of destitution, charity, and poor relief (which, of course, was eventually to become one of the most notorious sections of the entire book). Wordsworth had been composing a poem on just these themes since 1797—a poem that in 1798 he still considered an inte-

and "The Answer to Godwin"', *Review of English Studies*, NS 41 (1990), 229; Nicholas Roe, *Wordsworth and Coleridge: The Radical Years* (Oxford, 1988), 62, 233; Jonathan Wordsworth, *William Wordsworth: The Borders of Vision* (Oxford, 1982), 350–1. See also Kenneth Johnston, *Wordsworth and* The Recluse (New Haven, 1984), 3–52.

[13] Coleridge, *Collected Letters*, ed. Earl Leslie Griggs, 6 vols. (Oxford, 1956–71), i. 184 (Apr. 1797); i. 267 (Dec. 1796); i. 391 (Mar. 1798).

[14] Wordsworth, *Prose Works*, i. 103–4; see Alan Bewell, *Wordsworth and the Enlightenment: Nature, Man, and Society in the Experimental Poetry* (New Haven, 1989), 6–29.

[15] Hence Duncan Wu suggests that Wordsworth read the first *Essay* sometime before 14 Sept. 1798. The circumstantial evidence that Wordsworth was also familiar with subsequent editions of the *Essay* is suggestive, but somewhat less compelling, and my citations of Malthus's texts below will reflect this fact: Wu, *Wordsworth's Reading 1770–1799* (Cambridge, 1993), 94.

gral part of *The Recluse*, but which was subsequently to be entitled 'The Old Cumberland Beggar' when he chose to include it, substantially unmodified, in the second edition of *Lyrical Ballads* in 1800.

This poem has long occupied a central position within the critical canon of Wordsworth's early poetry. It 'stands as the most explicitly political verse' that he composed during this period, but also raises many of the same questions—of private morality and public policy towards the poor—that are addressed by Malthus's *Essay*.[16] As such, it has often been discussed in the context of the late-eighteenth-century poor law debate—a debate to which the *Essay on Population* was, of course, one of the most significant contributions. But the precise relation between Malthus's *Essay*, eighteenth-century 'political economy', and 'The Old Cumberland Beggar' remains unclear. Indeed, what might be described as the 'anti-economistic' interpretation of the poem's argument can prove something of an obstacle, not just to the accurate reconstruction of Wordsworth's initial response to Malthus, but also to our broader appreciation of the original grounds for the later, Lake school critique of political economy more generally.

'The Old Cumberland Beggar' grew out of an earlier, essentially descriptive poetic exercise, to which the author added an admonitory philosophical commentary in the spring of 1798; and this was more or less the form in which Wordsworth decided to publish it, two years later. The poem's argument centres on the claim that the aged and solitary beggar of the title, well known to the local villagers upon whose charity he relies, should be allowed to remain at large 'in the eye of Nature', rather than forced to endure the 'pent-up din' of the local workhouse. Only while he is at liberty will the charitable instincts of the local population be quickened, since

> Where'er the aged Beggar takes his rounds
> The mild necessity of use compels
> To acts of love . . .[17]

The poem has often prompted unease in its readers, though not always for quite the same reasons. Its didactic manner, and bluntly utilitarian justification for the social benefits to be derived from itinerant

[16] James Chandler, *Wordsworth's Second Nature: A Study of the Poetry and Politics* (Chicago, 1984), 84.

[17] Wordsworth, Lyrical Ballads *and Other Poems, 1797–1800*, ed. James Butler and Karen Green (Ithaca, NY, 1992), 233–4 (ll. 188, 173, 90–2). Subsequent references to line numbers will be provided in the text.

pauperism, have sometimes appeared to demand explanation, even exculpation.[18] The general tone of more recent criticism has itself been rather less charitable, and more insistently uncomfortable with the way in which the beggar's welfare is almost entirely subordinated to the moral edification of the rural society that maintains him.[19]

The utility for which the poem argues lies not in the beggar's suffering as such, but rather in the social 'visibility' of that suffering (a nice distinction, of course, from the old man's point of view). His regular interactions with the villagers are shown to possess a positive moral value chiefly for his benefactors, whose habitual acts of charity not only allow the possibility of enduring, active virtue, but also bind them together into a morally responsible community—albeit a community from which, except in the most idealized and abstract sense, the beggar is perforce excluded:

> 'Tis Nature's law
> That none, the meanest of created things,
> Of forms created the most vile and brute,
> The dullest or most noxious, should exist
> Divorced from good, a spirit and pulse of good,
> A life and soul to every mode of being
> Inseparably link'd. While thus he creeps
> From door to door, the Villagers in him
> Behold a record which together binds
> Past deeds and offices of charity
> Else unremember'd, and so keeps alive
> The kindly mood in hearts which lapse of years,
> And that half-wisdom half-experience gives
> Make slow to feel, and by sure steps resign
> To selfishness and cold oblivion cares.
>
> (ll. 73–87)

It is Wordsworth's stress upon the moral interdependence of human society, and the central role of charitable benevolence in sustaining it,

[18] Charles and Mary Lamb, *Letters*, ed. E. V. Lucas, 3 vols. (1935), i. 239–40 (Jan. 1801); Stephen Gill, 'Wordsworth's Breeches Pocket: Attitudes to the Didactic Poet', *Essays in Criticism*, 19 (1969), 385–401; David Sampson, 'Wordsworth and the Poor: The Poetry of Survival', *Studies in Romanticism*, 23 (1984), 31–59.

[19] See e.g. Robin Jarvis, 'Wordsworth and the Uses of Charity', in Stephen Copley and John Whale (eds.), *Beyond Romanticism: New Approaches to Texts and Contexts 1780–1832* (1992), 200–17; David Simpson, *Wordsworth's Historical Imagination: The Poetry of Displacement* (New York, 1987), 162–74.

that underlie the poem's exhortation, directed at certain proud and officious 'Statesmen', to reconsider the beggar's social value—to 'deem not this man useless' (l. 67).

This polemical insistence upon the social utility of pauperism suggests that 'The Old Cumberland Beggar' might be read in critical counterpoint to a more crassly utilitarian, quasi-Malthusian view of the dependent poor as little more than a 'redundant population'. There are indeed certain obvious attractions to such an approach. Wordsworth's fundamental stress upon the virtue of charitable benevolence seems in general terms quite compatible with that influential representation of political economy, later popularized by the Lake poets themselves, as an abstract and unfeeling science which reduces all human behaviour, in Coleridge's words, 'to debtor and creditor accounts on the ledgers of self-love'.[20] Even more suggestively, however, the poem ends by registering Wordsworth's distrust of the constricting, artificial, and overcrowded environment of the workhouse:

> May never House, misnamed of industry,
> Make him a captive; for that pent-up din,
> Those life-consuming sounds that clog the air,
> Be his the natural silence of old age.
>
> (ll. 172–5)

It is this concluding section of 'The Old Cumberland Beggar' that provides the most obvious justification for reading the poem within the context of contemporary economic argument. Wordsworth's final remarks on the workhouse system, in particular, invite interpretation as a barely disguised attack on an increasingly influential body of social thought, soon to be associated with the writings of Malthus and Jeremy Bentham, which sought to reduce the public provision of poor relief to a system of centralized administration and punitive deterrence (or, more euphemistically, 'less eligibility'), rather than collective moral responsibility.

It might seem quite unproblematic, then, that 'The Old Cumberland Beggar' has often been treated as an implicit critique of political economy as a legitimate approach to the problems of destitution and pauperism. Even if we allow for the fact that Wordsworth had not read Malthus's *Essay* when he first began the poem, it can still, with the

[20] Samuel Taylor Coleridge, *The Statesman's Manual* (1816), in *Lay Sermons*, ed. R. J. White (London and Princeton, 1972), 76.

benefit of hindsight, be interpreted as a pre-emptive blow against 'the economists just then emerging as a distinct force in politics', and the first offensive in a long war of attrition that involved not just Malthusian economics, but also the calculating spirit of Benthamite utilitarianism.[21] Some such interpretation of the poem was, indeed, encouraged by Wordsworth himself in later life. In 1843 he dictated a note on 'The Old Cumberland Beggar', which has often been printed with the poem and is frequently cited in its critical discussion. The 'Fenwick note', as it has come to be known, refers back to the period of the poem's composition in order to claim that

> The political economists were about that time beginning their war upon mendicity in all its forms & by implication, if not directly, on Alms-giving also. This heartless process has been carried as far as it can go by the AMENDED poor-law bill, tho' the inhumanity that prevails in this measure is somewhat disguised by the profession that one of its objects is to throw the poor upon the voluntary donations of their neighbours, that is, if rightly interpreted, to force them into a condition between relief in the union poor House & Alms robbed of their Christian grace & spirit, as being *forced* rather from the benevolent than given by them, while the avaricious & selfish, & all in fact but the humane & charitable, are at liberty to keep all they possess from their distressed brethren.[22]

The Fenwick note goes out of its way to identify the historical moment of 'The Old Cumberland Beggar' as the starting point for a fateful struggle between 'Christian grace and spirit' (implicitly identified with the sentiments of Wordsworth's poem), and the 'heartless' political imperatives of the new economic science, culminating in the (arguably) Benthamite and Malthusian provisions of the Poor Law Amendment Act of 1834. Wordsworth's claim is perhaps made more plausible by the fact that a defence of voluntary charity as a legitimate response to economic distress is common to both the 1843 note and the original poem. Yet it is the differences between the two documents that are most striking:

[21] David Bromwich, *Disowned by Memory: Wordsworth's Poetry of the 1790s* (Chicago, 1998), 35. See also, *inter alia*, Simpson, *Wordsworth's Historical Imagination*, 168; Mark Koch, 'Utilitarian and Reactionary Arguments for Almsgiving in Wordsworth's "The Old Cumberland Beggar"', *Eighteenth-Century Life*, NS 13 (1989), 23. Wordsworth's lack of familiarity with Bentham's writings of the 1790s is convincingly argued by John Rieder, who nevertheless persists in reading the poem as a critique of an 'emergent laissez-faire version of rational calculation'. See *Wordsworth's Counterrevolutionary Turn: Community, Virtue, and Vision in the 1790s* (1997), 69.

[22] William Wordsworth, *The Fenwick Notes*, ed. Jared Curtis (1993), 56.

the poem's telling refusal to identify charitable feeling with Christian morality, for example; but also, and above all, the Fenwick note's vigorous attack on 'political economists' as the scourge of charitable feeling, an association that is as conspicuously absent from the argument of the original poem as it is from the late-eighteenth-century debate on charity and poor law reform as a whole.

This is not, of course, to suggest that contemporary discussions of the poor relief question cannot provide an important and informative context for understanding Wordsworth's poem. In common with 'The Old Cumberland Beggar', critical commentators on the poor law at this time, whether outright abolitionists like Joseph Townsend, or administrative reformers such as Frederick Morton Eden, often tended to denigrate the workhouse system as damaging to the philanthropic, socially cohesive instincts of the population. Eden's *State of the Poor* (1797), for example, argued for the relative inefficacy of organized poor relief, and the positive value of private charity, as a means of preserving the nation's moral virtue.[23] The *Dissertation on Benevolence* (1795), by Coleridge's unitarian acquaintance George Dyer, took a similar line. Rational dissenting attitudes to charity placed a particular stress upon the importance of private philanthropy, partly because of their hostility to state interference in matters of conscience. Dyer was certainly willing to consider the argument that 'publick charities' such as workhouses and infirmaries, 'far from being blessings to a community, are rather its bane . . . the man who contributes largely to their support would be more usefully and more benevolently employed, in relieving the distresses of individuals'.[24] Several other contemporary philosophical discussions of the ethics of private charity can also provide us with valuable insights into the intellectual background of Wordsworth's poem. Godwin himself had composed an essay on just this theme, entitled 'On Beggars', for his *Enquirer* (1797); and William Paley, probably the most influential English moral philosopher of the period, had included a discussion

[23] See Gary Harrison's exhaustive contextualization of 'The Old Cumberland Beggar' in relation to eighteenth-century attitudes to charity: *Wordsworth's Vagrant Muse: Poetry, Poverty and Power* (Detroit, 1994), 139–71. Frederic Morton Eden, *The State of the Poor*, 3 vols. (1797); [Joseph Townsend], *A Dissertation on the Poor Laws* (1786). See also J. R. Poynter, *Society and Pauperism: English Ideas on Poor Relief, 1795–1834* (1969), 111–17.

[24] George Dyer, *A Dissertation on the Theory and Practice of Benevolence* (1795), 104, quoted in G. M. Ditchfield, 'English Rational Dissent and Philanthropy', in Hugh Cunningham and Joanna Innes (eds.), *Charity, Philanthropy and Reform: From the 1690s to 1850* (Basingstoke, 1998), 202.

of charitable benevolence in his *Principles of Moral and Political Philosophy* (1785). Godwin's 'On Beggars' proposed that paupers should not be regarded as 'useless' if they are rationally articulate, and demonstrate a transparent sincerity in their request for alms—an argument against which the 'natural silence' (l. 175) of Wordsworth's vacant and inscrutable old man stands as an obvious and extreme counterexample.[25] Godwin and Paley were also, of course, the two authors whom Wordsworth was to single out for attack in his *Essay on Morals* and it may not, therefore, be uncoincidental that the *Essay on Morals* goes on to illustrate its argument through a discussion of the different ways in which an affecting 'tale of distress' might elicit charitable relief from a disparate group of listeners.[26] The question of the proper relation of private and public charity was clearly a pressing one at this time. But, far from being the exclusive reserve of political economists and secular utilitarians, it seems to have exercised a whole range of different writers, including social reformers, moral philosophers, Anglican theologians, and religious radicals, many of whom expressed extreme dissatisfaction with existing forms of charity, both public and private, without adopting a particularly economistic or 'calculating' outlook.

From this perspective, Wordsworth's early hostility to the workhouse system seems neither so prescient, nor so clearly directed against the 'new' economic science, as the Fenwick note goes out of its way to suggest. It may well be that Wordsworth retrospectively identified 'The Old Cumberland Beggar' with the period of his original acquaintance with Malthus's *Essay*, and the first, obscure stirrings of secular utilitarian social reform. But there are good reasons to regard an association of this sort with suspicion. It makes more sense to read the Fenwick note, not as an authoritative insight into the origins of 'The Old Cumberland Beggar', but rather as a reflection of Wordsworth's personal and political concerns in 1843. Carlyle's *Past and Present* was published in this year, with its influential indictment of 'Benthamee Radicalism', 'Poor-law Prisons', and the widespread acceptance of 'Laissez-faire' as the only possible response to an 'ever-increasing population'—a critical manifesto that was itself strongly indebted to the spirit of the Lake school's

[25] William Godwin, *The Enquirer. Reflections on Education, Manners, and Literature* (1797), 192–3; William Paley, *The Principles of Moral and Political Philosophy* (1785), 37–8, 202–14. For a brief but illuminating comparison between Godwin's essay and Wordsworth's poem, see Gregory Dart, *Rousseau, Robespierre and English Romanticism* (Cambridge, 1999), 153–4.

[26] Wordsworth, *Prose*, i. 101.

attacks on political economy and the 'mechanical philosophy' in the 1810s and 1820s.[27] It was also during this period that his 1814 poem, *The Excursion*, which included Wordsworth's most sustained public attack on industrial manufactures, philosophical abstraction, and political economy, finally began to establish his reputation as a national poet of great spiritual and social importance. Wordsworth had recently attempted to capitalize upon this burgeoning celebrity by publishing a new collection, *Poems, Chiefly of Early and Late Years*, which, as Stephen Gill points out, was presented to the nation very much 'as a contribution towards social healing' and a reaffirmation of the contemporary relevance of the entire body of his work.[28]

It is thus unsurprising that the Fenwick note should read back into 'The Old Cumberland Beggar'—a poem that stood at the very beginning of Wordsworth's public literary career—a Lake school critique of political economy that, while something of a commonplace by the 1840s, had never been a distinctive feature of the poor law debate, or political argument more generally, in the 1790s. At least in terms of its original conception, 'The Old Cumberland Beggar' cannot be construed as a critique of 'political economists', despite its author's later willingness to rewrite his intellectual biography so as to suggest otherwise (a revisionary proclivity which, in other contexts, has long been recognized as a central element of his creative practice). Such a conclusion, however, leaves suggestively unresolved the true nature and significance of Wordsworth's—and the other Lake poets'—response to Malthusian ideas in the 1790s and early 1800s, and it is to this problem that we must now turn.

THE ORIGINS OF LAKE SCHOOL ANTI-ECONOMISM

The difficulty encountered at this point lies not so much in the task of recognizing the Lake poets' hostility to Malthusian doctrine, as in establishing its leading causes. A closer examination of the 1798 *Essay on Population* should not only make this point clearer, but might also suggest some of the surprising areas of compatibility, as well as divergence, between Malthus and his critics in the Lake school. In the first

[27] Carlyle, *Past and Present*, 248.

[28] William Wordsworth, *Poems, Chiefly of Early and Late Years* (1842); Stephen Gill, *Wordsworth and the Victorians* (Oxford, 1998), 26–7.

place, far from viewing poverty merely as the regrettable consequence of a redundant population, the 1798 *Essay* actually turns physical distress to moral good. In common with Wordsworth's argument in 'The Old Cumberland Beggar', Malthus maintained that virtue was inseparably linked to suffering: 'The sorrows and distresses of life form another class of excitements, which seem to be necessary, by a peculiar train of impressions, to soften and humanize the heart, to awaken social sympathy, to generate all the Christian virtues, and to afford scope for the ample exertion of benevolence.'[29] Notwithstanding Malthus's reference to 'Christian virtues', this statement quite succinctly expresses an ethical position that was fundamental to Wordsworth's poetry of the 1790s.[30] Indeed, in so far as his early work on *The Recluse* can be reconstructed with any reliability, it seems that the idea of moral truth as disclosed in human suffering was intended to provide the unifying thematic heart of the poem. Unlike Wordsworth, however, Malthus believed that the 'proper office of benevolence' was 'to soften the partial evils arising from self-love', and that the pursuit of individual self-interest was in fact the most widespread, and the most efficacious means of realizing the 'general good'.[31] This belief was common to a broad range of eighteenth-century social thought, including, of course, Adam Smith's *Wealth of Nations*. Yet, despite this important point of congruity with Smith's work, the most fundamental context for the Reverend Malthus's arguments in the first *Essay* is provided not by Scottish political economy, but rather by English natural theology.

The *Essay on Population* played a tremendously significant role in the historical transmission of eighteenth-century natural theology, an intellectual tradition that was to make a profound impression upon Victorian religious, social, and scientific thought.[32] In the most general terms, natural theology understood the distresses of the world to act as stimuli to the development of sympathy, benevolence, and religious virtue—qualities that would find their providential reward either in this life or in the next. This broadly utilitarian idea of Christian morality

[29] [Thomas Robert Malthus], *An Essay on the Principle of Population* . . . (1798), repr. for the Royal Economic Society (1926), 372.

[30] This point is also acknowledged by Bromwich, *Disowned by Memory*, 37 n.

[31] Johnson, *Wordsworth and* The Recluse, 7–9; [Malthus], *Essay* (1798), 294–5.

[32] Frank M. Turner, *Contesting Cultural Authority: Essays in Victorian Intellectual Life* (Cambridge, 1993), 101–27; see also Eric K. Heavner, 'Malthus and the Secularization of Political Ideology', *History of Political Thought*, 27 (1996), 408–30.

constituted the ethical component of natural theology, which linked the teleological structure of the natural world and human society (and all their manifest evils) to the stimulation of spiritual welfare, moral improvement, and worldly happiness. Natural theology has been described as 'the spiritual core of the British Enlightenment'—a clerical and conservative Enlightenment, that is, which sustained a convincing ideological reconciliation of science, commerce, and Christianity until at least the mid-nineteenth century.[33]

Malthus's own interpretation of this powerful body of thought in the first *Essay on Population* was not entirely conventional. Unlike more orthodox natural theologians, his polemic against Godwinian perfectibilism led him to reject the common understanding of the world as a 'state of trial', and to consider 'the world, and this life' as, instead, 'the mighty process of God . . . for the creation and formation of mind', a theodicy which, *contra* Godwin, necessarily disallowed the possibility of intellectual perfection in this world.[34] This was, however, only a partial (and temporary) aberration. In his concern to discover providential justifications for the institution of property and the pursuit of economic self-interest, his theological utilitarianism, and his avowedly inductive, experimental approach to the investigation of God's purpose on earth, Malthus was clearly working within the eighteenth-century tradition of natural theology associated above all at this time with the Whiggish and latitudinarian tendencies within Cambridge University.

While the political strength of latitudinarian and dissenting Cambridge, which was focused primarily upon the Subscription issue, failed to survive the conservative backlash of the 1790s, the intellectual hegemony of natural theology within the university persisted until well into the nineteenth century.[35] For young Cambridge radicals such as Wordsworth and Coleridge, natural theology therefore amounted to something like an intellectual orthodoxy against

[33] D. L. LeMahieu, *The Mind of William Paley: A Philosopher and his Age* (Lincoln, Nebr., 1976), 31; J. G. A. Pocock, 'Clergy and Commerce: The Conservative Enlightenment in England', in R. Ajello *et al.* (eds.), *L'Età dei Lumi: Studi Storici sul Settecento Europeo in Onore di Franco Venturi*, 2 vols. (Naples, 1985), i. 525–62.

[34] [Malthus], *Essay* (1798), 353; Waterman, *Revolution*, 99–101. For the more orthodox, 'probationary' theodicy, see William Paley, *Natural Theology* (1802), 561.

[35] Gascoigne, *Cambridge in the Age of Enlightenment*, ch. 7. On the later period, see Aileen Fyfe, 'The Reception of William Paley's *Natural Theology* in the University of Cambridge', *British Journal for the History of Science*, 30 (1997), 321–35.

which their own beliefs had to be tested and defined. In common with the traditions of English dissent—with which the two poets had much more direct sympathies—natural theology stressed the teleological structure of the natural world as a principal means of access to metaphysical truth and divine purpose. But in applying these beliefs to the structure of human society, natural theology was also committed to the providential defence of self-interest as the motive force of commercial civilization, in marked contrast to the Lake poets' benevolist understanding of moral nature. Even more importantly, however, the entire methodological orientation of natural theology was in certain fundamental respects incompatible with the philosophical principles adopted by Coleridge and Wordsworth in the mid-1790s. For writers such as Malthus and Paley, the natural world provided the opportunity to reconcile teleological 'reason' and biblical 'revelation' through the inductive exploration of God's creation. The 'constancy of the laws of nature' both formed the foundation, and constituted the proper object, of 'the faculty of reason'. The correct employment of that faculty would in turn reveal the providential tendency of natural laws to promote moral good.[36]

It was this prominence accorded to the exercise of reason that provided the immediate intellectual grounds upon which Wordsworth and Coleridge rejected Paleyite natural theology. Despite his praise for Paley's *Horæ Paulinæ* in his 1795 lectures on religion, Coleridge began to plan 'Strictures on Godwin, Paley &c &c' shortly afterwards; and by 1802 he was registering his antipathy to Paley's new-found political conservatism by identifying him with 'Pseudo-rationalists', including by implication the author of *Political Justice*.[37] However, it is Wordsworth's associationist defence of morally actuating 'habit' over the inefficacious exercise of 'reason' in the *Essay on Morals* that provides the most conclusive early example of the way in which natural theology, including by implication Malthus's *Essay*, could be assimilated to the poets' projected critique of Godwinian rationalism. Indeed, when Wordsworth dismissively alluded to 'such books as Mr Godwyn's, Mr. Paley's, & those of the whole tribe of authors of that class', he may

[36] [Malthus], *Essay* (1798), 355, 362; William Paley, *A View of the Evidences of Christianity*, 2nd edn., 2 vols. (1794), i. 1–3; id., *Natural Theology*, 439–73, 488–571.

[37] Samuel Taylor Coleridge, *Notebooks*, ed. Kathleen Coburn and Merton Christensen, 5 vols. (New York and London, 1957–), i. 161, 1187; id., *Lectures 1795 on Politics and Religion*, ed. Lewis Patton and Peter Mann (London and Princeton, 1971), 186.

very well have had in mind the author of the recently published *Essay on Population*.

But, if Wordsworth had little sympathy with Malthus on moral and theological grounds, he appears to have had a great deal more in common with the *Essay*'s views on politics and society. At several points in the first *Essay*, Malthus's concern to encourage the virtue of 'independence' amongst the lower classes is joined with a distrust of both 'luxury' and 'large manufactories, unfavourable both to health and virtue'. Such statements were typical examples of the kind of Old Whig or 'Country' party sentiment that Wordsworth, Coleridge, and Southey would all undoubtedly have both recognized and commended.[38] Wordsworth's well-known letter to Charles James Fox, for example, reiterates several of Malthus's complaints. This epistolary address to the Whig leader laments the 'rapid decay of the domestic affections among the lower orders of society', connects such affections with 'small independent *proprietors* of land', and argues that the decline of 'domestic feeling among the poor' has been caused by 'the spreading of manufactures through every part of the country, by the heavy taxes upon postage, by workhouses, Houses of Industry, and the invention of Soup-shops &c. &c. superadded to the encreasing disproportion between the price of labour and that of the necessaries of life . . .'. Wordsworth's implicit economic argument linking the provision of organized public poor relief with the high price of provisions and the decline of agrarian independence clearly echoes Malthus's argument in the *Essay on Population*, that the 'love of independence is a sentiment that surely none would wish to be erased from the breast of man: though the parish law of England, it must be confessed, is a system of all others the most calculated gradually to weaken this sentiment, and in the end, may eradicate it completely'.[39] Malthus's opposition to the existing poor laws, and limited support of county workhouses 'for cases of extreme distress', were qualified by his conviction that 'Many cases would undoubtedly be left for the exertion of individual benevolence', an assertion which is also broadly in accord with the argument of 'The Old Cumberland Beggar'. Indeed, if the latter poem contains any kind of implicit policy recommendation on poor law reform, then its

[38] [Malthus], *Essay* (1798), 67, 343, 321; Winch, *Riches and Poverty*, 253–5; Pfau, *Wordsworth's Profession*, 353.

[39] Wordsworth and Wordsworth, *Letters*, i. 312–15 (Jan. 1801); [Malthus], *Essay* (1798), 67–8; see also ibid. 84–5.

message seems entirely compatible with the abolitionist stance suggested both by the 1798 *Essay on Population*, and by Wordsworth's subsequent letter to Fox.[40]

Such affinities might seem surprising, at least in so far as they draw into uncomfortable proximity a poet endeavouring to capture the 'music of humanity', and the economist whose influence and reputation have done most to confirm the callous *in*humanity of the 'dismal science'. But they are by no means untypical of the close, complex, and often ambivalent relationship that existed between Malthusian argument and the politics of the Lake school during the late 1790s and early 1800s. That much, at least, is suggested by the rather belated manner in which the Lake poets' antipathy to Malthus first took shape, in 1804–5. It is true that, as early as May 1799, Coleridge confessed privately to Josiah Wedgwood that he found the *Essay on Population* 'extremely illogical', adding that, although he too had 'doubts' concerning the progressive nature of human society, they rested on 'other grounds' than those proposed by Malthus.[41] But it would clearly be overstating the case to interpret these isolated remarks as the first stirrings of a 'Romantic critique of political economy', particularly since, like Wordsworth, both Coleridge and Southey could easily have found common ground with Malthus on other important issues. Thus, for example, although Southey was strongly opposed to the idea of self-love as the governing principle of human society, his enduring hostility to manufactures and the commercial system had much in common with the agrarian bias of the *Essay on Population*.[42] In this respect, the politics of the *Essay* were influenced by the same diffuse tradition of Country ideology that also formed a principal component of Coleridge's political thought in the late 1790s.[43] Just as Malthus argued that English agriculture had not kept pace with the growth of manufactures in the previous century, so Coleridge began, around 1800, to warn of an 'overbalance of commerce' in the country's

[40] [Malthus], *Essay* (1798), 98. The abolitionist implications of 'The Old Cumberland Beggar' are also noted by Jarvis, 'Wordsworth and the Uses of Charity', 204.

[41] Coleridge, *Letters*, i. 517–18.

[42] Mark Storey, *Robert Southey: A Life* (Oxford, 1997), 158; David Eastwood, 'Ruinous Prosperity: Robert Southey's Critique of the Commercial System', *Wordsworth Circle*, 25 (1994), 72–6; Geoffrey Carnall, *Robert Southey and his Age: The Development of a Conservative Mind* (Oxford, 1960), 67–8.

[43] Nigel Leask, *The Politics of Imagination in Coleridge's Critical Thought* (Basingstoke, 1988), 9–45; John Morrow, *Coleridge's Political Thought: Property, Morality and the Limits of Traditional Discourse* (Basingstoke, 1990), chs. 1–2. See also Coleridge, *Lectures 1795*, 219, 223–4, 228.

economy. Since Coleridge was at this time publicly claiming some expertise in 'questions relative to political economy', we might even go so far as to speculate about the possible influence of the *Essay on Population* on this question.[44]

Perhaps just as significant, however, is the fact that neither Malthus nor Coleridge saw any necessary contradiction between their opinions on this issue and a fundamental respect for the inflexible laws governing the production and distribution of economic commodities. The clearest example of this attitude on Coleridge's part is his essentially Smithian view of the food scarcities and high prices that were responsible for serious and widespread distress in the years 1800–1. In a series of controversial newspaper articles written with Thomas Poole in October 1800, Coleridge denied that the scarcities could be attributed either to farmers stockpiling their harvests, or to the activities of forestallers and regraters of grain. Indeed, far from linking the riots, protests, and demonstrations sparked by the shortages to a traditionary moral economy, Coleridge chose to ascribe them instead to the 'false opinions' of 'mobs', whose '*feelings*' were perhaps understandable, but whose '*opinions*' betrayed their profound economic naivety.

I have often heard unthinking people exclaim, in observing differences of price in different parts of the country, What has become of Adam Smith's *level?* I, God knows, am no friend to those hard-hearted comparisons of human actions with the laws of inanimate nature. Water will come to a level without pain or pleasure, and provisions and money will come to a level likewise; but, O God! what scenes of anguish must take place while they are coming to a *level!* But still the sneer against Adam Smith, as to the simple fact, is absurd.[45]

In 1817 Coleridge would rework this passage, so as to render it more compatible with his post-war hostility to 'the reputed masters of Political Economy'.[46] In their original context, however, his remarks not only constituted an explicit defence of Smith's *Wealth of Nations*; they also expressed much the same sentiments as Malthus's *Investigation of the Cause of the Present High Price of Provisions*, which was published by

[44] [Malthus], *Essay* (1798), 315–20; Coleridge, *Essays on his Times in* The Morning Post *and* The Courier (1798–1817), ed. David V. Erdman, 3 vols. (London and Princeton, 1978), i. 223 (Mar. 19 1800); i. 245 (3 Oct. 1800).

[45] Coleridge, *Essays on his Times*, i. 253, 255. On the idea of 'moral economy' in relation to this period, see E. P. Thompson, *Customs in Common* (1991), 185–331.

[46] Coleridge, *A Lay Sermon* (1817), in *Lay Sermons*, 206, 140.

Johnson the next month. In his own contribution to the debate over food prices, Malthus similarly followed Smith in blaming the high price of grain on 'genuine' shortages rather than the speculation of hoarders and middlemen. He insisted that the parish allowance system currently in operation was inflationary in tendency, but he also argued that, given the extreme distress of the country, persisting in the use of such a scheme of poor relief was by this stage the only honourable course of action. Malthus's pamphlet was praised by the Lord Chancellor, and a copy seems to have found its way to William Pitt. Coleridge's articles, on the other hand, proved rather unpopular with many readers of the *Morning Post*, a paper that has been described as 'flexibly anti-ministerial' during this period.[47] Yet the arguments of both writers were potentially rather less sympathetic to the Pitt administration than the facts of their reception might at first suggest. Government and opposition writers alike tended to absolve forestallers and regraters from responsibility for the scarcities, for differing motives. For commentators such as Coleridge and Malthus, emphasizing the naturalness and inflexibility of economic laws could serve to draw attention to the extent to which blame for the present distresses lay with government policy, whether in prosecuting the war with France or, as Malthus argued, through the undue 'legislative interference' represented by 'the system of poor laws and parish allowances'.[48]

We might conclude that, despite the *Essay on Population*'s unsavoury theological provenance, many of its political and economic arguments would have proved entirely acceptable to Wordsworth and Coleridge. It may not, of course, have been quite so easy for the Lake poets to distinguish between theology and politics in this manner. Theological utilitarianism was an important resource for counter-revolutionary discourse during the 1790s (a fact that has often been obscured by the prominence accorded to the Burke–Paine controversy).[49] But it is also important to bear in mind that, for Wordsworth and Coleridge at least, the political

[47] [Thomas Robert Malthus], *An Investigation of the Cause of the Present High Price of Provisions* (1800), 3–5, 19–20; Winch, *Riches and Poverty*, 324; James, *Population Malthus*, 91; Coleridge, *Essays on his Times*, i, p. lxx.

[48] [Malthus], *Investigation*, 25, 8. See also Robert Waithman, *War Proved to be the Cause of the Present Scarcity* (1800). Pro-ministerial authors tended to stress the need for a more interventionist agricultural policy. See [Charles Long], *A Temperate Discussion of the Causes which have Led to the Present High Price of Bread* (1800); and Arthur Young, *The Question of Scarcity Plainly Stated* (1800).

[49] Thomas Philip Schofield, 'Conservative Political Thought in Britain in Response to the French Revolution', *Historical Journal*, 29 (1986), 601–22.

'apostasy' of other prominent natural theologians, such as William Paley and Richard Watson, provided a far more obvious target for polemical abuse than the Whiggish politics of the first *Essay on Population*. As early as 1793, Watson's shocked condemnation of the French regicides had provided the occasion for Wordsworth's unpublished republican tirade, the *Letter to the Bishop of Llandaff*. Coleridge, likewise, had been abusing the reactionary politics of the 'Reverend Moralist', William Paley, since 1795 (whilst continuing to plagiarize his biblical scholarship).[50] The often rancorous character of these attacks can be explained, in large part, by the fact that Watson and Paley were leading Cambridge divines both of whom had a reputation for political and religious toleration. Their complicity with the reactionary tendencies at work within the 'Whig University' after 1789 provoked widespread indignation amongst the local radical dissenting community. By 1796, Coleridge's Cambridge publisher Benjamin Flower was writing of Paley and Watson as 'apostatizing from many excellent sentiments they once professed, and floating down the stream of general corruption'. Watson's Pittite *Address to the People of Great Britain* of 1798 prompted further condemnation from George Dyer and Gilbert Wakefield, leading Cambridge unitarians who were also well known to Coleridge.[51] The 'apostasy' of Whig Cambridge must, then, have played an important part in shaping the attitudes of Coleridge and Wordsworth towards the Paleyite intellectual orthodoxy in which they were educated. But the important point remains that, given the contemporary ideological affiliations of natural theology, the moderate tone and agrarian, Foxite politics which underpinned Malthus's anti-utopian arguments may well have rendered the *Essay* relatively unobjectionable in comparison to what Wordsworth and Coleridge clearly regarded as the self-serving, counter-revolutionary betrayals of the Cambridge latitudinarian establishment.

It was only after the publication of the second, expanded edition of the *Essay on Population*, in 1803, that any kind of concerted Lake school opposition to Malthus's ideas really began to take shape. By then,

[50] Richard Watson (Lord Bishop of Llandaff), *A Sermon Preached before the Stewards of the Westminster Dispensary* (1793), 21–38; Coleridge, *Lectures 1795*, 69, 222, 310; id., *Essays on his Times*, i. 94 (10 Jan. 1800).

[51] Benjamin Flower, *National Sins Considered* (Cambridge, 1796), quoted in Gascoigne, *Cambridge in the Age of Enlightenment*, 243; see also William Burdon, *Three Letters Addressed to the Bishop of Llandaff* (Cambridge, 1795), 34; Gascoigne, *Cambridge in the Age of Enlightenment*, 216.

however, the scope of the original controversy had widened considerably. The 1798 *Essay* was initially conceived as a seasonable, and quite specific critique of two radical theoreticians of perfectibility, Godwin and Condorcet. But Malthus soon came to harbour much broader ambitions for his work. In preparing the second edition he greatly expanded the book's arguments and examples, made public his authorship, and wrote a new preface in which he expressed his hope that the revised *Essay* would transcend the circumstances of its original composition, and acquire instead 'a more practical and permanent interest'.[52] Yet, despite this aspiration, the polemical circumstances of its original appearance, as well as the turbulent political climate of 1803–4, continued to influence the second *Essay*'s immediate critical reception, in ways that complicated the responses of critics and admirers alike. This was perhaps particularly true of the Lake poets, whose reactions to the second *Essay* were further influenced by their diverse, and often compromised, attempts to renegotiate their earlier commitments to various forms of political and religious radicalism.

By the beginning of 1803, the Peace of Amiens, although less than a year old, was looking increasingly precarious. British violations of the treaty, together with fears of Napoleon's increasing strength, soon led to the Addington government's resumption of armed hostilities, and the appointment of Pitt's war ministry the following year. The renewal of the conflict with France also revived the Foxite opposition in Parliament; but, without doors, patriotic anti-gallicism revived with a vengeance, spurred on by a flood of cheap pro-war handbills and broadsheets.[53] Even the middle-class 'friends of peace', including such hitherto principled opponents of the war as William Frend, now found themselves arguing for the expediency of defensive war on explicitly patriotic grounds. It was the rise of this new 'liberal patriotism' that provided the opportunity for the Lake poets to make their own accommodation with the loyalist defence of war, and a more or less recantatory identification with popular patriotic sentiment against the 'Corsican Liberticide'.[54] By late 1802, Coleridge's political journalism

[52] Thomas Robert Malthus, *An Essay on the Principle of Population* . . . (1803), ed. Patricia James, 2 vols. (Cambridge, 1989), i. 1.

[53] Stella Cottrell, 'The Devil on Two Sticks: Franco-Phobia in 1803', in Raphael Samuel (ed.), *Patriotism: The Making and Unmaking of National Identity*, i. *History and Politics* (1989), 259–74.

[54] William Frend, *Patriotism; or, The Love of our Country* (1804); William Burdon, *Unanimity Recommended* (Newcastle upon Tyne, 1803); J. E. Cookson, *The Friends of*

for the *Morning Post* could be described as Bourbonist and 'anti-jacobin' in character, and in November of that year he published a sensational, condemnatory series of 'Letters to Fox'. Henceforth, Coleridge was to appear entirely unapologetic about his public opposition to the Foxite 'alarmists', and his newly assumed role as a journalistic abettor of the nation's 'patriotic valour'.[55]

The rhetorical gusto of Coleridge's articles is seldom marred by the anxiety that had marked his earlier ideological tergiversations, and betrays the mingled sense of vindication, sanctimony, and relief that was felt by all the Lake poets at finding their political sympathies in harmony at last with 'the sense of the country'.[56] Arriving home from a tour of Scotland with Dorothy and Coleridge in October 1803, Wordsworth signed up with the Grasmere volunteer militia and returned, with renewed vigour, to composing triumphalist sonnets on the war, at least one of which attained a pitch of aggressive jingoism sufficient to ensure its republication in the *Anti-Gallican* magazine.[57] Robert Southey, meanwhile, marvelled that the 'country was never so united & therefore never so strong'.[58] But, while Southey relished finding himself on the side of popular loyalist feeling, he persisted in identifying his enthusiasm for the total defeat of Napoleon with what he still liked to call his 'jacobinism'. Addington's diplomatic provocations, Southey suggested, 'have brought back the old temper of Englishmen. . . . There is an Anti-Gallican spirit abroad, most violent in those who were the most hostile to the last war.'[59]

It was against this backdrop, of invasion fears and renascent popular loyalism, that the second *Essay on Population* appeared. The *Essay*'s original provenance as a counter-revolutionary riposte to Godwinian

Peace: Anti-War Liberalism in England, 1793–1815 (Cambridge, 1982), 170; Coleridge, *Essays on his Time*, i. 425.

[55] Coleridge, *Essays on his Times*, i, pp. cvi–cvii, 424 (18 July 1803); John Colmer, *Coleridge: Critic of Society* (Oxford, 1959), 71–2.

[56] Coleridge, *Essays on his Times*, i. 434 (20 Aug. 1803).

[57] Kenneth Johnston, *The Hidden Wordsworth: Poet, Lover, Rebel, Spy* (New York, 1998), 805–7; Gill, *William Wordsworth*, 233–4; William Wordsworth, *Poetical Works*, ed. E. de Selincourt and Helen Darbishire, 5 vols. (Oxford, 1940–9), iii. 122. For a more detailed, and more qualified, treatment of the sonnets, see Alan Liu, *Wordsworth: The Sense of History* (Stanford, Calif., 1989), 427–36.

[58] Southey to William Taylor (13 July 1803), quoted in Storey, *Robert Southey*, 159.

[59] Robert Southey, *New Letters*, ed. Kenneth Curry, 2 vols. (New York, 1965), i. 314 (12 Sept. 1803).

radicalism continued to recommend it to many readers, particularly given the new mood of anti-Gallicism and national solidarity which was being drummed up by much of the press. The ongoing Malthus–Godwin debate was an issue that, although fading somewhat from public consciousness, had been kept alive by Samuel Parr's *Spital Sermon*, in addition to the efforts of the two main participants.[60] Certainly Malthus's reputation as the principal opponent of Godwin, together with the more orthodox theodicy of the second *Essay*, go a long way towards explaining his respectful treatment at the hands of the pugnaciously conservative *British Critic*, which began its measured, and by no means uncritical, review of the 1803 *Essay* with praise for the manner in which Malthus had demonstrated the 'futility' of Godwin's 'visionary theories'.[61]

But the groundswell of support for war also helped to determine critical responses to the second *Essay on Population* in a quite contrary manner, since the book's argument could also be interpreted as having distinctly pacific implications. Malthus argued for a society that would be 'Weak in offensive war', and commented sarcastically that a 'recruiting serjeant always prays for a bad harvest and a want of employment', sentiments which clearly reflected the author's links with prominent friends of peace, including William Frend, William Roscoe, and John Aikin.[62] At a time when erstwhile opponents of war such as Frend were turning to support the campaign against Napoleon, it is easy to see how the new edition of the *Essay* could have divided liberal opinion. To one contributor to the *Monthly Magazine*, for example, it seemed that anyone

> who bestows the least consideration on the state of this country, menaced from without by a most powerful and inveterate foe, and drawing the chief resources for its immense expenditure from manufactures and commerce extended over the globe, cannot for a moment doubt the necessity of a *great* population, not only for retaining the rank it has acquired among nations, but for its existence as an independent empire.[63]

[60] Samuel Parr, *A Spital Sermon* (1801); William Godwin, *Thoughts Occasioned by the Perusal of Dr. Parr's Spital Sermon* (1801).

[61] 'Malthus on the Principle of Population', *British Critic*, 23 (1804), 60. See also Clive Emsley, *British Society and the French Wars 1793–1815* (1979), 118; Waterman, *Revolution*, 145.

[62] Malthus, *Essay* (1803), ii. 101–2; see also ibid. i. 19; Winch, *Riches and Poverty*, 292–3.

[63] *Monthly Magazine*, 18 (Dec. 1804), 381.

It was at this moment that Malthus's reputation as a dour, celibatarian pessimist really began to gather strength, in counterpoint not to radical perfectibilism but to a new unanimity on the expediency and justice of war. Yet in many respects, the alterations and additions that Malthus had made to the 1803 *Essay* actually strengthened the case for regarding him as a melioristic social reformer. The *Monthly Review*, for one, was moved to protest that Malthus's speculations 'proceed from no gloomy views nor morose dispositions', but were motivated by 'the purest philanthropy and the most genuine benevolence'.[64]

Coleridge and Southey, meanwhile, were both attempting to salvage a measure of political integrity by grafting their vestigial reformism onto a rather virulent strain of popular loyalist rhetoric. In such circumstances, Malthus's pacific, moderate Whig pessimism provided an all too convenient foil for the Lake school's ideological accommodations with the Pittite war machine. Malthus's rhetorical indiscretions and tactless insensitivity (over the notorious 'Nature's feast' metaphor, for example) have never made it difficult to identify him as a reactionary defender of inequality and social division. Although this was clearly not a necessary response nor even, perhaps, a particularly accurate one, it was encouraged by the Lake poets' new-found identification with militant popular loyalism and the strongly perceived need for national fortitude and unanimity in the prosecution of the war. As Coleridge put it in a July 1803 attack on the divisive despondency of the parliamentary opposition, 'Patriotism and patriotic valour, like all other active virtues, are indissolubly wedded to hope'—a sentiment hardly exemplified by the *Essay on Population*.[65] The 'mobs' of hungry protesters whom Coleridge had castigated in 1800 for their ignorance of economic theory were now subsumed into a militantly patriotic *vox populi*. Viewed in this light, Malthus's providential arguments for the inevitability of '*misery & brutal Ignorance*' among the population were exposed as both wholly inappropriate, and more than ordinarily suspect, particularly since they reduced the noble passions of the British people to the 'physical Necessity' of 'Lust & Hunger', as Coleridge claimed in his marginal annotations to the 1803 *Essay*.[66] Coleridge seems even to have considered taking Godwin's side against Malthus, despite his long-standing

[64] *Monthly Review*, 43 (Jan. 1804), 67.

[65] Coleridge, *Essays on his Times*, i. 424.

[66] Coleridge, *Letters*, ii. 1026 (11 Jan. 1804); id., *Marginalia*, ed. H. J. Jackson and George Whalley, 6 vols. (London and Princeton, 1980–), iii. 806.

hostility to the atheistical rationalism of *Political Justice*. He was certainly willing to enter into an exchange of letters and notes with Southey, which culminated in the latter's vitriolic denunciation of the second *Essay on Population* in the *Annual Review* for 1803 (but published in 1804). Southey's article has often been discussed by historians of economic thought, and is sometimes regarded as the first public expression of an emergent 'Romantic' critique of political economy.[67] The private circumstances of the review's composition, however, are arguably just as revealing of the complex motivations underlying the Lake poets' initial reactions to the Malthusian controversy.

In January 1804 Coleridge wrote to Southey, accused the *Essay on Population* of sophistry and inconsistency, and encouraged his correspondent to use his review of the book to 'scourge' Malthus for encouraging the false opinion that Godwin sanctioned infanticide and abortion as a means of controlling population. But Coleridge's outrage was curiously short-lived. Two weeks later he wrote again, praising Southey's critical acumen to sycophantic excess, but then adding, 'In your Review of Malthus be exceedingly temperate & courteous & guarded in your language.' The reasons for Coleridge's circumspection begin to become clear, as he remarks immediately afterwards that 'Scott has reviewed Thalaba, I *hear*, in the Edinburgh Review / Thelwall has had a grand rumpus with the Ed[inburgh] Reviewers, written a pamphlet, of which a 1,000 copies have already sold & is said to have laid them prostrate & flat.'[68] Coleridge's remarks referred, in the first place, to the hostile review of Southey's *Thalaba the Destroyer* (written by Francis Jeffrey, rather than Scott), which had appeared in the first number of the *Edinburgh Review*, for October 1802. Jeffrey's comments did much to consolidate and popularize the idea of a modern '*sect* of poets', who would soon come to be more commonly referred to as the 'Lake school'.[69] It was thus of particular significance that the first few pages of Jeffrey's review should explicitly link the Lake poets' aesthetic principles with

[67] See especially the account in Winch, *Riches and Poverty*, 288–306; but also Bonar, *Malthus*, 374–6; Harold A. Boner, *Hungry Generations: The Nineteenth-Century Case against Malthusianism* (New York, 1955), 41–50; James, *Population Malthus*, 114–15, 121–2; William Petersen, *Malthus* (1971), 70–1.

[68] Coleridge, *Letters*, ii. 532 (11 Jan. 1804); ibid. ii. 538 (25 Jan. 1804).

[69] Although Wordsworth, Coleridge, and Southey were widely recognized as forming a distinct 'school' of poetry and politics from about 1800, the first association of the 'new school' with the 'Lakes of Cumberland' dates from 1807. See Peter A. Cook, 'Chronology of the "Lake School" Argument: Some Revisions', *Review of English Studies*, NS 28 (1977), 175–81.

political sedition and moral degeneracy. Most damagingly, perhaps, the productions of the 'new school' were identified with the 'antisocial principles, and distempered sensibility of Rousseau—his discontent with the present constitution of society—his paradoxical morality, and his perpetual hankerings after some unattainable state of voluptuous virtue and perfection'.[70] The revival of the idea of a radicalized poetic 'school' angered Wordsworth and Southey, and their mood was surely not helped by the publication of Peter Bayley's parodic treatments of the *Lyrical Ballads* shortly afterwards. Bayley's volume recalled the notorious *Anti-Jacobin* parodies of Southey's sentimental verse of the 1790s, which had been the first occasion on which the author was publicly identified with a 'NEW SCHOOL' of poetic and political radicalism.[71] To compound this ideological return of the repressed, just at the moment when the Lake poets' youthful radicalism was being publicly aired in the fashionable new *Edinburgh Review*, their old 'jacobin' acquaintance John Thelwall was involving himself in a paper war with exactly the same journal over its derogatory treatment of his *Poems, Chiefly Written in Retirement* (1801). And to make matters worse, Jeffrey's review had ridiculed Thelwall's verse as the product of a vulgar, levelling sensibility in terms that were at times uncomfortably similar to his earlier treatment of *Thalaba*.[72] In reminding Southey of these facts, and demanding he be 'exceedingly temperate & courteous & guarded', Coleridge clearly implied that too heated an attack on Malthus risked confirming the old radical sympathies of the Lake school just at the moment when Coleridge was most anxious to dispel such associations.

As it turned out, and perhaps emboldened by Coleridge's praise for the delicacy of his critical judgement, Southey seems to have decided that the best solution to the Lake poets' predicament would be to attack both Malthus *and* Godwin in equally offensive terms. He appears, moreover, to have been much less inhibited than Coleridge by the desire to disguise what remained of his reformist commitments. The published review argued that, because the *Essay on Population* wrongly insisted upon treating the sexual instinct as a rationally ungovernable 'passion

[70] [Francis Jeffrey], 'Southey's *Thalaba*', *Edinburgh Review*, 1 (Oct. 1802), 63–4.

[71] Wordsworth and Wordsworth, *Letters*, i. 433 (mid-Jan. 1804); Gill, *William Wordsworth*, 224–5; Peter Bayley, *Poems* (1803); 'The Friend of Humanity and the Knife-Grinder', *The Anti-Jacobin; or, Weekly Examiner*, 1 (27 Nov. 1797), 15.

[72] John Thelwall, *Poems Chiefly Written in Retirement* (1801); [Francis Jeffrey], 'Thelwall's *Poems*', *Edinburgh Review*, 2 (Apr. 1803), 197–202; John Thelwall, *A Letter to Francis Jeffray* [*sic*] (Edinburgh, 1804).

of physical necessity', its author was committed to denying the possibility of political and social improvement in a manner which implicitly attributed poverty, famine and disease to 'the will of God' rather than 'human institutions'—a position that Southey found both brutally reactionary and scandalously irreligious.[73] Godwin, meanwhile, was summarily dismissed as the philosophical equivalent of a quack doctor. But the reviewer's commitment to the 'improvement' of 'human institutions' was still plain enough. Indeed, by embracing a belligerent, Christianized version of Godwinian meliorism, Southey found a way publicly to reaffirm his political reformism at Malthus's expense.[74] The 'old temper of Englishmen', the revival of which he had previously extolled as a product of the renewed hostilities with France, was thus to be defended from Malthus's 'political bible of the rich, the sensual, and the selfish', and 'John Bull' rescued from emasculation and immiseration by schemes designed to 'starve the poor into celibacy'. The attack on Malthus thus allowed Southey to mark his distance from Godwin's equally 'sensual' and atheistical radicalism, while simultaneously vindicating his own manly, militantly patriotic version of the popular reformist platform.[75]

The circumstances in which Coleridge and Southey responded to the second edition of the *Essay on Population* strongly suggests that their declared antipathy to Malthus was largely dictated by a sense of their compromised relationship to the political radicalism they had espoused in the 1790s. Particularly in its inception, the Lake school critique of Malthus cannot be understood except by reference to the unstable ideological allegiances of the Lake poets themselves during this period. The encounter certainly cannot be reduced in any simple way to points of policy or principle, a conclusion that is reinforced by the fact that both Coleridge and Southey (the latter under the influence of John Rickman) continued to denounce Malthus in later years while implic-

[73] [Robert Southey], 'Malthus's Essay on Population', *Annual Review*, 2 (1803), 296–7. This is a broadly similar position to that outlined in the anonymous *Remarks on a Late Publication, entitled, 'An Essay on the Principle of Population . . .'* (1803 [1804]), which argued that 'public institutions' and 'private virtue' were the surest checks to vice and misery (*Remarks*, 62).

[74] David Craig, 'Republicanism Becoming Conservative: Robert Southey and Political Argument in Britain, *c.*1790–1817', University of Cambridge doctoral dissertation in progress, ch. 4.

[75] [Southey], 'Malthus's Essay', *Annual Review*, 2 (1803), 298–301, 295. On Southey's opinion of Malthus's pacifism, see Orlo Williams, *Lamb's Friend the Census-Taker: Life and Letters of John Rickman* (1912), 148.

itly acceding to many of his arguments, particularly on the efficacy of the poor laws.[76] Such considerations must also inform our approach to Wordsworth's own critical engagement with Malthus's *Essay* the following year, an encounter which reveals a similar (though significantly more pronounced) mixture of renunciation and qualified accommodation to that evinced by Southey and Coleridge. In Wordsworth's case, however, the imperative to formulate some sort of reply to Malthus was also intimately bound up with his developing poetic ambitions. The success of the second *Essay* suggested that Malthus's refutation of Godwin was, for many of its readers, rapidly acquiring the status of intellectual orthodoxy. For Wordsworth, therefore, the persuasiveness of Malthus's arguments would also have profound implications for *The Recluse*, in so far as that work still found its inspiration in the desire to create the kind of literary critique of rationalist thought which would, in Coleridge's words, effect 'a compleat and constant synthesis of Thought & Feeling'.[77]

WORDSWORTH, MALTHUS, AND THE 1805 *PRELUDE*

'I grieve that the Recluse sleeps', wrote Coleridge in February 1800; and although Wordsworth made a start on the 'great work' shortly afterwards, in the introductory poem that subsequently became *Home at Grasmere*, the project soon foundered as its author turned his attention to the second edition of the *Lyrical Ballads*.[78] It has often been assumed that Wordsworth's failure to make substantial progress on *The Recluse* can be explained by the obvious disjunction between the poem's high philosophical aspirations, which were inspired and nurtured above all by Coleridge, and, on the other hand, Wordsworth's own feeling that the work should remain true to its medium, and should therefore fully exploit the narrative and dramatic possibilities of the blank verse form.[79] Yet despite these enduring, and perhaps irresolvable difficulties, in late

[76] See Eastwood, 'Ruinous Prosperity', 75; Poynter, *Society and Pauperism*, 249–54; Winch, *Riches and Poverty*, 311–13.

[77] Coleridge, *Letters*, ii. 1034.

[78] Ibid. i. 575; Jonathan Wordsworth, 'On Man, on Nature, and on Human Life', *Review of English Studies*, NS 31 (1980), 2–29.

[79] See Bewell, *Wordsworth*, 7–13; and the editor's introduction to Wordsworth, *Home at Grasmere: Part First, Book First, of* The Recluse, ed. Beth Darlington (Ithaca, NY, 1977), 6–7.

1803 Wordsworth seems to have taken a renewed, even urgent interest in *The Recluse*. In March 1804 he wrote to Coleridge that he was 'very anxious to have your notes for the Recluse', and a few months later he was looking forward with great confidence to the completion of this, 'the chief object upon which my thoughts have been fixed these many years'. In large part, however, Wordsworth's enthusiasm more truly reflects his absorption in a rather different composition: the expansion of an earlier poetic memoir of his childhood into the autobiographical epic we know as the 'Thirteen Book' or '1805' *Prelude*.[80]

Whether the essential relation of this latter poem to *The Recluse* is best understood as propaedeutic, diversionary, or substitutive, it is clear that Wordsworth regarded it at this time as a 'tributary' to the 'larger and more important work'. Coleridge certainly suggested as much, if not more, in his declaration of 1804 that *The Recluse* promised to be 'the first & finest philosophical Poem, if only it be (as it undoubtedly will be) a Faithful Transcript of [Wordsworth's] own most august & innocent Life, of his own habitual Feelings & Modes of seeing and hearing'. The 1805 *Prelude*, as a 'transcript' of the growth of the poet's mind, clearly bears an extremely close relation to the 'philosophical Poem, containing views of Man, Nature, and Society', that Wordsworth was still promising the public in 1814.[81] One of the most significant aspects of this relation is the *Prelude*'s autobiographical enactment of *The Recluse*'s projected critique of Godwinian rationalism. Wordsworth's objections to 'lifeless words, & abstract propositions', which he had hitherto raised most explicitly in the *Essay on Morals*, were thus assimilated to an extended account of the poet's personal involvement with radical thought in general, and Godwinism in particular, during the mid-1790s.[82]

Readers with an interest in Wordsworth's political and philosophical development (and his poetic representations thereof) have tended to privilege Book X of the poem as a pivotal moment in the *Prelude*'s narrative of aesthetic, spiritual, and ideological self-discovery. It is here that Wordsworth provides a retrospective account of how, in the wake of the French revolutionary Terror and the Pitt government's repressive response to the domestic reform movement, he became a convert to the

80 Wordsworth and Wordsworth, *Letters*, i. 452, 518; Gill, *William Wordsworth*, 230–1.

81 Wordsworth and Wordsworth, *Letters*, i. 454; Coleridge, *Letters*, ii. 1034; William Wordsworth, *The Excursion, Being a Portion of the Recluse, a Poem* (1814), p. viii.

82 Wordsworth, *Prose Works*, i. 103–4.

'abstract' and rationalist speculations exemplified at the time by Godwin's *Political Justice*.[83]

> This was the time when all things tended fast
> To depravation; the Philosophy
> That promised to abstract the hopes of man
> Out of his feelings, to be fix'd thenceforth
> For ever in a purer element
> Found ready welcome.[84]

Although Godwin is not mentioned by name in Book X, the biographical evidence clearly suggests that he served as Wordsworth's 'philosophic mentor and guide' between 1794 and 1796, the period to which these lines seem to refer.[85] Certainly Coleridge, the 'dear Friend' to whom the *Prelude* was addressed, and the principal influence upon Wordsworth's renunciation of Godwinian philosophy, could hardly have mistaken this section of the poem for anything other than an allusion to Godwin's theory of rational benevolence, a moral system 'Which makes the human Reason's naked self / The object of its fervour' (x. 817–18). Wordsworth's description of a 'Philosophy' that abstracts 'the hopes of man / Out of his feelings' and ignores the 'accidents of nature, time, and place' (x. 822) clearly echoes Coleridge's own criticisms of Godwinian philosophy as a 'Stoical Morality which disclaims all duties of Gratitude and domestic Affection'.[86] In the *Prelude*, however, Wordsworth goes on to suggest that, as a result of his own over-intellectualized absorption in this abstracted form of moral speculation, he succumbed to an affective and imaginative debilitation, 'sacrificed / The exactness of a comprehensive mind', and embraced a 'scrupulous and microscopic' mentality fit only to serve a 'false imagination' (x. 842–7). The *Prelude*'s account of the author's involvement with Godwinian rationalism thus represents the episode as an important retrogressive moment in the development of his poetic faculties.

The next two books, under the title 'Imagination, how impaired and restored', attempt to establish a meaningful relation between Wordsworth's attainment of political and spiritual maturity and the

[83] See especially Roe, *Wordsworth and Coleridge*, 219–23; but also Michael H. Friedman, *The Making of a Tory Humanist: William Wordsworth and the Idea of Community* (New York, 1979), 105–10; Jonathan Wordsworth, *Borders of Vision*, 265–9.

[84] William Wordsworth, *The Thirteen Book* Prelude, ed. Mark L. Reed, 2 vols. (Ithaca, NY, 1991), i. 288–9 (Book X, ll. 805–10); further references will be given in the text.

[85] Roe, *Wordsworth and Coleridge*, 7.

[86] Coleridge, *Lectures 1795*, 164. See Roe, *Wordsworth and Coleridge*, 115–17.

fruition of his imaginative powers. An abiding love of nature, of poetry, and of common life is shown to have redeemed his unhealthy obeisance to abstract thought and narrow rationalism. Book XI is intended to demonstrate the centrality of 'Nature's presence' to the poet's consequent transformation into 'A sensitive and a creative Soul' (xi. 256–7), while Book XII has typically been interpreted as offering a complementary account of the *social* aspect of Wordsworth's poetic imagination. The two books together reprise the idea of 'love of nature leading to love of mankind', a synthesis of the natural and the social in an aesthetic sensibility analogous to that which Wordsworth had described in 1800 as a condition in which 'the passions of men are incorporated with the beautiful and permanent forms of nature'. Book XII can therefore be read as a more focused account of Wordsworth's growing concern with the poetic representation of 'Low and rustic life', which eventually issued in the *Lyrical Ballads*. But the three final books of *The Prelude* are also concerned, above all, to reaffirm Wordsworth's ongoing literary vocation as the author of *The Recluse*, the epic poem on 'Man, Nature, and Society' that he had yet to compose.[87] Hence, Book XII ends by portraying Wordsworth's poetic imagination as simultaneously responsive to both human society, and 'Nature's presence', thereby authorizing his final, triumphant intimation that 'a work of mine . . . might become / A power like one of Nature's' (xii. 309–12).

Despite its clear importance in the overall scheme of the poem, Book XII of the *Prelude* has rarely been discussed at any length, and critical attention has usually been focused on the brief 'Salisbury Plain' episode near its conclusion. Such relative neglect perhaps reflects the view that, for the most part, Book XII appears simply to recapitulate Wordsworth's earlier account of abstract philosophy and narrow book learning (now seemingly decontextualized from any clear historical context), in order to contrast them with the author's more direct, experiential acquaintance with the lower classes of society. But although Book XII contains a number of revealing parallels with the rejection of Godwinian rationalism earlier in the *Prelude*, Wordsworth's primary intention was not to return to Godwin, but rather to adapt and extend the arguments of Book X in order to answer Malthus's account of human nature and society in the *Essay on Population*.

Near the beginning of Book XII, Wordsworth relates how, after

[87] William Wordsworth, 'Preface' to *Lyrical Ballads* (1800), in *Prose Works*, i. 124; Johnston, *Wordsworth and* The Recluse, 199–206.

his disillusionment with philosophy and politics, he found 'Once more in Man an object of delight, / Of pure imagination, and of love' (xii. 54–5). In this renewed state of spiritual and intellectual equilibrium, he was at last

prepared to find
Ambition, folly, madness, in the men
Who thrust themselves upon this passive world
As Rulers of the world, to see in these,
Even when the public welfare is their aim,
Plans without thought, or bottom'd on false thought
And false philosophy: having brought to test
Of solid life and true result the Books
Of modern Statists, and thereby perceiv'd
The utter hollowness of what we name
The wealth of Nations, where alone that wealth
Is lodged, and how encreased . . .

(xii. 70–81)

The allusion to Smith's *Wealth of Nations* in the penultimate line is clear enough, and was made even more explicit in later versions of the poem.[88] Yet, perhaps because of the presumed naturalness of the opposition between 'political economy' and 'Romantic' poetics, this remark has usually been treated either as an isolated aside, with little specific bearing on Wordsworth's larger narrative of poetic self-discovery, or as a dismissive reference to the intellectual apologists for 'laissez-faire capitalism', against whom Wordsworth pitted his own, poetic representations of the labouring classes.[89] His reference to the 'wealth of Nations' has thus been understood in quite general terms, and implicitly opposed to the 'spiritual' wealth of poetry and the imagination. As a result, the poem's passing disavowal of Smith's text has actually proved rather misleading, since these lines serve to introduce an extended account of Wordsworth's intellectual engagement, not with Adam Smith, but with the much more urgent political and economic debate that had been sparked by the *Essay on Population*.

[88] William Wordsworth, *The Fourteen Book* Prelude, ed. W. J. B. Owen (Ithaca, NY, 1985), 246 (Book XIII, l. 78). The lines were also later reworked in the poem 'Humanity' (comp. 1829); see *Poetical Works*, iv. 105.

[89] Friedman, *Making of a Tory Humanist*, 197–8; Gayatri Chakravorty Spivak, 'Sex and History in *The Prelude* (1805): Books Nine to Thirteen', *Texas Studies in Language and Literature*, 23 (1981), 351–7; Kurt Heinzelman, *The Economics of the Imagination* (Amherst, 1980), 205–6.

Having discerned 'the utter hollowness of what we name / The wealth of Nations', Wordsworth's attention was turned instead to the corresponding, positive value of human 'dignity':

> and having gain'd
> A more judicious knowledge of what makes
> The dignity of individual Man,
> Of Man no composition of the thought,
> Abstraction, shadow, image, but the man
> Of whom we read, the man whom we behold
> With our own eyes; I could not but inquire,
> Not with less interest than heretofore,
> But greater, though in spirit more subdued,
> Why is this glorious Creature to be found
> One only in ten thousand? What one is
> Why may not many be? What bars are thrown
> By nature in the way of such a hope?
> Our animal wants and the necessities
> Which they impose, are these the obstacle?
>
> (xii. 81–95)

Wordsworth is at times rather too fond of expansive rhetorical interrogatives such as these. But although his obstinate questionings might at first seem somewhat vague, they would have struck those of his contemporaries who heard or read the 1805 *Prelude* (such as Coleridge and De Quincey) as a clear, and quite specific allusion to the Malthusian controversy. Book XII certainly goes on to address, at some length, the central claim of the *Essay on Population*—that the 'dignity of individual Man' must always be impeded by the natural and necessary operation of 'animal wants' and desires. Although, as we have seen, Malthus's *Essay* has often been regarded as a formative contribution to the secular science of economics, its notorious conclusions on the subject of population growth actually formed part of a much broader, Christian rationalist theodicy, which attempted to justify the existence of all moral and physical evil by invoking providential natural laws; and it is this fundamental supposition of Malthusian natural theology with which Wordsworth takes issue in Book XII of the *Prelude*. As Malthus put it in the first chapter of the 1798 *Essay*, 'nature has scattered the seeds of life abroad with the most profuse and liberal hand', yet 'Necessity, that imperious all pervading law of nature, restrains them within the prescribed bounds'. These 'prescribed bounds' are the bars imposed by nature on Wordsworth's 'hope', rendering both the 'passion between the sexes', and the struggle for subsistence entailed by such passion upon subsequent generations, immutable constants of our existence; with the result, according to Malthus, that 'misery and vice' must always afflict humanity to some degree.[90]

Coleridge and Southey had, in fact, already concluded that this argument constituted the foundation of the *Essay*'s entire case against human improvement. As Coleridge put it, 'The whole Question is this: Are Lust & Hunger both alike Passions of physical Necessity, and the one equally with the other independent of the Reason, & the Will?'[91] It is uncertain whether or not Wordsworth had access to the copy of the 1803 *Essay on Population* in which this marginal note appears, but he was in close contact with both Southey and Coleridge at this time, and probably saw the edition of the *Annual Review* that contained Southey's attack on Malthus, and in which Coleridge's remarks were reproduced practically verbatim.[92] Whatever the case, Wordsworth certainly wished to question the proposition that 'animal wants' are linked by a chain of causal necessity to human misery and vice; and to that extent Book XII strongly suggests his familiarity with the objections to Malthus's *Essay* which had recently been raised by Coleridge and Southey.[93] Indeed, the allusion to Malthusian doctrine in these lines is made even clearer in a manuscript revision of Book XII, line 94, in which Wordsworth refers to 'animal appetites & daily wants', or what Coleridge had described only slightly less euphemistically as 'Lust & Hunger' in his annotations to the second *Essay*. Wordsworth later settled on the revised, and more explicit, version of these lines.[94] Yet, just as he assumes his ideal reader's unprompted recognition that the 'Philosophy' to which he fell victim in Book X can be identified with Godwinism, so in Book XII of the 1805 *Prelude* Wordsworth frames his response to Malthus without overt reference to the *Essay on Population* or its author, both as a way of

[90] [Malthus], *Essay* (1798), 14–15; id., *Essay* (1803), i. 9–11. See also *Essay* (1798), 267–71.

[91] Coleridge, *Marginalia*, iii. 806.

[92] This inference is based upon Duncan Wu's argument that Wordsworth served as a 'contributor' to Southey's review of Bayley's *Poems*, which appeared in the same issue of the *Annual Review*, and which Wordsworth 'can be expected to have seen . . . in MS and in print'. See Wu, *Wordsworth's Reading 1800–1815* (Cambridge, 1995), 197.

[93] See *Thirteen Book* Prelude, ii. 215, 943–4 (MS A, DC MS 52).

[94] See *Fourteen Book* Prelude, 247, 1085 (Bk. XIII, l. 91).

marking his distance from the vulgar, abstracted polemic of contemporary 'moral philosophy', and as a means of sustaining that sense of knowing intimacy with his audience which is such a constant feature of the *Prelude*'s narrative style.

Wordsworth's 'meditations' upon the possible impediments placed by nature and necessity on plebeian dignity are described as having inspired him with the 'anxious wish'

> To ascertain how much of real worth
> And genuine knowledge, and true power of mind
> Did at this day exist in those who liv'd
> By bodily labour . . .
>
> (xii. 98–101)

> To frame such estimate
> I chiefly look'd (what need to look beyond?)
> Among the natural abodes of men,
> Fields with their rural works, recall'd to mind
> My earliest notices, with these compared
> The observations of my later youth
> Continued downwards to that very day.
>
> (xii. 105–11)

After reflecting upon these wanderings among the labouring classes, Wordsworth restates the challenge of Malthusian doctrine, claiming that the 'lonely roads' were 'schools' of human nature, in which he was

> call'd to make good search
> If man's estate, by doom of Nature yoked
> With toil, is therefore yoked with ignorance,
> If virtue be indeed so hard to rear,
> And intellectual strength so rare a boon . . .
>
> (xii. 173–7)

The *Essay on Population* argues that nature imposes upon humanity 'the necessity of constant exertion' but that, despite such labours, the effect of the 'law of nature' is always to produce 'misery and vice'.[95] However, particularly in the first edition, the *Essay* also emphasizes the structural equivalence of intellectual and corporeal wants. Hence the 'passions, and the wants of the body' stimulate the exertion of mind, and call forth

95 [Malthus], *Essay* (1798), 394, 15–16; see also id., *Essay* (1803), i. 9.

'intellectual wants' that are equally insatiable, as a result of the constantly impinging claims of physical survival. The 'infinite variety of nature' further ensures that, like the thirst for bodily sustenance, the 'thirst of knowledge' can never be satisfied.[96] For Malthus, therefore, material and intellectual deprivation alike provide an unending providential stimulus to human improvement. Wordsworth's rather less sanguine interpretation of this theodicy, on the other hand, reduces Malthus's argument to the simple proposition that 'man's estate' will always be 'by doom of Nature yoked' to both 'toil' and 'ignorance'. It is the truth of this claim that, Wordsworth recalls, he resolved to test in his travels upon the 'lonely roads' (xii. 163).

In the 'walks' that made up this 'good search', Wordsworth claims both to have discovered spiritual equilibrium, and to have heard from the 'lowly men' whom he encountered, 'A tale of honour; sounds in unison / With loftiest promises of good and fair' (xii. 183–4). It is this direct experience of humble society that assures him of the dignity of common life, and consequently of the insufficiency of arguments for the inevitability of suffering and inequality:

> . . . in those wanderings deeply did I feel
> How we mislead each other, above all
> How Books mislead us, looking for their fame
> To judgements of the wealthy Few, who see
> By artificial lights; how they debase
> The Many for the pleasure of those few;
> Effeminately level down the truth
> To certain general notions for the sake
> Of being understood at once, or else
> Through want of better knowledge in the men
> Who frame them, flattering thus our self-conceit
> With pictures that ambitiously set forth
> The differences, the outside marks by which
> Society has parted man from man,
> Neglectful of the universal heart.
>
> (xii. 205–19)

The attack on book learning at this point might recall the critique of Godwinism in Book X, but the 'Books' in question hardly embody the kind of radically egalitarian philosophy expounded in the *Enquiry*

96 [Malthus], *Essay* (1798), 377; ibid. 379–80.

Concerning Political Justice.[97] It seems far more credible to view these lines as a reapplication of that critique to the *Essay on Population* and, more specifically, to Malthus's argument that any community which has escaped the 'savage' state must necessarily become stratified into an unequal society of 'proprietors' and 'labourers'.[98] Wordsworth's implicit accusation that Malthusian doctrine gave spurious philosophical credibility to the oppression of the poor was becoming an increasingly familiar one at this time. William Hazlitt was to make much the same point in his *Reply to the Essay on Population* (1807), when complaining that 'it is neither generous nor just, to come in aid of the narrow prejudices and hard-heartedness of mankind, with metaphysical distinctions and the cobwebs of philosophy'. And Southey's 1804 review, which Wordsworth had probably read, concluded 'No wonder that Mr. Malthus should be a fashionable philosopher! He writes advice to the poor for the rich to read; they of course will approve his opinions . . .'.[99] Throughout this period, in fact, the *Essay on Population* was consistently depicted by its critics as one of the most pernicious contemporary defences of political and economic inequality, and a culpable perversion of 'philosophical' authority in the interests of the powerful and the wealthy.

In formulating his own response to Malthusian doctrine, Wordsworth was perhaps also influenced by Southey's contention that 'human institutions' rather than the 'laws of nature' must bear some responsibility for the degradation of the labouring classes and the material inequality of society. The *Prelude* certainly assumes that those who survive through 'bodily labour' are compelled to live by

> labour far exceeding
> Their due proportion, under all weight
> Of that injustice which upon ourselves
> By composition of society
> Ourselves entail.
>
> (xii. 101–5)

But the most fundamental aspect of Wordsworth's answer to the *Essay on Population* is drawn from his encounters upon the 'lonely roads' with 'Vagrants' and 'Bedlamites', together with his direct

[97] See Johnston, *Wordsworth and* The Recluse, 201.

[98] [Malthus], *Essay* (1798), 287–8; id., *Essay* (1803), i. 322–3.

[99] William Hazlitt, *A Reply to the Essay on Population* (1807), 4–5; [Southey], 'Malthus's Essay', *Annual Review*, 2 (1803), 301.

observation of 'the natural abodes of men' and 'Fields with their rural works' (xii. 124, 158–9, 107–8). His wanderings provided 'Hope to my hope, and to my pleasure peace' (xii. 179), by assuring him of the inner dignity of humanity's 'universal heart', whatever its external appearance (xii. 219).

> the lonely roads
> Were schools to me in which I daily read
> With most delight the passions of mankind,
> There saw into the depth of human souls,
> Souls that appear to have no depth at all
> To vulgar eyes.
>
> (xii. 163–8)

Wordsworth's association of political education and social feeling with his walks upon the 'lonely roads' may have been influenced by John Thelwall's *Peripatetic* (1793), an experimental literary work that is known to have informed *The Excursion* (the only part of *The Recluse* published in Wordsworth's lifetime) and which also extolled the virtues of 'peripatetic habits' and 'rural life' in opposition to the dubious benefits of cities and commercial wealth.[100] The subtitle of Thelwall's poem, 'Sketches of the Heart, of Nature and Society', certainly suggests its connection with Wordsworth's *Recluse*, which was similarly to have comprised 'views of Nature, Man and Society'.[101] But unlike Thelwall's 'democratic pedestrian rambles' (as he described his own peripatetic enquiries into popular opinion), Wordsworth's educative excursions in Book XII of the *Prelude* are framed as a direct refutation of Malthus's *Essay*. In this respect, too, the poet's travels anticipate *The Excursion*, in which it is the character of the 'Wanderer' who figures as the preeminent Wordsworthian critic of unfeeling economists and the Malthusian 'fear / Of numbers'.[102]

Like Wordsworth's peripatetic 'estimate', the *Essay on Population* was also avowedly experimental in method. 'It is an acknowledged truth in philosophy', Malthus declared in the 1798 edition, 'that a just theory will always be confirmed by experiment', and he went on to stress that 'experience' is 'the true source and foundation of all

[100] John Thelwall, *The Peripatetic; or, Sketches of the Heart, of Nature and Society*, 3 vols. (Southwark, 1793), i. 14, 38, 176–7.

[101] Judson Stanley Lyons, *The Excursion: A Study* (New Haven, 1950), 35–7.

[102] John Thelwall, 'Report on the State of Popular Opinion', *Tribune*, 2 (1796), 185; Wordsworth, *Excursion*, 403; id., *Poetical Works*, ix. 363–4.

knowledge'.[103] Wordsworth's account of the means by which he brought the *Essay*'s bookish arguments to the test of 'solid life and true result' attempts to expose both the empirical poverty of Malthus's experimental method, and the consequent superficiality of his understanding of social differences between the 'Many' and the 'few'. Against Malthus's 'artificial lights', Wordsworth claims to find a more profound truth in the insights he has derived from those 'observations' and 'notices' that have been his gift since early youth. It is not bookish speculation, but rather his unmediated experience of 'solid life', which allows Wordsworth to claim a superior insight into the 'human souls' of the rural poor, just as the Fenwick note of 1843 suggests that his early conviction of the social utility of pauperism was ultimately derived, not from intellectual contemplation, but from his having observed an aged beggar as a child, 'with great benefit to my own heart'.[104]

That Wordsworth should include such an extended discussion of Malthusian ideas in the 1805 *Prelude* is hardly surprising, given the fierceness and topicality of the debate, the relevance of the *Essay on Population* to Wordsworth's literary and philosophical preoccupations, and the recent public involvement of both Southey and Coleridge in the Malthusian controversy. Yet the *Prelude*'s elaborate autobiographical critique of the *Essay* has gone unrecognized, even amongst those scholars anxious to draw the two writers into meaningful historical relation.[105] The explanation for this oversight perhaps lies in the fact that Book XII's attack on 'abstract' thought and book learning are more usually associated with Wordsworth's response to Godwinian radicalism. The poet's references to 'false thought / And false philosophy'; his implied contempt for intellectual systems that reduce 'Man' to 'Abstraction, shadow, image'; and his opposition between 'solid life' and mere 'Books': all these recall the attack on Godwin in Book X, and certainly suggest a degree of thematic continuity between the *Prelude*'s earlier critique of radical thought and the concerns of Book XII. But the burden of Wordsworth's argument in the latter book can far more easily be

103 [Malthus], *Essay* (1798), 6, 17.

104 Wordsworth, *Fenwick Notes*, 56. On Wordsworth and walking, see Robin Jarvis, *Romantic Writing and Pedestrian Travel* (Basingstoke, 1997); Celeste Langan, *Romantic Vagrancy: Wordsworth and the Simulation of Freedom* (Cambridge, 1995); Anne D. Wallace, *Walking, Literature, and English Culture: The Origins and Uses of Peripatetic in the Nineteenth Century* (Oxford, 1993).

105 See e.g. Thomas Pfau's comparative reading of poetic and sexual 'reproduction' in Malthus and Wordsworth: *Wordsworth's Profession*, 341–62.

interpreted as anti-Malthusian than anti-Godwinian in orientation. Moreover, as the *Essay on Morals* clearly demonstrates, Wordsworth had already come to the conclusion that his criticisms of Godwin had an equally urgent application to Paleyite natural theology—an intellectual system of which Malthus's 1803 *Essay* was one of the most important contemporary expositions.[106]

In the context of *The Prelude*'s overall thematic structure, the significance of Wordsworth's extended critique of Malthusian ideas in Book XII lies in the fact that, just as in the discussion of Godwin in Book X, Wordsworth goes on to suggest a link between his renunciation of the *Essay on Population* and the assumption of his poetic vocation. Reflecting on his peripatetic observations of 'the natural abodes of men', his consequent insights into 'Nature', 'the power of human minds', and 'men, as they are men within themselves' (xii. 224–5), Wordsworth recounts how he was led to make a profound declaration of aesthetic intent.

> Of these, said I, shall be my Song, of these
> If future years mature me for the task,
> Will I record the praises, making Verse
> Deal boldly with substantial things, in truth
> And sanctity of passion speak of these
>
> (xii. 231–5)

He was, henceforth, resolved to take as his 'theme'

> No other than the very heart of man
> As found amongst the best of those who live
> Not unexalted by religious hope,
> Not uninform'd by books, good books though few,
> In Nature's presence: thence may I select
> Sorrow that is not sorrow, but delight,
> And miserable love that is not pain
> To hear of, for the glory that redounds
> Therefrom to humankind and what we are.
>
> (xii. 239–48)

These lines are commonly taken to refer to some period in Wordsworth's life between his post-Godwinian 'crisis' and the first results of his

[106] Paley had by now publicly announced his conversion to Malthus's population principle: see *Natural Theology*, 540.

imaginative enquiry into the 'very heart of man' in the creative watershed of 1797–8 that produced the *Lyrical Ballads*, *The Ruined Cottage*, and the plan for *The Recluse*.[107] Indeed, the poet's heightened intimacy with 'Nature', 'the power of human minds', and 'men, as they are men within themselves' contains a distinct echo of the proposed subject matter of *The Recluse*, the poem 'On Man, on Nature, and on Human Life', as he was to describe it in the 1814 'Prospectus'.[108] But, although Wordsworth closely associates the 'wanderings' that led to his declaration of poetic vocation with the experiential refutation of Malthusian doctrine, the first *Essay on Population* was in fact published just *after* the extended period of spiritual recovery and creative consolidation to which Wordsworth appears, on purely external biographical evidence, to be referring in these lines. It seems, nevertheless, that he wished to imply that Malthus's *Essay*, as well as Godwinian philosophy, provided a vital catalyst for his creative self-realization. Book XII, we might therefore conclude, subtly distorts Wordsworth's intellectual development in order to suggest that it was his 'anxious' engagement with the doctrines soon to be associated with the *Essay on Population* which helped to precipitate his devotion to a poetry of nature and common life.

There is in fact no unequivocal indication within the *Prelude* itself of precisely which periods of Wordsworth's life are depicted here. Like so much of the poem, Book XII 'skilfully dissolves clear temporal boundaries' within Wordsworth's spiritual autobiography, deliberately overlaying experiences, thoughts, and emotions from disparate periods in the poet's life to form a richly patterned chronological palimpsest. The revisionary process was, in this respect, vital to Wordsworth's compositional method; and the last three books of the *Prelude*, in particular, contain a great deal of poetry transposed from drafts of earlier passages.[109] Thus, in Book XII, it seems likely that material originally intended for Book VIII is first decontextualized, and then reimagined as 'an explicit résumé of the [political and philosophical] critique

[107] Mark L. Reed, *Wordsworth: The Chronology of the Early Years 1770–1799* (Cambridge, Mass., 1967), 187, 189–90; id., 'Introduction' to Wordsworth, *The Thirteen Book* Prelude, i. 50; Jarvis, *Romantic Writing and Pedestrian Travel*, 104–5. Johnston suggests the even earlier period of 1791 to 1795: *Wordsworth and* The Recluse, 200.

[108] Wordsworth, *Excursion*, x; id., *Home at Grasmere*, 100–1.

[109] Reed, *Early Years*, 191; Jonathan Wordsworth, 'Revision as Making: *The Prelude* and its Peers', in Robert Brinkley and Keith Hanley (eds.), *Romantic Revisions* (Cambridge, 1992), 35.

implicit in the earlier Books', but one which can now be seen to be directed at Malthus rather than Godwin.[110] In the process, Wordsworth's critical engagement with Malthus is symbolically conflated with the creative efflorescence of 1796–8 in which the *Lyrical Ballads* were composed, and *The Recluse* was first planned. The *Prelude* is thus able to absorb the trial of Malthus by 'solid life' into the broader account, in Books XI–XIII, of the creative and spiritual reawakening that Wordsworth experienced in the wake of his disillusionment with the French revolution and his rejection of Godwinian rationalism. It is perhaps a measure of its significance to his authorial self-conception that Wordsworth may still have been engaged in this artful piece of autobiographical elision forty years later, when he suggested to Elizabeth Fenwick that his 1798 poem, 'The Old Cumberland Beggar', was his first critical response to the 'political economists'.[111]

There were good public, polemical reasons in 1805, as in 1843, for Wordsworth to define his poetic genius in opposition to Malthusian ideas, but the most fundamental explanation is provided by the *Prelude*'s rationale as a 'tributary' to *The Recluse*. During the late 1790s, Wordsworth was strongly influenced by the synthesis of pantheistic religion and associationist psychology that Coleridge had formulated in direct opposition to the 'Stoical Morality' of Godwin's *Political Justice*. His work on *The Recluse* from this early period suggests that Wordsworth was attempting to give poetic realization to a Coleridgean critique of rational benevolence in which the 'intensity' of private, domestic, and local attachments was understood to promote, rather than obscure, the ends of 'universal philanthropy'.[112] Although significant elements of this pantheistic and associationist version of benevolist philosophy continued to inform the 1805 *Prelude*, Wordsworth's earlier vision of the 'One Life' had by this time been largely replaced by something more nearly

[110] Paul Hamilton, *Wordsworth* (Brighton, 1986), 123. The compositional history of the 1805 *Prelude* is notoriously complex. In brief, about half of Book XII, including much of the response to Malthus, appears to have been originally intended for Book VIII (MS Y, DC MS 48, comp. Oct. 1804). See Wordsworth, *The Prelude: 1799, 1805, 1850*, ed. Jonathan Wordsworth *et al.* (New York, 1979), 517–20; id., *The Thirteen Book* Prelude, 42–58. The material from MS Y suggests that Wordsworth was already considering some kind of response to Malthus in the drafts for Book VIII, before deciding that it would be more appropriate to move this material to Book XII. In doing so, he seems to have made his allusions to the *Essay* much clearer.

[111] Wordsworth, *Fenwick Notes*, 56.

[112] Coleridge, *Lectures 1795*, 163; Jonathan Wordsworth, *Borders of Vision*, 22–3, 131–2.

approximating 'the Christian twofold love of God and one's neighbour, to be attained through a life perfectly attuned to the rhythms of Nature'.[113]

Moreover, by 1805 the broader ideological landscape in which *The Recluse* had originally been conceived was also considerably altered. Perhaps most importantly, Godwin's ideas possessed nothing like the intellectual currency they had enjoyed in the 1790s when, as Hazlitt recalled, 'he blazed as a sun in the firmament of reputation'. The remarkably rapid waning of Godwin's influence was closely associated with the success of Malthus's *Essay*, which was by far the most influential, and indeed controversial, attempt to refute the arguments of *Political Justice*.[114] In vanquishing Godwin, therefore, the *Essay on Population* also offered an indirect, but nevertheless profound challenge to the continued meaning and relevance of *The Recluse*, at least to the extent that the poem continued to be associated by Wordsworth and Coleridge with a projected critique of Godwin originally formulated in the late 1790s, but which by 1804 must have seemed increasingly obsolete, both personally and publicly. The *Prelude*, of course, was conceived by Wordsworth as a way of facilitating *The Recluse*, by providing the autobiographical authorization for his high literary vocation. But, in the changed circumstances of 1804–5, Wordsworth seems to have decided to structure the *Prelude*'s account of his self-discovery as a poet around his creative struggles with both Godwin *and* Malthus. Once incorporated into his literary autobiography, Wordsworth's extended engagement with Malthusian ideas could serve both as the completing counterpart to his critique of abstract philosophy in Book X, and as a vital preliminary to the articulation of his own, poetic vision of 'nature, man and society' in *The Recluse*. Nevertheless, in marked contrast to his unequivocal rejection of Godwinian rational benevolence, *The Prelude* wilfully fails to transcend certain fundamental claims of Malthusian doctrine.

Book XII of the 1805 *Prelude* begins with the typically Wordsworthian assertion that 'Genius' finds in nature 'His best and purest Friend' (xii. 8, 10). Nature provides the spiritual composure and creative energy which allows the poet to find 'in Man an object of delight, / Of pure imagination and of love' (xii. 53–5). In 1798, such sentiments would

[113] Jonathan Wordsworth, *Borders of Vision*, 286.

[114] Hazlitt, *Spirit of the Age*, 31; William St Clair, *The Godwins and the Shelleys: The Biography of a Family* (1989), 197–9, 240.

perhaps have reflected the poet's imaginative rejection of Godwinian rationalism in the visionary recognition of a pantheistic 'One Life'. In Book XII of the *Prelude*, however, the concept of 'nature', as the medium for both poetic imagination and the love of mankind, is developed in contradistinction, not to Godwinian rationalism, but rather to the stern and inflexible 'law of nature' implied by Malthusian natural theology. This latter idea of 'nature' is associated with the 'bars' to dignity imposed by 'animal wants'; it is the 'doom of Nature' that yokes 'man's estate' with 'ignorance' and 'toil'. And, as 'vulgar Nature', it is the antithesis of Wordsworthian 'love'.

> There are those who think that strong affections, love
> Known by whatever name, is falsely deem'd
> A gift, to use the term which they would use,
> Of vulgar Nature, that its growth requires
> Retirement, leisure, language purified
> By manners thoughtful and elaborate
>
> (xii. 185–8)

Although this passage can certainly be read as an attack on the didactic, polite culture of 'the *déraciné* Godwinian intelligentsia', as E. P. Thompson described it, it was a culture that was also shared by Malthus's *Essay*.[115] In a striking passage in the 1798 *Essay* (directed against the theory of rational benevolence), Malthus argued that 'benevolence', while noble and even godlike, is 'generated perhaps, slowly and gradually from self-love'. It is this latter instinct that, Malthus noted elsewhere, 'the inevitable laws of nature' have decreed must always remain the providential 'main-spring of the great machine': benevolence is a prerogative only of 'the most enlightened minds', while self-interest will always be the fundamental rule of human conduct amongst 'the unenlightened'.[116] In 1803 Malthus altered his position somewhat, arguing (after Paley) that, while 'benevolence' is a 'natural passion', it is our duty to train it up into habits conformable to the test of utility and the will of God, and thereby 'to purify and exalt the human mind'. But while he also argued forcefully in the second *Essay* for the education of the lower orders, Malthus remained convinced that

[115] E. P. Thompson, 'Disenchantment or Default? A Lay Sermon' (1969), repr. in *The Romantics: England in a Revolutionary Age* (Woodbridge, 1997), 34. For Godwin's views on education and benevolence, see his *Enquirer*, 1–6; and id., *An Enquiry Concerning Political Justice, and its Influence on General Virtue and Happiness*, 2 vols. (1793), i. 341–60.

[116] [Malthus], *Essay* (1798), 207, 294–5.

the 'poor are by no means inclined to be visionary', and that the best that could be hoped for was to impress upon them their own self-interest in acquiring 'habits of prudence and foresight'.[117]

Wordsworth was extremely reluctant to countenance Malthus's claims for the psychological primacy of self-interest. Yet the *Prelude* does admit the practical applicability of Malthus's arguments to some of the most wretched scenes of human life. 'Love cannot be', for example, in circumstances in which 'labour in excess and poverty / . . . preoccupy the ground / Of the affections'; nor in 'cities, where the human heart is sick, / And the eye feeds it not, and cannot feed'. 'Thus far, no further', it seems, is the Malthusian 'inference good'. Wordsworth thus appears to concede the inevitable absence of benevolent 'love' in the two situations that Malthus himself had identified as the principal barriers to the improvement of the labouring classes: extreme poverty and unchecked urbanization. In such circumstances 'Nature's self' is opposed by 'a deeper nature'—the loveless law of selfishness and 'animal wants' (xii. 197–204). To that extent, the *Prelude* fails to provide an outright refutation of the *Essay on Population*, as Wordsworth finds himself challenged to discover a source of human 'dignity' at the deepest instinctual level, and in the most impoverished situations. Indeed, what James Chandler describes as Wordsworth's 'second nature' is, at least in Book XII, determined far less by Burkean ideas of prescription and tradition than by the influential account of providential necessity articulated in the *Essay on Population*.[118] The breach between 'Nature's self' and the Malthusian 'deeper nature' is never adequately resolved in Book XII's descriptions of human society; it both justifies, and simultaneously ironizes, Wordsworth's compulsive discrimination between the inner and the outer nature of 'man'. Ultimately, the poem attempts to deny this loveless substratum of human nature through its assimilation to a sanctified, benevolent conception of 'Nature's self', leading Wordsworth to declare his conviction

> Not only that the inner frame is good,
> And graciously composed, but that no less
> Nature through all conditions hath a power
> To consecrate, if we have eyes to see,
> The outside of her creatures, and to breathe

[117] Malthus, *Essay* (1803), ii. 157–8; ibid. ii. 128, 153.
[118] Chandler, *Wordsworth's Second Nature*, pp. xviii–xix.

> Grandeur upon the very humblest face
> Of human life.
>
> (xii. 280–6)

But Wordsworth's declarations leave suggestively unresolved the tension between the beauty and dignity of 'the depth of human souls', of 'men, as they are men within themselves' (xii. 167, 225), and a bestial deeper nature, which is implicitly identified by Book XII with Malthusian doctrine, and which Wordsworth seems content to suppose operative in the most deprived circumstances; in 'cities, where the human heart is sick', or in situations in which the imperative of labour precludes all 'grace / Of culture' (xii. 202, 195–6).[119] In this context, the ancestral vision of Salisbury Plain that concludes Book XII, of the ancient Briton's 'rattling spear' and the 'sacrificial Altar, fed / with lining men', suggests Wordsworth's barely suppressed fears of an atavistic cruelty hidden in the depths of human nature (xii. 324, 331–2).

Jonathan Wordsworth has argued that 'the internal voice of imagination' was too strong in the 1805 *Prelude* to allow a genuine poetic identification with 'the still sad music of humanity'. Kenneth Johnston makes the similar claim that Wordsworth 'constantly tried, and constantly failed, to integrate a vision of imaginatively redeemed society into *The Recluse*'s epic mission'; and James Averill identifies Book XII as the moment at which Wordsworth's creative struggle to vindicate his radical social vision of the imagination, as a transfiguring vehicle of human suffering, finally falters and expires.[120] But Book XII also suggests that Wordsworth's ultimate failure to recuperate his earlier vision of 'general human-heartedness' stemmed not just from the overbearing operations of the egotistical sublime, but also from his inability—or unwillingness—to provide an unqualified refutation of Malthusian natural theology, a failure that undermined once and for all the generalized vision of social love originally promised in 1798.

[119] *The Prelude* thus cautions against reducing the differences between 'Romanticism' and 'political economy' to a disagreement over the 'natural' or 'artificial' causes of human suffering. For related discussions, see Winch, *Riches and Poverty*, 420–1; Stephen Copley, 'The "Natural Economy": A Note on Some Rhetorical Strategies in Political Economy—Adam Smith and Malthus', in Francis Barker *et al.* (eds.), *1789: Reading Writing Revolution* (Essex, 1982), 160–9.

[120] Jonathan Wordsworth, *Borders of Vision*, 306–7, 286–7; Johnston, *The Hidden Wordsworth*, 710; James H. Averill, *Wordsworth and the Poetry of Human Suffering* (Ithaca, NY, 1980), 276–7. See also Carl Woodring, *Politics in English Romantic Poetry* (Cambridge, Mass., 1970), 113.

Wordsworth's partial, tacit, and distinctly uneasy accommodation with Malthusian argument in the penultimate Book of the *Prelude* can best be accounted for as a consequence of his enduring sympathies with Malthus's agrarian politics. Indeed, it is precisely Wordsworth's repression of the reformist elements of Malthus's position, and his implicit depiction of the *Essay* as a defence of the interests of the 'Few' at the expense of the 'Many', that allows his covert appropriation of the more agrarian or 'physiocratic' elements of the *Essay*'s argument, and their redirection against Malthus himself. Hence, for example, Wordsworth's strictures on the spiritually deadening environment of the 'great City' are closely integrated with his response to Malthusian doctrine, in spite of the first *Essay*'s persistent hostility to urbanization, and forthright defence of agrarian 'independence' (xii. 120).[121] The same appropriative strategy seems to be at work towards the start of Book XII, in the allusion to Smith's *Wealth of Nations* that introduces Wordsworth's lengthy discussion of the *Essay on Population*. There is no evidence that Wordsworth had any first-hand familiarity with Smith's book, and there was little or no precedent in 1805 for treating Smith's text as a metonym for 'economic discourse' in general, still less for Malthus's distinctive and original synthesis of natural theology and political economy.[122] It seems more likely that Wordsworth's declaration of the 'utter hollowness' of the 'wealth of Nations', and his determination to discover 'where alone that wealth / Is lodged, and how encreased', takes its lead from Malthus's own extensive critique of Smith in the *Essay on Population*—a critique that Malthus himself had shown to have direct implications for '*the proper definition of the wealth of a state*'.[123] The *Essay* was certainly quite clear that the 'professed object of Dr. Adam Smith's inquiry . . . the nature and causes of the wealth of nations' is too often assumed to have a direct relation to 'the happiness and comfort of the lower orders of society'. Malthus's point, upon which Wordsworth seems to have drawn in his own allusion to Smith, was that an increase in the 'wealth' of a nation—'the stock or revenue of the society'—is not necessarily 'convertible into a proportional quantity of provisions'. In the worst case, when surplus revenue is invested in improvements to 'manufacturing

[121] [Malthus], *Essay* (1798), 67, 343, 321.

[122] On the fallacy of assuming that its contemporaries regarded Smith's text as in any sense a foundational work, see Richard F. Teichgraeber III, 'Adam Smith and Tradition: The *Wealth of Nations* before Malthus', in Collini *et al.* (eds.), *Economy, Polity, and Society*, 101–2.

[123] [Malthus], *Essay* (1798), 327; emphasis in original.

machinery', not only will the price of provisions refuse to fall, but there will also be an increase in the number of labourers moving from agriculture to the city to engage in unhealthy and uncertain occupations. 'The increasing wealth of the nation,' he concluded, 'has had little or no tendency to better the condition of the labouring poor. They have not, I believe, a greater command of the necessaries and conveniencies of life; and a much greater proportion of them, than at the period of the [Glorious] revolution, is employed in manufactures, and crowded together in close and unwholesome rooms.'[124] Distaste for urban environments, concern for the 'condition of the labouring poor', and impatience with selective definitions of national wealth: all these aspects of the *Essay on Population*'s argument were selectively reworked in Book XII of the *Prelude* as Wordsworth struggled to impose upon his compromised relationship with Malthusian political economy the appearance of straightforward disagreement.

In this Wordsworth was perhaps more successful than he had the right to expect. His tacit appropriation of Malthus's agrarian critique of Adam Smith has indeed been interpreted as an unproblematic reflection of the Romantic antipathy to 'political economy' in general, an antipathy that is naturally assumed to have included the *Essay on Population*. Wordsworth's initial attitude was far more ambivalent and self-ironizing than this, but the 1805 *Prelude* nevertheless constitutes a foundational moment in the Lake school's long campaign against the 'mechanical' and unfeeling abstractions of economic science. His critical engagement with Malthusian ideas must, however, also affect to our more general understanding of Wordsworth's shifting ideological loyalties. It has often been suggested that the politics of the *Prelude* were centrally informed by its author's abiding commitment to some form of agrarian humanism, which mediated his turn from heterodox republicanism to the conservative defence of church and state.[125] But 'agrarianism' is, of course, an extremely broad category, and to understand its polemical role in the *Prelude* also requires an appreciation of the ambivalent attitude to commercial wealth evident in Malthus's economic thought. Wordsworth's complex reaction to the *Essay*'s agrarian

[124] Ibid. 303–13; cf. id., *Essay* (1803), i. 380–409. His criticisms of Smith did not, however, diminish Malthus's typically polite and respectful attitude to *The Wealth of Nation*'s contribution to political economy; see Winch, *Riches and Poverty*, 237, 272.

[125] See e.g. Friedman, *Making of a Tory Humanist*; Kenneth MacLean, *Agrarian Age: A Background for Wordsworth* (New Haven, 1950); John Williams, *Wordsworth: Romantic Poetry and Revolution Politics* (Manchester, 1989).

bias certainly provides a neglected clue to the difficulties and compromises attendant upon his progressive identification with conservative political opinion. Yet the *Prelude*'s response to Malthus is also suggestive of a certain continuity between the radical critique of Godwin, originally formulated by Wordsworth and Coleridge in the 1790s, and that later, Lake school attack on the 'abstract' and unfeeling science of political economy which took shape in the post-war years. To that extent, the critique of Malthus in Book XII of the *Prelude* not only constitutes a missing link in Wordsworth's autobiographical aetiology of creative genius; it also provides an important insight into the ideological origins of the Lake poets' 'mature' political conservatism.

CHAPTER TWO

Moral Culture and the March of Mind: Education and Economics in the Early Nineteenth Century

The language of politics and morals in later eighteenth-century British society was suffused with expressions of wonder, fascination, and alarm at the growing power of 'commerce', the ubiquitous influence of which extended from public finance to domestic economy, high fashion to popular politics.[1] Many contemporary writers, finding their professional identity and status directly caught up in these changes, were particularly preoccupied by the nexus between commerce, morals, and the diffusion of learning through the printed page. The growth of a middle-class reading public, the shift from aristocratic patronage to the literary marketplace, and the end of perpetual copyright all testified to the dramatic changes in the 'polite' culture of eighteenth-century Britain brought about by the commercialization of literature and learning.[2] Perhaps just as importantly, however, these changes also helped to stimulate anxious reflection on the relationship between new wealth, moral propriety, and the concomitant progress of intellectual enlightenment amongst the labouring and 'mechanical' classes of society.

'The vast influx of riches . . . amongst the lower ranks of men', warned the Archdeacon of Lincoln, John Gordon, in 1771, 'helps to lift them up, in dress and other accommodations, to a fancied level with their superiors: which the diffused state of learning amongst us still

[1] Neil McKendrick *et al.*, *The Birth of a Consumer Society: The Commercialization of Eighteenth-Century Society* (1982).

[2] John Brewer, *The Pleasures of the Imagination: English Culture in the Eighteenth Century* (1997), 125–97.

further enables them, with some shew, to support'.[3] Gordon regarded such developments as an urgent threat to the existing social order, and a principal source of irreligion, blasphemy, and sedition. Many other late-eighteenth-century moralists shared similar fears about the corrupting influence of commercial wealth. The Catholic Whig Joseph Berington, for example, conceded that the 'wealth of England and its power have, surely, been promoted by its commerce with other nations, and by its manufactures at home: But,' he went on, 'they also have been the source of many evils; and our present depravity of manners takes its principal strength from them'. Berington, however, drew a rather more positive conclusion from this gloomy reflection than Gordon had done, and went on to argue that the moral depravity of the nation could best be remedied by a renewed commitment to popular education and the rapid extension of Sunday schools throughout the country.[4]

The Sunday schools movement of the 1780s (of which Berington was a leading supporter) was perhaps the most obvious manifestation of a much broader concern with the role of paternalistic educational intervention in the moral character of the populace.[5] Widespread concern about national decline, particularly after 1776, often found expression in complaints about the corruptions of commerce and luxury, and the corresponding need for the moral elevation of the populace through 'disciplinary, moral and social reforms'—an agenda that went on to exert a powerful influence on early nineteenth-century discussions of education and the poor laws.[6] Political economists and social reformers thus found themselves united in their concern, not just with the production and distribution of material commodities in a complex commercial society, but also with the more intangible, moral and epistemic 'economies'

[3] John Gordon, *The Causes and Consequences of Evil Speaking against Government* (1771), 12.

[4] Joseph Berington, *An Essay on the Depravity of the Nation, with a View to the Promotion of Sunday Schools* (Birmingham, 1788), 15. On Berington, see Robert Hole, *Pulpits, Politics and Public Order in England 1760–1832* (Cambridge, 1989), 26–7.

[5] Robert J. Hind, 'Working People and Sunday Schools: England, 1780–1850', *Journal of Religious History*, 15 (1988), 199–218; Thomas Walter Laqueur, *Religion and Respectability: Sunday Schools and Working Class Culture, 1780–1850* (New Haven, 1976), 21–62.

[6] Kathleen Wilson, *The Sense of the People: Politics, Culture and Imperialism in England, 1715–1785* (Cambridge, 1995), 269; Joanna Innes, 'Politics and Morals: The Reformation of Manners Movement in Later Eighteenth-Century England', in Eckhart Hellmuth (ed.), *The Transformation of Political Culture: England and Germany in the Late Eighteenth Century* (Oxford, 1990), 57–118.

linking the national dynamics of wealth and poverty to those of virtue, vice, and the diffusion of knowledge.

These issues became central to the second, 1803 edition of the *Essay on Population*, via Malthus's recommendation of 'moral restraint' from procreation as a check to the operation of the population principle. The ethical resource of moral restraint held out the possibility of a permanently raised living standard for the labouring classes (and therefore exposed Malthus to the charge of self-contradiction, as both Coleridge and Southey noted). Its successful operation was predicated upon the education of the lower orders in those habits of sobriety, industry, and self-control which, Malthus supposed, were in their own long-term interests. Deriving from Paleyite theological utilitarianism, the idea of moral restraint brought Malthus back within the fold of mainstream Anglican social theory by answering orthodox criticisms relating to the problem of evil in the first edition. In the process, however, Malthus provided a powerful justification for the progressive social diffusion of the moral precepts of Christianity, the principles of political economy, and the basic literacy skills necessary for their effective inculcation.

For Malthus, the only effective means of encouraging 'preventive' checks to population, such as moral restraint, was to 'infuse' into 'the lower classes of society . . . a portion of that knowledge and foresight which so much facilitates the attainment of this object in the educated part of the community'. The manners and intellect of the lower orders had therefore to be raised to a point at which they could exercise moral circumspection and rational foresight, in a manner similar to their social superiors. The means to this end, for Malthus, lay in 'the establishment of a system of parochial education', much as Adam Smith had recommended in the *Wealth of Nations*, but supplemented with instruction in 'a few of the simplest principles of political economy'. In this case,

> the parochial schools would, by early instruction and the judicious distribution of rewards, have the fairest chance of training up the rising generation in habits of sobriety, industry, independence, and prudence, and in a proper discharge of their religious duties; which would raise them from their present degraded state, and approximate them in some degree to the middle classes of society, whose habits, generally speaking, are certainly superior.[7]

[7] Malthus, *Essay* (1803), ii. 151–5.

But the moral elevation of the lower orders would not only improve their material condition as a class; it would also have important collateral benefits for society as a whole. Malthus conceded that this might at first appear paradoxical. A populace acquainted with the true explanation for poverty might be expected to provide 'a tempting opportunity to governments of oppressing their subjects at pleasure, and laying the whole blame on the laws of nature and the imprudence of the poor'.[8] This, as we have seen, was certainly Southey's opinion. But Malthus's Whiggish instincts led him, on the contrary, to the rather different conclusion that the progress of 'civil liberty' and 'rational freedom' could only be quickened by the widespread diffusion of the natural principles revealed by the *Essay on Population*.

His conviction on this issue was based on the belief that, if the lower orders' 'poverty and distress' were to be blamed entirely upon the 'iniquity of government', without regard to the laws of natural necessity, potential demagogues would be provided with the perfect excuse to foment civil unrest and political disaffection in a dishonest manner, by falsely promising to ameliorate the condition of the people. On this analysis, a typical example of eighteenth-century Country party rhetoric, such provocations could lead only to a succession of violent revolutions in government, and the alternating rule of 'tyranny' and the 'mob'. A system of national, parochial education for the lower classes would thus also serve to increase the civil liberty and political independence of the mass of society: 'an instructed and well-informed people would be much less likely to be led away by inflammatory writings, and much better able to detect the false declamation of interested and ambitious demagogues, than an ignorant people'.[9]

This perhaps conveys something of the intensely politicized character of the debate on popular education in this period, as well as the important contribution made by Malthusian political economy on this issue. Indeed, while the educational content of Malthus's Christianized economics began as a reflex of his Foxite politics, it went on to influence both reformist English Whigs and prominent 'liberal Tory' evangelicals such as the Scottish clergyman and social reformer Thomas Chalmers. But the increasing prominence of political economy in discussions of national prosperity and the diffusion of knowledge was by no means confined to the question of popular education. Its enduring

[8] Malthus, *Essay* (1803), ii. 122.
[9] Ibid. ii. 154.

debt to the sophisticated, self-scrutinizing intellectual preoccupations of the Scottish Enlightenment meant that early nineteenth-century political economy often found itself equally concerned with the fate of higher, more 'refined' forms of learning and literature within complex commercial societies.

'THE PROPER AND LIBERAL CULTURE OF THE MIND': DUGALD STEWART AND ENLIGHTENMENT

Over the course of the eighteenth century, Scottish society experienced a number of important, and far-reaching, alterations to its formal educational structures. A national system of parochial schooling, funded by local taxation, had been enacted in law between 1616 and 1696, and thereafter developed with such success that the parochial system became an important model for many nineteenth-century English educational reformers. There were also innovations in the Burgh schools, which proved increasingly willing to reorientate their curricula in order to accommodate the more vocational subjects demanded by the professional and mercantile classes.[10] The universities, meanwhile, experienced a concerted intellectual reaction against both clericalism and scholasticism in the years after 1707. In their place, the 'liberal arts' were given a renewed centrality, 'as a vital forming-process for the character of citizens in a modern Scottish *res publica*'—a broadly 'Commonwealth' Whig conception of gentlemanly learning that also remained congruous with 'rich local traditions of Calvinist and humanist scholarship' dating back to the Reformation.[11]

As this new, secular educational ideology established itself within the Scottish universities in the first half of the century, its advocates found themselves less vulnerable to the more pious criticisms of the Kirk, but also increasingly obliged to defend the civic function of the learned scholar in terms of the commercializing ethos of an 'improving'

[10] Donald J. Witherington, 'Education and Society in the Eighteenth Century', in N. T. Phillipson and Rosalind Mitchison (eds.), *Scotland in the Age of Improvement: Essays in Scottish History in the Eighteenth Century*, new edn. (Edinburgh, 1996), 169–99.

[11] Peter Jones, 'The Scottish Professoriate and the Polite Academy, 1720–46', in Istvan Hont and Michael Ignatieff (eds.), *Wealth and Virtue: The Shaping of Political Economy in the Scottish Enlightenment* (Cambridge, 1985), 90; David Allan, *Virtue, Learning and the Scottish Enlightenment: Ideas of Scholarship in Early Modern History* (Edinburgh, 1993), 232.

Scottish society.[12] If this eventually lent a rather systematic, professionalized character to some branches of humanistic enquiry within the universities, it also contributed to the formation of a much more diffuse sense of intellectual community. The social and intellectual milieu of the Scottish Enlightenment included not just the university, but also a number of other less formal institutions, including the coffee house, the essayistic periodical, and voluntary associations such as the famous Select Society. The ideal of 'polite learning', which has often been identified with the Addisonian Anglicization of Scottish high culture, united the university professoriate with a wider intelligentsia of schoolmasters, doctors, and lawyers, as well as a provincial aristocratic elite self-consciously committed to reviving the country's fortunes through economic and intellectual improvement rather than political or military participation. This in turn required a positive reconceptualization of commercial civilization, in its relations to both polite learning and the ideals of civic virtue apparently emasculated by the Act of Union.[13] But if the intellectual life of late-eighteenth-century Scotland was, as a result, increasingly centred around the values of rational enquiry and cultural refinement as the historical correlates of economic progress, uncomfortable questions nevertheless remained concerning the broader relevance and utility of 'polite learning' in a rapidly 'improving' society.

Adam Smith's discussion of the division of labour, and its effects on the intellectual and moral frame of the 'common people', forms one of the most celebrated contemporary engagements with this issue. Book V of *The Wealth of Nations* devotes considerable space to education in the context of 'the expence [*sic*] of public works and public institutions'. Smith was quite confident that men of 'some rank and fortune' could turn to private education to furnish themselves with 'every accomplishment which can recommend them to the publick esteem'. Their subsequent employments would be of sufficient complexity to prevent any weakening of the understanding, and would allow in addition 'a good deal of leisure, during which they may perfect themselves in every branch either of useful or ornamental

[12] Richard B. Sher, *Church and University in the Scottish Enlightenment: The Moderate Literati of Edinburgh* (Princeton, 1985), 326–8; Allan, *Virtue, Learning*, 162–3.

[13] The terms of this account are most closely associated with the work of Nicholas Phillipson. See, *inter alia*, his article on 'The Scottish Enlightenment', in Roy Porter and Mikulàs Teich (eds.), *The Enlightenment in National Context* (Cambridge, 1981), 19–40.

knowledge . . .'.[14] However, the public education of the lower classes remained a clear necessity in a 'civilized and commercial society', since the division of labour within humbler occupations tended to induce mental torpor and a narrowing of understanding, unconducive to either moral or intellectual improvement:

In the progress of the division of labour, the employment of the far greater part of those who live by labour, that is, of the great body of the people, comes to be confined to a few very simple operations; frequently to one or two. But the understandings of the greater part of men are necessarily formed by their different employments. The man whose whole life is spent in performing a few simple operations, of which the effects too are, perhaps, always the same, has no occasion to exert his understanding, or to exercise his invention in finding out expedients for removing difficulties which never occur. He naturally loses, therefore, the habit of such exertion, and generally becomes as stupid and ignorant as it is possible for a human creature to become.

Such a condition incapacitated the labourer with respect not just to 'the ordinary duties of private life', but also to the more public responsibilities entailed by 'the great and extensive interests of his country'. The solution, for Smith, was public education of the 'common labourer' through a national system of parochial schools.[15] Scholarly discussion of this famous passage has focused on the issue of how much priority Smith gave to safeguarding the private and public virtue of the labourer through education, over the just satisfaction of the material needs of the many realizable through the operations of the division of labour and the 'invisible hand'.[16] But the fact that he felt compelled to confront this dilemma at all is also suggestive of a broader disjunction between a restrictive ideal of polite, educated scholarship, and the wider moral and social implications of accelerating commercialization.

Smith's account of the division of labour and popular education might thus be taken to exemplify a latent paradox inherent in the Scottish 'commercial humanist' account of the mutually supportive relation between commercial progress, polite learning, and civic

[14] Adam Smith, *An Inquiry into the Nature and Causes of the Wealth of Nations* (1776), ed. R. H. Campbell *et al.*, 2 vols. (Oxford, 1976), ii. 784.

[15] Ibid. ii. 781–6; see also id., *Lectures on Jurisprudence*, ed. R. L. Meek *et al.* (Oxford, 1978), 539–40.

[16] Donald Winch, *Adam Smith's Politics: An Essay in Historiographic Revision* (Cambridge, 1978), 111–20; Istvan Hont and Michael Ignatieff, 'Needs and Justice in the "Wealth of Nations" ', in id. (eds.), *Wealth and Virtue*, 8.

virtue.[17] But the terms of that account were complicated still further by the French Revolution. Events in France after 1789 appeared to many British observers to invite explanation as the violent political consequences of the diffusion of 'speculative' knowledge and opinion by infidel *philosophes*; and counter-revolutionary argument was quick to link the explosive political agency of a radicalized French literary class to its alliance with a restless, politically ambitious commercial interest. The Revolution controversy thus called into question the compatibility of oligarchic constitutional monarchy with the growing political influence of commercial and manufacturing wealth, creating a series of ideological fissures within the discourse of 'polite letters' through which eighteenth-century English society had integrated the regulative ethical norms of courtly *politesse* with the expansive, and potentially unrestrained marketplace of 'intellectual commerce'. Such developments were to prove particularly troubling for the Scottish Whig intelligentsia, who had done much to popularize the ideology of Addisonian 'politeness' amongst the country's ruling elite; and this perhaps goes some way to explaining the frequency with which Smith's *Wealth of Nations*, and the doctrine of trade liberalization, were damned by association with radical ideas in the counter-revolutionary atmosphere of the early 1790s.[18] For Scottish commercial humanism, the intellectual character of the English counter-revolution constituted a challenge not just to the legitimacy of the revolutionary regime but also, more indirectly, to an already compromised ideological synthesis of learning, virtue, and commercial civilization. It is no coincidence that in 1802, when a group of young Edinburgh Whigs set up a new literary review in defiance of the reactionary oligarchy of Henry Dundas, the lead article of the very first number was given over to a spirited refutation of the influence of 'philosophers' in fomenting the French Revolution.[19]

The leading representative of Scottish Whig thought in this oppressive, post-revolutionary period was Dugald Stewart, Professor at

[17] On 'commercial humanism', see J. G. A. Pocock, *Virtue, Commerce, and History: Essays on Political Thought and History, Chiefly in the Eighteenth Century* (Cambridge, 1985), 194.

[18] Lawrence E. Klein, *Shaftesbury and the Culture of Politeness: Moral Discourse and Cultural Politics in Early Eighteenth-Century England* (Cambridge, 1994); Emma Rothschild, 'Adam Smith and Conservative Economics', *Economic History Review*, 2nd ser., 45 (1992), 74–96.

[19] [Francis Jeffrey], 'Mounier, De l'Influence des Philosophes', *Edinburgh Review*, 1 (Oct. 1802), 1–18.

Edinburgh University from 1785 to 1820 and, at least during the first part of the nineteenth century, 'the most influential philosophy teacher in the West outside Germany'.[20] Stewart's attempts to forge a system of 'speculative' moral and political philosophy after 1789 were guided by his wish to reconcile inductive method with a defence of abstract, general principle as a guide to legislation, a project that made the science of 'political economy' an essential resource for the enlightened statesman. In the controversial first volume of his *Elements of the Philosophy of the Human Mind* (1792), Stewart argued that the unique complexity of contemporary European civilization was making recourse to 'ancient prejudices' increasingly unreliable: the 'violent revolutions which, at different periods, have convulsed modern Europe, have arisen, not from a spirit of innovation in sovereigns and statesmen; but from their bigoted attachment to antiquated forms, and to principles borrowed from less enlightened ages'.[21] But, if the *Elements* can be regarded from this perspective as a critical response to counter-revolutionary attacks on 'abstract' and dehistoricized political forms, they also constituted a defence of the role of learning and literature in progressive commercial society in opposition to the more nostalgic, muscular Whiggism of Adam Ferguson's *Essay on the History of Civil Society* (1767).

For Ferguson, Stewart's predecessor in the Chair of Moral Philosophy at Edinburgh, literary 'exertions of imagination and sentiment' flourished with most 'vigour' amongst a 'forward and aspiring people', the pre-eminent example of which was classical Greece, 'divided into many little states, and agitated, beyond any spot on the globe, by domestic contentions and foreign wars'.[22] The emasculatory dangers of excessive refinement in modern society were understood by Ferguson to arise from the subdivision of arts, professions, and ranks, which tended 'to withdraw individuals from the common scene of occupation'. Alienation from this animating arena of public virtue could therefore be identified as one of the most acute dangers of the progress of letters, for, when 'libraries are furnished, and every path of ingenuity is occupied', we 'become students and admirers, instead of rivals; and substitute the

[20] Nicholas Phillipson, 'The Pursuit of Virtue in Scottish University Education: Dugald Stewart and Scottish Moral Philosophy in the Enlightenment', in id. (ed.), *Universities, Society, and the Future* (Edinburgh, 1983), 85.

[21] Dugald Stewart, *Elements of the Philosophy of the Human Mind*, 3 vols. (1792–1827), i. 245.

[22] Adam Ferguson, *An Essay on the History of Civil Society* (Edinburgh, 1767), 272–3.

knowledge of books, instead of the inquisitive or animated spirit in which they were written'. The potentially unlimited accumulation of wealth (and the equally unlimited desire for such accumulation) would not merely corrupt public spirit in a highly commercial society; it also threatened to submerge a vigorous and heroic literary tradition beneath a welter of superficial knowledge acquired purely for its own sake.[23]

For Stewart, however, the most instructive models for the science of politics should be drawn neither from prescriptive, and dangerously ossified historical forms, nor from the anachronistic martial ideals of Fergusonian civic humanism, but rather from the progressive civilization of European society since the Reformation. Perhaps the single most important justification for this change of emphasis can be traced to his assertion that 'in modern Europe, in consequence of the invention of printing, and the liberty of the press, public opinion has acquired an ascendant in public affairs, which it never possessed in those states of antiquity from which most of our political examples are drawn'.[24] Stewart argued that, although the rise of printing relied first and foremost upon technological innovation, it should nevertheless be regarded as a glorious advance in the 'natural history of man'. The *Elements*' celebration of the rise of European print culture since the sixteenth century, which promised to 'widen the circle of science and civilization' and diffuse a principled appreciation of good government, allowed him to align the rise of manufactures and commerce with the development of enlightened civilization in a naturalized historical *telos*.[25] The 'rapid communication, and the universal diffusion of knowledge, by means of the press, render the situation of political societies essentially different from what it ever was formerly, and secure infallibly, against every accident, the progress of human reason'. The science of politics had to adapt to these comparatively new, and still rapidly evolving features of contemporary European society, and 'they are to be the most successful statesmen, who, paying all due regard to past experience, search for the rules of their conduct in the peculiar circumstances of their own times, and in an enlightened anticipation of the future history of mankind'.[26] By 1821, when he published the second

[23] Adam Ferguson, *An Essay on the History of Civil Society* (Edinburgh, 1767), 333–4.
[24] Stewart, *Elements*, i. 245.
[25] Ibid. i. 263–5.
[26] Ibid. i. 238.

part of his *Dissertation Exhibiting the Progress of Metaphysical, Ethical, and Political Philosophy, since the Revival of Letters in Europe*, Stewart's speculative science of politics was centrally premissed upon the development of a cosmopolitan 'Republic of Letters' since the Reformation, a unique historical phenomenon which demanded that the philosopher disregard 'all diversities of language and of geographical situation' and direct his attention instead 'to the intellectual progress of the species in general'.[27]

But despite the increasing intellectual homogenization of European letters, Stewart refused to endorse Ferguson's argument that the creative imagination was increasingly impoverished by the progress of civilization. The nostalgic belief that imagination was 'in its state of highest perfection in those rude periods of society, when the faculties shoot up wild and free', was simply not credible, since such undisciplined mental flights lacked the quality of reflexivity necessary to a 'cultivated imagination' that had 'acquired such a degree of activity as to delight in its own exertions'.[28]

> It is . . . in times of general darkness and barbarism, that what is commonly called originality of genius most frequently appears: and surely the great aim of an enlightened and benevolent philosophy, is not to rear a small number of individuals, who may be regarded as prodigies in an ignorant and admiring age, but to diffuse, as widely as possible, that degree of cultivation which may enable the bulk of a people to possess all the intellectual and moral improvement of which their nature is susceptible.[29]

It is hardly surprising that Stewart's reflections on the political and social value of the 'cultivated imagination' have been marginalized by an overdetermined identification of 'culture' and its cognates with a 'Romantic' sensibility. Stewart's progressive Whiggism was profoundly antipathetic to that 'originality of genius' which has commonly been regarded as a central, defining characteristic of the Romantic artist, but which he would clearly have regarded as the product of undisciplined intellectual primitivism. Stewart's alternative conception of mental cultivation promised, in the words of Nicholas Phillipson, to 'release the imagination from its dependence on fantasy, and harness it to the cause of virtue', animating the legislator with the spirit of enlightened civic

[27] Dugald Stewart, 'Dissertation . . . Part II', in *Supplement to the Fourth, Fifth, and Sixth Editions of the Encyclopaedia Britannica*, 6 vols. (Edinburgh, 1816–1824), v. 1.

[28] Dugald Stewart, *Philosophical Essays* (Edinburgh, 1810), 524–5.

[29] Stewart, *Elements*, i. 27.

responsibility.[30] In this respect, Stewart seems to have been drawing on a more general interest amongst the Scottish professoriate with the 'culture of the mind' as a branch of practical ethics, a pedagogic ideal that was originally inspired by Baconian notions of scholarship and learning as forms of mental 'husbandry'.[31] For Stewart, however, the cultivated imagination constituted an essential prerequisite not just of the speculative thinker, but also of the progressive legislator, thereby supplanting the role of Fergusonian civic virtue in his political philosophy. The primary vehicle for its exertions in the cause of good government was, moreover, to be found in neither heroic literature nor impassioned oratory, but rather in the new science of political economy.

Stewart's influential lectures on this subject dramatically extended the intellectual range of political economy, stressing its affiliations with moral philosophy, and drawing the study of government and jurisprudence into the orbit of a discipline elevated far beyond the narrow consideration of wealth and demographics.[32] Its notionally 'scientific' status nevertheless remained extremely important. Indeed, for Stewart and his Whig students, political economy offered a way of sustaining a spirit of moderate reformism in the reactionary intellectual atmosphere after 1789, by dissociating specific constitutional questions from the legitimating methodological grounds of political science, and distinguishing the productive economic relations disclosed by the Whig 'experimental philosophy' from the violent excesses of French revolutionary ideology.[33] It also promised, therefore, to redeem the pedagogic social function of political theorists from association with the reckless propagandizing of radical *philosophes*. Because political economy was of more immediate relevance to the happiness of a people than their particular system of government, Stewart's lectures recommended popular education in its principles as an essential precondition of constitutional reform but also,

[30] Phillipson, 'The Pursuit of Virtue', 96.

[31] See Charles Stewart-Robinson, 'The Pneumatics and Georgics of the Scottish Mind', *Eighteenth-Century Studies*, 20 (1987), 296–312.

[32] Knud Haakonssen, 'From Moral Philosophy to Political Economy: The Contribution of Dugald Stewart', in V. Hope (ed.), *Philosophers of the Scottish Enlightenment* (Edinburgh, 1984), 211–32; Salim Rashid, 'Political Economy as Moral Philosophy: Dugald Stewart of Edinburgh', *Australian Economic Papers*, 26 (1987), 145–56.

[33] See Donald Winch, 'The System of the North: Dugald Stewart and his Pupils', in Stefan Collini *et al.*, *That Noble Science of Politics: A Study in Nineteenth-Century Intellectual History* (Cambridge, 1983), 36–8; Biancamaria Fontana, *Rethinking the Politics of Commercial Society: The* Edinburgh Review *1802–1832* (Cambridge, 1985), 81–105.

more generally, as a 'means of encouraging among the body of the people habits of industry, and . . . regularity of morals'.[34]

This process of popular enlightenment was accelerating as a result of 'the wide circulation of occasional pamphlets, and . . . periodical journals,—those cheap and enticing vehicles of information, which adapt themselves to the rapid, and often capricious changes of general curiosity, and communicate, even to the indolent and dissipated, some imperfect knowledge of the course of political events, and of the progress of scientific improvement'. Yet the gradualist emphasis of Stewart's Whig politics demanded that the insights of political philosophy be entrusted in the first instance to the 'speculative few'. He was thus inclined to discriminate the 'intellectual habits that are formed by the pursuit of science or of literature' from those appropriate to the 'active engagements of business'.[35]

In his lectures on political economy, Stewart discussed the process of specialization in relation to intellectual as well as 'mechanical' pursuits.[36] Unlike Smith, who had been confident of the ease with which a man of 'rank and fortune' could acquire and maintain a level of education appropriate to his station, Stewart recognized that the division of labour, and all its attendant dangers, had already begun to impinge upon the higher spheres of intellectual production. 'Nothing', he maintained in the *Elements*, 'can be more evident, than the necessity of limiting the field of our exertion, if we wish to benefit society by our labours'. There seemed, moreover, to be 'no profession or pursuit which has not habits peculiar to itself; and which does not leave some powers of the mind dormant, while it exercises and improves the rest'. Hence 'the proper and liberal culture of the mind' must depend on 'a variety of those occupations which literature and science afford, added to a promiscuous intercourse with the world, in the habits of conversation and business'.[37]

Stewart went on in the lectures on political economy to argue that the development of European print culture and the emergence of the republic of letters since the Reformation had created the preconditions for the gifted philosopher to contribute to a more general

[34] Dugald Stewart, 'Lectures on Political Economy', in *Collected Works*, ed. William Hamilton, 11 vols. (Edinburgh, 1854–60), viii. 49.

[35] Ibid. ix. 343; Winch, 'The System of the North', in Collini *et al.*, *That Noble Science*, 36; Dugald Stewart, *Outlines of Moral Philosophy* (Edinburgh, 1793), 60–1.

[36] Stewart, 'Lectures on Political Economy', in *Works*, ix. 315.

[37] Stewart, *Elements*, i. 21–3.

process of enlightenment. While, in the 'mechanical arts . . . the number of individuals who can be made to contribute their labours to a common stock, is comparatively limited', in the intellectual sphere, by contrast, 'a combination is formed, by means of the press, among all the powers which genius and industry can display in the most remote ages and nations'. Stewart thus combined Smith's insight into the intellectually debilitating consequences of the division of labour with his own emphasis on the role of a 'speculative' philosophical class as the guardians of European enlightenment. The accumulating 'observations and conjectures of obscure individuals' were to be gathered and synthesized by the cultivated philosopher, in his capacity both as the adviser of statesmen, and as the agent of a broader and more gradual process of material and intellectual improvement.[38]

USEFUL KNOWLEDGE AND THE INTELLECTUAL DIVISION OF LABOUR

Stewart's pedagogic influence on a generation of Whig writers and politicians was profound, and extended from James Mackintosh and John Russell to Francis Jeffrey—the editor of the *Edinburgh Review*—and his leading contributors, Henry Brougham and Francis Horner. The *Edinburgh* rapidly established a reputation as the most influential literary review in Britain, and the contributors' keen interest in political economy made it an important vehicle for the popularization of the works of Smith, Malthus, and Ricardo amongst middle-class reading audiences. This new generation of intellectual ambassadors from late Enlightenment Scotland consolidated the influence of Stewart's post-revolutionary reconception of the scope and methods of political science upon English liberal Whiggism. But Stewart's teachings also played an important role in the emergence of utilitarian radicalism in the years after Waterloo, through their influence on another of his pupils, James Mill. For both utilitarians and liberal Whigs, the emergence of relatively large-scale institutions of adult education in the 1820s, along with the continued growth of reading societies and a popular periodical press, not only gave Stewart's faith in print culture and the diffusion of knowledge a prophetic ring; they also suggested the need for a

[38] Stewart, 'Lectures on Political Economy', in *Works*, ix. 339; id., *Elements*, i. 267.

systematic sociology of knowledge and belief, adapted to the rhythms of early industrial society and predicated upon the insights and arguments of political economy.

The early nineteenth-century middle-class movement to educate the working classes, or certain sections thereof, in the principles of economic science was inspired by the belief that, once the truths of political economy were simplified and disseminated, the curse of social unrest and Luddite machine breaking would fade, and the virtues of capital accumulation and socio-economic aspiration become clear to the productive classes of society. The prospectus of the Manchester Mechanics' Institute, set up in 1824, proclaimed the benefits of science to the mechanic and artisan as 'of practical application' to their trade, by allowing them to gain 'a more thorough knowledge of their business, acquire a greater degree of skill in the practice of it, and be qualified to make improvements and even new inventions in the arts which they respectively profess'.[39] The ideological presuppositions shaping the curricula of those mechanics' institutes under middle-class control were based, to a large extent, upon a perceived need to mould certain sectors of the nascent industrial workforce to new patterns of economic production.[40] The popularization of those scientific principles determining the pace of technological and economic advance was central to this project, since their assimilation by the labour elite to be shaped by the institutes could only further quicken the rate of economic progress and diminish the incidence of social conflict.

The revolutionary wars with France saw a new importance attached by political argument to the formation and potential derangements of the public mind. As the Napoleonic threat receded, and Liverpool's government attempted to secure the peace, national cohesion and social stability were frequently understood to depend upon the populace's urgent recognition of the essential interrelatedness of society that had been revealed by political economy. J. R. McCulloch, for example, maintained the 'intimate connection' of a popular political economy to 'all the best interests of society . . . There is no other [science], indeed, which comes so directly home to the everyday occupations and business of mankind.'[41] During the war, the national debt was often invoked as a

[39] Quoted in A. E. Dobbs, *Education and Social Movements 1700–1850* (1919), 173.

[40] See Berg, *Machinery Question*, 149.

[41] J. R. McCulloch, *A Discourse on the Rise, Progress, Peculiar Objects, and Importance of Political Economy* (Edinburgh, 1824), 1–2.

source of embattled solidarity, uniting the nation in mutual ties of moral and economic obligation.[42] The economic crisis into which the country was plunged after 1815 gave rise to similar arguments for social cohesion in the face of potentially divisive economic forces, but one that constructed a national self-image on the basis of the productive relations underpinning the prospects of recovery, rather than the ties of fiscal and martial 'confidence'.

Thus, while the image of political economy amongst the genteel and professional classes was increasingly tinged with a fatalistic expectation of cyclical economic crisis, popular political economy managed to function simultaneously as a lesson in collective humility before the immutable laws governing human society, and a clarion call to national economic renewal, social stability, and popular enlightenment.[43] Henry Brougham, for example, argued that by disseminating sound political knowledge and the principles of economics through 'cheap publications' it would be possible to harmonize the relation between workers and their masters: 'I can hardly imagine . . . a greater good being rendered to the men, than expounding to them the true principles and mutual relations of population and wages.'[44] The movement for the diffusion of political economy among the labouring classes, broadly analogous in its aims to the wartime publications of evangelicals such as Hannah More, could thus be seen as a way of awakening the populace to the merits of economic, as well as spiritual, concord and aspiration: where More's *Cheap Repository Tracts* left off, Jane Marcet and Harriet Martineau took over with works such as *Conversations in Political Economy* and 'The Hill and the Valley'.[45] Ironically enough, the practice of rationalist 'method', which had often been identified with the worst excesses of French revolutionary philosophy, was now in the service of a popular science dedicated to a mass ideology of victorious economic recovery.[46] It is certainly

[42] See below, pp. 153–6.

[43] Maxine Berg, 'Progress and Providence in Early Nineteenth-Century Political Economy', *Social History*, 15 (1990), 365–75.

[44] Henry Brougham, *Practical Observations on the Education of the People* (1825), 5.

[45] Jane Marcet, *Conversations in Political Economy* (1816); Harriet Martineau, *Illustrations of Political Economy*, 9 vols. (1832–4); Max Goldstrum, 'Popular Political Economy for the British Working Class Reader in the Nineteenth Century', in Terry Shinn and Richard Whitley (eds.), *Expository Science: Forms and Functions of Popularization* (Dordrecht, 1985), 259–73; on More and Martineau, see Catharine Gallagher, *The Industrial Reformation of English Fiction 1832–1867* (Chicago, 1985), 36–61.

[46] See David Simpson, *Romanticism, Nationalism, and the Revolt against Theory* (Chicago, 1993).

true that the theoretical rigour of 'high' economic argument was considerably softened in the process of its dissemination; but the schematized, analytical character of 'classical' theory also suggests the many points of connection between secular political economy and the broader character of the post-war 'scientific movement'. 'We are advancing from a reading to a scientific population', the Benthamite *Westminster Review* announced approvingly in 1824, an observation that the author probably considered as applicable to the spheres of politics and economics as to the new vogue for natural philosophy.[47]

Enthusiasm for the social and economic virtues of a popularly diffused culture of scientific enquiry extended from utilitarian radicals such as Mill and the *Westminster* reviewers to liberal Whigs like Henry Brougham. But it also formed a significant component of the self-improving and individualistic spirit of popular radicalism exemplified by such figures as Richard Carlile and Francis Place. The network of 'zetetic' societies which, inspired by Carlile's *Republican* magazine, sprang up across the country during the 1820s can best be understood as subaltern, politically and religiously radicalized versions of the mechanics' institutes, blending the latter's nonconformist, scientific culture of self-improvement with an underground tradition of free thought which looked back to the infidel societies of the 1790s. Typical of an emergent 'respectable' radicalism which tended to shun both the physical solidarity of the mass platform and the bacchanalian, morally degrading atmosphere of 'pothouse politics', the zetetic educational programme remained broadly congruent with the Benthamite and liberal Whig promotion of 'useful knowledge'.[48] Yet, while the zetetics remained committed to the 'equalization of knowledge' through discussion, experimentation, and the liberating practice of infidel free thought, middle-class radicals such as James Mill came to consider that the progressive division of labour in advanced commercial societies would necessarily impose itself on the realm of learning, and necessitate the differentiation of a privileged class of 'cultivated' individuals, secure from the myopic, enervated intellectual condition encouraged by increasingly mechanical and repetitive forms of labour. As the most

[47] [W. J. Fox], 'Men and Things in 1823', *Westminster Review*, 1 (Jan. 1824), 8; Berg, *Machinery Question*, ch. 7.

[48] Iain McCalman, 'Popular Radicalism and Freethought in Early Nineteenth-Century England: A Study of Richard Carlile and his Followers, 1815–32', Australian National University MA (1975).

effective, and eclectic, middle-class radical publicist of this period, Mill provides an important example of the ways in which early nineteenth-century educationalists confronted this central problematic of liberal thought.

Mill arrived in London in 1802 after an intensive period of study under Stewart at Edinburgh University and a brief, disillusioning career as an itinerant preacher. After several years of prolific journalistic activity, including occasional contributions to the *Edinburgh Review*, he published the monumental *History of British India* in 1817, a work that secured him the post of Assistant Examiner in the East India Company. By this time, however, Mill was playing a vital part in the middle-class reform movement, centred around Jeremy Bentham, that his son John was later to name 'philosophic radicalism'. Mill was far more than merely a propagandist for Benthamite ideas, as has sometimes been suggested: he introduced a significant degree of rationalist, conjectural historicism to the utilitarian analysis of society, as well as strengthening the links between Bentham's 'felicific' account of human motivation and Scottish associationist psychology.[49] Most importantly, however, Mill allied the cause of political economy with the aspiration to a rigorously utilitarian science of society, drawing Ricardo into the philosophic radical party and vigorously promoting the plebeian diffusion of political economy as an essential precondition for realizing the greatest happiness of the greatest number.

From at least as early as 1807, when he published a sharply critical response to William Spence's *Britain Independent of Commerce*, Mill's economic writings diverge significantly from Stewart's rather more physiocratic reading of the *Wealth of Nations*.[50] Beyond such theoretical differences, however, Mill remained adamant that he owed to Stewart 'the taste for the studies which have formed my favourite pursuits, and which will be so till the end of my life'.[51] His enthusiasm for popular political economy, in particular, was firmly grounded in Stewart's historicized account of the relation between political science and the

[49] James Mill, *The History of British India*, 3 vols. (1817). On Mill and Reidian associationism, see Robert A. Fenn, *James Mill's Political Thought* (New York, 1987).

[50] James Mill, *Commerce Defended* (1808). However, Mill clearly saw some kind of affiliation between utilitarian radicalism and the politics of Quesnay and the French *Économistes*. See [Mill], 'Economists' (1819), in *Supplement to the . . . Encyclopædia Britannica*, iii. 712–15.

[51] Letter to M. Napier (1821), quoted in Winch, 'System of the North', in Collini *et al.*, *That Noble Science*, 61.

growth of the press and public opinion since the Reformation. Following Stewart, Mill saw the advent of print culture as the final stage in a hierarchized conjectural history of the legible sign, a development that clearly marked European civilization out from the representational poverty of more 'primitive' societies. His analysis of Hindu civilization in the *History of British India* allowed Mill to launch a covert attack upon Ferguson's description of the invention of writing as a natural progression from the savage but noble gratifications of epic poetry (as exemplified by Ossian), and hence as more or less continuous with 'traditional' social forms. Mill's argument was related to his belief that, beyond narrative poetry, the Hindus had nothing even approximating to a reliable historiographic practice. Because they had been unable to utilize the development of letters and the reliable accretion of knowledge in the form of 'permanent signs', they had failed to progress beyond an essentially oral, bardic culture—resulting, as far as Mill was concerned, in a remarkable collective propensity to embellishment and distortion. This position might seem a little ironic given its articulation within what one commentator has described as 'an example of the parochialism of Rationalist history so extreme as to be almost a caricature'.[52] But it was, nevertheless, an important corollary of the associationist psychology that Mill would later codify in the *Analysis of the Phenomena of the Human Mind*, and implied that, unlike the spoken word, 'permanent' or legible signs could function as vehicles for the progressive formation of useful knowledge and opinion because of their endurance over time. This obvious but fundamental property facilitated the inculcation of ever more reliable ideational trains in the individual mind, as well as allowing the historical accretion of knowledge that Stewart had identified, in his own treatment of the subject, as an essential precondition of the growth of civilization.[53]

But Mill also shared his teacher's fascination with the profound political consequences of the emergence of print culture in Europe, and followed Stewart's conjectural historical semiology in arguing that such a departure required a complete reorientation of existing political and educational structures. 'The art of printing exists,' Mill declared. 'And

[52] Mill, *History of British India*, i. 364; Duncan Forbes, 'James Mill and India', *Cambridge Journal*, 5 (1951), 28. See also Javed Majeed, *Ungoverned Imaginings: James Mill's* The History of British India *and Orientalism* (Oxford, 1992).

[53] See James Mill, *Analysis of the Phenomena of the Human Mind*, 2 vols. (1829), i. 87–90; Stewart, *Elements*, i. 441–9.

the irresistible progress of the information which it diffuses necessitates, not a change merely, but a perfect revolution, in the art of governing mankind.'[54] Deriding Whiggish appeals to the popular element of the constitution as vain attempts to conceal political corruption behind the carnivalesque 'fever and tumult' of unreformed elections, Mill proposed instead the diffusion of 'good sense . . . reading and knowledge'. The only truly effective safeguard against the 'sinister' interests of despotic government, he argued, lay in the unfettered collision of diverse opinion. In this way, the 'knowledge which all the individuals in the society possess' is 'brought, as it were, to a common stock or treasury', just as Stewart had argued that the 'free commerce of ideas' effected by the press allowed the disparate products of the intellectual division of labour to be brought to a 'common stock . . . one vast engine' of intellectual improvement.[55]

This liberal identification of a transparent public culture of print as a precondition and guarantor of enlightened government also derived certain important elements from Bentham's own understanding of the efficacy of the press in facilitating the operations of 'publicity' and 'opinion'. As early as 1802, when Étienne Dumont published his influential edition of Bentham's jurisprudential theory, these two concepts had become central to the latter's understanding of the safeguards against bad government available to the 'indirect' legislator.[56] Bentham conceived the regulative function of the public eye in terms of the 'panoptic' principle informing his penal theory, with the essential difference that efficient publicity for the operation of the 'moral sanction' of opinion in civil society as a whole required a more decentred vehicle for the regulative operation of inspection. This he found in the press, by means of which 'instruction descends from the government to the people, and remounts from the people to the government; the more liberty the press enjoys the easier it is to ascertain the current of opinion, so as to act with certainty'.[57]

[54] [James Mill], 'The Ballot', *Westminster Review*, 13 (July 1830), 2.

[55] [id.], 'Edinburgh Review on Parliamentary Reform', *Westminster Review*, 4 (July 1825), 231; James Mill, 'Liberty of the Press', in *Essays* (1823), 2nd edn. (n.d. [1828]), 28; Stewart, 'Dissertation Part III', in *Works*, i. 505.

[56] See Jeremy Bentham, *Traités de Législation civile et pénale* (1802), ed. Étienne Dumont; trans. Robert Hildreth as *The Theory of Legislation* (1931), 432–4.

[57] Ibid. 443. On the moral sanction, see id., *An Introduction to the Principles of Morals and Legislation* (1781), ed. J. H. Burns and H. L. A. Hart (Oxford, 1996), 35 n.

Bentham's stress on the 'principle of publicity' and the liberty of the press remained central components of the utilitarian programme of radical reform and constitutional codification in the 1810s and 1820s.[58] His *Plan of Parliamentary Reform*, for example, identified the visual realm of print and the written word as the ideal medium for the exercise of political power—to the extent that, while the proposed scheme of 'virtual universal suffrage' included women, it excluded those among the population who lacked the application to learn to read. For Bentham, it was the interiority of the acts of reading and writing, their reliance upon visual perception rather than the collective aural experience exploited by the demagogue, that guaranteed their essential rationality, figuring a moment of self-communion and political empowerment which, like the 'absolute and imperturbable secrecy' of the ballot, secured the moral and political primacy of the self-interested individual elector as a precondition for the legislative pursuit of the public good.[59]

Mill was strongly influenced by Bentham's stress on the utility of 'publicity', popular education, and the liberty of the press as essential to good government. He went on, however, to draw these concerns into conjunction with his interest in popular political economy. The end of government was to secure 'the greatest possible happiness of society', and, according to Mill, this was to be achieved above all 'by insuring to every man the greatest possible quantity of the produce of his labour'. This in turn could best be achieved by securing for every individual an accurate knowledge of his own best interest, as revealed by the science of political economy.[60] The Political Economy Club was founded by Mill in 1821 in the belief that the press was 'the grand instrument for the diffusion of knowledge, or error', and members were therefore enjoined 'to study the means of obtaining access to the public mind through as many as possible of the periodical publications of the day and to influence as far as possible the tone of such publications in favour of just principles of Political Economy'.[61] Yet Mill's educational thought continued to be informed by a far more historicized understanding of the

[58] See e.g. id., *On the Liberty of the Press and Public Discussion* (1821).

[59] Bentham, *Plan of Parliamentary Reform* (1817), pp. cii–cv.

[60] James Mill, 'Government', in *Essays*, 5. The gendering here is deliberate, since Mill believed the interests of women to be identical, for all practical purposes, with those of the *paterfamilias*.

[61] *Political Economy Club, Minutes of Proceedings*, 6 vols. (1860–1921), iv. 39, quoted in Joseph Hamburger, *James Mill and the Art of Revolution* (New Haven, 1963), 48.

ongoing process of intellectual and material specialization—an understanding which also suggested the necessity of a new discursive medium for the textual diffusion of useful knowledge.

The economic verities that Mill was so anxious to disseminate amongst the labouring classes were derived for the most part from his friend David Ricardo, the financier and radically inclined Member of Parliament whose writings played a central part in the establishment of 'classical' economic theory. Perhaps to an even greater extent than Malthus's *Essay*, Ricardo's *Principles of Political Economy*, which was first published in 1817, invites interpretation as a decisive refashioning of the discourse of political economy. The conventional, polite prose of *The Wealth of Nations* and the *Essay on Population* was abandoned by writers such as Ricardo and Mill, in favour of dense, closely argued, and logically structured treatises, a stylistic reformation which has traditionally been interpreted as paralleling the shift away from empirical observation towards the deductive, a priori methodology characteristic of the classical school.[62] This reorientation could, until relatively recently, also be understood as the initial moment in the abnegation, by an emergent middle-class intelligentsia, of interest in the broader, 'richer' science of society promised by Scottish Enlightenment thought, prefiguring the wider failure of nineteenth-century Britain to produce a totalizing vision of social and material relations comparable to the continental development of sociology and Marxism.[63]

But it is perhaps more useful to approach the innovations and discontinuities within political economy during this period as reflections of rather more complex, and more localized ideological conflicts. Indeed, the charge of Ricardian deductivism which coloured methodological disputes in the 1820s and 1830s was often strongly informed by the desire to cast intellectual discredit upon the alliance between Ricardian economics and middle-class radicalism. While the Lake school tended towards the wholesale denunciation of political economy as irredeemably selfish and soulless, Christian and Tory economists such as Richard Whately and Richard Jones mounted a more discriminating, 'inductivist' attack on the new school which probably contributed to

[62] T. W. Hutchison, *On Revolutions and Progress in Economic Knowledge* (Cambridge, 1978), 26–57.

[63] For a critical response to this argument, see Lawrence Goldman, 'A Peculiarity of the English? The Social Science Association and the Absence of Sociology in Nineteenth-Century Britain', *Past and Present*, 114 (1987), 133–71.

the lasting perception of Ricardian methodology as excessively abstract and a priori—and hence also as the product of Ricardo's exposure to utilitarian political philosophy.[64] It is James Mill, one of the most prominent Benthamite radicals at this time, who has generally been credited as the primary influence upon Ricardo's reconception of the scope and methods of political economy. But it seems increasingly untenable to describe Mill's contribution in terms of a decisive methodological rupture, since it appears both that there was a significant Smithian element to Ricardo's approach in the *Principles*, and that Mill himself was decisively influenced by the practice of inductive investigation on the basis of general principles as taught by his old Edinburgh Professor, Dugald Stewart.[65]

The *Elements of Political Economy* was published by Mill in 1821 as a 'school-book' of Ricardian principles, potentially comprehensible by any interested student of 'ordinary understanding'. The text was aimed in practice somewhere between the artisanal audiences of the mechanics' institutes and the non-specialist middle-class reader, while the organization of the work grew out of Mill's education of his son in the principles of Ricardian economics. As such, and despite its failure to attain the circulation for which he hoped, the *Elements* can be regarded as Mill's most significant attempt to refashion the discourse of popular political economy, so as to adapt the insights and methods of Ricardo's *Principles* to a working-class audience increasingly prone to intellectual debilitation through the division of labour.

The preface to the *Elements* adumbrates the interpretative method, couched in the language of associationist psychology, that the author considered best suited to the text's organization:

> They who are commencing the study ought to proceed slowly, and to familiarize themselves with the new combinations of ideas, as they are successively presented to them. If they proceed to a subsequent proposition before they are sufficiently imbued with the first, they will of course experience a difficulty, only because they have not present to their memory the truth which is calculated to remove it. If they who begin the study of mathematics were to content themselves with merely reading and assenting to the demonstrations, they would soon arrive at doctrines, which they would be unable to comprehend,

[64] Hilton, *Age of Atonement*, 51.

[65] Neil de Marchi, 'The Case for James Mill', in A. W. Coats (ed.), *Methodological Controversy in Economics: Historical Essays in Honor of T. W. Hutchinson* (Greenwich, Conn., 1983), 155–84; Fontana, *Rethinking*, 79–111.

solely because they had not, by frequent repetition, established in their minds those previous propositions, on which the evidence of the subsequent ones depends.[66]

The 'deductive' method for which Mill's essay on 'Government' was to become so notorious is clearly in evidence here in the presentation of the *Elements* as a kind of Euclidean proof, every stage of which must be grasped sequentially by the careful reader. In his essay on 'Education' Mill argued that the end of all successful pedagogy must be to produce and reinforce beneficial trains of ideas in the mind; that is, associations which both motivate actions, and encourage predictions about the future consequences of those actions, tending to maximize utility. The *Elements* go on to provide a basic historical framework for this claim, in Mill's suggestion that the need for such associational trains is increased, as the productive processes of society become more complex:

> Science is not implied in putting forth the hand, and using. But when labour is to be employed, and the objects of desire can be multiplied only by a pre-concerted plan of operations, it becomes an object of importance to ascertain completely the means of that multiplication, and to frame a system of rules for applying them with the greatest advantage to the end.[67]

It is a truism of classical economics that the division of labour takes place on the expectation of future exchange: it requires some conception of the relation between the projected mode of production to the future state of the market before the most efficient organization of labour can be undertaken. Mill restates this idea in his chapter on production, claiming that, in an 'artificial and opulent state of society', in which only a highly complex division of labour could release the greatest productive power, 'the most perfect philosophical analysis of the subject would be the first operation to be performed; the next would be an equally perfect philosophical synthesis'.[68] This account of the intellectual discipline appropriate to complex economic activity, deriving from Stewart's 'experimental' inductivism, is directly analogous to the interpretative method which Mill recommends to the reader of the *Elements*—the individual analysis of each proposition as a link in an inferential chain

[66] James Mill, *Elements of Political Economy* (1821), 3rd edn., rev. (1826), pp. iii–iv.
[67] Ibid. 2.
[68] Ibid. 13.

leading finally to the synthetic comprehension of the whole system of political economy.[69]

Mill clearly believed that the 'philosophic' method of analysis and synthesis necessary to the organization of intellectual and physical labour should govern all useful interpretative exertions in an 'artificial and opulent state of society', and not just the ideal reader of political economy. His political essays, which were composed around the same time as the *Elements*, certainly share the latter's distinctive methodology. The essay on 'Education', for example, argues that 'Very unconnected, or very general instructions, are all that can be given upon this subject, till the proper decompositions and recompositions are performed; in other words, till the subject is first analysed, and then systemized; or, in one word, *philosophized* . . .'.[70] This two-stage process serves as a guide not only to the method of the essay, but also to all productive human activity, since a 'man is sagacious in devising means for the production of events when his ideas run easily in trains which are at once agreeable to knowledge, that is, to the trains of events, and at the same time new in combination'. The important distinction here is that between 'knowledge', and what Mill called 'sagacity'. The former consists in a systematic correspondence between causal trains of ideas in the mind, and similar trains of events in the world. But *productive* acts are only made possible by the further, synthetic faculty of 'sagacity', which produces 'a peculiar train, at once correspondent with nature, and adapted to the end'.[71] The historical origins, and the archetypal instance, of this latter mental process are, according to the *Elements*, to be found in the institution of the division of labour.

Mill's philosophic method can best be understood as an attempt to find new ways of minutely dividing and recombining complex ideas to produce ever more efficient processes of intellectual labour among his readers. It was necessary for uninformed students to 'familiarize themselves with the new combinations of ideas, as they are successively

[69] On Stewart and Mill, see de Marchi, 'The Case for James Mill', 163–4; on analysis and synthesis, see Redman, *Rise of Political Economy*, 128–31.

[70] Mill, 'Education', in *Essays*, 32; see also 'Jurisprudence', in ibid. 7–8, 'Government', in ibid. 3–4. Those essays that bear the strongest methodological connections to Mill's work on political economy—'Education', 'Government', 'Jurisprudence', and 'Liberty of the Press'—were first published in 1819–21, in the *Supplement* to the *Encyclopaedia Britannica*, and it was over the same period that Mill developed the structure of a schoolbook of political economy in the course of his son's education, and then composed and published the first edition of the *Elements* in 1820–1.

[71] Mill, 'Education', in *Essays*, 32; see also ibid. 15.

presented to them', before moving on to further combinations. The process of mental production would thus replicate the efficient division of labour, which required the organizer of labour and capital to contemplate the 'vast aggregate of materials . . . in its elements; to resolve it into those elements; and carefully and comprehensively to pass them under review'.[72] Furthermore, just as the 'foundation' of the division of labour 'is laid, in the fact, that an operation, which we perform slowly at first, is performed with greater and greater rapidity by repetition', so the student of political economy is enjoined to practise a form of reading whereby the 'frequent repetition' of individual trains of ideas will establish clearly in the reader's mind 'those previous propositions, on which the evidence of the subsequent ones depends'.[73]

Macaulay's review of Mill's essay on 'Government' attacked it as a 'ceremonial of logic' deriving from the antiquated philosophy of medieval scholasticism.[74] Yet Mill seems to have conceived of his mode of argument as a form of discourse peculiarly *modern* in its allowance for the debilitation of intellect produced by the complex subdivisions of productive labour in an advanced state of civilization. Mill's method in the *Elements* represented an attempt to substantiate his belief that the 'moral' influences of domestic and institutionalized education—and, in particular, those mental habits deriving from the political structure of society—could produce 'a very high degree of intellectual acquirements . . . a firm foundation may be laid for a life of mental action, a life of wi[s]dom, and reflection, and ingenuity, even in those by whom the most ordinary labour will fall to be performed'.[75]

Yet he was also inclined to the conclusion not only that such intellectual acquirements could be limited by physical factors such as health and diet, but also that the division of labour must necessarily prove deleterious to the 'mental excellence' of the mechanic. The essay on 'Education' cites Adam Smith's 'important remark' that the

> division and subdivision of labour . . . confines the attention of the labourer to so small a number of objects, and so narrow a circle of ideas, that the mind receives not that varied exercise, and that portion of aliment, on which almost every degree of mental excellence depends . . . The minds, therefore, of the great

[72] Mill, *Elements*, pp. iii, 13–14. [73] Ibid. 10, iv.

[74] [Thomas Babington Macaulay], 'Mill's Essay on Government, Utilitarian Logic and Politics', *Edinburgh Review*, 44 (Mar. 1829), 159–89.

[75] Mill, 'Education', in *Essays*, 40.

body of the people are in danger of really degenerating, while the other elements of civilization are advancing, unless care is taken, by means of the other instruments of education, to counteract those effects which the simplification of the natural processes has a tendency to produce.[76]

Mill's associationist pedagogy offered one solution to this difficulty, by transposing the principles governing the division of labour to the exertions of the individual intellect. But he was also driven to recognize the necessity of an intellectually privileged social class, as the only means of preventing the further fragmentation of the public mind into discrete, disconnected epistemic fields. This role was to be filled by the 'middle rank'; that class which is 'both the most wise and the most virtuous part of the community'. Because of its medial social position, this rank of society could best regulate the collective accumulation of knowledge and belief. All those 'who have attentively considered the formation of opinions in the great body of society' must concur that 'the opinions of that class of people, who are below the middle rank, are formed, and their minds are directed by that intelligent and virtuous rank, who come the most immediately in contact with them, who are in the constant habit of intimate communication with them . . . whose opinions they hear daily repeated, and account it their honour to adopt'.[77] This imitative principle was an important component of Mill's educational theory, but it also found application, as it had for Bentham, in the political realm. The tendency of the public mind to fragment into 'sinister', interest-bound factions could be traced in part to the imitative communication of psychological trains between 'the minds of all those individuals by whom we are surrounded . . . [which] pass with extraordinary frequency through our own minds, and must, unless where extraordinary means are used to prevent them from producing their natural effect, engross to a proportional degree the dominion of our minds'.[78] Opinion should flow through society unconstrained by partial, sinister interests, just as Bentham had argued. But Mill also came to believe that such mobility had to be regulated and stabilized by an extensive middle class that would prevent the sort of melodramatic 'contagion of passions' exploited during the war by the nationalistic rhetoric of the government and aristocracy.

[76] Ibid. 30. [77] Id., 'Government', in *Essays*, 31–2.
[78] Id., 'Education', in *Essays*, 44.

The terms of Mill's controversial essay on 'Government' might be viewed as a compromise between the universalist tenor of Benthamite utilitarianism and an emergent political idiom that represented the middle class as agents of national progress and stability in the years leading up to the first Reform Act.[79] But it must also be stressed that the privileging of a particular social rank as the bearer of economic and intellectual civilization was integral to discussions of the progress of learning and opinion in complex, specialized economies from the later eighteenth century onwards and, as we have seen in the case of Dugald Stewart, was justifiable in terms of the putative relation between the intellectual progress of society and the mental effects of the division of labour. In this case, the contradictions within Mill's political thought should be seen as far more deeply rooted in the two principal constituents of early nineteenth-century liberal ideology—Scottish Enlightenment Whiggism and utilitarian radicalism. It was the former strain of thought, just as much as the more localized political language of the 1820s, to which Mill was concerned to adapt Benthamite doctrine through his defence of the 'middle class'. In 1821, in the *Elements of Political Economy*, he argued that

> All the blessings, which flow from that grand and distinguishing attribute of our nature, its progressiveness, the power of advancing continually from one degree of knowledge, one degree of command over the means of happiness, to another, seem, in a great measure, to depend upon the existence of a class of men who have their time at their command . . . It is by this class of men that knowledge is cultivated and enlarged; it is also by this class that it is diffused; it is this class of men whose children receive the best education, and are prepared for all the higher and more delicate functions of society, as legislators, judges, administrators, teachers, inventors in all the arts, and superintendants in all the more important works, by which the dominion of the human species is extended over the powers of nature.[80]

The luxury and indolence that characterized the aristocratic temperament rendered it unconducive to habits of both intellectual and physical productivity.[81] Mill's allusion to the 'men of middling fortunes' as the 'cultivated' agents of the march of the mind implied, on the other hand, that this class formed the principle locus for the 'union . . . of

[79] See Dror Wahrman, *Imagining the Middle Class: The Political Representation of Class in Britain,* c.*1780–1840* (Cambridge, 1995), 256–60.

[80] Mill, *Elements*, 63.

[81] Id., 'Government', in *Essays*, 7.

copiousness and energy; this possession of numerous ideas, with the masterly command over them', which education should aim to inculcate, and which would tend to maximize the productive capacities of the individual upon whom such gifts were bestowed.[82]

Liberal political economy envisioned society as unified not by the prescriptive ties of language and tradition, but through the interrelation and mutual reliance of productive processes. 'Like the different parts of a well constructed machine,' McCulloch wrote, 'the inhabitants of a civilized country are all mutually dependent on and connected with each other'.[83] This necessitated a sociology of knowledge equally attendant to the intangible, epistemic networks of belief underpinning the material operations of society. Useful knowledge should ideally inform and regulate every level of productive activity. 'Literature and education become valuable in a national point of view only as they are diffused,' Mill insisted.[84] But his utilitarian political economy also recognized the necessity of a 'general, commanding, and complete view' of the epistemic and economic structure of society:

> is it not necessary, for effecting a combination of all . . . [the objects of political economy], so exquisite as to make them conspire, in the best possible manner, to the production of a particular effect, that the arrangement should be made by some pervading mind which takes a comprehensive view of the whole; which leaves nothing out of its consideration; which contemplates every part of the great co-operation; marks wherever there is any thing either too much or too little, where any one thing stands in the way of another, where any thing is wanting to the complete operation of another thing; and which, by help of this knowledge, places and proportions every thing?[85]

This was a belief reiterated by the Tory economist Richard Jones, who projected a vision of the 'scattered artizans of other realms collected, here, into workshops and manufactories, the eye of a superior enforcing everywhere steady and continuous labour; knowledge and science importing to human industry a sovereign power over the material world'.[86] Beyond purely economic considerations, a significant motivation behind such desires was the growing perception that, outside

[82] Id., *Elements*, 64; id., 'Education', in *Essays*, 15. See also [id.], 'Chas, Sur la Souveraineté', *Edinburgh Review*, 17 (Feb. 1811), 417.

[83] J. R. McCulloch, *The Principles of Political Economy* (1825), 147.

[84] [James Mill], 'State of the Nation', *Westminster Review*, 6 (Oct. 1826), 268.

[85] [Id.], 'Whether Political Economy is Useful?', *London Review*, 2 (Jan. 1836), 561.

[86] Richard Jones, *Literary Remains*, ed. William Whewell (1859), 12, quoted in Berg, *Machinery Question*, 126.

the confines of the workshop or factory, the urban labouring mind was becoming more and more inscrutable to coherent analysis. One educationalist reported in 1845 that 'the inner life of the classes below us in society is never penetrated by us. We are profoundly ignorant of the springs of public opinion, the elements of thought and the principles of action among them . . .'.[87] The statistical movement of the 1830s was the first attempt to extend the analytic capacity of political economy to areas such as education and health, and thus to render the wider social field, including that of educationally inculcated mass opinion, 'more or less the subject of calculation from given facts'.[88]

In 1826, however, it seemed to Mill quite unproblematic that its intrinsic qualities and medial class position made the 'pervading mind' of the cultivated middle rank peculiarly suited to the panoptic superintendence of the social machine. His writings on economics and education might, therefore, begin to suggest how the rhetorical invocation of a 'cultivated' class peculiarly resistant to the historical process of intellectual specialization could be seen as a distinctive component of liberal political thought, even amongst doctrinaire, 'first-generation' philosophic radicals. Certainly Mill's abandonment of a strict Benthamite universalism, and his promotion of the middle ranks as the guardians of 'refined' learning and the vehicles of popular enlightenment, not only recall Stewart's idea of a speculative and cultivated philosophical class, but also prefigure his son John's interest in the Coleridgean 'clerisy' as a potential bulwark against the homogenizing tendencies of mass society.

The elder Mill's political aspirations were, however, primarily focused upon the sphere of 'useful' scientific and economic knowledge, and reflect the philosophic radicals' broader distrust of discursive 'fiction' as a tool of corrupt politicians and 'sinister' interests—a prejudice that also conditioned their attitude to imaginative, entertaining, or 'polite' literature. Within the pages of the *Edinburgh Review*, by contrast, the popularization of political economy proved increasingly relevant to

[87] *Minutes of the Committee of Council on Education* (1845), i. 266–7, quoted in Richard Johnson, 'Educational Policy and Social Control in Early Victorian England', *Past and Present*, 49 (1970), 104.

[88] Brougham, 'Discourse of the Objects, Pleasures, and Advantages of Political Science', in *Works*, 11 vols. (1855–61), vii. 384. M. J. Cullen, *The Statistical Movement in Early Victorian Britain: The Foundations of Empirical Social Research* (Hassocks, 1975), ch. 5.

the discussion of polite literature and learning and, more specifically, to the problematic issues surrounding the role of humanistic literary culture in a rapidly commercializing society.

'THE BEST MUSE OF ALL ELEGANCE AND REFINEMENT': WHIG POLITICS AND POLITE LETTERS IN THE *EDINBURGH REVIEW*

Despite its rapid rise to fame as the pre-eminent literary periodical of the day, the *Edinburgh's* preoccupations and perspective remained deeply politicized in character. Its ideological energies, particularly in its early years, were often devoted to steering a defensive, moderate line between radicalism and reaction, in a bid to preserve the damaged reputation of the Foxite party from association with 'zealous and infatuated partizan[s] of democracy' such as the radical Whig historian William Belsham. Although the Napoleonic ascendancy greatly simplified the review's attitude to Anglo-French hostilities, and seemed to promise a return of principled 'candour' to the 'great and interesting discussions' of domestic political controversy, the review was still being charged with 'jacobin' sympathies by conservative polemicists as late as 1809.[89] Indeed, the *Edinburgh*'s very existence was to a large extent the direct product of the virtual disintegration of the Whig opposition during the 1790s, and the corresponding strength of the Pittite reaction, which together deprived its founders of any prospect of easy professional advancement in careers more directly dependent on political patronage, and which must therefore have done much to mitigate any scruples they might have entertained concerning the 'ungentlemanly' status of paid journalism.[90]

These circumstances certainly go some way to explaining the sceptical critical outlook of Francis Jeffrey, the *Edinburgh*'s editor and chief literary reviewer, whose contributions to the periodical often seem engaged in tacit critical dialogue with Stewart's more aggressive apologetic for the continued diffusion of knowledge in the post-revolutionary period. The historical sociology of literature and learning underpinning Jeffrey's

[89] 'Belsham's Memoirs of the Reign of George III', *Edinburgh Review*, 2 (Apr. 1803), 181; [Francis Jeffrey], 'Gentz, État de l'Europe', ibid. 1; [Richard Wharton], *Remarks on the Jacobinical Tendency of the Edinburgh Review* (1809).

[90] Fontana, *Rethinking*, 11; Michael Fry, *The Dundas Despotism* (Edinburgh, 1992), 278–9.

review essays for the first decade of the *Edinburgh*'s life—a period roughly conterminous with the wartime ascendancy of loyalist conservatism—was concerned above all with the progressive erosion of the conditions under which serious literary and intellectual endeavour might be fostered. This gloomy perspective inspired Jeffrey with one of the first comparative arguments for the non-emergence of a dynamic English intelligentsia, on the grounds that, while in the salon culture of *ancien régime* France, 'men of letters . . . mingled far more extensively with the polite world', the 'great scholars and authors' of 'England' had traditionally remained much more aloof from the metropolitan environment of politics and polite society, leading to the incapacity of the elevated thinker to maintain any significant, efficacious influence on manners and opinions. The dispirited tone of this observation contrasts strikingly with Hume's earlier celebration of the alliance between the 'learned' and 'conversible' worlds constitutive of high Enlightenment sociability.[91] But Jeffrey also believed that the solipsistic tendencies of the country's intellectual class had been even further exacerbated by the French Revolution, the greatest evil of which he declared to have been 'the injury done to the cause of rational freedom, and the discredit in which it has involved the principles of political philosophy'. Unlike writers such as Millar and Stewart, the last representatives of a now fading Scottish Enlightenment, Jeffrey could no longer maintain unbridled confidence in the speculative philosopher's aspiration, which the *Edinburgh* still shared up to a point, 'to break down the old and unfortunate distinction between the wisdom of the academician and the wisdom of the man of the world'.[92]

Jeffrey's disagreements with Stewart on the importance of metaphysics and 'speculative' philosophy are evident as early as his account of Stewart's *Life of Reid*, in 1804.[93] But it was his 1813 review of Madame de Staël's rather more optimistic view of literary culture, in *De la littérature*, that gave Jeffrey the opportunity to develop these themes into a broader account of the contemporary degeneration of polite learn-

[91] [Francis Jeffrey], 'Correspondance de Madame du Deffand et de Mademoiselle de Lespinasse', *Edinburgh Review*, 15 (Jan. 1810), 463; David Hume, *Essays, Moral and Political*, 2 vols. (Edinburgh, 1742), ii. 1–8.

[92] [Francis Jeffrey], 'Mémoires de Bailly', *Edinburgh Review*, 6 (Apr. 1805), 137; [id.], 'Craig's Life of Millar', *Edinburgh Review*, 9 (Oct. 1806), 87.

[93] [Francis Jeffrey], 'Stewart's Life of Dr. Reid', *Edinburgh Review*, 3 (Jan. 1804), 267–87; George E. Davie, *The Social Significance of the Scottish Philosophy of Common Sense* (Dundee, 1973).

ing. The review reflected Jeffrey's growing disdain for the reading public, 'the ingenious frequenters of circulating libraries and the lively inquirers after new books *in duodecimo*', whose shallow sensibilities seemed untouched by the tragic drama of the revolution. This growing body of literary consumers was interested principally in poetry and the fine arts, which 'habituate the mind to transitory and passive impressions' and which seemed, therefore, to be entirely compatible with 'the greatest and most debasing corruption of manners'.[94] Because studies of Jeffrey's literary criticism have for the most part been concerned with his often rather unsympathetic responses to canonical Romantic poetry, it can easily be forgotten that his negative characterization of the poetic sensibility is developed in contrast to more 'virtuous' forms of humanistic learning; namely, 'philosophy, eloquence, history, and those other departments of learning which refer chiefly to the heart and the understanding, and depend upon a knowledge of human nature, and an attentive study of all that contributes to its actual enjoyments'.[95] The general neglect of this field of intellectual endeavour was understood by Jeffrey as one of the most regrettable consequences of a refined, commercial state of society. In a significant concession to Stewart's conjectural historical sociology, he noted the value of printing and the 'perfect communication that is [thereby] established all over Europe', and suggested that empirical knowledge 'which admits of demonstration will advance . . . and extend itself'. His principal objective, however, was to convince his readers that the progressive accumulation of knowledge had ended the age of heroic literary endeavour, those 'vigorous and independent excursions' of the intellect exemplified by the works of Bacon, Shakespeare, Taylor, and Hooker.[96]

In their place, Jeffrey discerned the fragmentation of learning into a confusing multitude of superficial literary forms united only by their transient mediocrity; a condition that he considered explicable in terms of 'that minute subdivision of labour which is the great secret of the mechanical arts, but [which] can never be introduced into literature without depriving its higher branches of all force, dignity, or

[94] [Francis Jeffrey], 'Madame de Staël, Sur la Littérature', *Edinburgh Review*, 21 (Feb. 1813), 1, 7–8; see also [id.], 'Correspondance Littéraire et Philosophique de Grimm', *Edinburgh Review*, 21 (July 1813), 265–6. Fontana, *Rethinking*, 173–5.

[95] [Jeffrey], 'Sur la Littérature', ibid., 21 (Feb. 1813), 7.

[96] Ibid. 11–12, 17.

importance'.[97] He went on, however, to give this by now familiar complaint a distinctly Malthusian turn. The increase of 'wealth and luxury', which previously figured as the great corrupter of national literature, was now also identified with the growth of manufactures and a redundant labouring population subject to the inevitable, ruinous fluctuations of an industrialized economy. Yet the corresponding Malthusian argument for working-class education, which Jeffrey went on to endorse, ran directly counter to his civic critique of 'refined' letters. The diffusion amongst the lower orders of 'a good system of education, habits of foresight and self-control, and rigid economy' would, it seemed, be accomplished *in spite of* the more '*general* progress of refinement and intelligence', since this latter tendency was in fact encouraging moral corruption rather than restraint, fostering an atmosphere of 'sensuality and selfishness' which threatened to terminate in the imposition of despotic government upon an effete and decadent people.[98]

The internal contradictions of Jeffrey's position can best be understood as a product of his attempts to combine a Fergusonian, deteriorationist view of polite learning with the more ameliorative attitude to the diffusion of knowledge amongst the lower classes implied by Malthusian social thought. From around the late 1810s, the former, civic humanist component of his critical stance was increasingly at odds with the growing influence of Broughamite educational thought on the *Edinburgh*'s political agenda. This latter development meant that, by the early 1820s, the review could be unambiguously identified as a supporter of non-denominational mass education, a cause for which it frequently argued in distinctly Malthusian terms. Meanwhile, within doors, the findings of Brougham's Select Committee on education led to the establishment of a Charity Commission, charged with a wide-ranging investigation of educational endowments stretching from plebeian institutions of popular instruction to the country's grammar schools.[99] This broad focus was entirely in accord with the *Edinburgh*'s identification of the cause of educational reform with its attacks on the corrupt alliance of aristocratic and ecclesiastical interests. After 1821, the review vigorously championed the cause of church reform,

97 Ibid. 20; see also [id.], 'The Works of Dr. Franklin', *Edinburgh Review*, 8 (July 1806), 329.

98 [Jeffrey], 'Sur la Littérature', ibid., 21 (Feb. 1813), 22–4; emphasis in original.

99 Brian Simon, *The Two Nations and the Educational Structure 1780–1870* (1960), new edn. (1974), 94–5; 'Education of the Poor', *Edinburgh Review*, 30 (Sept. 1818), 486–502.

condemning clerical abuses and the wastefulness of Anglican endowments in terms that provoked a spate of aggrieved High Church pamphleteering.[100] The *Edinburgh* tended to depict the unreformed state of educational endowments as detrimental to the intellectual condition of the 'lower orders', whose chance of a reasonable parish education at the hands of the established church was often negligible, while confining 'the means of literary and scientific instruction . . . to a few hundred families of the highest rank and greatest wealth'.[101] High Church hostility to national education, together with the effete and exclusive training provided by the grammar schools and the two great universities, reflected the concerted antipathy of church and aristocracy to the inevitable advance of general intelligence—a point that helped to justify the review's increasingly vigorous defence of the 'middle class' as an educationally disadvantaged, but intellectually and economically vital section of the community.[102] The cause of grammar school and university reform could, thus, be reconciled with the existing economic arguments for popular education by demonstrating the value of an extensively educated middle class to social cohesion, material progress, and political stability.

The sceptical, deteriorationist sociology of polite learning that had characterized Jeffrey's literary reviewing during the war years was clearly incompatible with this objective; and by 1825, when he took on a review of McCulloch's *Discourse on Political Economy*, it is clear that a dramatic reorientation of his earlier position had taken place. The review is important not just as an indicator of the increasing Broughamite influence on the *Edinburgh*, but also as a demonstration of how liberal–Whig educational thought in the 1820s could use the language of political economy to draw together 'scientific' popular education and 'refined' middle-class learning and literature into a harmonious vision of social cohesion and material progress. Jeffrey began by suggesting that political economy, 'in the exercise of its primary and direct

[100] See e.g. Henry Phillpotts, *A Letter to Francis Jeffrey* (Durham, 1823); Augustus Campbell, *A Reply to the Article on Church Establishments in . . . the Edinburgh Review* (1823); G. F. A. Best, *Temporal Pillars: Queen Anne's Bounty, the Ecclesiastical Commissioners, and the Church of England* (Cambridge, 1964), 247–50.

[101] [Henry Brougham], 'High Church Opinions on Popular Education', *Edinburgh Review*, 42 (Apr. 1825), 222–3.

[102] [Id.], 'High Church National Education', *Edinburgh Review*, 35 (July 1821), 509–14; [D. K. Sandford], 'Classical Education', *Edinburgh Review*, 25 (July 1821), 302–14; Fontana, *Rethinking*, 155–7; Wahrman, *Imagining*, 303.

functions, aims only at the multiplication of . . . lower gratifications', and might therefore seem incompatible with the claims of religion, as well as 'Intellect, Imagination and Taste'. Yet, despite this apparent concession to an emergent conservative critique of economic science, Jeffrey went on to argue that, in its indirect results, political economy was in fact 'the best muse of all elegance and refinement, the surest guarantee for justice, order and freedom, and the only safe basis for every species of moral and intellectual improvement'.[103] The increased productivity of labour secured by a widely diffused knowledge of political economy would lead to more leisure and material comfort, which in turn would provide the stimulus to more refined intellectual pursuits. In 1813 Jeffrey had argued that, in an 'advanced stage of society', the 'passion' and 'warmth' of poetry and the arts were sacrificed to the prying, metaphysical spirit of barren 'philosophy'.[104] Now, however, it appeared possible to integrate the notionally rival claims of science and the arts into a progressive vision of material and intellectual improvement. 'While enjoyments are multiplied and refined, therefore, intellect is developed—and brings with it far higher and more precious enjoyments than those for the sake of which it was first called into action.'[105]

In wealthy manufacturing countries in which the science of political economy was well understood, not only did the 'intelligent artisan' enjoy more 'comforts and luxuries', but his labour was directed towards ever more challenging 'efforts of skill and ingenuity'. Following Maxine Berg, we might understand this argument in terms of an early nineteenth-century 'view of science as a cultural antidote to the division of labour'.[106] Brougham, for example, insisted that the 'mere gratification of curiosity' in scientific matters, quite apart from the practical benefits of experimental enquiry, 'elevates the faculties above low pursuits, purifies and refines the passions, and helps our reason to assuage their passion'.[107] Jeffrey similarly suggested that it was not merely inferential, ratiocinative powers of mind that were exercised and developed by new forms of production, but rather that the worker would benefit by 'the gradual cultivation and improvement of all his intellectual faculties, the

[103] [Francis Jeffrey], 'Political Economy', *Edinburgh Review*, 43 (Nov. 1825), 1–2.
[104] [Id.], 'Correspondance Littéraire et Philosophique de Grimm', ibid., 21 (July 1813), 294–5.
[105] [Jeffrey], 'Political Economy', ibid., 43 (Nov. 1825), 3.
[106] Ibid. 4–5; Berg, *Machinery Question*, 150.
[107] Henry Brougham, *A Discourse of the Objects, Advantages, and Pleasures of Science*, 2nd edn. (1827), 5.

enlargement of his views, the development of his moral sensibilities, and the infinite multiplication of his best capacities of enjoyment'. Thus the 'pursuit of those vulgar comforts and venal luxuries' typical of advanced economies, which Jeffrey had previously associated with political and moral corruption in his 1813 review of de Staël, was now redescribed such that it only seemed 'at first sight to terminate in selfishness and sensuality', but in fact constituted the only route by which 'the body of any society ever becomes intelligent, moral, or refined'.[108]

This allowed Jeffrey to integrate all classes of society into a hierarchized schema linking increasing prosperity and happiness to progressive levels of intellectual refinement and moral cultivation. Jeffrey was particularly concerned that the 'richer classes' improve their knowledge of political economy, so as to maintain their 'intellectual superiority' in 'those branches of knowledge on which they and their immediate dependents are most likely to come into direct collision'. A shared knowledge of the truths of economic science would prevent combinations and strikes, and promote the cause of 'general prosperity'. But Jeffrey's argument clearly embraces the cause of virtuous humanistic learning as well as the more strictly scientific laws governing economic relations. For liberal–Whig educationalists, the morally and materially efficacious aspects of the diffusion of knowledge were intimately connected. Capital accumulation sustained by foresight and scientific learning would in turn provide the stimulus to 'higher' and more extensive intellectual pursuits, for both the individual and the community. Hence, unlike his earlier, Fergusonian critique of the commercialization of literature, Jeffrey's educational rhetoric of progressive cultivation and refined learning successfully reconciled a broadly Malthusian stress on the moral elevation of the lower orders with a forthright defence of polite letters.

This argument was based on the widespread contemporary assumption that, despite the progressive diffusion of knowledge, the political and social order would continue to rely upon the maintenance of distinct ranks, within and across which the progressive forces of intellectual and socio-economic aspiration could be brought to bear. The result would be a nation in which, in Macaulay's words, the 'whole society is equably rising in intelligence; where the distance between its different orders remains the same, though every order

108 [Jeffrey], 'Political Economy', *Edinburgh Review*, 43 (Nov. 1825), 5.

advances'.[109] Macaulay was writing in the *Edinburgh*, in 1826, on the new London University, an institution with tremendous symbolic importance for its Whig and philosophic radical supporters, as a vital first step towards consolidating the benign influence of the 'middle classes' upon a rapidly advancing popular mind. The poet Thomas Campbell, for example, argued in favour of the new university on the grounds that the

> middling rich—that is, all above the working classes and beneath the enormously rich—form a momentously important mass of society. . . . it is desirable that all portions of it should be well-educated. If money (as it undeniably is) be the means of influence, wherever there is money there ought to be cultivated intellect; and the education that is to keep the most influential body of the people liberal in their opinions, solid in their information, and respectably intellectual in their tastes and pursuits, that education is of a consequence which cannot be overrated.[110]

The founding of London University has often been described as a 'utilitarian' project, a term that might cause some difficulties for historians of the academic discipline of English Literature, to whom the university's creation of the first chair in English Language and Literature (held in the first instance by the evangelical cleric Thomas Dale) might seem a somewhat incongruous addition to the philistine, Benthamite educational programme that the idea of utilitarian pedagogy typically conjures up.[111] Yet supporters of the new university such as Campbell were less inspired by the ideological eccentricities of doctrinaire Benthamism than by a broader, liberal–Whig discourse of 'cultivated intellect', which recognized the social utility of both polite literature and political economy, and which drew together the defence of popular and middle-class education into a common, but subtly differentiated language of moral cultivation and intellectual refinement. In this case, the institutional development of English Literature might be regarded not

[109] [Thomas Babington Macaulay], 'The London University', *Edinburgh Review*, 43 (Feb. 1826), 317.

[110] Thomas Campbell, *Reprint of Mr. Campbell's Letter to Mr. Brougham* (1825), 1.

[111] D. J. Palmer, *The Rise of English Studies: An Account of the Study of English Language and Literature from its Origins to the Making of the Oxford English School* (1965), ch. 2, draws attention to the evangelical, as well as the utilitarian, influence on the university's founders. See also Franklin E. Court, *Institutionalizing English Literature: The Culture and Politics of Literary Study, 1750–1900* (Stanford, Calif., 1992), 44–5. On the rival London chair, established in 1835, see Alan Bacon, 'English Literature Becomes a University Subject: King's College, London as Pioneer', *Victorian Studies*, 29 (1986), 598.

merely as a vernacular alternative to the traditional emphasis on the Classics at Oxford and Cambridge, nor simply as a lineal descendant of 'rhetoric and belles lettres' in the eighteenth-century Scottish academy.[112] Rather, the study of what Macaulay described as 'our own literature, second to none that ever existed, so rich in poetry, in eloquence, in philosophy', formed part of a much broader redefinition of the idea of polite humanistic learning, the object of which was to adapt the older social functions of the *literae humaniores* to a new understanding of the diffuse pedagogic influence of an educated 'middle rank' upon the moral culture of the British nation as a whole.[113]

WILLIAM ROSCOE, SAMUEL BAILEY, AND THE CASE FOR BOURGEOIS PHILISTINISM

James Mill's support for the new London University was quite compatible with the *Edinburgh* reviewers' arguments for the political and economic importance of an intellectually refined middle class. Yet, unlike Macaulay, Mill would hardly have attached much importance to the study of poetry at the new university—his 'cultivated' middle ranks seem less like a literary intelligentsia than the panoptic superintendents of a vast social machine. 'There are few parishes', he suggested in 1826, 'in which there is not some centrical spot, in which a reading-room, and a small library of useful books, might not be resorted to without inconvenience by most of the inhabitants'. But the ultimate focus for the country's mental energies was to be found, not in the intellectual resorts of the plebeian autodidact, but rather in the new university, from which, Mill believed, would emerge the intellectual overseers of its material and epistemic economy. Through this institution the middle class would be granted 'the grand faculty of judging soundly of all the circumstances which affect the happiness and prosperity of the individual, the family, and the state', and thus permitted to shape, through the progressive diffusion of useful knowledge, the mental capacities of the broader

112 Robert Crawford (ed.), *The Scottish Invention of English Literature* (Cambridge, 1998).

113 [Macaulay], 'The London University', *Edinburgh Review*, 43 (Feb. 1826), 329–34. The education of the nation's colonial subjects was also the subject of some debate at this time. See below, pp. 174–6, and Gauri Viswanathan, *Masks of Conquest: Literary Study and British Rule in India* (1990).

community for political and economic behaviour conducive to the greatest happiness of the greatest number.[114]

But, despite Mill's somewhat managerial approach to the business of education, the outright identification of middle-class radicalism in this period with a kind of vulgar, technocratic philistinism would be highly misleading. For the majority of both utilitarians and liberal Whigs, the social stratification and economic specialization typical of complex commercial society seemed to require not just the diffusion of materially productive forms of scientific knowledge but also a morally salutary species of literary refinement that would be universalist enough to encourage moral propriety through its diffusion amongst the lower classes, but which could also imply, for its more privileged possessors, a release from the debilitating effects of merely 'mechanical' pursuits.[115]

The utilitarian hostility to fiction and imagination would naturally render a figure such as Mill an anathema to defenders of that later understanding of 'culture' which, after Arnold, came to be identified above all with the cause of imaginative literature. But if in this respect the terms of Victorian social criticism seem to have resulted in a partial and anachronistic view of early nineteenth-century political and social thought, then much the same misrepresentation can be seen to inform the enduring image of the early Victorian bourgeoisie as the quintessential embodiment of philistine rationalism. According to John Seed, a 'kind of moralized caricature, at least partly constructed through nineteenth-century fiction, has obscured the strengths and the capacity for adaptation which enabled the middle class to extend their hegemony throughout this period'.[116] Indeed, the 'alleged closure of a whole class within a narrow utilitarian discourse', which Seed identifies as a long-standing obstacle to an adequate appreciation of the religious sensibil-

[114] [James Mill], 'State of the Nation', *Westminster Review*, 6 (Oct. 1826), 269–70.

[115] On the continuities and transformations within nineteenth-century Whiggism, see J. W. Burrow, *Whigs and Liberals: Continuity and Change in English Political Thought* (Oxford, 1988).

[116] John Seed, 'Unitarianism, Political Economy and the Antinomies of Liberal Culture in Manchester, 1830–50', *Social History*, 7 (1982), 1. For some reservations concerning the generic anti-capitalist orientation of the nineteenth-century novel, see Neil McKendrick, '"Gentlemen and Players" Revisited: The Gentlemanly Ideal, the Business Ideal and the Professional Ideal in English Literary Culture', in id. and R. B. Outhwaite (eds.), *Business Life and Public Policy: Essays in Honour of D. C. Coleman* (Cambridge, 1986), 98–136; and see also G. R. Searle, *Morality and the Market in Victorian Britain* (Oxford, 1998), 7.

ities of the early nineteenth-century urban bourgeoisie, has also tended to limit our understanding of secular middle-class ideology in this period, by confining our attention to the select, metropolitan milieu of the Bentham circle.

The partial nature of such a perspective can only briefly be suggested here, through a consideration of two provincial middle-class writers, William Roscoe of Liverpool and Samuel Bailey of Sheffield. A 'self-made role model and icon of the mercantile élite', Roscoe combined a prominent, if not particularly successful career as a Liverpool banker with his celebrated biographical studies of Renaissance Italy, together with subsidiary interests in botany, poetic composition, and textual editing (he produced an important new edition of Pope in 1824).[117] Despite his deep commitment to the liberal politics of the 'friends of peace', Roscoe's involvement with issues of national political significance was balanced by his participation in the civic, political, and cultural life of his home town. He served as the Whig Member of Parliament for Liverpool in 1806–7 and was a dedicated supporter of both the local Anti-Slavery Society and the Liverpool Royal Institution.[118] Like Roscoe, the Sheffield merchant Samuel Bailey enjoyed a wider political and philosophical reputation that was strongly grounded in his local celebrity. Bailey played an active part in the Sheffield Literary and Philosophical Society, one of the many lecture and discussion societies that were a central feature of male middle-class intellectual life at this time.[119] Indeed, it was precisely their immersion in the self-confident bourgeois culture of the early nineteenth-century provincial town that allowed Roscoe and Bailey not only to sustain their commitments to reformist politics, but also to defend an ideal of polite learning that embraced both science and literature as integral components of commercial civilization.

[117] John Belchem and Nick Handy, 'Second Metropolis: The Middle Class in Early Victorian Liverpool', in Alan Kidd and David Nicholls (eds.), *The Making of the British Middle Class? Studies of Regional and Cultural Diversity since the Eighteenth Century* (Stroud, 1998), 59.

[118] Henry Roscoe, *Life of William Roscoe*, 2 vols. (1833). For a recent attempt to reintegrate the Roscoe circle into Romantic literary historiography, see Daniel Sanjiv Roberts, *Revisionary Gleam: De Quincey, Coleridge, and the High Romantic Argument* (Liverpool, 2000).

[119] Leonore Davidoff and Catherine Hall, *Family Fortunes: Men and Women of the English Middle Class, 1780–1850* (1987), new edn. (1992), 419–21, 442–3; Howard M. Wach, 'Culture and the Middle Classes: Popular Knowledge in Industrial Manchester', *Journal of British Studies*, 27 (1988), 382.

The American man of letters Washington Irving, who met Roscoe shortly after arriving in England in 1815, described him as having achieved a perfect 'union of commerce and the intellectual pursuits', thus demonstrating 'how beautifully they may be brought to harmonize, and to benefit each other'. Although there were tensions between Liverpool's dissenting intelligentsia and some sections of the commercial middle classes (particularly on the slavery issue), Irving's remarks indicate the depth of Roscoe's ideological investment in the values of commercial civilization.[120] This much is strongly suggested by his lecture 'On the Origin and Vicissitudes of Literature, Science, and Art, and their Influence on the Present State of Society', which was originally delivered at the opening of the Liverpool Royal Institution in 1817, and later published in both Liverpool and London. The 'vicissitudes' in question centred on the problematic relation between the diffusion of learning, and the growth of commerce and industry. 'The effect of manufactures', Roscoe argued,

> is different; and upon the whole not so conducive perhaps as agriculture to the formation of intellectual character. Inasmuch, however, as they tend to increase the wealth of a country, they may be classed amongst those occupations which form the texture of the web of which letters and arts are the ornaments; but it is much to be feared that the unavoidable tendency of these employments is to contract or deaden the exertions of the intellect, and to reduce the powers both of mind and of body to a machine, in which the individual almost loses his identity and becomes only a part of a more complicated apparatus.[121]

Roscoe's analysis, as well as the fastidiously intellectualized manner in which he represents the plight of the industrial worker, recall nothing so much as the Scottish commercial humanist debate on the mentally debilitating effects of the division of labour. It is unsurprising, then, that the lecture goes on to cite Dugald Stewart's argument that the arts, sciences, and commerce are all mutually supportive in an advanced state of civilization.[122] Although its enduring commitment to trade at the expense of industrial modernization would eventually prove its undoing,

[120] [Washington Irving], *The Sketch Book of Geoffrey Crayon, Gent.* (1820), 29; S. G. Checkland, 'Economic Attitudes in Liverpool, 1793–1807', *Economic History Review*, NS 5 (1952–3), 58–75.

[121] William Roscoe, *On the Origins and Vicissitudes of Literature, Science, and Art, and their Influence on the Present State of Society* (Liverpool, 1817), repr. in *Pamphleteer*, 11 (1818), 522.

[122] Ibid. 532.

Liverpool was in this respect rather more typical of the early nineteenth-century provincial town than more heavily industrialized areas, and Roscoe's reservations about the effects of manufactures certainly reflect this fact.[123] But, like Stewart, Roscoe was far from conceding that the effects of industrial society were wholly pernicious, and argued instead that the rise of the manufacturing system was ultimately redeemed by the moral and cultural leadership of the middle class, on the grounds that, in a truly progressive society, 'improvement is not merely confined to . . . producing a better and cheaper article, but is in many instances extended to . . . ameliorating the condition and cultivating the understanding of the persons employed, particularly of the young'. 'Not only in the metropolis,' he went on, 'but in many of the great commercial towns of the United Kingdom, academical institutions are formed, and literary societies established . . . calculated to promote the great object of intellectual improvement'—an expression of middle-class civic pride all the more remarkable given the contemporary immiseration of large swathes of Liverpool's labouring population.[124]

Roscoe's Anglicized, bourgeois version of Scottish commercial humanism attempted to sustain the moral and cultural legitimacy of nineteenth-century industrial conditions, in the face of widespread poverty and social dislocation, by extending the potential benefits of polite learning to the labouring classes in an intellectual hierarchy of cultural diffusion and emulation. But in this respect, the arguments of Scottish Enlightenment thinkers such as Dugald Stewart converged with an ideological defence of commerce and polite letters which had been current within English literary culture since at least the 1780s. Vicesimus Knox's popular series of *Essays, Moral and Literary* (1782), for example, suggests a concerted attempt to transcend earlier, 'civic' critiques of the alliance between literature and commerce.[125] Knox retained a conventional, moralizing concern with the corrupt contemporary taste for superficial literary diversions such as novel reading, and stressed the

[123] John Belchem, 'Introduction: The Peculiarities of Liverpool', in id. (ed.), *Popular Politics, Riot and Labour: Essays in Liverpool History 1790–1840* (Liverpool, 1992), 1–3.

[124] Roscoe, *Origins and Vicissitudes of Literature*, 522 n., 524.

[125] Robert W. Uphaus, 'Vicesimus Knox and the Canon of Eighteenth-Century Literature', *The Age of Johnson*, 4 (1991), 345–61. Earlier attacks on the corrupting influence of commerce upon humanistic learning include Oliver Goldsmith, *An Enquiry into the Present State of Polite Learning in Europe* (1759); and [John Brown], *An Estimate of the Manners and Principles of the Times* (1757). See also John D. Scheffer, 'The Idea of Decline in Literature and the Fine Arts in Eighteenth-Century England', *Modern Philology*, 34 (1936–7), 155–78.

corresponding virtues of classicism and polite learning. Yet he also gave the merchant and manufacturer a central place within the modern republic of letters. 'To the honour of the commercial order in the community,' he insisted elsewhere, 'they have usually paid attention to the state of literature, and have greatly contributed to the diffusion of polite learning . . .'. Knox thus sought to preserve 'merchants, traders, and mechanics' from the vagaries of fashion and the shallow aspiration to literary fame that threatened to debase the cause of learning, while securing their broader cultural enfranchisement as morally and intellectually 'serious' literary consumers.[126] By 1817, however, it was no longer necessary to make such concessions to the sterner idiom of an increasingly marginalized civic critique. Indeed, Roscoe's confident invocation of Dugald Stewart gives some indication of the diversity of contemporary middle-class representations of the relationship between commerce and the arts, as Scottish Enlightenment thought gradually penetrated the ideological milieu of the provincial English intelligentsia, supplementing not just the liberal belletrism of Vicesimus Knox, but also rational dissent, evangelicalism, and the more secular, utilitarian sensibility exemplified by Samuel Bailey of Sheffield.

The 'Hallamshire Bentham', as Ebeneezer Elliott called Bailey, is now rather a neglected figure. Yet his attitude to the relation between political economy, the diffusion of knowledge, and the 'polite arts' made Bailey much more representative of 'progressive' middle-class attitudes in the early nineteenth century than a more eccentric writer like Bentham, whose personal reputation has done much to consolidate the historical representation of the liberal temper in this period as inherently antipathetic to the products of the imagination. Like the more plebeian mechanics' institutes, the 'Literary and Philosophical' societies which attracted men such as Bailey and Roscoe gave a central place to the educational and self-improving value of 'scientific' knowledge. But such study was by no means considered incompatible with an interest in 'polite literature', as Bailey's eclectic textual companion, intended 'for Discussion in Literary Societies', makes clear.[127] Institutions of middle-

[126] Vicesimus Knox, *Liberal Education* (Dublin, 1781), p. vi; id., *Essays Moral and Literary*, new edn., enlarged, 2 vols. (1782), i. 245: see also ibid. i. 68–71, 247–52; ibid. ii. 108–10, 292–5.

[127] [Samuel Bailey], *Questions in Political Economy, Politics, Morals, Metaphysics, Polite Literature, and other Branches of Knowledge; for Discussion in Literary Societies, or for Private Study* (1823).

class adult education such as the Manchester 'Lit. and Phil.' had been a prominent feature of urban provincial life in England since at least the 1780s, and there is little suggestion that the rise of utilitarian radicalism made any essential impact on their pursuit of humanistic literary edification in tandem with popular scientific enquiry. It is unsurprising, therefore, that Bailey's own reflections upon the 'diffusion of knowledge'—a central trope not just of the popular education movement but also of the civic self-conception of the urban middle class—gave mutually supportive roles to the pursuit of scientific and humanistic learning.[128]

Bailey is chiefly remembered as a political economist whose attempted refutation of Ricardo's labour theory of value contributed to the refinement and reorientation of classical economic doctrine in the 1820s.[129] But four years prior to his contentious involvement in the debate over Ricardian theory, Bailey achieved a measure of celebrity with the publication of his *Essays on the Formation and Publication of Opinions* (1821), an extended philosophical analysis of the psychological production and social circulation of knowledge and belief. Bailey's deterministic account of belief formation was quite compatible with Mill's associationism, and resulted in the favourable reception of the work in the *Westminster Review*. But the *Essays* also clearly reveal their author's interest in political economy, and his willingness to see the two subjects in broadly similar terms:

> the extrication of mankind from error will be most readily and effectually accomplished by perfect freedom of discussion . . . to check inquiry and attempt to regulate the progress and direction of opinions, by proscriptions and penalties, is to disturb the order of nature, and is analogous, in its mischievous tendency, to the system of forcing the capital and industry of the community into channels, which they would never spontaneously seek, instead of suffering private interest to direct them to their most profitable employment.[130]

In his *Dissertation* on Ricardo, Bailey went on to argue that value can be measured only relatively, as a function of the subjective quanta of

128 Wach, 'Culture and the Middle Classes', 376.

129 [Samuel Bailey], *A Critical Dissertation on the Nature, Measure, and Causes of Value* (1825); Maurice Dobb, *Theories of Value and Distribution since Adam Smith: Ideology and Economic Theory* (Cambridge, 1973), 99–102; Hilton, *Age of Atonement*, 166–7.

130 [Samuel Bailey], *Essays on the Formation and Publication of Opinions* (1821), 99–100; [James Mill], 'Formation of Opinions', *Westminster Review*, 6 (July 1826), 1–23.

human desire intentionally directed at different commodities.[131] Similarly, in the *Essays*, it is only 'by the comparison and collision of opinions, [that] truth will be separated from error and emerge from obscurity'. To attempt to curtail the liberty of the press and stop up the 'thousand channels' by which ideas circulate in the public mind would lead only to violent and sudden 'revolutions in public sentiment', mimicking the way in which the protectionist regulation of commerce appeared to exacerbate the cyclical effects of economic depression.[132] Indeed, it seems quite possible that it was his investigation of this political economy of opinion that first led Bailey to his conclusions about the relative nature of commodity values in the *Dissertation*. The progress of universal education and the diffusion of knowledge appeared to him as natural, and ultimately as inevitable, as the laws of supply and demand themselves. The 'silent march of thought', operating through the press, 'is rousing the intellect of nations, and happy will it be for them if there be no rash interference with the natural progress of knowledge'.[133]

This might seem to typify the reductive economism that is often regarded as a central feature of Benthamite social thought, and certainly recalls the proselytizing attitude to the march of the mind which, as we have seen, was later to be satirized in Peacock's fictional character of Mr Mac Quedy, the pedantic disciple of political economy and intellectual sparring partner of Mr Skionar, the 'transcendental' Romantic poet.[134] The first attempt to reconcile these supposedly incommensurable intellectual types is commonly dated from John Stuart Mill's belated discovery of the Lake poets, and thus identified with a 'second generation' of philosophic radicals more or less receptive to the 'Romantic' sensibility. Bailey, however (writing as early as 1821), does not appear to have recognized any necessary incompatibility between the claims of science and literary taste. Indeed, the *Essays on Opinions* also include a sophisticated defence of imaginative, morally improving literature which invites comparison with the kinds of literary nationalism more commonly associated with some form of Romantic ideology.

[131] [Bailey], *Critical Dissertation*, 98.

[132] Boyd Hilton, *Corn, Cash, Commerce: The Economic Policies of the Tory Governments 1815–1830* (Oxford, 1977), 200–1, 211–12. Cf. David Ricardo, *On the Principles of Political Economy and Taxation*, ed. Piero Sraffa and M. H. Dobb (Cambridge, 1951), 133–4 and ch. 19.

[133] [Bailey], *Essays on . . . Opinions*, 145, 160, 164.

[134] Peacock, *Crotchet Castle*, chs. 2, 6.

In his 'Essay on the Variety of Intellectual Pursuits' Bailey declared that the sciences 'are so connected, if by nothing else, at least by the general logical principles pervading the whole, that they throw light on each other'. But, despite the essential interrelatedness of scientific endeavour, he went on to note with some concern the ever-increasing 'multiplicity of knowledge, and the consequent division of intellectual labour'. This process threatened to alienate 'that numerous body of people, not destitute of mental culture, who come under the denomination of general readers'. While, with respect to the sciences, it remained possible for the committed student to avoid the ignominy of becoming an 'intellectual artizan' by securing a good grounding in 'general information', the proliferation of intellectual pursuits nevertheless tended to deprive the reading public at large of 'copiousness of ideas and comprehensiveness of views'. Bailey found the antidote to such mental debilitation in the realm of moral and aesthetic judgement, that

large class of subjects, in which almost all men of cultivated minds can take an equal interest; subjects which relate to man himself . . . The elementary knowledge required in topics relating to morals, manners, and taste, is possessed by all, the terms in which they are treated of form the common language of daily intercourse, and every mind feels itself competent to pronounce on the positions in the expression of which they are employed.[135]

We can therefore understand Bailey to have held two distinct, but interrelated, models of the 'public mind'. On the one hand, he clearly recognized the importance of the universal diffusion of rationally derived scientific knowledge, exemplified by political economy, 'that noble creation of modern times'. In a liberal society enjoying mass literacy, such knowledge would proceed gradually 'downwards', from 'men of high station, learning, and abilities', thereby avoiding those 'violent transitions' of opinion that resulted from the imposition of artificial restraints upon free discussion.[136] Like Mill, however, Bailey also recognized that, despite the best efforts of the mechanics' institutes and the Society for the Diffusion of Useful Knowledge, the stratified nature of modern commercial society would necessarily tend to impoverish the public mind. While Mill's answer to this problem lay in the elevation of the cultivated middle ranks to philosophic foremen in the workshop

135 [Bailey], *Essays on . . . Opinions*, 242–6.
136 Ibid. 118, 158–9.

of the world, Bailey responded by attributing a new importance to the literary field of 'morals, manners, and taste' as a universal and socially cohesive 'common language', which permeated the public mind instantaneously rather than through a hierarchized process of gradual diffusion. It would, however, be anachronistic to read into this distinction any sense of incommensurability between the spheres of 'science' and 'culture'. Bailey understood the social field of knowledge and opinion as much more connected than this—if not for the mechanic, whose socio-economic station seemed to favour a predominantly scientific education, then at least for those of Bailey's peers with the leisure and resources to participate in the book clubs and debating societies which were springing up all over industrial England in this period as 'dual expressions of civic and middle-class identity'.[137]

In a subsequent work Bailey suggested that there 'is a certain measure of intelligence, or rather there is a certain set of notions, which every one inevitably imbibes, even the lowest of society; a certain atmosphere of knowledge breathed in common by all; and these notions depend on the state of knowledge amongst those whose particular business it is to apply themselves to its cultivation'. It was not inconceivable that the progress even of the scientific intellect, augmented by the press and institutions of mass education, might eventually broach the gap between rarefied thought and popular intellect; for in the contemporary condition of society, in which the means of publicizing opinion were ever-increasing, 'the diffusion may be effected with the instantaneousness of lightning . . . the world has become an immense whispering gallery, and the faintest accent of science is heard throughout every civilized country as soon as uttered'. The utilitarian argument for the political value of 'publicity' was predicated upon a similar, idealized vision of a wholly transparent epistemic field in which private opinion, circulating universally and with minimal restraint, would continually transform itself into authoritative knowledge of the public good—much as Adam Smith's 'invisible hand' was understood to harmonize the operations of the free market.[138]

For Bailey, however, this idea of the instantaneous communication and synthesis of myriad private opinions and sentiments was realized most completely not through the diffusion of popular political economy

[137] Wach, 'Culture and the Middle Classes', 376.

[138] [Samuel Bailey], *Essays on the Pursuit of Truth* (1829), 181, 187–8; [id.], *The Rationale of Political Representation* (1835), ch. 3, sect. 4.

and a scientific appreciation of the material workings of society, but rather in the affective power of literature to create a truly communal sense of identity. Unlike the diffusion of knowledge facilitated by scientific reputation, which was inevitably slowed by 'the division of labour in the intellectual world', the

> fame of a poet, or a moralist . . . pervades all society, not as a matter of fact, but as a matter of feeling. It is not merely the echo of his merits that reaches us, but it is his own voice to which we listen. His noble sentiments, his beautiful images, his brilliant wit, his felicitous expressions, mingle themselves with our intellectual being, and constitute a part of the public mind.[139]

In this case, the idea of a national literary culture sustained by the affective power of poetic genius, a notion conventionally associated with Romantic ideology, can be identified as the sublimated, aestheticized aspect of a liberal public sphere rendered ideally impervious to the progressive fragmentation of the national intellect.

Literary and cultural historians have often assumed some kind of fundamental antagonism within nineteenth-century intellectual life, between the Romantic, anti-capitalist values of a gentrified literary intelligentsia, and the bourgeois philistinism of liberal ideologues such as Bentham and Mill. Such a perspective would not, however, have been shared by Samuel Bailey and his fellow members of the Sheffield Lit. and Phil., who seem more likely to have concurred with Roscoe that 'there exists no necessity for our separating the ideas of utility and of pleasure'.[140] Even within the notionally philistine intellectual environment of secular, utilitarian radicalism, it remained both possible and, in Bailey's case, even desirable to defend a vision of national literature compatible with the idea of poetic genius, and a shared 'mental culture' unified by the affective products of the creative imagination.

THOMAS CHALMERS AND THE EVANGELICAL ECONOMY OF THE GOSPEL

The publication of John Bird Sumner's *Treatise on the Records of the Creation*, in 1816, is commonly regarded as the first really influential vindication of Malthusian ideas within the intellectual framework provided by Paleyite natural theology. The *Treatise* legitimized Christian

[139] [Bailey], *Essays . . . on Opinions*, 242.
[140] Roscoe, *Origins and Vicissitudes of Literature*, 531.

political economy for a new generation of Anglican intellectuals, and established the population principle, in Sumner's words, as a 'mighty engine which, operating constantly and uniformly, keeps our world in that state which is most agreeable to the design of the creation, and renders mankind the spontaneous instruments of their Maker, in filling and civilizing the habitable globe'.[141] Sumner's stirring pieties did much to rescue the moral and religious reputation of the population principle from freethinking neo-Malthusian radicals such as Francis Place and the young J. S. Mill. No one, however, elaborated and applied the lessons of Christian economics more single-mindedly than Thomas Chalmers, the Malthusian 'arch-Parson' who was perhaps the single most influential churchman of the early nineteenth century.

As presbyterian minister of the rural parish of Kilmany, near St Andrews, Chalmers was active from around 1811 in establishing a local branch of the British and Foreign Bible Society, urging the importance of scriptural education as a means by which to 'reform the improvident habits of the people', and hence discourage both pauperism and moral dissipation.[142] In 1815, Chalmers moved to the parish of Tron, in Glasgow. This was already a very deprived part of the city, and Chalmers's arrival more or less coincided with the onset of post-war depression, which brought further extremes of poverty to large sections of its labouring population. Glasgow had been a stronghold of the national handloom weavers' union up until 1812, when manufacturers had refused to pay a legally prescribed minimum wage, and local union leaders had been imprisoned after organizing a scrupulously lawful protest strike.[143] It was in this context, of widespread, extreme physical hardship and the political repression of organized labour, that Chalmers set about transforming Tron into an exemplary model of the spiritually redemptive capacities of the free market, in a social experiment that would do much to seal his popularity with the liberal Tories of Lord Liverpool's post-war government.

[141] John Bird Sumner, *A Treatise on the Records of the Creation*, 2 vols. (1816), ii. 175; Waterman, *Revolution*, 150–1.

[142] Thomas Chalmers, *The Influence of Bible Societies, on the Temporal Necessities of the Poor* (1814), 4th edn. (Edinburgh, 1818), 18.

[143] Stewart J. Brown, *Thomas Chalmers and the Godly Commonwealth in Scotland* (Oxford, 1982), 95–6; E. P. Thompson notes that the 'treatment of the Glasgow weavers' leaders was [only] the most outrageous example of the general predicament of trade unionists at this time'. See Thompson, *The Making of the English Working Class* (1963), 542.

Although the national resurgence of popular political radicalism after 1815 placed evangelical educational thought under a certain amount of pressure, it retained a central place in the agenda of Christian political economy. Sumner's *Treatise* 'imbedded the concept of moral restraint within a larger theodicy which included the beneficence of the market economy, [and] the key importance of universal public education', as a means of encouraging the informed deferral of personal gratification through the exercise of 'improvable reason'.[144] A year later, in the fifth edition of the *Essay on Population*, Malthus once more stressed that popular instruction in the true causes of the present distresses would tend to diminish, rather than exacerbate, radical clamour for constitutional reform, by demonstrating the relative powerlessness of government action to influence the disruptive forces of economic and demographic change. Yet, despite such arguments, when Malthus's friend William Otter came to consider these questions in an assize sermon in 1820, he noted a renewed 'disposition to impute a considerable share of the bad spirit, which has lately appeared in the nation, to the general diffusion of Education amongst the poor'.[145]

As a consequence, evangelical educationalists such as Otter and Chalmers tended to place even greater stress upon the 'moralizing' element of mass pedagogy, in opposition to the secular rationalism of the scientific educational movement embraced by utilitarians, liberal Whigs, and 'respectable' radicals. Where Sumner had provided an essentially Paleyite, consequentialist justification for mass education on the grounds that it improved knowledge of one's own best interests, subsequent evangelical educationalists tended, rhetorically at least, to de-emphasize the rationalist, utilitarian elements of Christian political economy in favour of an organic language of moral and spiritual nurture. For Otter, who protested that 'the instruction given under the sanction of our Church to the poor, is entirely consistent with good policy at the present season', the 'mental cultivation' of the people was necessary as a means not only of raising living standards, but also of instilling 'moral discipline' into their relations with employers and the state, and encouraging a proper sense of Christian humility.[146] But the challenge of secular popular education also raised the question of the established

[144] Sumner, *Treatise*, ii. 17; Waterman, *Revolution*, 170.

[145] Malthus, *Essay* (1803), i. 133–6; William Otter, *Reasons for the Education of the Poor at the Present Crisis* (1820), 2.

[146] Ibid. 5–7.

church's pedagogic role, and the relative value of endowed forms of education and learning—issues upon which Chalmers soon became an important and influential commentator.

The core assumption of Chalmers's social thought was the necessity of transplanting Scotland's traditional, parochial system of education and poor relief to the nation's growing urban centres, thereby replacing the impersonality and bureaucracy of the English Poor Laws with the charitable instincts that would be fostered among urban parishioners by their revitalized sense of communal identity and responsibility. In 1816 Chalmers set up Glasgow's first parochial Sunday school society on an aggressively evangelical model that proved influential both in Glasgow and further afield.[147] Three years later, following his controversial articles on pauperism for the *Edinburgh Review*, Chalmers persuaded the town council to place him in charge of poor relief for the new parish of St John's, with a view to achieving the eventual abolition of legal relief and demonstrating in its place the financial and moral sufficiency of charitable donation bolstered by moral restraint and a pious work ethic. By this time, however, Chalmers's growing reputation as a preacher and social reformer had turned him into something of a national celebrity. In 1817 he had visited London, where his 'prophetic fury', as Hazlitt called it, impressed not only the Clapham Sect, but also several members of Liverpool's government, famously reducing George Canning to tears.[148]

These circumstances certainly lend some support to Boyd Hilton's argument for a degree of convergence between post-war liberal Toryism and an evangelical free-trade ethic, of which Chalmers was the foremost exponent at this time, and which

> may be characterized as static (or cyclical), nationalist, retributive, and purgative, employing competition as a means to education rather than to growth. Its psychological premiss was not self-interest but the supremacy of economic conscience, the latter innate in man yet needing to be nurtured into a habitude through the mechanisms of the free market, with its constant operation of temptation, trial, and exemplary suffering.[149]

[147] Brown, *Thomas Chalmers*, 103; Thomas Chalmers, *Considerations on the System of Parochial Schools in Scotland* (Glasgow, 1819).

[148] [Hazlitt], *Spirit of the Age*, 93; Brown, *Thomas Chalmers*, 109.

[149] Hilton, *Age of Atonement*, 69–70; see also id., 'Chalmers as Political Economist', in A. C. Cheyne (ed.), *The Practical and the Pious: Essays on Thomas Chalmers* (Edinburgh, 1985), 141–56.

Chalmers's first attempt to elaborate this liberal economic theodicy came in his *Commercial Discourses* (1820), in which he set out to reconcile traditional Christian virtue with the more worldly realities of self-interested economic behaviour:

God may combine the separate interests of every individual of the human race, and the strenuous prosecution of those interests by each of them, into a harmonious system of operation, for the good of one great and extended family. But if, on estimating the character of each individual member of that family, we shall find that the main-spring of his action is the urgency of selfish inclination; and that to this his very virtues are subordinate; and that even the honesties which mark his conduct are chiefly, though, perhaps, insensibly due to the selfishness which actuates and occupies his whole heart;—then, let the semblance be what it may, still the reality of the case accords with the most mortifying representations of the New Testament.[150]

Chalmers thus sought to augment Adam Smith's treatment of the 'sympathetic' faculty as the moral foundation of human society with a sterner and more overtly Christian ethic. He saw a distinct role for 'the beauteous of character . . . that kindliness of feeling, which one look or one sigh of imploring distress can touch into liveliest sympathy'. But while this mundane and ultimately self-regarding virtue underpinned the operation of 'confidence . . . the very soul and life of commercial activity', it was in the last resort subordinate to 'the sublime of character . . . that high sense of honour, which no interest and no terror can seduce from envy of its obligations'.[151] This latter trait conformed to the 'inward and spiritual graces' of religious observance and moral self-restraint, and introduced an explicitly redemptive aspect to the pursuit of worldly gain.

The *Commercial Discourses* sought to explain how society could operate as a 'moral mechanism' by awakening individual economic agents to a consciousness of their sinful condition. The ultimate end of this state of trial was not any 'external' melioration such as the abolition of rank and

[150] Thomas Chalmers, *The Application of Christianity to the Commercial and Ordinary Affairs of Life, in a series of Discourses*, 2nd edn. (Glasgow, 1820), 77.

[151] Ibid. 40, 73. Chalmers might thus be interpreted as teasing apart two intimately connected aspects of Adam Smith's moral theory. The latter certainly suggested on one occasion that the internalized moral injunctions of the sympathetic 'impartial spectator' could be identified with 'the most sublime and godlike motive'. See Smith, *The Theory of Moral Sentiments* (1759), ed. D. D. Raphael and A. L. Macfie (Oxford, 1976), 311; see also Athol Fitzgibbons, *Adam Smith's System of Liberty, Wealth, and Virtue: The Moral and Political Foundations of* The Wealth of Nations (Oxford, 1995), ch. 5.

inequality but rather an inward, 'moral and spiritual change' in the individual—and this was to be accomplished by 'evangelizing human life, by impregnating its minutest transactions with the spirit of the gospel'.[152] The greatest obstacle to such a mission in contemporary Britain was, Chalmers believed, the growth of densely populated urban environments, the inhabitants of which were increasingly alienated from supervision and instruction by the church. Education, and the problematic relation between Christian learning and commercial society, therefore became central themes of Chalmers's *Christian and Civic Economy of Large Towns* (1821–6), an ambitious attempt to reconcile the views of 'political economists' and 'Christian philanthropists' in an overarching analysis of the 'moral economy' of the nineteenth-century city.[153]

The *Christian and Civic Economy* spurned the academic enquiries of 'our abstract politicians' in favour of an investigation of the 'moral habit of the labouring classes, as founded on their religion'. The growth of commerce required the imposition of free market principles, but a Christianized, Malthusian political economy would also recognize the necessity

> to go forth among the people, and there to superinduce the principles of an efficient morality, on the mere principles of nature—and there to work a transformation of taste and of character—and there to deliver lessons, which, of themselves, will induce a habit of thoughtfulness, that must insensibly pervade the whole system of a man's desires and his doings; making him more a being of reach, and intellect, and anticipation, than he was formerly—raising the whole tone of his mind, and infusing into every practical movement, along with the elements of passion and interest, the elements of duty, and of wisdom, and of self-estimation.[154]

The parochial school was a key agency for such moral reformation, providing 'a fountain of scholarship in every parish' by introducing the 'softening and humanizing effects' of learning to the humblest community; and it was therefore essential to introduce similar institutions of moral improvement to overcrowded urban environments. But at this point in his argument Chalmers recognized a potential difficulty. In large towns, the intellectual energies of the church appeared con-

152 Chalmers, *Application of Christianity*, 156, 167–8, 135.

153 Chalmers, *The Christian and Civic Economy of Large Towns*, 3 vols. (Glasgow, 1821–6), i. 3.

154 Ibid. i. 4, 9–10.

tinually to be sapped, as 'the literature of theology' was vulgarized and degraded by 'the employments of ordinary business'. The superficial concerns of the 'unlearned public' could all too easily tempt the pious Christian away from the church and 'general cultivation' towards a selfish absorption in commercial pursuits alone. In sharp contrast to the past glories of Scottish theological literature, there was now 'a constant withdrawment of the more conspicuous members of our establishment from the solitude of their first parishes. But it is withdrawment into a vortex which stifles and destroys them'—a 'withdrawal', that is, into the 'pestilential' moral and intellectual atmosphere of the great towns.[155]

Yet, despite conceding the vitiating influence of the town, Chalmers went on to suggest that, by introducing the parochial system to a dense urban area, the intellectual 'excitement' fostered by the latter's 'great literary public' could actually be harnessed to the cause of theological learning. Under such an arrangement, the urban poor would be provided with the moral 'culture' necessary to elevate their spiritual and material condition, while their clergyman would in turn be quickened by the social 'excitement' of a great commercial town without succumbing to the enervating spirit of selfishness. The 'thriving interchange of commodities' that Chalmers had celebrated in the *Commercial Discourses* would thereby be translated to the 'busy movement of [moral] circulation over a given space' provided by parochial education; and the Christian 'sublime' reconciled with the 'beauteous' moral aspect of commercial society.[156] Such a conjunction was predicated on a localist ethic, redolent of neo-Burkean idealizations of traditional social relations, which opposed the 'kindliness of select and limited intercourse' typical of the parochial system to 'the cold lustre of a wider and more public management' of education and poor relief. Under a 'parochial economy' the virtues of thrift, independence, and charity would replace an institutionalized pauperism, just as the 'subdivisions of locality' would encourage social order and quieten political unrest.[157]

Chalmers's *Christian and Civic Economy* was conceived as an explicit alternative to the educational philosophy of the mechanics' institutes, and offered moral culture in place of instruction in the science of political economy, on the grounds that

155 Ibid. i. 22–3, 44–51.
156 Ibid. i. 48, 103; id., *Application of Christianity*, 79.
157 Chalmers, *Christian and Civic Economy*, i. 74; ii. 70, 41.

a system of political economy may take effect upon men, who do not understand the steps or *rationale* of the process. It is not necessary, for example, that the philosophy of Malthus should be studied by our common people, ere they shall come under the operation of that moral and preventive check, through which we are taught, by his philosophy, that labourers might attain to a greater comfort and sufficiency than they are now in possession of. It is not necessary, for this purpose, to read lectures, or to circulate tracts among them, which shall expound the theory of population, in order that they may realize the benefits which would ensue from a right practical application of this theory. The same object is accomplished by the ordinary and general processes, whether of spiritual or of scholastic culture. A lettered and religious population will exemplify the truth of this system, though ignorant of all its doctrines, and therefore totally unacted upon by its authority.[158]

Economic prosperity would follow not from the combination of labour encouraged by a potentially radicalized economic theory, but rather through the checks to population and pauperism offered by a 'busy process of moral and mental culture'. Rejecting the pedagogic imperatives of the secular movement for scientific education and popular political economy, Chalmers recommended instead that the cause of national education would best be served by a Christianized moral discourse diffused by an intellectually vibrant clerical caste. 'It is mainly to the learning of the priesthood', he wrote, 'that Christianity has kept her ground on the higher platform of cultivated and well-educated humanity, and that she enters so largely, as a bright and much-esteemed ingredient, into the body of our national literature'.[159]

Such arguments intersected with Chalmers's belief that educational endowments should remain firmly under the control of the established church. While members of the Clapham Sect tended to support both non-denominational and Anglican educational schemes, Chalmers maintained a more conservative attitude, a fact which might help to explain his refusal of the chair of Moral Philosophy at London University, despite fervent attempts by Henry Brougham and Zachary Macaulay to persuade him otherwise.[160] In the same year he published

[158] Chalmers, *Christian and Civic Economy*, iii. 380–1. See also id., 'On Political Economy, in Connexion with the Moral State and Moral Prospects of Society', in *Works*, 25 vols. (Glasgow, 1836–42), xx, ch. 15. But cf. id., 'On Mechanics Schools and on Political Economy as a Branch of Popular Education', *Glasgow Mechanics' Magazine*, 5 (3 June 1826), 217–21, quoted in Berg, *Machinery Question*, 163.

[159] Chalmers, *Christian and Civic Economy*, iii. 403; ibid. i. 306.

[160] Ernest Marshall Howse, *Saints in Politics: The 'Clapham Sect' and the Growth of Freedom* (1953), new edn. (1971), 98–9; Brown, *Thomas Chalmers*, 177.

a treatise *On the Use and Abuse of Literary and Ecclesiastical Endowments*, a vigorous affirmation of the mutual interdependence of higher learning and established religion as preconditions for the elevation of 'plebeian taste'. Learning should not, he argued, be treated as a 'marketable commodity' and left to the otherwise inviolable laws of supply and demand. Indeed, a particular text could become 'a permanent addition to the classic and literary wealth of the nation' only if its author was endowed and therefore 'fully possessed with his subject'. Moreover, in the related case of established religion, it 'is quite palpable, that the people do not seek after the article of Christian instruction as they would after an article of ordinary merchandise'. Chalmers therefore made a strict distinction between the unrestrained market forces guiding the moral and spiritual culture of society at large, and the necessity for an endowed class of clerical scholars and educators charged with regulating the 'moral economy' of commercial society so as to promote the cause of both Christian virtue and theological enquiry.[161]

Now these concerns—with church establishment, the corrupting influence of the marketplace upon literature and learning, and the intellectual and spiritual function of an endowed intelligentsia—have all traditionally been identified far more readily with the 'Romantic' social criticism of Samuel Taylor Coleridge. John Stuart Mill certainly recognized this parallel, when he compared Coleridge to 'the other great defender of endowed establishments, Dr Chalmers'.[162] We are used to thinking of the Lake poets as resolute opponents of what Coleridge called the 'overbalance of the commercial spirit', and there are certainly significant differences between the interventionist prescriptions of Lake school conservatism and the spiritualized capitalism of Chalmers's evangelical economics. But on the important point of education, both evangelical political economists and the Lake poets argued for the suspension of the laws of the market; and it is here that we can see the common political and intellectual ground behind their shared reliance on the rhetoric of 'cultivation'—namely, a belief in an active, interventionist process of moral, civic, and spiritual nurture.[163] On the other hand, when liberal Whigs and philosophic radicals employed the same language, it

[161] Chalmers, *On the Use and Abuse of Literary and Ecclesiastical Endowments* (Glasgow, 1827), 33–4, 24, 50–1, 112, 124; Waterman, *Revolution*, 230–40.

[162] John Stuart Mill, 'Coleridge', *London and Westminster Review*, 33 (Mar. 1840), 289.

[163] Mainstream Anglican ecclesiastical reformers made a similar point: see e.g. Richard Yates, *Patronage of the Church of England* (1823), 21–3.

was, as we have seen, primarily directed at the rhetorical differentiation of the intellectual attainments and pursuits of the leisured yet virtuous middle class from the mental debilitation attendant upon the increasingly specialized and 'mechanical' pursuits of the labouring classes.

In common with Wordsworth, Chalmers developed a parochial, socially particularist defence of the values of localism. Like Walter Scott, he sought to recuperate a sense of 'organic community' apparently extinguished by the cosmopolitan rationalism of the Scottish Enlightenment.[164] But in striking contrast to the literary conservatism of the Lake school, his arguments had consistent and unapologetic recourse to the language of political economy. While Chalmers openly embraced a Christianized version of the 'dismal science', Wordsworth, Coleridge, and Southey all came to harbour a deep distrust of economic discourse, which they regarded as a particularly pernicious manifestation of a reductive, secularizing 'mechanical philosophy'. This, it should now be clear, was by no means an obvious position to take, however satisfyingly it seems to conform to an anachronistic explanatory schema predicated upon the 'two cultures' of science and literature. Its clarification will therefore require some renewed attention to the Lake poets' economic and political opinions in the years after 1805.

[164] Brown, *Thomas Chalmers*, 12, 211.

CHAPTER THREE

The Politics of Apostasy: Coleridge, Wordsworth, and Lake School Literary Conservatism

The work that is usually regarded as the summation of Coleridge's social and political thought, *On the Constitution of Church and State*, did not make a particularly auspicious entrance onto the public stage, despite its topical appearance in December 1829, in the wake of the Catholic Emancipation Act. The habitual intellectual intricacies of Coleridge's writing made *Church and State* at best a rather oblique intervention in the emancipation debate, and the book's slightly belated appearance can only have compounded the impression of its original readers that it was less a policy document than an esoteric effusion of the kind increasingly expected from the Sage of Highgate. From 'the elevation to which he transports us', observed the *Eclectic Review*, 'the misty exhalations of thought which come rolling one over another, apparently the sport of accident or impulse, but governed by unknown laws of association,—often assume forms of grandeur and beauty which delight the fancy, although they obscure or conceal the field of intellectual vision'.[1] The *Eclectic*'s remarks constitute one of the earliest examples of a familiar strain of nineteenth-century Coleridgeana, most memorably exemplified by Carlyle's account of the 'formidable apparatus' of Coleridge's table talk, comprising just enough 'logical swim-bladders' and 'transcendental life-preservers' to sustain the sage in 'the high seas of theosophic philosophy', while leaving his hapless audience floundering in the 'unintelligible deluge'.[2]

Such responses do much to explain why *Church and State* found so few admirers in what remained of Coleridge's lifetime. Yet its profound

[1] 'Church and State', *Eclectic Review*, 3rd ser., 6 (July 1831), 1–2.

[2] Thomas Carlyle, *The Life of John Sterling* (1851), 73–4.

effect on a handful of influential, and surprisingly diverse, early readers, including Julius Hare, F. D. Maurice, and John Henry Newman, ensured that Coleridge's discussion of the 'National Church' coloured the entire spectrum of Victorian ecclesiology, from the Oxford Movement to liberal Anglicanism. Of all his prose works, *Church and State* actually did most, in the end, to rescue Coleridge from the charge of obscurantist irrelevance, and established his nineteenth-century reputation as a theologian and social critic of considerable importance. In 1856 the Cambridge divine F. J. A. Hort declared it 'his last and most important work', and the reverential tone in which this judgement was delivered suggests that it was no longer a particularly contentious assertion.[3]

Coleridge's defence of the national church was still exerting some influence in the mid-twentieth century, most notably via T. S. Eliot's *The Idea of a Christian Society* (1939). Thereafter, however, the significance of *Church and State* gradually shifted to a rather different, if not entirely unrelated context. From Leavisite literary pedagogy to Raymond Williams's Marxist humanism, and on to more recent (and more critical) analyses of the relationship between 'culture', hegemony, and the idea of the state, Coleridge's work now figured as the originary moment in a long tradition of English educational and social thought.[4] The central importance of *Church and State* seemed, on this reading, to lie in Coleridge's concept of 'cultivation', an educational ideal embodied in the labours of the public intellectual class he termed the 'clerisy'. Cultivation, 'the harmonious developement [*sic*] of those qualities and faculties that characterise our humanity' could thus be contrasted with 'civilization', the intellectual and material growth of a particular society, which Coleridge associated with the 'progressive' forces of commerce and manufacturing, the secular arts and sciences, and the 'mercantile and commercial class' of the community.[5] Thus, as *Church and State* took its place at the beginning of a putative tradition of 'cultural' thought, Coleridge simultaneously emerged as

[3] Stephen Prickett, *Romanticism and Religion: The Tradition of Wordsworth and Coleridge in the Victorian Church* (Cambridge, 1976), 31–3; F. J. A. Hort, 'Coleridge', *Cambridge Essays* (1856), 348.

[4] Francis Mulhern, *The Moment of 'Scrutiny'* (1979), 306; Raymond Williams, *Culture and Society 1780–1950* (1958); David Lloyd and Paul Thomas, *Culture and the State* (New York, 1998), 61–70.

[5] Samuel Taylor Coleridge, *On the Constitution of Church and State* (1829), ed. John Colmer (London and Princeton, 1976), 42–3.

a pre-eminent Romantic critic of economic modernity and its intellectual products.

A broadly similar pattern emerges from the reception history of William Wordsworth's *Excursion* (1814), the most ambitious publication of the poet's lifetime, and the text that stood at the heart of the Wordsworthian canon for much of the nineteenth century. Francis Jeffrey's notorious attack on the poem as a 'tissue of moral and devotional ravings' had a tangible effect on *The Excursion*'s early reception, and the first edition still 'had not cleared its 500-copy printing twenty years later'.[6] Yet *The Excursion* did eventually find a new generation of readers, who recognized the poem as a profound commentary on the myriad public arguments and private agonies that tend now to be collectively, and often rather summarily, referred to as the Victorian 'crisis of faith'. As a result, and although early reviewers did note its author's anxious attempts to come to terms with the gathering pace of urbanization and industrial growth, nineteenth-century readers tended to subordinate *The Excursion*'s discussion of such issues to more explicitly spiritual concerns, and to focus their appreciation on Wordsworth as the pre-eminent poet of a sanctified natural landscape. Even Ruskin, whose reading of the poem clearly played some considerable part in clarifying his distaste for utilitarian materialism and economic science, nevertheless considered it 'a thoroughly religious book'.[7]

It was only with Leslie Stephen's essay on 'Wordsworth's Ethics', in 1876, that a fully blown secular reading (or perhaps 'strong misreading') of *The Excursion* became possible. For Stephen, who viewed the poem as the coherent expression of an ethical and social 'philosophy', Wordsworth's discussion of the factory system represented an astute response to the fragmentation of the individual 'social unit' under the pressure of the division of labour. Such claims formed part of a broader reinterpretation of the Wordsworthian corpus as a proleptic engagement with the great intellectual antitheses of late-nineteenth-century social and political thought—individualism and collectivism, utilitarians and intuitionists—and thus as an unlikely precursor of Stephen's own, equally idiosyncratic version of evolutionary naturalism. In response,

[6] [Francis Jeffrey], 'Wordsworth's Excursion', *Edinburgh Review*, 24 (Nov. 1814), 4; Gill, *Wordsworth and the Victorians*, 17.

[7] 'Wordsworth's Excursion', *British Critic*, 2nd ser., 3 (May 1815), 463; John Ruskin, *Letters from Venice*, ed. John Lewis Bradley (New Haven, 1955), 92 (14 Dec. 1851); id., *Fors Clavigera*, 5 vols. (London and Kent, 1871–7), vol. i, letter v, 16–17.

Matthew Arnold turned the anachronism implicit in Stephen's approach on its head, in his well-known complaint that *The Excursion*'s concluding plea for a national education system would not be out of place at a Social Science Congress.[8] But, while Arnold's valuation of the poem's literary qualities has persisted more or less unchallenged until quite recently, *The Excursion*'s concluding discussion of manufacturing and education has gradually taken on a new significance, as a central document of Wordsworth's mature political thought. As such, the poem has inspired some quite diverse interpretations—serving, for example, as a demonstration of its author's political apostasy, a vindication of his enduring radical sympathies, and even as the literary manifesto of an English 'environmental tradition'.[9] Yet, despite such heterogeneous critical responses, a shared impression remains of the poem's final books as a portentous and far-sighted critique of nineteenth-century industrial society.

The shifting terms of the Lake poets' historical influence and critical reception, together with their abiding reputation as the first, prophetic critics of high capitalist society, have left Wordsworth and Coleridge somewhat isolated from the orthodox 'Toryism' that is commonly supposed to represent their nearest point of reference within contemporary political discourse once they had abandoned the radicalism of their youth. Some of their opinions, particularly in old age, invite identification with that protectionist, authoritarian, and High Church tendency usually referred to as 'Ultra' Toryism. But this term only really begins to make sense in the mid-1820s, while such an association is further problematized by the apparent eccentricities of the Lake poets' political judgements (such as Coleridge's opposition to the 1815 Corn Law), together with the rather unconventional manner of their reconciliation with the Church of England.[10] Coleridge's precocious engagement with the 'mythological school' of continental biblical criticism seems to have remained abstruse enough to pass most of the Anglican establishment

[8] Leslie Stephen, 'Wordsworth's Ethics', in *Hours in a Library*, 3rd ser. (1879), 214–16; Matthew Arnold, 'Preface' to *Poems of Wordsworth*, ed. Arnold (1879), p. xxi. See also F. W. H. Myers, *Wordsworth* (1881), 90–4.

[9] See e.g. E. P. Thompson, 'Disenchantment or Default?', in *The Romantics*; Mary Wedd, 'Industrialization and the Moral Law in Books VIII and IX of *The Excursion*', *Charles Lamb Bulletin*, NS. 81 (1993), 5–25; Jonathan Bate, *Romantic Ecology: Wordsworth and the Environmental Tradition* (1991).

[10] James J. Sack, *From Jacobite to Conservative: Reaction and Orthodoxy in Britain, c.1760–1832* (Cambridge, 1993), 6.

by. But Wordsworth's 'Natural Methodism', as the *Quarterly* described it, was far more obviously suspect, and provoked a great deal of critical casuistry, if not outright condemnation, amongst *The Excursion*'s more pious admirers, which persisted even after the publication of *Ecclesiastical Sketches* in 1822.[11] Given the intense doubts that continued to surround the question of Wordsworth's religion, it does not seem entirely adequate to assert, with E. P. Thompson, that the poet fell back into a 'traditional', and ideologically unproblematic, allegiance to 'paternalism, Anglican doctrine, [and] fear of change'.[12]

Such difficulties of classification perhaps begin to explain why the two principal Lake poets' political and social opinions have often seemed unusually isolated from those of their immediate contemporaries, at least once they left behind the radical milieu of the 1790s. Some version of Lake school 'apostasy' is generally accepted; but, while we are familar enough with the turbulent political events that shaped their early radicalism, the context of their subsequent turn to conservatism remains rather less clear. Even the most detailed studies of Coleridge's political thought have tended to reinforce a sense of his ideological isolation, by viewing his trajectory from radical to conservative as an illuminating but idiosyncratic response to what J. G. A. Pocock has called 'the end of early modernity'—a putative crisis in the conventional terms of political discourse in which the dual traditions of civic humanism and the Scottish Enlightenment each suffered a sea change, and which Coleridge could surmount only by exploiting such exotic intellectual resources as German transcendentalism and seventeenth-century English political philosophy.[13] The ideological identity of Wordsworth's later poetry, meanwhile, has tended to be either displaced into a 'proto-Victorian moment', or assimilated to a broad tradition of 'Tory humanism' and Burkean veneration for prescriptive custom.[14]

[11] [Charles Lamb and William Gifford], 'Wordsworth's Excursion', *Quarterly Review*, 12 (Oct. 1814), 105; [James Montgomery], 'Wordsworth's Excursion', *Eclectic Review*, 2nd ser., 3 (Jan. 1815), 19–21.

[12] Thompson, 'Disenchantment or Default?', in *The Romantics*, 67.

[13] J. G. A. Pocock, 'Empire, Revolution and the End of Early Modernity', in id. *et al.* (eds.), *The Varieties of British Political Thought, 1500–1800* (Cambridge, 1993), 283–317; Morrow, *Coleridge's Political Thought*; Leask, *Politics of Imagination*.

[14] Alison Hickey, *Impure Conceits: Rhetoric and Ideology in Wordsworth's 'Excurson'* (Stanford, Calif., 1997), 22; Friedman, *Making of a Tory Humanist*, 92; Chandler, *Wordsworth's Second Nature*, *passim*. Chandler's somewhat overstated case for the Burkean presence in Wordsworth's verse argues that the poet capitulated to an ideological programme derived from the *Reflections* as early as 1798.

Wordsworth, Coleridge, and Southey all undoubtedly came to feel an uncommonly close affinity with Burke, whose transition from Rockinghamite Whig to fevered reactionary seemed in many ways to foreshadow their own post-revolutionary ideological odyssey. But while Burke's *Reflections on the Revolution in France* did become an increasingly important point of reference for the Lake school, as for many other nineteenth-century writers and politicians, it cannot be regarded as the sacred text of first-generation 'Romantic conservatism', as is often assumed, without considerable qualification. In the broadest terms, the development of the Lake poets' political and social thought is best understood in terms of the continuities and contradictions pertaining between their vestigially radicalized commitment to agrarian virtue (whether Godwinian, Foxite, or neo-Harringtonian in origin), and the establishment conservatism to which they all sought, with varying degrees of enthusiasm, to conform. The 'Genius of Burke' provided one way of finessing some of the contradictions of such a position, and was also broadly compatible with Wordsworth's perennial attachment to the defence of customary social and political forms.[15] Yet the Lake poets must also have been aware that the mainstream of British political conservatism often proved extremely reluctant to discover its governing values in Burke's ambivalent posthumous reputation.[16] An adequate contextualization of the Lake school's 'apostasy', however defined, must therefore also be prepared to explore their ideological relation to that dominant, Pittite tradition within the political establishment which proved increasingly receptive to some version of 'liberal' values during the early decades of the nineteenth century.

If there was one feature of the Lake poets' literary conservatism that did mark them out particularly clearly from their Tory and high Anglican contemporaries, it was the depth of their commitment to the cause of popular education. Their immersion in the dissenting radical culture of the 1790s left Wordsworth and Coleridge, in particular, with an enduring enthusiasm for the intellectual enlightenment of the 'lower orders', even if the nature and ends of such education were increasingly subordinated to the defence of church and state. Their close involvement with the politics of popular education persisted into the 1810s and 1820s, a period in which conservative social thought experienced a

[15] Wordsworth, *Fourteen Book* Prelude, vii. 512.

[16] See James J. Sack, 'The Memory of Burke and the Memory of Pitt: English Conservatism Confronts its Past, 1806–1829', *Historical Journal*, 30 (1987), 623–40.

sustained challenge from Whigs, liberals, and philosophic radicals, many of whom, as we have seen, were willing to invoke the insights of political economy in support of their own arguments for non-denominational, and even secular, forms of popular education and the 'diffusion of knowledge'. From this perspective, Coleridge's mounting antipathy to political economy, and concomitant defence of spiritual 'cultivation', seem far more directly concerned with educational and ecclesiastical politics than with the moral iniquities of commerce and industrialization. Indeed, both *Church and State* and *The Excursion* display a much greater degree of toleration for the 'commercial spirit' than is commonly supposed, despite their authors' continued conviction of the vital, stabilizing influence exercised by landed property, and the potential evils of manufacturing and trade. The resultant tensions and ambivalences might well testify to the Lake poets' continuing debt to the agrarian politics of their youth but, conversely, they also suggest the extent to which Wordsworth and Coleridge actively sought some form of intellectual and imaginative accommodation with the ideological ascendancy of liberal Toryism. Before expanding on these remarks, however, it will be necessary to look in a little more detail at the changing nature of conservative attitudes to popular education, which provide an important preliminary context for understanding the Lake School's shifting political loyalties in the early years of the nineteenth century.

COUNTER-REVOLUTION, 'CULTIVATION', AND CONSERVATIVE EDUCATIONAL DISCOURSE

In February 1807, the brewer and Whig politician Samuel Whitbread introduced a bill of poor law reform into the House of Commons. Whitbread's wide-ranging plan was extremely ambitious, and reflected not just his self-appointed mission to claim the leadership of the Foxite party in parliament, but also his desire to secure the industry and independence of the poorest members of society. To this latter end, the bill's most significant proposals included changes to the settlement laws, the establishment of a 'National Poor's Fund', a parochially funded scheme of cottage building, and a system of public education for the children of the poor.[17] But, despite his faith in the immediate necessity for such reforms, the speech in which Whitbread presented his proposals to the

[17] Poynter, *Society and Pauperism*, 207–22.

Commons also registered his fundamental suspicion of the poor law as a whole, claiming that it 'has served to degrade those whom it was intended to exalt, to destroy the spirit of independence, throughout our land; to hold out hopes which cannot be realized; to encourage idleness and vice; and to produce a superfluous population, the offspring of improvidence, and the early victim of misery and want'. Given such sentiments, it should come as no surprise that Whitbread went on to praise the influence that Malthusian ideas had exercised upon the climate of debate. The *Essay on Population*, he claimed, 'has completed that change of opinion with regard to the poor laws, which had before been in some measure begun'. Whitbread objected to the specific, practical conclusions Malthus had reached on this issue; but, while he expressed reservations about Malthus's plan of reform, by which 'the poor laws would absolutely cease, after the expiration of a very short period', he himself looked forward to the 'gradual abolition' of those laws at some point in the not too distant future.[18]

Despite such differences of emphasis, it is easy to understand why contemporary observers quickly came to associate the *Essay on Population* with the new bill, particularly after Malthus published his *Letter to Samuel Whitbread*, a broadly supportive contribution to the controversy over Whitbread's plan. Malthus declared himself particularly sympathetic to the proposed system of national education, which, by elevating the intellectual condition of the lower orders, would tend to reduce their dependence on parochial relief and stimulate their political and economic autonomy.[19] Indeed, Whitbread's plan of national education—which was eventually consigned to a separate bill of its own—was not just 'the first time that popular education was discussed at the highest level'; it also marked a turning point in political arguments on this issue, by giving Malthusian social theory a prominent place in the debate on national education, and thus preparing the way for Sumner, Chalmers, and the evangelical Malthusianism of

[18] Samuel Whitbread, *Substance of a Speech on the Poor Laws* (1807), 3–15; Roger Fulford, *Samuel Whitbread 1764–1815: A Study in Opposition* (1967), 179–80. Even fervent abolitionists were prepared to concede the immediate utility of Whitbread's bill: see John Berkeley Monck, *General Reflections on the System of the Poor Laws* (n.d. [1807]).

[19] John Bone, *The Wants of the People, and the Means of Government* (1807), 46–8; Thomas Jarrold, *A Letter to Samuel Whitbread* (n.d. [1807]), 10–11; Thomas Robert Malthus, *A Letter to Samuel Whitbread* (1807), 34–5. David Eastwood's claim that Whitbread's approach was 'radically different' from that of Malthus seems overstated: *Governing Rural England: Tradition and Transformation in Local Government 1780–1840* (Oxford, 1994), 125.

the 1810s and 1820s.[20] Whitbread invoked the educational recommendations of Malthus and Adam Smith in defending his proposals on poor law reform, and followed the second *Essay on Population* in stressing the political, as well as material, benefits of popular education. National schools, and the opportunity of saving, would lead to independence, industry, and frugality. But moreover, 'in a political point of view, nothing can possibly afford greater stability to a popular government than the education of your people'.[21]

Whitbread's arguments were calculated to revive a growing consensus on the desirability of popular education that had taken shape within the political and religious establishment during the late eighteenth century, before disintegrating in the counter-revolutionary atmosphere of the 1790s. The Sunday school movement of the 1780s had struck a powerful chord amongst politicians, evangelicals, and social reformers anxious to encourage the moral regeneration of society. After 1789, however, it became increasingly difficult to justify any further extension of popular education, owing to an influential interpretation of the French Revolution that attributed its outbreak, in the words of one popular contemporary account, to the process whereby 'literature and riches became more diffused among the middle and inferior orders of society'.[22] On both sides of the Revolution debate, the diffusion of knowledge and the growing importance of commercial wealth were yoked together as powerful catalysts for the downfall of the *ancien régime*. The barrister and magistrate John Bowles, for example, 'one of the most successful loyalist writers' of the 1790s, traced the lamentable rise of revolutionary 'infidelism' and 'philosophy', in both France and Britain, to the imperialist and mercantile expansion of European power. The 'new and most copious sources of wealth and prosperity' that were thereby opened had, Bowles argued, operated 'in conjunction with the art of printing, to produce a great and sudden Revolution in the minds and manners of civilized Nations'.[23]

[20] Laqueur, *Religion and Respectability*, 129.

[21] Whitbread, *Substance of a Speech*, 23–36.

[22] John Moore, *A View of the Causes and Progress of the French Revolution*, 2 vols. (1795), i. 25.

[23] Emma Vincent, '"The Real Grounds of the Present War": John Bowles and the French Revolutionary Wars, 1792–1802', *History*, 78 (1993), 393; John Bowles, *Reflections on the Political and Moral State of Society, at the Close of the Eighteenth Century* (1800), 128.

In many cases, such arguments represented little more than an extension of earlier attacks on the heretical tendencies of Enlightenment erudition.[24] But the counter-revolutionary critique of the mutual corruption of commerce and literature found its most original and sophisticated expression in the writings of Edmund Burke, whose outraged account of an incendiary alliance between the 'political Men of Letters' and the French professional and commercial classes proved extremely influential in shaping British perceptions of the Revolution.[25] Although Burke's analysis was by no means the only one available, the basic terms of his argument gained widespread acceptance, thanks at least in part to their conformity with the socio-historical assumptions of the Scottish Enlightenment. Moderate Whig supporters of the Revolution such as James Mackintosh, for example, were willing to accept the reality of an alliance between 'philosophers' and 'literature' with the 'commercial, or monied interest', but argued that it represented a socially beneficial and intellectually enlightening conjunction that had secured the freedom and prosperity of the British people after 1688, and had manifested itself in such sudden and dramatic fashion in France only as a result of the political inertia of the *ancien régime.*[26]

The resultant controversy over the 'literary' causes of the French Revolution was undoubtedly made far more urgent by the publishing sensation of Thomas Paine's *Rights of Man* Part Two, over one and a half million copies of which were in circulation by 1809.[27] The incredible success of this godless bible of English jacobinism scandalized the political establishment, and seemed to vindicate the reactionary identification of the diffusion of knowledge with the spread of seditious opinion. Even politically conservative defenders of popular education had to endure the suspicions of those counter-revolutionary ideologues convinced that literate reflection amongst the working classes would breed only discontent and rebellion. Evangelicals and philanthropists such as Hannah More and Thomas Bernard remained convinced of the utility of their educational work in maintaining traditional structures of deference and

[24] See e.g. William Purkiss, *Influence of the Present Pursuits in Learning as they Affect Religion* (Cambridge, 1786).

[25] Edmund Burke, *Reflections on the Revolution in France* (1790), in *Writings and Speeches*, ed. Paul Langford, vol. viii, *The French Revolution 1790–94*, ed. L. G. Mitchell (Oxford, 1989), 160; Pocock, *Virtue, Commerce, and History*, 193–212.

[26] James Mackintosh, *Vindiciæ Gallicæ* (1791), 136–9, 123–4.

[27] Richard D. Altick, *The English Common Reader: A Social History of the Mass Reading Public 1800–1900* (Chicago, 1957), 70.

power. But they often found themselves defending their beliefs against what Bernard described as 'absurd prejudices' against educating the poor.[28]

Malthus himself thought it probable that the 'circulation of Paine's Rights of Man . . . has done great mischief among the lower and middling classes of people in this country'. He was adamant, however, that the 'arguments which have been urged against instructing the people appear to me to be not only illiberal, but to the last degree, feeble'. The principal such argument against 'a system of national education in England is, that the common people would be put in a capacity to read such works as those of Paine, and that the consequences would probably be fatal to government'. As we have seen, Malthus was so confident of the falsity of this assumption that he went onto the offensive against the enemies of popular education, claiming that a knowledge of the 'real nature' of the people's situation 'so obviously tends to promote peace and quietness . . . that those who would still object to the instruction of the people may fairly be suspected of a wish to encourage their ignorance, as a pretext for tyranny, and an opportunity of increasing the power and influence of the executive government'.[29] Such arguments were designed to assuage counter-revolutionary fears; but they were also clearly informed by a reformist Whig agenda, which viewed popular education as the principal means of preserving the independence of the lower orders from corrupt and demagogic government. It is little wonder, then, that they appealed to Whitbread, whose defence of 'the general diffusion of knowledge' also reflected a distinctly Whiggish political sensibility.[30]

The Malthusian argument for popular education was, however, by no means straightforwardly identifiable with the radical platform. Indeed, this was one of its principal recommendations to reformist Whigs such as Whitbread, who had found themselves politically isolated by the triumph of counter-revolutionary Pittite loyalism, and who failed to realize the degree to which, by appearing to compromise their allegiance to the more radical elements of the Foxite legacy, they risked forfeiting their leadership of a renascent popular reform movement. Whitbread's proposals could hardly be described as informed by the

[28] *Reports of the Society for Bettering the Condition and Increasing the Comforts of the Poor*, ii. report lxi, quoted in Poynter, *Society and Pauperism*, 95.

[29] Malthus, *Essay* (1803), ii. 126, 153–4.

[30] Whitbread, *Substance of a Speech*, 24.

kind of 'utopian' educational ideals that conservative pedagogues attacked as 'injurious and absurd'—they were, after all, explicitly predicated upon the Malthusian principle that 'man' is 'born to labour as the sparks fly upwards: that a certain portion of misery is inseparable from mortality; and that all plans for the lodging, cloathing, and feeding of all mankind, with what may be called comfort, are quite impossible in practice'.[31] Malthus's enduring reputation as the intellectual nemesis of Godwinian radical hubris only lent an additional layer of respectability to a scheme of national education and poor law reform explicitly indebted to the principles of the *Essay on Population*.

The influence of Malthusian ideas upon early nineteenth-century educational and social thought was extremely diverse, ranging from the Enlightenment Whiggism of Francis Jeffrey to the evangelical conservatism of Thomas Chalmers. Indeed, while the first *Essay* had been primarily concerned with the refutation of radical perfectibilism, the 'achievement of Malthus's second *Essay* . . . was to wrest the idea of "progress" from the grasp of the Jacobins and to make it instead the legitimate property of reformist whigs and subsequently of a new generation of post-war "liberal conservatives" '.[32] It can certainly be argued that Whitbread was the first such reformist English Whig to recognize this fact, by deploying the fatalistic language of Malthusian natural theology in support of a national system of popular education. Just as Dugald Stewart sought to dissociate himself from a beleagured Whig reformism by embracing the supposedly pre-political language of economic science, so Malthusian rhetoric provided Whitbread with a medium in which he could continue to pursue the diffusion of knowledge while attracting a minimum of counter-revolutionary opprobrium.

Like Stewart, however, Whitbread quickly discovered that such tactics would prove only partially successful. The spectre of revolutionary France continued to form a potent warning against the extension of learning amongst the lower classes. 'I can scarcely conceive it possible', wrote one Justice of the Peace of Whitbread's bill,

that the events which have so recently occurred in France should have escaped the honourable Gentleman's recollection; neither is it probable that a person of his extensive information should not have been aware, that the revolution, which is rapidly changing the face of the European

[31] Patrick Colquhoun, *A New and Appropriate System of Education for the Labouring People* (1806), 12; Whitbread, *Substance of a Speech*, 7.

[32] Waterman, *Revolution*, 142.

continent, has been principally ascribed to the education of the lower orders . . .[33]

Such a response was by no means untypical of Whitbread's more reactionary critics. Reminding his readers of the publishing sensation enjoyed by 'the notorious Thomas Paine', another anonymous commentator suggested that 'the very ignorance which this bill proposes to remove, tended in a considerable degree to the saving of our country from all the horrors in which a neighbouring country has been involved'.[34]

Yet despite such objections, which were conceded, to a greater or lesser extent, by many influential members of the Commons, Whitbread's education bill (unlike his poor law proposals) did survive long enough to reach the House of Lords. Indeed, the parochial schools bill's eventual rejection by the Lords must be attributed not to Parliament's wholesale rejection of national education *per se*, but rather to the religious implications of Whitbread's plan. For one thing, his bill shifted responsibility for education from the clergy to the magistracy, and hence appeared to undermine the degree to which popular instruction could remain the legitimate province of the established church.[35] The resultant suspicions of the bill's dissenting character amongst the Lords were only confirmed by the fact that Whitbread explicitly endorsed the non-denominational educational system of the Quaker Joseph Lancaster as a model for his parochial schools.[36]

Lancaster's much publicized *Improvements in Education* (1803) was the subject of some controversy at this time. The novelty of the *Improvements* had already been questioned by Sarah Trimmer, who identified the 'original inventor' of Lancaster's educational techniques as the Revd. Andrew Bell, a retired tutor of the mixed-race 'orphan' children of British soldiers in India (whose pedagogic method was therefore often referred to as the 'Madras' system).[37] There were certainly a number of practical

[33] [Daniel Carpenter], *Reflections Suggested by Mr. Whitbread's Bill* (1808), 4–5.

[34] *Remarks Upon 'A Bill . . . for Promoting and Encouraging of Industry amongst the Labouring Classes of the Community'* (1807), 11; see also [John Leslie], *A Summons of Wakening* (Hawick, 1807), 147–8; [W. Randall], *The Warning Voice* (1807), 15–16.

[35] *Parliamentary Debates*, 1st ser., ix. 1174–8; Poynter, *Society and Pauperism*, 215; R. A. Soloway, *Prelates and People: Ecclesiastical Social Thought in England 1783–1852* (1969), 367–70; Alan Richardson, *Literature, Education, and Romanticism: Reading as Social Practice 1780–1832* (Cambridge, 1994), 90–1.

[36] Whitbread, *Substance of a Speech*, 33–4.

[37] Sarah Trimmer, *A Comparative View of the New Plan of Education* (1805), 20.

differences between these rival educational schemes, although they shared the basic innovation of employing the most able students as disciplinary and pedagogical 'monitors', with the result that the sheer numbers of students capable of being instructed by one teacher expanded quite dramatically. It was principally for this reason that 'monitorial' pedagogy came to be inextricably bound up with early nineteenth-century debates on popular education. However, the most important point at issue in the claims and counter-claims of the two men's supporters was the religious content of the education to be provided by the monitorial method. Lancaster's *Improvements* argued that, while it was necessary to make the instruction of the industrious classes a 'national concern', it 'ought not to be made subservient to the propagation of the peculiar tenets of any sect'.[38] Trimmer's support for the Anglican Bell, on the other hand, was closely linked to her conviction 'that children should be educated in the doctrines and tenets of the *national religion*'.[39]

Certainly, Whitbread's enthusiastic defence of Lancaster's *Improvements in Education* in the face of orthodox religious 'bigotry and prejudice' laid him wide open to the accusation that the schools bill was dangerously anti-establishment in character.[40] The most concerted such charge was levelled by the anti-jacobin pamphleteer John Bowles, whose *Letter to Samuel Whitbread* conceded 'the utility of the mechanical part' of the monitorial system, but found the 'religious part' of Lancaster's educational writings 'liable to the most serious and weighty objections'.[41] Bowles argued that, if Lancaster's system 'be really intended to be compatible with the safety of the national Church, it must be made subservient to the propagation of the faith of that Church: and indeed it must be founded on the principle, that *the youth who partake of its benefits must be brought up as members of the establishment*'.[42] A non-denominational education was simply equivalent to a schismatic education; and for loyalist ideologues such as Bowles, religious schism was still the most palpable threat to the constitutional fabric of church and state.

[38] Joseph Lancaster, *Improvements in Education, as it respects the Industrious Classes of the Community* (1803), pp. iii–iv.

[39] Trimmer, *Comparative View*, 9.

[40] Whitbread, *Substance of a Speech*, 34. In a note appended to the published version of his speech, Whitbread acknowledged Bell as well as Lancaster. The damage, however, seems already to have been done.

[41] John Bowles, *A Letter to Samuel Whitbread*, 2nd edn. (1808), 2; see also [Carpenter], *Reflections*, 5.

[42] Bowles, *Letter*, 26–7.

The debate on Whitbread's parochial schools bill certainly gave a new prominence and urgency to the Bell–Lancaster controversy; and it may not, therefore, be entirely uncoincidental that the Lake poets' first public involvement in this issue occurred soon afterwards. In May 1808 Coleridge interrupted his Royal Institution lecture series on the principles of poetry with a discourse on education, ending with a eulogy on Bell, and a controversial personal attack on Joseph Lancaster. Coleridge's loyalties seem to have been determined, above all, by religious politics. 'I am a zealous *subject*', he confided in his subsequent correspondence with Bell, 'and a convinced and fervent son of the Church of England'. Lancaster's schools, by contrast, constituted 'a very dangerous attack on our civil and ecclesiastical establishments'.[43] Wordsworth and Southey soon joined with Coleridge in his support for Bell's system, and Wordsworth even went so far as to experiment with the monitorial method himself, in the local school at Grasmere.[44]

The alacrity and enthusiasm with which the Lake school embraced the Bellite cause, as well as the note of anxiety in Coleridge's letters on Lancaster, suggest the very real political and constitutional threat that non-denominational popular education seemed to pose at this time. The Royal Lancasterian Association included in its membership not just Baptists and Quakers, but also radicals and reformist Whigs such as Francis Place, James Mill, and Henry Brougham. The membership of the West London branch of the association had a yet more radical reputation, particularly after Sir Francis Burdett made a donation of £1,000.[45] The Benthamite philosophic radicals also became involved, a development that culminated in the publication of Bentham's *Chrestomathia*, a plan for a 'superior Lancasterian school', which was to be organized on monitorial and panoptic principles, in order to maximize the intellectual and economic 'profit' and minimize the disciplinary and financial 'expense' of each child's education.[46] But the Lancasterian cause was also championed in the far more influential

[43] Samuel Taylor Coleridge, *Lectures 1808–1819 On Literature*, ed. R. A. Foakes, 2 vols. (London and Princeton, 1987), i. 95–109; id., *Letters*, iii. 106–7 (May 1808).

[44] See R. A. Foakes, '"Thriving Prisoners": Coleridge, Wordsworth and the Child at School', *Studies in Romanticism*, 28 (1989), 187–206; Richardson, *Literature, Education, and Romanticism*, 91–103.

[45] J. Ann Hone, *For the Cause of Truth: Radicalism in London 1796–1821* (Oxford, 1982), 238–47; Simon, *The Two Nations*, 149.

[46] Jeremy Bentham, *Chrestomathia* (1815–17), ed. M. J. Smith and W. H. Burston (Oxford, 1983), pp. xi, 55.

Edinburgh Review, while its founder enjoyed visits from a 'noble army' of admiring aristocrats and bishops, royal audiences, and finally the patronage of George III himself.[47] The early momentum of the association did not last, thanks in no small part to the erratic personality of its founder. But, for a while at least, the prospect of large sections of the lower orders being educated outside the control of the established church, and under the superintendence of a reformist—and even radical—political interest, seemed very real indeed.

Much of Lancaster's early success can be attributed to the fact that, by defending the teaching of reading, writing, and arithmetic as essential preliminaries to moral and religious education, his supporters could credibly represent the former set of attainments as relatively uncontroversial. It seemed increasingly uncharitable to combine, as some Anglican polemicists attempted to do, arguments for retaining the church establishment's control over religious instruction with the claim that 'a general diffusion of the knowledge of writing and arithmetic . . . would have an evil tendency on the virtue and happiness of the lowest orders, by giving them the possession of qualities higher than they can find means of exercising honestly'.[48] Bell himself was forced to make a humiliating retraction after suggesting in 1807 that the 'children of the poor' should not be educated 'in an expensive manner, or even taught to write and to cypher', since 'there is a risque of elevating, by an indiscriminate education, the minds of those doomed to the drudgery of daily labour, above their condition, and thereby rendering them discontented and unhappy in their lot. It may suffice to teach the generality, on an economical plan, to read their Bible and understand the doctrines of our holy religion.'[49] Such claims quickly began to seem too crudely reactionary a response to the Lancasterian challenge, particularly once

[47] See e.g. [Sydney Smith], 'Mrs. Trimmer on Lancaster's Plan of Education', *Edinburgh Review*, 9 (Oct. 1806), 177–84; [id., or Henry Hallam], 'Lancaster's Improvements in Education', ibid. 11 (Oct. 1807), 61–73; David Salmon, *Joseph Lancaster* (1904), 17.

[48] John Weyland, *A Letter to a Country Gentleman on the Education of the Lower Orders* (1808), 38.

[49] Andrew Bell, *An Analysis of the Experiment in Education, made at Egmore, near Madras* (1797), 3rd edn. (1807), 90–1; Joseph Fox, *A Comparative View of the Plans of Education, as Detailed in the Publications of Dr. Bell and Mr. Lancaster* (n.d. [1808]), 38–40; [Henry Brougham], 'Education of the Poor', *Edinburgh Review*, 17 (Nov. 1810), 63–4; Andrew Bell, *Elements of Tuition, Part II. The English School* (1814), 416–17. Dorothy Wordsworth may well have helped Bell to prepare his self-exculpatory commentary on the offending passage. See Robert Southey and Charles Cuthbert Southey, *Life of the Rev. Andrew Bell* (1844), ii. 420–1.

Malthus and Whitbread began to insist upon a direct link between popular morality and informed habits of rational foresight. In turn, however, the very success of these new arguments for popular education forced conservative social critics to refine their own vision of national schooling in some interesting and prescient ways.

This much is certainly suggested by Bowles's second public response to Whitbread, *Education of the Lower Orders* (1808). Bowles's first *Letter* had been dominated by the distinction between non-denominational and Anglican education, and the corresponding argument that a 'national' system of education must teach the 'national', established religion, a claim that led to predictably hostile reviews in the liberal press.[50] In the subsequent work, Bowles sought to answer his critics with a more sophisticated version of his argument, which distinguished between moral and religious education, on the one hand, and a technical or purely utilitarian training, on the other. Bowles once again expressed his support for Bell's Madras system, and conceded that non-denominational educationalists, such as Lancaster, were often largely concerned with basic training in reading, writing, and arithmetic. But he went on to argue that there was no necessary connection between the possession of such skills and 'the practice of religion and virtue':

> Now, reading and writing (to say nothing in this place of arithmetic), are in themselves mere arts, the utility of which depends solely on the application. They are the appropriate means for the acquisition and diffusion of science. But science, their proper object, even in its highest state of perfection, may be, and frequently is, unaccompanied by any regard for religion and virtue. The above arts are not, however, exclusively applied to the acquisition and diffusion of science. They are sometimes converted into engines of the most extensive and lasting mischief. They are not infrequently employed in disturbing the order of civil society, in promoting anarchy and confusion, infidelity and vice.[51]

Bowles's pre-eminent example of such 'mischief' was, of course, provided by Paine's *Rights of Man*. His reactionary political instincts had clearly not abandoned him, and he continued to deny the desirability of teaching writing and arithmetic to the poor. But, unlike previous conservative educationalists such as Bell and Patrick Colquhoun, Bowles seems to have realized that to condemn the further extension of popular

[50] See *Monthly Review*, 53 (July 1807), 329–40; *Critical Review*, 11 (June 1807), 174–82.

[51] John Bowles, *The Education of the Lower Orders* (1808), 9–10.

literacy as 'utopian' and impolitic would simply play further into the hands of his critics.

Instead, he made a qualitative distinction between 'instruction' and 'education'. While the former

> is simply the means of imparting knowledge . . . education actually prepares and qualifies youth for the stations which they are to occupy in society . . . By instruction the mind is informed, and the understanding enlarged; by education the heart also is cultivated, the manners, habits, and dispositions are properly moulded, and the whole man is trained up to virtue and usefulness.[52]

Hence, while part of his argument for the social utility of a national religious education continued to rely on a conventional register of vice, virtue, and moral training, Bowles laid an equal and corresponding stress on the necessity of educative 'moral cultivation' as a way of moulding the lower orders to their particular social station and responsibilities. Education, properly understood, should make the individual aware both that 'He owes personal duties to himself', defined in essentially religious terms, and that 'he owes relative duties to those to whom he is associated by ties of family connexion, of friendship, of neighbourhood, of civil subjection, of a common country, of a common nature . . . Education, therefore, in order to answer its true purpose, must correspond with the compound character which he is to sustain . . .'.[53] Bowles was clearly moving towards an understanding of popular pedagogy in which the nature of the education provided was determined both by universal moral and spiritual needs, and by the circumscribed social identity and expectations of a particular individual or class. This was in contrast to mere 'instruction', a form of learning equivalent to 'science', and which could be applied in any situation, and made subservient to any end, no matter how subversive or schismatic. This clearly represents a departure from earlier, less sophisticated forms of conservative argument, which had opposed 'visionary' schemes of 'universal' instruction simply by reference to the need to restrict learning *in toto*, so as not to spread disaffection with existing social and political conditions. Bowles's response to Whitbread's parochial schools bill thus looked forward, in its own way, to the kinds of issues that would become increasingly central to educational debate in the succeeding decades, including the distinction between secular and religious instruction, and

[52] John Bowles, *The Education of the Lower Orders* (1808), 32.
[53] Ibid. 53, 37–8.

the appropriate role of national education in furthering material well-being and popular morality.

Bowles's close acquaintance during the 1790s with leading counter-revolutionary propagandists such as John Gifford, the editor of the *Anti-Jacobin Review*, would probably have alienated such erstwhile butts of loyalist ridicule as Coleridge and Southey. Nevertheless, his interventions in the Whitbread debate provide an excellent example of the way in which the ecclesiastical politics of popular education were instrumental in shaping the kinds of conservative educational rhetoric that are now more readily associated with the Lake school. Bell went on to participate in the High Church Hackney Phalanx and the National Society for the Education of the Poor in the Principles of the Established Church.[54] But his reflections on the distinction between 'education' and 'instruction', while an innovative response to the Lancasterian challenge, were unsustained. High Anglican educational thought remained largely paralysed by counter-revolutionary anxieties, and mired in disputes with the more evangelical tendency represented by the British and Foreign Bible Society, an interdenominational alliance which had pledged itself to the distribution of the Bible without the Church of England prayer book.[55]

The Lake poets were increasingly unembarrassed by their links with 'red-hot' Anglicans such as Wordsworth's brother Christopher and convinced, on political and constitutional grounds, that popular education should remain under the control of the established church. But, unlike more mainstream High Churchmen, they also shared a much stronger attachment to the positive value of popular education, a disposition that can be traced back to their early commitment to political and religious radicalism, and what Coleridge had described in 1796 as 'the diffusion of that general knowledge which should be the basis or substratum of politics'.[56] This certainly explains Southey's willingness, in the early stages of the controversy, to defend Lancaster against the 'calumnious bigotry' of his Anglican opponents, and his subsequent attempts to excuse Bell's 'error' in succumbing to the reactionary argument against popular education. For Southey, there was no necessary contradiction between the 'general diffusion of

[54] Soloway, *Prelates and People*, 374.

[55] Hole, *Pulpits*, 187–95.

[56] Gill, *William Wordsworth*, 343; Samuel Taylor Coleridge, *The Watchman* (1796), ed. Lewis Patton (London and Princeton, 1970), 14.

knowledge' and his growing conviction that the 'constitution of church and state . . . is the pride and strength of England', for the simple reason that the only way to render that constitution 'perpetual' was 'by training up the children of the people from generation to generation in the way they should go'.[57]

Coleridge, likewise, consistently gave his support to the Anglican cause in the educational debates of this period, while showing himself uncommonly receptive to arguments for the rapid extension of popular instruction. Although in principle opposed to a national system of non-denominational education, he declared himself 'a sincere friend' to the interdenominational Bible Society, and carefully distinguished his distaste for Lancasterian educational doctrine from his support for the Society's declared objects. 'An earnest advocate for national education,' he wrote in 1814, 'I cannot but be friendly to the societies, who exert their attentive powers in dispersing the best of books, the comfort of the comfortless, and the poor man's infallible receipt to make poverty itself a mine of imperishable wealth'.[58] Coleridge's sentiments derived, in large part, from his belief that the further diffusion of learning was quite simply unstoppable. 'Reflection, and stirrings of Mind, with all their Restlessness and all their Imperfections and Errors, are come into the World', he noted in his ill-fated periodical *The Friend*, in 1809.

> The Powers that awaken and foster the Spirit of Curiosity and Investigation, are to be found in every Village; Books are in every Cottage. The Infant's cries are hushed with *picture-Books*; and the Child sheds his first bitter Tears over Pages which will render it impossible for him, when a Man, to be treated or governed as a Child. The Cause of our disquietude must be the means of our Tranquillity . . . In an Age in which artificial knowledge is received almost at the Birth, Intellect and Thought alone can be our Upholder and Judge.[59]

Such convictions, which Coleridge carried with him from the 1790s, clearly allowed him to respond to the challenges facing conservative educational thought in this period with much greater flexibility than a more orthodox Anglican inheritance would have allowed.

[57] [Robert Southey], 'Mr. Jos. Lancaster's Plan for Educating Poor Children', *Annual Review*, 5 (1807), 232; [id.], 'Bell and Lancaster's Systems of Education', *Quarterly Review*, 6 (Oct. 1811), 292, 304.

[58] Coleridge, *Essays on his Times*, ii. 397 (2 Nov. 1814).

[59] Samuel Taylor Coleridge, *The Friend* (1809–10, 1818), ed. Barbara E. Rooke, 2 vols. (London and Princeton, 1969), ii. 86.

As early as 1809, Coleridge had begun to formulate a response to the challenge of secular and non-denominational education which was, in certain respects, strikingly similar to that offered by Bowles the previous year. True 'education', he maintained in *The Friend*, 'consists in *educing*, or to adopt Dr. Bell's own expression, *eliciting* the faculties of the Human Mind, and at the same time subordinating them to Reason and Conscience; varying the means of this common end according to the sphere and particular mode, in which the Individual is likely to act and become useful'.[60] Like Bowles's *Education of the Lower Orders*, Coleridge thus attempted to redefine 'education' as a process of moral and spiritual cultivation adapted to a given individual's particular social and economic station. He went beyond Bowles, however, in grafting a Platonic conception of educational psychology onto a more traditional language of social order and moral discipline. The resultant definition of popular instruction, which was directly inspired by the Bell–Lancaster debate, became a recurrent theme of Coleridge's educational and social thought, up to and including *Church and State*. In *The Statesman's Manual* of 1816, for example, Coleridge restated his definition of education as a process of 'educing the faculties and forming the habits; the means varying according to the sphere in which the individuals to be educated are likely to act and become useful', and contrasted it with Lancasterian educational theory, which assumed merely that 'a national education will have been realized when the People at large have been taught to read and write'.[61]

By now, however, Coleridge had also discovered, in an abstruse fusion of Kant and German biblical criticism, a rather sophisticated means of reconciling the evangelical imperative of the Bible Society with the Anglican establishment's concern with hierarchy and social control. *The Statesman's Manual* reimagined the Bible as a kind of hermetic *Ur*-text, whose stratified yet interpenetrative symbolic meanings could integrate the extension of popular instruction into a sacralized, hierarchical sociology of knowledge. The semantic interpenetration of literal and metaphorical, particular and general, 'the translucence of the Eternal through and in the Temporal' that characterized the biblical text could thus be transposed onto the field of social differentiation, where they figured the manner in which the 'neighbourliness' and 'consanguinity' of parochial affections and circumscribed class identities were reconciled

[60] Ibid. ii. 288 n.

[61] Coleridge, *Lay Sermons*, 40. See also id., *Lectures 1808–1819*, i. 585.

by the pure reason, uniting the 'one life' of the nation, and ultimately mankind, through the claims of transcendent moral duty.[62]

The manifest eccentricities of this argument do not seem to have troubled their author, and Coleridge even presumed to send a copy of *The Statesman's Manual* to the Prime Minister, Lord Liverpool.[63] Indeed, Coleridge's educational prescriptions seemed to their author to be all the more relevant in a post-war period experiencing economic dislocation, social unrest, and the rapid growth of political and religious radicalism. He certainly must have been aware of contemporary fears of a return to the explosive political situation of the 1790s, as a literate but 'semi-educated' population became progressively alienated from the teachings of the established church. The secular educational initiatives of liberal Whigs and philosophic radicals seemed only to be exacerbating this situation, and by the time Coleridge came to write *Church and State*, in 1829, mechanics' institutes and the University of London had joined 'tract societies' and 'Lancasterian schools' as the pernicious educational institutions of 'Liberalists and Utilitarians'—the antitheses of that genuine education which could be provided only by a 'permanent, nationalized, learned order, a national clerisy or church'.[64]

Church and State clearly displays Coleridge's long-standing involvement with ecclesiastical educational politics, most obviously in the great importance he placed on theology and the national church, as the only legitimate sources of 'NATIONAL EDUCATION, the *nisus formativus* of the body politics, the shaping and informing spirit, which *educing*, *i.e.* eliciting, the latent *man* in all the natives of the soil, *trains them up* to citizens of the country, free subjects of the realm'. But as this quotation suggests, *Church and State* also registers Coleridge's increased willingness to elide the distinction, implicit in his earlier writings, between the universal necessity of moral and spiritual cultivation, and the contingent differences in educational practice appropriate to differing socioeconomic situations. The civic training of the population as 'free subjects of the realm' was thus absorbed into a universalized sphere previously identified exclusively with religion and morality. This change of emphasis was as much the result of Coleridge's growing disillusionment

[62] Id., *Lay Sermons*, 28–30, 63. Cf. Leask, *Politics of Imagination*, 165–73. On Coleridge and the higher criticism, see E. S. Shaffer, *'Kubla Khan' and the Fall of Jerusalem: The Mythological School in Biblical Criticism and Secular Literature 1770–1880* (Cambridge, 1975).

[63] Coleridge, *Letters*, iv. 757–63 (28 July 1817).

[64] Id., *Church and State*, 68–9.

with the intellectual condition of the country's traditional ruling class as it was of his long-standing concerns with popular education.[65] The important distinction was now that between 'cultivation' and 'civilization', the former drawing together Christian education and social discipline into a seamless unity and counterposing them to 'all the so called liberal arts and sciences, the possession and application of which constitute the civilization of a country'.[66]

That political economy should have fallen into this latter category seems clear enough. Coleridge's political writings after 1808 consistently identify economic science as the exemplary product of a reductive, materialistic empiricism—the 'mechanico-corpuscular' theory which he believed to have exerted a profound influence on the intellectual and political life of the eighteenth century, in both Britain and France. Political economy thus emerged as the most debased intellectual product of 'civilization', and the antithesis of that civic and spiritual 'cultivation' which should be supplied by the nation's clerisy. Yet, despite his profound hostility to economic discourse, Coleridge was always reluctant to offer a sustained critical engagement with the new science on its own terms. It is certainly hard to imagine the author of the *Lay Sermons* embarking on a transcendental critique of the labour theory of value, let alone finishing it. Yet neither does it seem sufficient in this case to invoke the familiar, question-begging identification of English conservative ideology with an anti-rationalist sensibility operating primarily at the level of feeling rather than argument.

Coleridge certainly recognized the strong affiliations between political economy and secular or nonconformist educational argument, and this must have played an important part in conditioning his growing distaste for both Malthus and Smith. According to our report of his 1808 lectures, Coleridge's discussion of the education of the poor incorporated an intemperate attack upon Malthus, as well as Lancaster.[67] It is certainly significant that his first public criticism of the author of the *Essay on Population* should have occurred in the course of a diatribe on popular education. The association of the *Essay* with nonconformist educational schemes was also encouraged by the *Edinburgh Review*, which

[65] John Morrow, 'Coleridge and the National Church', in Gordon J. Schochet (ed.), *Empire and Revolutions* (Washington, 1993), 344–5.

[66] Coleridge, *Church and State*, 46–8. For some interesting reflections on the implications of this change of emphasis, see Lloyd and Thomas, *Culture and the State*, 67–70.

[67] Coleridge, *Lectures 1808–1819*, i. 108.

repeatedly championed the cause of non-denominational, Lancasterian national schools while simultaneously popularizing the Malthusian argument that positive checks on population required 'intelligence and knowledge . . . pretty generally diffused' among the populace.[68] Moreover, both Malthus and Whitbread had recommended Adam Smith's arguments for popular parochial education in *The Wealth of Nations*, a work which also included an extended attack on church establishments and public endowments as inefficient and potentially corrupt means of supporting popular education. That Coleridge was deeply disturbed by the secularizing, anti-establishment tendency of such arguments is suggested by his Swiftian 'Modest Proposal for Abolishing the Church of England' (1812). Under a 'free trade and a free religion', he wrote, in a mockery of Lancasterian educational rhetoric, every 'sect will . . . have fair play, and things being suffered to find their level, every doctrine will fetch its just price and no more'.[69]

But the political dimension of Coleridge's hostility to economic discourse has deeper roots than this. It is no coincidence that his first aspersions on 'economists' (Malthus not yet having been honoured with this title) emerged in the course of his intricate, quasi-Kantian critique of French revolutionary ideology in *The Friend*. In common with many other counter-revolutionary writers, Coleridge seems to have assumed that prominent physiocrats such as Quesnay and Turgot must have played a leading role in the intellectual fomentation of the Revolution. Burke himself had implied as much, in his attacks on 'sophisters, oeconomists, and calculators' in the *Reflections*, while Paine's *Rights of Man* had identified the 'moral maxims and systems of œconomy' of the physiocrats, along with the writings of Montesquieu, Voltaire, Rousseau and Raynal, as catalysts of that 'spirit of political enquiry [which] began to diffuse itself through the nation' in late-eighteenth-century France.[70] An association of revolutionary ideology with the physiocratic doctrine of free trade was in fact a recurrent element of British political discourse in the years after 1789, and one that also had important

[68] [unidentified author, poss. Thomas Robert Malthus], 'Disquisitions on Population', *Edinburgh Review*, 16 (Aug. 1810), 471.

[69] Smith, *Wealth of Nations*, ii. 788–814; Coleridge, *Essays on his Times*, ii. 345–6 (1 Apr. 1812). See also ibid. ii. 394–5 (2 Nov. 1814).

[70] Burke, *Writings and Speeches*, viii. 127; Thomas Paine, *Rights of Man* (1791), 87; Salim Rashid, 'Economists and the Age of Chivalry: Notes on a Passage in Burke's *Reflections*', *Eighteenth-Century Studies*, 20 (1986), 56–61.

repercussions for the reputations of Scottish economists such as Stewart and Smith.[71] Coleridge was thus conforming to well-established precedent when he identified the French revolutionary 'system' with 'Rousseau's *Du Contrat Social*, and the Writings of the French Economists, or as they more appropriately entitled themselves, *Physiocratic* Philosophers'.[72]

The French revolutionary philosophy, according to *The Friend*, 'denies all rightful origin to Governments, except as far as they are derivable from Principles contained in the REASON of Man, and judges all the relations of men in Society by the Laws of moral necessity, according to IDEAS . . . co-essential with the Reason . . .'.[73] The damning flaw in this position was not the veneration of rational 'Ideas', of which *The Friend* wholeheartedly approved, but rather the proper limits of their application. Coleridge denied the capacity of universal ideas of reason to dictate the organizing principles of a given community, on the grounds that it was the particular historical circumstances of a people that determined the form of government best suited to it. 'Reason never acts by itself, but must cloath itself in the Substance of individual Understanding and specific Inclination, in order to become a Reality and an Object of Consciousness and Experience.'[74] Ignoring this maxim, Rousseau and the 'Economists' misguidedly attempted to transpose pure reason, the Kantian arbiter of private morality alone, into the contingent public realm of political organization and civic responsibility. Revolutionary France necessarily failed to witness the emergence of an enlightened *volonté générale*, since, once proclaimed as the constitutional basis of the state, the universal principles of reason rapidly degenerated into a purely abstract form of political discourse, unmodified by habitual personal attachments of kinship, community, or class. Such abstract speculations quickly found their way into 'public opinion', which was consequently transformed into a superficial, volatile, and dangerously contagious form of mass consciousness. Increasingly disjoined from its origins in high philosophical argument, such opinion was ever more prone to vacuous semantic distortion, since the 'more abstract the notions' of the radical ideologues were, 'with the closer affinity did they combine with the

[71] On Smith's reputation in the 1790s, see Rothschild, 'Adam Smith'.

[72] Coleridge, *Friend*, ii. 105.

[73] Ibid. ii. 105.

[74] Ibid. ii. 132. On Coleridge and Burke, see Dierdre Coleman, *Coleridge and* The Friend *(1809–1810)* (Oxford, 1988), ch. 6.

most fervent feelings and the immediate impulses to action' of the populace.[75]

Coleridge did not concern himself with the doctrine for which the physiocrats were best known—that land is the sole source of wealth. His attitude to the *économistes* was overwhelmingly conditioned by their presumed complicity in the intellectual inspiration of the Revolution. He was aware that 'several of the French Economists, although devotees of Rousseau . . . did yet declare them for a pure Monarchy'.[76] But even this muddled admission did not sway his argument, since the Rousseauvian veneration of the general will and the physiocratic attachment to absolute monarchy were both inspired by the same desire to elevate pure reason to the status of public law—and they were both, in this sense, potentially revolutionary systems of thought. Moreover, by severing the dictates of reason from their only legitimate ground in the self-determining freedom of the individual moral agent, the 'System of the Economists' overturned the 'sacred Principle' that 'a Person can never become a Thing, nor be treated as such without wrong'.[77] This insight was of lasting and fundamental importance to Coleridge's understanding of both the physiocratic contribution to revolutionary thought, and the intellectual defects of political economy more generally. To treat society as a 'self-regulating Machine', he argued in the midst of the post-war depression in 1817, was to forget that 'Persons are not *Things* . . . Man does not find his level'.[78]

It was on these grounds that Coleridge came to regard political economy as a dangerously radical intellectual system, which wilfully confused the spheres of abstract reason and the contingent art of government: private 'freedom' and public 'liberty'. There was no difference in this respect between the revolutionary legislator and the opponent of factory regulation—both displayed a '*Physiocratic* . . . contempt for all that distinguishes or rather that forms the chasm . . . between man & beast'.[79] His criticisms of political economy, which have often been regarded as an influential response to the excesses of early nineteenth-century capitalism, were primarily inspired by Coleridge's analysis of French revolutionary ideology, and only

75 Coleridge, *Friend*, ii. 107.

76 Ibid. ii. 129.

77 Ibid. ii. 124–5.

78 Coleridge, *Lay Sermons*, 205. See also ibid. 76.

79 Id., *Letters*, iv. 856 (May 1818); cf. Rothschild, 'Adam Smith', 82–3.

latterly—and selectively—applied to the laissez-faire spirit supposedly at large in post-war Britain. But the counter-revolutionary origins of Coleridge's antipathy to political economy also suggest that his attempts to reach some kind of ideological compromise with the 'spirit of commerce' were more sustained, and significant, than might otherwise be expected.

FROM THE NATIONAL DEBT TO THE NATIONAL CHURCH

By 1809, when Coleridge undertook his critique of French revolutionary ideology in *The Friend*, the revival of popular radicalism in England seemed to imply that the same analysis could, *mutatis mutandis*, also be applied rather closer to home. Having exposed 'the theory of Rousseau and the French Economists', Coleridge went on to argue that the same misguided 'System' was at work in the political writings of Major John Cartwright.[80] In yoking together such dissimilar figures as Rousseau and Cartwright, Coleridge was clearly working both at a high degree of abstraction, and at an equally elevated level of polemic. His discussion of Cartwright's principles was, however, tempered by a certain respect for this venerable figurehead of the English reform movement. Coleridge's real anxiety—and the likely grounds of his parallel between English radicalism and Rousseauvian political philosophy—was that Cartwright's misguided but largely benign political arguments might be subject to the same kinds of demagogic manipulation that had proved so explosive in revolutionary France.

Coleridge seems to have been particularly concerned in this respect by the growing influence of William Cobbett's *Weekly Political Register*, and what he clearly regarded as its editor's refractory, intemperate, and inflammatory appeals to the plebeian reading public. The *Political Register* certainly provided an important foil for Coleridge's somewhat loftier conception of political journalism. He declared to correspondents that *The Friend* was 'the very same sort of publication, as Cobbett's Political Journal', but with the crucial difference that, whereas Cobbett concerned himself with 'Passions' and 'personality . . . the Events and political Topics of the Day', *The Friend* was to be grounded on 'true PRINCIPLES . . . in Criticism, Legislation, Philosophy, Morals, and

[80] Coleridge, *Friend*, ii. 123–49.

International Law'.[81] In contrast to the passional appeal of Cobbett's *Register*, *The Friend*'s professed aim, of referring his readers' 'opinions' to 'absolute Principles', was to be accomplished by means of its abstruse and highly intellectualized content, which, its author hoped, would exclude from his audience most of the 'ordinary readers of periodical publications' and attract instead those 'scattered and solitary minds . . . always labouring somewhere in the service of truth and virtue'. *The Friend*'s ambitions of influencing the moral and intellectual character of the country at large were not diminished by this strategy, however, since 'by the sleep of the multitude, the energy of the multitude may be prepared', a sentiment suggestive of the textual hermeticism that Coleridge was developing through his acquaintance with German biblical criticism.[82]

In marked contrast to the esoteric political conservatism of *The Friend*, Cartwright's reformist political agenda might easily 'be *made* tempting to the Vulgar', a goal that seemed most likely to be attained by radical representations of plebeian suffering, 'fitted to excite the *fury* of the Multitude', combined with reckless 'promises of turning the current of the public Revenue into the channels of individual Distress and Poverty, so as to bribe the Populace by selfish hopes'. Cartwright's sense of patriotism and honour would not permit him to sanction such rabble-rousing, since he was 'incapable of aiding his arguments by the poignant condiment of personal slander, incapable of appealing to the envy of the Multitude by bitter declamation against the follies and oppressions of the Higher Classes!'[83] On the contrary, these incendiary representations of the 'public Revenue' were the preserve of demagogic politicians and radical journalists such as Cobbett and Paine; and, in the twelfth number of *The Friend*, Coleridge set about demonstrating that his own views on the wartime economy and public finance were, like his politics, soundly bottomed on 'principle'.

Coleridge's essay on taxation appeared in *The Friend* in November 1809, and was thereafter quickly reprinted in the *Courier* newspaper. It marked a dramatic reorientation of his attitudes to commerce and the government revenue, which had previously reflected a quite consistent Country hostility to the 'monied interest', as a corrupter of morals and

[81] Coleridge, *Letters*, iii. 197 (18 Apr. 1809); ibid. iii. 143 (14 Dec. 1808); Coleman, *Coleridge and* The Friend, 40–3.

[82] Coleridge, *Friend*, ii. 276, 273, 260.

[83] Ibid. ii. 134, 137.

a threat to constitutional stability.[84] Coleridge never entirely escaped the legacy of his early agrarianism, and his subsequent defence of the national debt, commerce, and taxation was usually qualified by a stress on the countervailing constitutional importance of the landed interest. Nevertheless, *The Friend* marked a permanent and important departure in Coleridge's political and economic thought, and one that cannot properly be appreciated in isolation from certain broader changes in the nature of British political discourse, precipitated by the nation's ongoing struggle against Napoleonic France.

In the six years between 1803 and 1809, Britain's annual war expenditure more than doubled to £44 million, an alarming rise in spending that necessitated a commensurate increase in revenue from taxation and borrowing.[85] Yet by 1808 Napoleon's 'Continental System' of economic blockade had halved the value of Britain's trade with mainland Europe, causing serious disruption to the country's commerce and manufactures, and further radicalizing the provincial manufacturing population. The growing demands on the public finances, combined with the economic and social impact of the Continental System and the retaliatory Orders in Council, provoked a great deal of anxious reflection on the origins of the nation's resources, and the continued strength of the British 'fiscal–military state'.[86] The country's military and economic predicament certainly helps to explain what Henry Brougham described as the 'sensation' excited by the publication of William Spence's *Britain Independent of Commerce* in 1807. Because Spence's tract argued that the nation's wealth flowed principally from agriculture, he could also confidently assert that 'her riches, her prosperity, and her power are intrinsic, derived from her own resources, independent of commerce'—and thus also, by implication, independent of Napoleon's continental blockade.[87]

This qualified revival of the principles of physiocracy seemed calculated to reawaken a patriotic faith in the nation's economic self-

[84] See e.g. Coleridge, *Essays on his Times*, iii. 143–4. Morrow, *Coleridge's Political Thought*, 93–6.

[85] Norman J. Silverberg, 'Financial and Monetary Policy of Great Britain during the Napoleonic Wars', *Quarterly Journal of Economics*, 38 (1924), 215–17.

[86] On the 'fiscal–military state', see John Brewer, *The Sinews of Power: War, Money and the English State, 1688–1783* (1989).

[87] [Henry Brougham], 'Spence on Commerce', *Edinburgh Review*, 11 (Jan. 1808), 429; William Spence, *Britain Independent of Commerce* (1807), 35; Bernard Semmel, *The Rise of Free Trade Imperialism: Classical Political Economy and the Empire of Free Trade Imperialism 1750–1850* (Cambridge, 1970), 56–60, 79–80.

sufficiency. *Britain Independent of Commerce* quickly went through four editions, and attracted numerous replies from across the political spectrum. Opponents of the war were particularly anxious to refute an argument which threatened to undermine the causal connection between peace, commercial renewal, and national prosperity. James Mill's *Commerce Defended* (1808), for example, combined a vigorous defence of commerce and manufactures as important sources of national wealth with an attack upon the 'lamentable continuance of wars, almost always nourished by puerile prejudices and blind passions'. Rejecting Spence's position as that of a doctrinaire physiocrat, Mill argued that by diverting the country's resources into the maintenance of the armed forces—a species of unproductive consumption supported by extensive taxation—the war prevented the accumulation of reproductive capital in manufactures, as well as agriculture, and therefore robbed the country of the riches it could expect to acquire in peacetime.[88]

The politics of the Spence–Mill controversy were, however, rather more complicated than this; for while it was clear to many observers that the war effort could not be sustained without the system of taxation and long-term public credit which had been put in place by Pitt, this was precisely the 'system' that popular radicals such as Cobbett condemned as a vehicle of political corruption and economic privation, while simultaneously arguing (against liberals such as Mill) for the continuation of the war. Cobbett's radical patriotism endorsed both the vigorous prosecution of the struggle against Napoleon, and the extirpation of the commercial, or 'monied' interest, whose self-interested machinations lay behind the growth of stock-jobbing, public debt, and taxation. Spence's *Britain Independent of Commerce* certainly provided the justification for a broadly anti-commercial stance, despite its author's qualified support for manufacturing industry, and this explains the alacrity with which Cobbett reprinted lengthy extracts from Spence's pamphlet, along with commentary, in a controversial series of articles entitled 'Perish Commerce!' Spence was clearly rather bemused to find himself described as 'a Jacobin and a Leveller', who had lifted his economic theories from the pages of the *Political Register*. Nevertheless, Cobbett was adamant that Spence's 'politico-economical principles' revealed him as an unwitting ally of the radical campaign against the 'commercial system', the tendency of which was

[88] James Mill, *Commerce Defended*, 74. See also William Roscoe, *Considerations on the Causes, Objects and Consequences of the Present War* (1808), 111–13 n.; Cookson, *Friends of Peace*, 63–5.

to draw the real wealth of the whole country towards the metropolis, there, upon the labour of the working classes, to maintain, in idleness and luxury, innumerable swarms of place-men, pensioners, tax-gatherers, jews, jobbers, singers, parasites, and buffoons, while, at the same time, its financial operations render nine men out of ten either directly or indirectly dependant [*sic*] upon the minister of the day . . .[89]

Spence would never have endorsed such claims, although he wisely chose to avoid provoking Cobbett's enmity by a direct attack on the *Register*'s political principles.[90] The differences between the two writers did, however, emerge very clearly on the contentious issue of taxation and the national debt. Arguing from under-consumptionist principles, Spence maintained that the national debt 'has been of the greatest service to our wealth and prosperity', by converting 'superfluous capital into consumable revenue' and disseminating economic benefits 'amongst every branch of society'. Spence used a similar physiocratic logic to defend the benefits of extensive taxation, which he claimed diverted the wealth of the landed classes away from the indulgence of luxuries and into government expenditure, which was in turn quickly expended on 'food and manufactures, and is thus returned to the society which has advanced it'.[91] Cobbett, however, found nothing of value in such arguments. Spence, he remarked incredulously, 'no where throws out even a hint, that the taxes are too heavy'. An extensive public revenue could not even be justified as a way of subsidizing the employment of a displaced manufacturing population in public works, since this would only perpetuate the discredited commercial system and the government's deep-seated prejudice against the interests of the agricultural population. According to Cobbett, the current system of taxation should be viewed primarily as an instrument of corruption and exploitation—an uncompromising stance that was to exert a pervasive influence on radical and Whig representations of the Pittite legacy in the years to come.[92]

89 *Cobbett's Weekly Political Register*, 12 (7 Nov. 1807), 713–14 (hereafter *Political Register*).

90 Spence, *Britain Independent of Commerce*, 4th edn. (1808), 70 n.

91 Ibid. 1st edn., 70–4 n. See also Thomas Chalmers, *An Enquiry into the Extent and Stability of the National Resources* (Edinburgh, 1808), 227–53; Ronald L. Meek, *The Economics of Physiocracy: Essays and Translations* (1962), 313–44.

92 *Political Register*, 12 (7 Nov. 1807), 706; ibid. 12 (22 Nov. 1807), 836–43; Philip Harling, *The Waning of 'Old Corruption': The Politics of Economical Reform in Britain, 1779–1846* (Oxford, 1996), 94–5.

Coleridge's own contribution to the debate, in the *Friend* essay 'On the Vulgar Errors Respecting Taxes and Taxation', constituted a vigorous defence of the 'commercial system' in defiance of Cobbett's radical critique. Coleridge would probably have been aware of Spence's debt to the French physiocrats, if only through Brougham's review in the *Edinburgh*.[93] He may also have seen the letter to the *Political Register* in which Spence acknowledged his debts to 'the French Economists', and implied that Cobbett was vulgarizing physiocratic ideas to suit a virulently anti-commercial position—an assertion that would have suggested a worrying parallel with the demagogic popularization of revolutionary philosophy in France.[94] However, at no point in his essay on taxation did Coleridge explicitly connect physiocratic agrarianism with radical politics, a point that further suggests the extent to which his critique of 'Physiocrats' and 'Economists' in *The Friend* was essentially counter-revolutionary in origin, and had relatively little to do with the agrarian doctrine of Quesnay and Turgot.

Coleridge's essay followed a broadly Spencean line in discerning, in the contingent circumstances of the wartime economy, a beneficent tendency towards the circulative redistribution of wealth, together with a heightened awareness of national solidarity and self-sufficiency. But, in marked contrast to *Britain Independent of Commerce*, Coleridge chose to celebrate these developments as functions of the economy's commercial, rather than agrarian, dynamism. Hence *The Friend* treated taxation as itself 'a part of Commerce', with the result that 'the Government may be fairly considered as a great manufacturing House', engaged in the stimulative 'dispersion of . . . capital through the whole Population'. The essay describes how, by stifling trade, 'a principal source of Civilization, the origin of a *middle Class*', Napoleon fostered the growth of the national debt and taxation and thus, in effect, turned the commercial energy of the nation back upon itself.[95] The growth of public credit had, in turn, intensified national solidarity by attaching a sense of 'immediate Self-interest' to public duty, generating 'Patriotism and national Fervour' and a recognition of the financial and moral interdependence of all ranks in society. The national debt 'has wedded in indissoluble union all the interests of the State, the landed with the

[93] [Brougham], 'Spence on Commerce', *Edinburgh Review*, 11 (Jan. 1808), 429–31.

[94] *Political Register*, 12 (12 Dec. 1807), 922.

[95] Coleridge, *Friend*, ii. 160–1; cf. id., *Essays on his Time*, ii. 76 (21 Dec. 1809).

commercial, and the man of independent fortune with the stirring Tradesman and reposing Annuitant'.[96]

This fortuitous redoubling of the country's economic energies was also intimately connected with the development of Britain's expanding communications networks. The national debt had formed the country's roads, rivers, and canals into 'the veins, arteries, and nerves, of the State', channelling the 'commercial Current' such that 'every pulse in the Metropolis produces a correspondent pulsation in the remotest Village'.[97] But the ubiquitous and interconnective power of public credit is matched in *The Friend* by the rapid expansion of printed communications, which seemed to operate in tandem with the national debt to bind together the nation's commercial and epistemic energies:

> Newspapers, their Advertisements, Speeches in Parliament, Law-courts, and Public Meetings, Reviews, Magazines, Obituaries, and (as affording occasional commentaries on all these) that diffusion of uniform opinions, of Behaviour and Appearance, of Fashions in things external and internal, have combined to diminish, and often to render evanescent, the distinctions between the enlightened Inhabitants of the great city, and the scattered Hamlet.[98]

The intellectual origins of Coleridge's changed attitudes to public debt can be traced to a variety of eighteenth-century texts, including James Steuart's *Inquiry into the Principles of Political Economy* and Burke's *Letters on a Regicide Peace*.[99] A more immediate inspiration, however, was provided by certain important developments within contemporary political argument. The celebration of the nation's commercial wealth was by no means restricted to the friends of peace at this time, but was also frequently employed in defence of the government's prosecution of the war. Ministerial writers found it easy to reply to 'those who now raise a clamour about the galling load of our taxation' by pointing to the country's 'commercial greatness', 'flourishing cities', and abundance of 'productive capital', all of which could be invoked to demonstrate the strength of the 'national spirit'.[100] Even Coleridge's old friend Gould Francis Leckie, whose political temperament veered, in certain respects,

[96] Coleridge, *Friend*, ii. 162–3.

[97] Ibid.

[98] Ibid. ii. 28.

[99] William F. Kennedy, *Humanist versus Economist: The Economic Thought of Samuel Taylor Coleridge* (1958), new edn. (Westport, Conn., 1978), 26–8; Winch, *Riches and Poverty*, 327–9.

[100] John Pern Tinney, *Reflections on Some Questions Relative to the Present State of the Nation* (Salisbury, n.d. [1808]), 81, 45–7.

towards an unreconstructed form of high Toryism, was prepared to locate the combative vigour of the nation with the commercial, rather than the landed interest:

> The nature of the government, by the support it gives to good faith in all transactions, has afforded to the freedom of commerce, the valuable aid of public credit. In this empire every thing is activity and enterprise, and the moral sentiments of the people give it a splendid superiority over the profligate nations of the continent. These are, probably, the intellectual springs from which the British energy originates . . .[101]

Leckie's rhetoric suggests a certain modulation in the language of patriotism, whereby an older set of collective martial virtues such as 'independence' and 'liberty' were progressively supplemented by references to the 'energy', 'activity', and 'interdependence' of the people; terms that had fewer associations with Country ideology, and were more easily accommodated to a new recognition of the role played by the commercial and manufacturing classes in sustaining the war effort.

Such developments were part of a broader reorientation of political discourse which, as J. E. Cookson has argued, prefigured the emergence of 'liberal Toryism' in the years after Waterloo.[102] A number of statistical surveys made at the turn of the century had already done much to diffuse an awareness of the economic importance of manufacturing and agriculture relative to overseas trade, bolstering confidence in the possibility of economic autarchy based on the nation's 'internal resources', and helping to 'allay anxiety about the country's economic capacity to continue fighting a war of unprecedented magnitude'.[103] In circumstances such as these, it became increasingly easy to ridicule the doom-laden strictures of recalcitrant peacemongers such as Anna Barbauld, whose poem *Eighteen Hundred and Eleven* foresaw Britain's impending downfall in the banking and business failures of 1810–11, an economic crisis that could be traced directly to the fragility of Britain's overseas markets:

[101] Gould Francis Leckie, *An Historical Survey of the Foreign Affairs of Great Britain*, 2 pts. (1808), i. 10.

[102] J. E. Cookson, 'British Society and the French Wars, 1793–1815', *Australian Journal of Politics and History*, 31 (1985), 192–203. See also Frank Gorman, 'Pitt and the "Tory" Reaction to the French Revolution 1789–1815', in H. T. Dickinson (ed.), *Britain and the French Revolution 1789–1815* (Basingstoke, 1989), 28.

[103] J. E. Cookson, 'Political Arithmetic and War in Britain, 1793–1815', *War and Society*, 1 (1983), 42.

The golden tide of Commerce leaves thy shore,
Leaves thee to prove the alternate ills that haunt
Enfeebling Luxury and ghastly Want . . .[104]

Barbauld's poem was universally condemned as imprudent and unpatriotic, and it is perhaps a measure of the growing redundancy of such pacific economic pessimism that even the more liberal sections of the 'respectable' press proved reluctant to endorse her gloomy vision of 'London's faded glories', even during a period of widespread economic hardship and social unrest.[105] An altogether more acceptable attitude to the nation's economic dynamism informed the well-known peroration on commerce at the conclusion of William Huskisson's *Question Concerning Depreciation*, which located the country's resources in 'the immense and increasing produce of its territory:—in the unwearied extension of its manufacturing industry:—in the elastick and expansive force of its legitimate commerce: —all mutually aiding and fostering each other:—all fed and put in motion by capital, the genuine growth of progressive accumulation . . . .'[106] Huskisson's emphasis upon the dynamic, 'mutually aiding' resources of agriculture, manufacturing, and 'legitimate' commerce formed an increasingly influential element of political and economic discourse at this time, and is strongly suggestive of a convergence between the language of patriotism and the ideological origins of liberal Toryism.

Such sentiments were certainly a recurrent theme of Coleridge's writings during the remainder of the war. A 'true patriot', he maintained in *The Friend*, should seek the happiness of the individual members of the community, but should also promote

whatever tends to bind them more closely together, as a People; that as a multitude of parts and functions make up one human body, so the whole multitude of his Countrymen may, by the visible and invisible influences of religion, language, laws, customs, and the reciprocal dependence and re-action of trade and agriculture, be organized into one body politic.[107]

[104] Anna Lætitia Barbauld, *Eighteen Hundred and Eleven, a Poem* (1812), 5–6.

[105] Ibid. 12; *Monthly Review*, 67 (Apr. 1812), 428–32.

[106] William Huskisson, *The Question Concerning the Depreciation of our Currency* (1810), 153.

[107] Coleridge, *Friend*, ii. 326; see also id., *Essays on his Times*, ii. 236 (29 July 1811), ii. 304 (19 Sept. 1811), ii. 383 (29 Sept. 1814); id., *Biographia Literaria* (1817), ed. James Engell and W. Jackson Bate, 2 vols. (London and Princeton, 1983), i. 213.

The twin imperatives of solidarity and interdependence are reflected in the predominance of organic, physiological imagery in Coleridge's descriptions of the 'agricultural' and 'commercial' interests, 'as necessary to each other, as the veins to the blood, as closely intertwined as the nerves and muscles with the flesh-fibres of the body'.[108]

Of course, what might cautiously be described as the 'liberalization' of Coleridge's political opinions was far from being either complete or straightforward. For one thing, he continued to maintain his youthful hostility to manufactures as a source of moral turpitude, disease, poverty, and irreligion—even if the 'moral and physical evils of manufactories' were now carefully distinguished from the civilizing tendencies of 'commerce'.[109] A nagging ambivalence about the wider implications of public credit was also a feature of the 1809 *Friend*, in which Coleridge warned that the funding system had 'greatly modified' the Constitution, and assured his readers that he would elaborate further upon the 'injurious effects' of the national debt 'on the Literature, the Morals, and religious Principles' of the country.[110] Coleridge made good on this promise eight years later in the *Lay Sermon* of 1817, in which he responded to post-war depression and government retrenchment with a damning critique of the 'overbalance of the commercial spirit'. This, he maintained, had come about through the absence or insufficiency of the 'counterweights' provided by 'Religion', 'the ancient feeling of rank and ancestry', and 'a learned and philosophic Public'.[111] Coleridge was adamant that nothing in the *Lay Sermon* was 'incompatible' with his earlier defence of taxation, and he continued to extol the 'subliming and expanding warmth of public credit'. But he was also prepared, somewhat self-contradictorily, to date the overbalance of the commercial spirit from the institution of paper money and the national debt in the early eighteenth century.[112]

Coleridge's inconsistency on such issues reflects a more general difficulty facing conservative moralists and social critics during this period, deriving from the need to reconcile an older, eighteenth-century association of mobile wealth, luxury and corruption with an increasingly popular identification between patriotic virtue, national solidarity, and

[108] Coleridge, *Essays on his Times*, ii. 128 (7 May 1811).
[109] Ibid. ii. 304 (19 Sept. 1811); cf. id., *Lectures 1795*, 223–5.
[110] Coleridge, *Friend*, ii. 167, 162.
[111] Coleridge, *Lay Sermons*, 202–3, 169–89.
[112] Ibid. 214, 168.

commercial prosperity; a dilemma that, particularly within evangelical discourse, often involved recourse to 'religious' or 'moral' checks on the less wholesome tendencies of commercial society.[113] In Coleridge's case, such reservations found uncommonly intellectualized expression in the identification of 'commerce' with 'the outward world' of sensation and appearance, as opposed to a more fundamental stress upon the 'nurture and evolution of humanity'—an insight that directly informs the distinction between 'civilization' and 'cultivation' in *Church and State*.[114] However, Coleridge's hesitations concerning the benefits of commercial society also reflected a fear that the patriotic 'energy' coursing through the arteries of the nation might be prone to the same kinds of intellectual and moral derangement that had destroyed the French *ancien régime*. He continued to associate wartime taxation with a range of broader social changes which 'have made us a World of Readers', including urbanization, the growth of the periodical press, and the rise of the novel.[115] But Coleridge also retained serious doubts about the intellectual rigour of the reading public thus unleashed. The institution of the Whig commercial order after the Glorious Revolution, he suggested in *The Friend*, had led to the widespread diffusion of 'literary' rather than rigorously principled 'intellectual' power. Coleridge's brave new 'World of Readers', united into a single body politic by the pulsations of commercial intercourse, could at times seem perilously similar to the overwrought public mind of revolutionary France, in which, 'in the remotest Villages, every tongue was employed in echoing and enforcing the Doctrines of the Parisian Journalists'.[116]

Nevertheless, Coleridge's economic analysis of the nation's wartime resources had an important positive influence upon the subsequent development of his political and social thought. He remained consistent in looking back on the war—and more specifically on the peninsular campaign—as having brought about a 'national unanimity unexampled in our history since the reign of Elizabeth', a historical analogy that strongly suggests the extent to which his faith in an organic national community was inspired by the ideological milieu of the Napoleonic Wars.[117] Coleridge also remained in awe of the increasing

[113] See e.g. Patrick Colquhoun, *A Treatise on Indigence* (1806), 34–5, 146–8; Richard Raikes, *Considerations on the Alliance between Christianity and Commerce* (1806).

[114] Coleridge, *Friend*, i. 508.

[115] Id., *Lectures 1808–1819*, i. 186.

[116] Id., *Friend*, ii. 58, 107.

[117] Id., *Biographia*, i. 189.

complexity and interdependence of commercial society that had been stimulated by the national debt; its capacity to bind the nation together through the ties of social propriety and intellectual interconnection. He went on in the *Lay Sermon* to praise 'the expansion and systematic movements of our trade; and the consequent inter-dependence, the arterial or nerve-like *net-work* of property, which make every deviation from outward integrity a calculable loss to the offending individual himself from its mere effects', while in the 1818 edition of *The Friend* he asserted that, 'without trade and literature, mutually commingled, there can be no nation'.[118]

Coleridge's fascinated exploration of the relationship between national solidarity, public credit, and economic interdependence played an important part in shaping his subsequent concern, in *Church and State*, with the constitutional necessity of a 'balance' between the forces of 'permanence' and 'progression', land and commerce. His ideological defence of the fiscal–military state was inspired by its apparent effectiveness in uniting the nation's disparate interests; but also by the autarchic economic energy created through taxation and the 'productive circulation' of wealth, a process that mirrored the self-sustaining patriotic vigour of the beleaguered British people themselves.[119] It was these factors which, in Coleridge's opinion, helped to seal military victory. 'We conquered by compelling *reversionary* power into alliance with our existing and natural strength,' he wrote in the *Lay Sermon*.[120] However, Coleridge was also increasingly convinced that the spirit of commerce required the 'counterbalances' provided by religion, 'rank and ancestry', and a 'philosophic Public'. There was, as a result, a gradual transposition of Coleridge's rhetoric from an economic to a spiritual register: the church, rather than public credit, would henceforth regulate social order and foster learning, taking on in the process elements of an earlier, 'civic' defence of landed property. Already in 1817, under the influence of his developing ideas about the role of the church in maintaining social order, Coleridge was reimagining the 'reversionary', stimulative power of the wartime finances in spiritual terms, such that it now became the 'living principle of Christianity' that was characterized by the 'ampli-

[118] Id., *Lay Sermons*, 127; id., *Friend*, i. 507, quoted in Leask, *Politics of Imagination*, 215. See also Coleridge, *Essays on his Times*, ii. 430 (25 July 1816); ibid. ii. 487 (31 Mar. 1818).

[119] Id., *Lay Sermons*, 157.

[120] Ibid. 159; emphasis in original.

tude of its present, and the immensity of its reversionary, wealth'.[121] In both the *Biographia Literaria* and *Church and State*, Coleridge used the institution of the national church to reconcile the circulative and socially cohesive nature of the nation's wartime fiscal policy with the perceived necessity of bringing the influence of endowed, landed property to bear upon the excrescences of commercial society: 'the revenues of the church are in some sort the reversionary property of every family, that may have a member educated for the church, or a daughter that may marry a clergyman. Instead of being foreclosed and immovable, it is in fact the only species of landed property, that is essentially moving and circulative.'[122] The national debt was thus replaced by the 'nationalty', and the circulative, reversionary powers of the fiscal–military state displaced onto the national church, balancing the restless spirit of commerce with the 'permanency' of landed property and the moral authority of Christian 'cultivation'.

It is now clear that it was the unrelenting pressures of war which did most to consolidate and extend the British state in the long eighteenth century, while simultaneously redefining the experience and representation of national identity in some quite fundamental ways.[123] The Coleridgean ideal of 'cultivation', as an attempt to clarify the relationship between Christianity, nationhood, and the state, was inevitably shaped by the same forces, and reflected the same concern with the integration of the country's material and moral resources that had been given such urgency by the revolutionary conflict. Victory over France appeared to offer the prospect of European, and even global, military ascendancy. But it also seemed to Coleridge to have left a moral and political vacuum in the place of the militarized nation state, dangerously exacerbating the destabilizing effects of political radicalism, secularizing social reform and the 'commercial spirit'. Of course, the end of the struggle against France did not end Britain's military overseas commitments. The dramatic extension of the nation's global imperial power was already evident by the latter stages of the Napoleonic wars. But the broader issue of British imperial power was, except perhaps for the case of Ireland, tangential to Coleridge's more domestic concerns, in *Church and*

[121] Ibid. 179.

[122] Coleridge, *Biographia*, i. 227; id., *Church and State*, 76.

[123] See Brewer, *Sinews of Power*; Lawrence Stone (ed.), *An Imperial State at War: Britain from 1689 to 1815* (1994); Linda Colley, *Britons: Forging the Nation 1707–1837* (New Haven, 1992), ch. 7. J. E. Cookson makes some qualifying criticisms of Brewer and Colley in *The British Armed Nation 1793–1815* (Oxford, 1997), 3–11.

State, with constitutional and social 'balance'. The question of empire, and its relation to the nation's internal social order, did, however, play an important part in Wordsworth's ongoing attempts to produce an epic philosophical poem that would speak to the most urgent concerns of his own age, as well as the timeless judgement of posterity.

'THE MASTER IDOL OF THE REALM': THE POLITICAL ECONOMY OF WORDSWORTH'S *EXCURSION*

The creative momentum established by the completion of the 1805 *Prelude* carried Wordsworth forward to the 'chief object' of his literary ambitions, and the following summer, Dorothy reported excitedly that 'William goes on rapidly with the Recluse'.[124] But although she remained enthusiastic, her brother's progress soon slowed, as he ran up against a series of false starts and wrong turnings. *The Recluse* only gradually took shape over the next seven years, as Wordsworth extended the narrative of his 1798 poem, *The Ruined Cottage*, eventually introducing the character of the Solitary, a disillusioned misanthrope who fulfilled something of Coleridge's wish that the poem should include an address to those 'who, in consequence of the complete failure of the French Revolution, have thrown up all hopes of the amelioration of mankind'.[125] The textual evidence for the poem's compositional history is slight, but that which is available suggests that it was as late as January 1813 when Wordsworth embarked on the final, concentrated burst of composition and reorganization which produced *The Excursion*; the first 'portion' of *The Recluse* to be presented to the public, in August 1814, and the only one to be published in the poet's lifetime.[126] The story of *The Ruined Cottage* forms the centre of Book I of *The Excursion*; thereafter the 'Wanderer' (a character modelled on the visionary 'Pedlar' who recounts this initial tale) prevails upon his auditor, the poet-narrator, to travel with him to meet the Solitary. Together they attempt to win back this faithless sceptic to piety

[124] Wordsworth and Wordsworth, *Letters*, ii. 61 (23 July 1806).

[125] Coleridge, *Letters*, i. 527 (Sept. 1799).

[126] Wordsworth and Wordsworth, *Letters*, ii. 64 (5 Jan. 1813). The compositional history of *The Excursion* is even more tangled than that of *The Prelude*. The best available account is provided by Mark L. Reed in *Wordsworth: The Chronology of the Middle Years 1800–1815* (Cambridge, Mass., 1975), 656–86. Reed tentatively dates the greater part of Books VIII and IX to the period between January 1813 and May 1814—a conclusion that is supported by the internal evidence presented below, including Wordsworth's borrowings from Southey's December 1812 article on the poor laws.

and hope, eventually persuading him to return with them to meet the Pastor of a Lakeland church, in whose edifying company they spend several thousand lines of blank verse, before the poem finally ends on a note of irresolution with the Solitary bidding his companions farewell, his redemption apparently incomplete.

In the poem's preface, Wordsworth explained that he had chosen to publish *The Excursion* out of sequence, since, unlike the autobiographical 'preparatory' poem, *The Prelude*, 'the second division of the Work was designed to refer more to passing events, and to an existing state of things', with the result that 'more continuous exertion was naturally bestowed upon it, and greater progress made here than in the rest of the Poem'.[127] The intense period of composition that immediately preceded *The Excursion*'s publication undoubtedly gave Wordsworth the opportunity to incorporate a sufficient amount of polemical material into the concluding two books to justify their being regarded as his most sustained public statement of his political and social thought, albeit one that is somewhat complicated by its dramatic presentation within *The Excursion*'s poetic narrative.

Running through the Wanderer's speeches in Books VIII and IX of *The Excursion* is a restatement of the central themes of *The Prelude*, Book XII, which Wordsworth clearly continued to regard as fundamental to his 'philosophical Poem, containing views of Man, Nature, and Society'.[128] In the 1805 poem, Wordsworth had questioned the Malthusian 'bars . . . thrown / By nature' in the way of a fully realized human 'dignity'. In *The Excursion*, 'Economists' are once again associated with 'such Wisdom as condemns / A native Briton to . . . inward chains'.[129] *The Prelude*'s answer to Malthus had claimed that the 'bars' to human dignity and benevolence were derived not from the universal 'animal wants' of lust and hunger, but from the artificial conditions of 'cities, where the human heart is sick' and wherever 'labour in excess and poverty / . . . preoccupy the ground / Of the affections'.[130] Much the same assumptions underpin the Wanderer's association of child

[127] Wordsworth, *Excursion*, p. vii.

[128] Ibid. p. viii.

[129] Wordsworth, *Thirteen Book* Prelude, xii. 83–93; id., *Excursion*, 372. All quotations are taken from the 1814 edition of the poem, but further references will be given in the text using the corresponding book and line references (in this case viii. 283, 297–8) to the slightly revised 1850 edition, reproduced in vol. v of *Poetical Works*, ed. Selincourt and Darbishire.

[130] Wordsworth, *Thirteen Book* Prelude, xii. 94, 202, 197–9.

labourers' stultifying 'inward chains' with the brutalizing conditions of the country's cotton mills (viii. 283–98).

In a further parallel with the argument of *The Prelude*, Book XII, such considerations are bound up with a more profound reflection on the inequalities of the human condition. 'Alas! what differs more than man from man! / And whence that difference?', the Wanderer asks, in his final speech (ix. 206–7), restating Wordsworth's rhetorical question in Book XII of *The Prelude*: 'Why is this glorious Creature to be found / One only in ten thousand?' The poet of *The Prelude* claims only to have answered this question in the course of his youthful 'wanderings' on the 'lonely roads' and among 'the natural abodes of men'.[131] But the Wanderer, who seems blessed with greater experience and authority, is much more immediately forthcoming:

> whence that difference? whence but from himself?
> For see the universal Race endowed
> With the same upright form!—The sun is fixed,
> And the infinite magnificence of heaven,
> Within the reach of every human eye;
> The sleepless Ocean murmurs for all ears;
> The vernal field infuses fresh delight
> Into all hearts. Throughout the world of sense
> Even as an object is sublime or fair,
> That object is laid open to the view
> Without reserve or veil; and as a power
> Is salutary, or an influence sweet,
> Are each and all enabled to perceive
> That power, that influence, by impartial law.
> Gifts nobler are vouchsafed alike to all;
> Reason,—and, with that reason, smiles and tears;
> Imagination, freedom in the will,
> Conscience to guide and check; and death to be
> Foretasted, immortality presumed.
>
> (ix. 207–25)

The Wanderer's answer might seem supremely confident compared to that which emerges from Wordsworth's peripatetic plumbing of 'the depth of human souls' in Book XII of *The Prelude*.[132] Indeed, it is lines such as these that come closest to confirming Francis Jeffrey's descrip-

[131] Wordsworth, *Thirteen Book* Prelude, xii. 90–1, 205, 163, 107.
[132] Ibid. xii. 166.

tion of *The Excursion* as 'decidedly didactic . . . a series of long sermons or harangues' that reduce Wordsworth's blank verse to the condition of lifeless dogma. Nevertheless, the complacent self-assurance of the Wanderer's speech also belies a certain contradiction implicit in his defence of the salutary and universal power of 'nature'.[133]

At the beginning of Book IX the Wanderer extols the conclusion of human life—and by implication his own situation—as an 'eminence' from which we may hope to receive 'Fresh power to commune with the invisible world', and thus to discern the providential 'mighty stream of tendency'. But, he continues,

> Them only can such hope inspire whose minds
> Have not been starved by absolute neglect;
> Nor bodies crushed by unremitting toil;
> To whom kind Nature, therefore, may afford
> Proof of the sacred love she bears for all;
> Whose birth-right, Reason, therefore, may ensue.
>
> (ix. 81–101)

Nature remains, as it did in much of *The Prelude*, a maternal, nurturing presence, the ubiquitous medium of a universal and 'sacred love'. Yet the 'Reason' necessary for the realization of such pious hopes remains a 'birth-right' which is merely 'vouchsafed to all' (ix. 221). Wordsworth's repeated use of such contractual, quasi-legalistic language figures human 'Reason', and all that flows from it, as a right rather than an inalienable possession—as an entail rather than innate.[134] And in this case, responsibility for the nurture of the higher faculties amongst the lower classes shifts from 'nature' to more contingent, human institutions of education.

Hence, despite his praise for 'every genial Power of heaven and earth' which alternately brings 'enjoyment, knowledge, health, / Beauty, or strength' to the Parson's children, the Wanderer's final speech in *The Excursion* ends with an extended plea to 'British Lawgivers', for a programme of state-sponsored national education on the principles of the Madras school (ix. 265, 269–70, 399). Bell's system 'affords

[133] [Jeffrey], 'Wordsworth's Excursion', *Edinburgh Review*, 24 (Nov. 1814), 5. The question of the Wanderer's authority is discussed in Susan Wolfson, *The Questioning Presence: Wordsworth, Keats, and the Interrogative Method in Romantic Poetry* (Ithaca, NY, 1986), 93–125.

[134] Cf. Simpson, *Wordsworth's Historical Imagination*, 191–4; and see also the Pastor's remarks on the inadequacy of reason in v. 485–523.

marvellous facilities' for instituting such a plan, Wordsworth enthused in a note to this section of the poem, 'and it is impossible to overrate the benefit which might accrue to humanity from the universal application of this simple engine under an enlightened and conscientious government' (ix. 299 n.). But, although convinced that a national system of popular schooling was an urgent necessity, Wordsworth was also notoriously unwilling to forgo the educational adequacy of Nature's 'sacred love'.[135] This is perhaps most strongly suggested by his metaphorical conflation of national education with the 'filial bond' between mother and infant which had grounded his benevolist moral psychology in Book II of *The Prelude*.[136] The Wanderer thus announces his belief that, 'far as kindly Nature hath free scope / And reason's sway predominates, even so far, / Country, society, and time itself' participate in 'one maternal spirit, bringing forth / And cherishing with ever-constant love' (ix. 105–12). The right to education 'the lisping Babe proclaims / To be inherent in him', and the 'rude Boy . . . by process indirect / Declares his due'. This unconscious 'plea',

like a prayer
That from the humblest floor ascends to heaven,
It mounts, to reach the State's parental ear;
Who, if indeed she own a Mother's heart,
And be not most unfeelingly devoid
Of gratitude to Providence, will grant
The unquestionable good . . .

(ix. 311–31)

Yet, despite Wordsworth's repeated attempts to represent the state in these maternal, quasi-naturalized terms, the Wanderer's implicit contention that 'this Imperial Realm' has thus far failed in her parental duties continues to require the supervenient intendance of divine 'Providence'. It is indeed a measure of Wordsworth's uncertainty on this issue that, when the Wanderer breaks off, making way for the Pastor to deliver the poem's climactic final speech, his naturalized, nurturing representations of the state are displaced by the 'paternal splendors' of a sterner and more orthodox Christian vision (ix. 620).

[135] See Simpson, *Wordsworth's Historical Imagination*, 196–200; Foakes, '"Thriving Prisoners"', 202–4; Hickey, *Impure Conceits*, 105–30; Richardson, *Literature, Education, and Romanticism*, 106.

[136] Wordsworth, *Thirteen Book* Prelude, ii. 263.

Many of the shifts in emphasis between *The Prelude* and *The Excursion* on these issues can be traced to the influence of Southey's 1811–12 articles on education, population, and the poor in the *Quarterly Review* and, in particular, to his December 1812 review of Colquhoun's *Treatise on Indigence*. Much of this article comprised a restatement of the basic argument of Southey's 1804 review of the *Essay on Population*. By 1812, however, Southey was placing a new emphasis on emigration as a means of venting surplus population, and praising 'Dr. Bell's discovery' as a way of moralizing an increasingly faithless, dissolute, and radicalized labouring population. Wordsworth incorporated both these aspects of Southey's article into the final two books of *The Excursion*, in which the Wanderer argues that, by combining the 'discipline of virtue' with a vigorous emigration policy, the state might dispel 'the fear / Of numbers crowded on their native soil' (ix. 352–64). Just as he had used Southey's 1804 review of the *Essay on Population* to develop his own reply to Malthus in *The Prelude*, so Wordsworth turned once again to Southey's political journalism, in 1813, as he relocated the concerns of *The Prelude*'s Book XII to the Wanderer's speeches in the final books of *The Excursion*.[137]

Southey's renewed attack upon Malthusian social policy seems to have been triggered by the wave of Luddite machine-breaking and popular disaffection accompanying the economic crisis of the previous two years. Food rioting swept the country in the summer of 1812, and the Prime Minister's assassination was greeted with open celebration in many areas. 'Sheer insurrectionary fury', according to E. P. Thompson, 'has rarely been more widespread in English history'.[138] Southey's analysis of the situation in the *Quarterly* laid much of the blame for the volatile state of the country on the 'rapid increase of manufactures'. The evils of the 'manufacturing system' were manifold: it encouraged the growth of cities, destroyed 'local attachments', and undermined both the patriotism and the deference of the labouring population. But the growth of manufactures had also produced widespread physical and mental debility, and left large sections of the population without moral or religious education—an omission that

[137] [Robert Southey], 'Inquiry into the Poor Laws, &c.', *Quarterly Review*, 8 (Dec. 1812), 353. Wordsworth's borrowings from this article are noted by Richardson, *Literature, Education, and Romanticism*, 98; and Hickey, *Impure Conceits*, 15 and n. 48. On emigration policy and the Tory press, see Anna Gambles, *Protection and Politics: Conservative Economic Discourse, 1815–1852* (Woodbridge, 1999), 75.

[138] Thompson, *Making*, 570.

had been encouraged by Adam Smith's secular and materialistic view of 'man' as a 'manufacturing animal', a mere 'instrument' of gain without virtues, duties, or an immortal destiny. Yet the vitriolic urgency of Southey's article had rather less to do with humanitarian Christian compassion than with the imminent threat of insurrection. Even if an 'organized plan for effecting revolution in this country' was unlikely to exist, he warned, 'it by no means follows that the preparatory work of revolution is not going on', and the brutalized, itinerant, and amoral condition of the labouring population made such a threat all the more palpable.[139]

The final books of *The Excursion* are clearly indebted to Southey's critique of the manufacturing system, particularly in the Wanderer's descriptions of child labour and night-working.[140] But they also display a more pervasive nostalgia, shared with the poet-narrator, for the 'old domestic morals of the land' (viii. 236):

I have lived to mark
A new and unforeseen Creation rise
From out the labours of a peaceful Land,
Wielding her potent Enginery to frame
And to produce, with appetite as keen
As that of War, which rests not night or day,
Industrious to destroy!

(viii. 89–95)

The Wanderer's repeated warnings about the 'potent Enginery' of industrialization in Books VIII and IX may well reflect contemporary fears of insurrection and popular immorality. But they also indicate Wordsworth's enduring debt to the radical politics that had shaped his outlook in the 1790s—a connection most clearly suggested by the Wanderer's symbolic association of industrial work discipline with the Norman yoke (viii. 170–3).[141]

The fact that such attitudes suggest a degree of consistency, even integrity, in the Lake poets' social and political thought helps to explain the prominence commonly accorded to the Wanderer's admonitions on the exploitation of the manufacturing population. Wordsworth himself stressed the prescience of the Wanderer's 'apprehensions' in the Fenwick

[139] [Southey], 'Inquiry into the Poor Laws', *Quarterly Review*, 8 (Dec. 1812), 337–44.
[140] Cf. ibid. 338–9, and Wordsworth, *Excursion*, viii. 156–95, 285–96.
[141] Cf. Mark Schoenfield, *The Professional Wordsworth: Law, Labor and the Poet's Contract* (Athens, Ga., 1996), 220–1.

notes of 1843.[142] Yet, to a far greater degree than Southey's *Quarterly* journalism, the final books of *The Excursion* also mark a determined attempt to move beyond the radical agrarianism of Wordsworth's youth. This is signalled most dramatically by the Solitary's interjections, which repeatedly undercut the lapsarian narrative of pastoral independence and virtue to which both the Wanderer and poet-narrator show themselves susceptible. At the beginning of Book VIII, for example, the Solitary first compares the Wanderer's employment as a pedlar with that of a knight errant, before assimilating the Wanderer's occupation to a bathetic, but only semi-ironic, defence of commercial humanist values, in which itinerant pedlars figure as the agents of rural civilization, their 'moving magazines' softening 'blind prejudice; / Raising, through just gradation, savage life / To rustic, and the rustic to urbane' (viii. 69–71). This rather quaint example of progressive stadial historiography passes uncontested, yet the Wanderer goes on to mourn the fact that any 'romantic interest' in the pedlars' occupation has been extinguished by urbanization, industrialization, and the 'stately roads / Easy and bold, that penetrate the gloom / Of England's farthest Glens' (viii. 109–11). Undiscouraged, the Solitary continues to challenge the moral priority accorded by the Wanderer to rural life, culminating in the description of a brutish ploughboy whose intellectual condition poses just as great a threat to social order as that of the urban poor:

no Town
Nor crowded City may be taxed with aught
Of sottish vice or desperate breach of law,
To which in after years he may be rouzed.

(viii. 421–5)

His final challenge, 'pointedly addressed' to the Wanderer, 'what liberty of mind is here?', is conceded in the following book, in his interlocutor's admission that the 'ignorance' of the rural poor 'is not less / Nor less to be deplored' than that of the towns (viii. 433–6; ix. 176–7).

Even more telling, however, than the Solitary's sceptical subversion of a complacent pastoral nostalgia are the qualifications and ambivalences that repeatedly surface in the Wanderer's own speeches, which strongly suggest his willingness to embrace the new industrial order, provided it is guided by Christian moral values:

[142] Wordsworth, *Fenwick Notes*, 86–90.

I rejoice,
Measuring the force of those gigantic powers,
That, by the thinking Mind have been compelled
To serve the Will of feeble-bodied Man.
For with the sense of admiration blends
The animating hope that time may come
When, strengthened, yet not dazzled, by the might
Of this dominion over Nature gained,
Men of all lands shall exercise the same
In due proportion to their Country's need;
Learning, though late, that all true glory rests,
All praise, all safety, and all happiness,
Upon the Moral law.

(viii. 204–16)

The Wanderer's remarks on this point are usually either passed over or dismissed as a half-hearted endorsement that stands in an awkward, contradictory relation to his previous statements.[143] Such a reaction does not, however, seem to have been characteristic of the poem's first readers. Francis Jeffrey, for example, praised the 'picturesque' quality of Wordsworth's 'lively and impressive appeal on the injury done to the health, happiness, and morality of the lower orders, by the unceasing and premature labours of our crowded manufactories'; but Jeffrey did not perceive any contradiction between such representations and Wordsworth's apparent hope that 'the farther improvement and the universal diffusion of these arts may take away the temptation for us to embark so largely in their cultivation'.[144] The Wanderer's ambivalence seems to have been entirely understandable, even to the poem's harshest critics, at a time when the national economic benefits of the manufacturing system seemed increasingly compromised by the irreligion, moral dissolution, and political radicalism of the new industrial towns.

Wordsworth's attitudes might, then, appear to have most in common with those 'liberal Tories' who 'did not welcome the machine, but . . . did believe it was here to stay'.[145] The Wanderer's mixed feelings on this issue can certainly be viewed as a reflection of Wordsworth's ongoing attempts to reconcile his earlier agrarian inclinations with a commit-

143 Friedman, *Making of a Tory Humanist*, 225–7; Hickey, *Impure Conceits*, 100.

144 [Francis Jeffrey], 'Wordsworth's Excursion', *Edinburgh Review*, 24 (Nov. 1814), 25–6.

145 Berg, *Machinery Question*, 16.

ment to commerce and manufacturing as vital components of the country's wartime resources, in much the same manner as Coleridge's political writings after 1808. Such a tendency can be detected as early as 1809, in Wordsworth's lengthy pamphlet on the *Convention of Cintra.* Although the *Cintra* tract identified the 'Artisan and the Merchant' as 'men of classes perhaps least attached to their native soil', the commercial and manufacturing interests were readily subsumed in 'the solemn fraternity which a great nation composes', as Wordsworth's growing commitment to a rhetoric of patriotism and national solidarity impelled him to moderate the anti-commercial attitudes that continued to inform the language of radicals such as Cobbett. 'Mechanic Arts, Manufactures, Agriculture, [and] Commerce' were now united as 'those products of knowledge which are confined to gross—definite—and tangible objects . . .'. The 'outward', material benefits of all such 'arts' had, according to Wordsworth, to be supplemented by the deeper, imaginative resources supplied by 'the genial and vernal inmate of the breast', an infusion that was as vital to maintaining the martial energy and moral legitimacy of the British nation as it had been to the Iberian patriots.[146]

Much the same attitude is apparent in Wordsworth's first letter to Captain Charles William Pasley of 1811, in response to the latter's *Essay on the Military Policy and Institutions of the British Empire.* Pasley was a celebrated war hero, whom Coleridge had known in Malta, and whose *Essay* recommended a 'vigorous system' of imperial expansion and economic exploitation in response to Napoleon's economic blockade. 'The first soldier I ever sighed for,' admitted Jane Austen (somewhat archly), after reading the *Essay*, her feelings apparently having been aroused by the 'extraordinary force & spirit' of Pasley's book. Wordsworth was also rather smitten, and confessed himself not only 'much interested' but also 'in a high degree instructed' by the *Essay.*[147] However, Wordsworth's letter to Pasley was primarily intended to signal some of his objections to the book, and in particular his concern at the

[146] William Wordsworth, *Concerning the Relations of Great Britain, Spain, and Portugal . . . as Affected by the Convention of Cintra* (1809), in *Prose*, i. 305–26; Gordon Kent Thomas, *Wordsworth's Dirge and Promise: Napoleon, Wellington, and the Convention of Cintra* (Lincoln, Neb., 1971). On the vestigial radicalism informing Wordsworth's nationalistic rhetoric, see Dierdre Coleman, 'Re-Living Jacobinism: Wordsworth and the Convention of Cintra', *Yearbook of English Studies*, 19 (1989), 144–61.

[147] Charles William Pasley, *An Essay on the Military Policy and Institutions of the British Empire* (1810), 2nd edn. (1811), 111; Jane Austen, *Letters*, ed. Deirdre Le Faye, 3rd edn. (Oxford, 1995), 198. Wordsworth and Wordsworth, *Letters*, ii. 474 (28 Mar. 1811).

pessimistic tone in which the *Essay* represented the nation's economic wealth. Reviewing the debate initiated by Spence's *Britain Independent of Commerce*, Pasley had concluded that the comparative advantages enjoyed by Britain in commerce, manufactures, and public finances were destined to be eroded by the consolidation of the French economy and tax revenue, leaving a 'vigorous system of external war and even of conquest' the only means of achieving ultimate victory.[148] Wordsworth responded by pointing out that Pasley had overlooked the profound influence on national resources exerted by 'the characters of the two nations, and of the two Governments'. Unlike France, the British government provided a credible 'security for Capital . . . so that the mechanic arts and inventions may thereby be applied in such a manner as that an overplus may arise from the labour of the Country which shall find its way into the pocket of the State for the purpose of supporting its military and civil establishments'. The 'manufacturing capitalists' emerge from Wordsworth's letter as vital bulwarks of the struggle against Napoleon, and, on the eve of the Luddite disturbances, their activities seemed perfectly integrated with the 'laws, the regulations, the customs, the moral character, and the physical enginery of all sorts, through means, and by aid of which, labour is carried on in this happy Land . . .'.[149]

Although by 1813 Wordsworth was considerably less assured on this point, he retained a significant degree of faith in commerce and manufactures as a potential reserve of patriotic 'energy'. 'Our country has a mighty and daily-growing forest of this sort of wealth,' Wordsworth had written of industrial manufacturing in 1811, 'whereas, in France, the trees are not yet put in the ground'.[150] The same metaphor recurs, in a rather more extended form, in *The Excursion*, as the Wanderer marvels at the gathering pace of urbanization:

> Meanwhile, at social Industry's command,
> How quick, how vast an increase! From the germ
> Of some poor Hamlet, rapidly produced
> Here a huge Town, continuous and compact,
> Hiding the face of earth for leagues—and there,
> Where not a habitation stood before,
> The Abodes of men irregularly massed

148 Pasley, *Essay*, 18–51, 128.
149 Wordsworth and Wordsworth, *Letters*, ii. 475–6 (28 Mar. 1811).
150 Ibid. ii. 477.

Like trees in forests—spread through spacious tracts,
O'er which the smoke of unremitting fires
Hangs permanent, and plentiful as wreaths
Of vapour glittering in the morning sun.

(viii. 117–27)

The forces of urbanization are thus symbolically integrated with the rural environment, as the 'forests' of the new industrial towns emerge organically, from the 'germ / Of some poor Hamlet', obscuring a rural landscape that is now blankly denaturalized, a 'barren wilderness erased, / Or disappearing' (viii. 129–30). Despite his subsequent reflections on the 'darker side / Of this great change' (viii. 151–2), the Wanderer's views should be taken seriously, not least because of their apparent conformity with the poet's own attempts to reconcile his deep-seated agrarian sensibilities with the patriotic celebration of the nation's commercial power. Wordsworth's wartime rhetoric had proved increasingly amenable to the forces of commerce and manufacturing, in much the same way as the Wanderer's regret at the passing of an older, more 'romantic' world modulates into a panegyric on the symbiotic integration of the nation's economic resources. The organic, quasi-arboreal expansion of the industrial towns is thus hailed as a

triumph that proclaims
How much the mild Directress of the plough
Owes to alliance with these new-born Arts!
—Hence is the wide Sea peopled,—and the Shores
Of Britain are resorted to by Ships
Freighted from every climate of the world
With the world's choicest produce. Hence that sum
Of Keels that rest within her crowded ports,
Or ride at anchor in her sounds and bays;
That animating spectacle of Sails
Which through her inland regions, to and fro
Pass with the respirations of the tide,
Perpetual, multitudinous! Finally,
Hence a dread arm of floating Power, a voice
Of thunder, daunting those who would approach
With hostile purposes the blessed Isle,
Truth's consecrated residence, the seat
Impregnable, of Liberty and Peace.

(viii. 130–47)

However incompatible with the more traditional view of Wordsworth, as an unflinching defender of rural values, the Wanderer's speech remains a powerful vision of the nation's commercial and manufacturing wealth as the guarantor of Britain's imperial, maritime power in the post-Napoleonic era; albeit a power which also conferred the obligation to subject those baser, secularizing and materialistic tendencies of the manufacturing 'philosophy' to a higher, 'Moral law' (viii. 224–5).

The years immediately preceding the publication of *The Excursion* were marked by the new Liverpool administration's increasing receptivity to the case for trade liberalization. In 1812 the Orders in Council were revoked, following a concerted and vocal campaign by provincial merchants and manufacturers. Of more direct relevance to the politics of *The Excursion*, however, was the debate on the renewal of the East India Company's charter, which took place in the first half of 1813, and which resulted in the revocation of the Company's monopoly on Indian trade. While Britain's provincial mercantile and manufacturing interests hoped that this measure would enlarge their export markets, the government's qualified conversion to the cause of liberalization stemmed from its desire to encourage certain strategic imports from India, such as raw cotton and sugar, as a way of regulating prices and controlling inflation.[151] Such considerations certainly played a part in persuading the *Quarterly Review* to throw its weight behind the anti-monopolists, albeit in more measured tones than its rivals at the *Edinburgh*. But the *Quarterly* was also firmly persuaded of the moralizing effects of colonization and trade, declaring that it had always been 'the constant and invariable effect of commercial intercourse, for the more refined and civilized to enlighten and improve those who were less so'.[152]

The emergent political consensus on the merits of a less restrictive imperial trade was facilitated by the perceived self-interest of the Company and the London merchant community, combined with a growing willingness to acknowledge the economic contribution that provincial manufacturing and trade had made to the war effort, and a

[151] Anthony Webster, 'The Political Economy of Trade Liberalization: The East India Company Charter Act of 1813', *Economic History Review*, 2nd ser., 43 (1990), 404–19. Cf. Gambles, *Protection and Politics*, 158–65.

[152] [John Barrow], 'Papers Respecting the E. I. Company's Charter', *Quarterly Review*, 8 (Dec. 1812), 260–9; cf. [James Mill], 'East India Monopoly', *Edinburgh Review*, 20 (Nov. 1812), 471–93; [George Ellis], 'Macpherson's European Commerce with India', *Quarterly Review*, 15 (Sept. 1812), 114–44.

new conviction of the British Empire's broader civilizing mission. The 'improving' rhetoric with which the *Quarterly* promoted the case for colonization and freer trade is certainly echoed in *The Excursion*, as the Wanderer surveys 'the wide waters, open to the power, / The will, the instincts, the appointed needs / Of Britain', and anticipates the future importance of colonization in diffusing Christian civilization across the empire:

> Earth's universal Frame shall feel the effect
> Even 'till the smallest habitable Rock,
> Beaten by the lonely billows, hear the songs
> Of humanized society; and bloom
> With civil arts, and send their fragrance forth,
> A grateful tribute to all-ruling Heaven.
>
> (ix. 375–91)

The impending victory over Napoleon promised to consolidate not just Britain's military supremacy, 'a dread arm of floating Power', but also its moral responsibility to the post-war world sustained by the 'new-born arts' of economic modernity.

However, the final books of *The Excursion* also suggest Wordsworth's receptivity not just to a secular imperialist rhetoric of material 'civilization', but also to the related, '"providentialist" Christian evangelicalism' that was rapidly emerging as 'an important component of Britain's new imperialism'.[153] This is most clearly apparent in the Pastor's prayer to the 'universal God' with which the poem concludes:

> Spread the law,
> As it is written in thy holy book,
> Throughout all Lands; let every nation hear
> The high behest, and every heart obey . . .
>
> (ix. 639–42)

The Pastor's ardent plea, that 'thy Word prevail' throughout the globe, might seem like an uncontroversial expression of nineteenth-century imperialist ideology. Within their original context, however, his declarations implicated *The Excursion* in an impassioned controversy over the relationship between British imperialism and Christian missionary activity that came to a head in the charter debate of 1813. An

[153] C. A. Bayley, *Imperial Meridian: The British Empire and the World 1780–1830* (1989), 177; Jonathan Mendilow, *The Romantic Tradition in British Political Thought* (1986), 73–4.

evangelical campaign had been in progress since 1805 both to compel the East India Company to admit missionaries into the subcontinent, and to persuade the government to establish an Indian episcopacy. The debates on the renewal of the Company's charter intensified evangelical efforts, and prompted a flood of around 900 petitions on the issue from across the country, signed by 'near half a million of persons', while William Wilberforce pursued the objective within doors, in some of the most celebrated speeches of his parliamentary career.[154] The evangelical campaign has been called one of the 'greatest mobilizations of public opinion Britain had ever seen'.[155] It was also, at least on its own terms, a resounding success. The government's resolutions on the charter issue conceded 'that it is the duty of this country to promote the interest and happiness of the native inhabitants of the British dominions in India, and that such measures ought to be adopted, as may tend to the introduction among them of useful knowledge, and of religious and moral improvement'.[156] The Charter Act of 1813 established an Anglican bishopric at Calcutta, with Archdeacons in Calcutta, Madras, and Bombay; secured limited access for missionaries engaged in the diffusion of 'useful Knowledge' and 'religious and moral Improvement'; and required that the Company spend the equivalent of £10,000 per annum on 'the Revival and Improvement of Literature and the Encouragement of the learned natives of India, and for the Introduction and Promotion of a Knowledge of the Sciences among the Inhabitants of the British Territories in India'. In effect, the 1813 charter amounted to a statutory obligation upon the British nation 'to undertake the education of the native subjects, a responsibility which it did not officially bear even toward its own people'.[157]

That Wordsworth must have taken a keen interest in these developments seems clear. He not only enjoyed long-standing connections with evangelicals such as Thomas Clarkson and Francis Wrangham, but one of his most important ideological mentors, Robert Southey, was the

[154] *Evangelical Magazine and Missionary Chronicle*, 21 (Aug. 1813), 321; William Wilberforce, *Substance of the Speeches . . . on the Clause in the East-India Bill for Promoting the Religious Instruction and Moral Improvement of the Natives of India* (1813); Ford K. Brown, *Fathers of the Victorians: The Age of Wilberforce* (Cambridge, 1961), 270–80; Eric Stokes, *The English Utilitarians and India* (Oxford, 1959), 27–35.

[155] Cookson, *British Armed Nation*, 244.

[156] *Parliamentary Debates*, 1st ser., xxvi. 562–3.

[157] *Public General Statutes*, 53 Geo. III., c. 155, secs. 49, 33, 42; Viswanathan, *Masks of Conquest*, 23.

leading spokesman on this issue for the *Quarterly Review*, and had been a vocal supporter of Christian missions and an Indian church establishment since the early 1800s.[158] Although Southey confessed to 'doubts' over the monopoly issue, his support for missions was unambiguous, easily overcoming his distrust of the dissenting contribution to the missionary cause, and marking him out as a powerful ally of the Claphamites. Wilberforce himself wrote to Southey in May 1813, to beg for 'facts or suggestions which tend to prove either the duty . . . practicability, or policy of endeavouring . . . to christianise the natives of Hindostan', information that he clearly intended to incorporate into his parliamentary speeches on the issue.[159]

The significance of the East India issue for the final books of *The Excursion* lies in the new prominence that it gave to the cause of Christian teaching and moral improvement as integral components of Britain's post-war imperial responsibilities. However, while the evangelical campaign remained strongly focused on India at this time, Wordsworth was particularly anxious to stress the equal necessity for moral and religious education rather closer to home:

> O for the coming of that glorious time
> When, prizing knowledge as her noblest wealth
> And best protection, this Imperial Realm,
> While she exacts allegiance, shall admit
> An obligation, on her part, to *teach*
> Them who are born to serve her and obey;
> Binding herself by Statute to secure
> For all the Children whom her soil maintains
> The rudiments of Letters, and to inform
> The mind with moral and religious truth
> Both understood, and practised,—so that none,
> However destitute, be left to droop
> By timely culture unsustained, or run
> Into wild disorder; or be forced
> To drudge through weary life without the aid

[158] Richard E. Brantley, *Wordsworth's 'Natural Methodism'* (New Haven, 1975); Majeed, *Ungoverned Imaginings*, 79–85.

[159] Robert Southey, *Life and Correspondence of the Late Robert Southey*, ed. Charles Cuthbert Southey, 6 vols. (1849–50), iv. 28 (Mar. 1813); William Wilberforce, *Correspondence*, ed. Robert Isaac Wilberforce and Samuel Wilberforce, 2 vols. (1840), ii. 264 (28 May 1813). Southey's reply does not appear to be extant, although Wilberforce gratefully acknowledged receipt of his 'obliging, and I can truly assure you, most gratifying letter' (ibid. ii. 265).

Of intellectual implements and tools;
A savage Horde among the civilized,
A servile Band among the lordly free!

(ix. 293–310)

The Excursion has sometimes been regarded as ahead of its time in this respect, in so far as it 'anticipated by nearly fifty years the national education act of 1870'.[160] But it hardly seems coincidental that Wordsworth's calls for a domestic system of 'national education' in Britain coincided precisely with the moment at which 'British Law-givers' bound themselves 'by Statute' to the cause of education and evangelization in the broader, imperial sphere. Some evangelicals, including Wordsworth's friend Francis Wrangham, were equally committed to the cause of national schools in England, and Christian education in India.[161] But the Wanderer's diffuse, visionary rhetoric positively encourages a conflation of the domestic and colonial subjects of 'this Imperial Realm', and, as Alan Richardson points out, exposes the threat posed to Britain's 'colonial ambitions . . . by a "savage horde" *within* England, its uncivilized and restive lower orders'.[162]

The Excursion's imaginative identification of Britain's imperial and domestic civilizing missions finds its most powerful and complex realization in the imaginative evocation of druidical, pagan savagery with which the Pastor introduces his final prayer of thanksgiving to the 'eternal King':

Once, while the Name, Jehovah, was a sound,
Within the circuit of this sea-girt isle,
Unheard, the savage Nations bowed their heads
To Gods delighting in remorseless deeds;
Gods which themselves had fashioned, to promote
Ill purposes, and flatter foul desires.
Then, in the bosom of yon mountain cove,
To those inventions of corrupted Man
Mysterious rites were solemnized; and there,
Amid impending rocks and gloomy woods,
Of those dread Idols, some, perchance, received

[160] Woodring, *Politics in English Romantic Poetry*, 136.

[161] See e.g. Francis Wrangham, *The Gospel Best Promulgated by National Schools* (1808), in *Sermons, Practical and Occasional*, 3 vols. (1816); id., *A Dissertation upon the Best Means of Civilizing the Subjects of the British Empire in India* (1805).

[162] Richardson, *Literature, Education, and Romanticism*, 100.

Such dismal service, that the loudest voice
Of the swoln cataracts (which now are heard
Soft murmuring) was too weak to overcome,
Though aided by wild winds, the groans and shrieks
Of human Victims, offered up to appease
Or to propitiate. And, if living eyes
Had visionary faculties to see
The thing that hath been as the thing that is,
Aghast we might behold this spacious Mere
Bedimmed with smoke, in wreaths voluminous,
Flung from the body of devouring fires,
To Taranis erected on the heights
By priestly hands, for sacrifice . . .

(ix. 682–705)

The intertextual associations of this passage resonate back to Wordsworth's *Salisbury Plain* poem of 1793, through to the vision of druidical sacrifice at the end of *The Prelude*, Book XII, and on to *The Excursion* itself, where it serves as an implicit rebuke to the Wanderer's qualified endorsement of pagan myth in Book IV.[163] Situated within the political and religious context of 1813, however, the reappearance of this abiding Wordsworthian motif at the very climax of *The Excursion* also evokes the many vivid, and often detailed accounts of Hindu polytheism, idolatry, immolation, and infanticide that suffused the evangelical campaign for the Christianization of the empire in the years immediately preceding the poem's publication. 'Evangelical anti-Hinduism' reached a new pitch of intensity in the years leading up to 1813, as leading propagandists for the missionary cause, such as Wilberforce, Buchanan, and Southey, all pressed the case for Christianization by dwelling in fascinated horror on scenes of 'dread Idols', 'foul desires', and 'human victims' very similar to that which Wordsworth's Pastor conjures on the Lakeland shore.[164]

Supporters of the evangelical cause were also willing to heighten the visceral impact of their accounts by imagining Hindu atrocities taking place within Britain itself. Lord Teignmouth, for example,

[163] See Liu, *Wordsworth*, 190–201.

[164] David Kopf, *British Orientalism and the Bengal Renaissance: The Dynamics of Indian Modernization 1773–1835* (Berkeley, Calif., 1969), 129–44; Wilberforce, *Substance of the Speeches*, 44–54; Claudius Buchanan, *Colonial Ecclesiastical Establishment* (1813), 126–40; [Robert Southey], 'Account of the Baptist Missionary Society', *Quarterly Review*, 1 (Feb. 1809), 217–20.

a former governor-general of India and a prominent Claphamite, remarked that,

> Were the same superstitions, or the same barbarous and licentious rites, which are now exhibited on the banks of the Ganges, to be practised on the banks of the Thames, or even in the remotest part of the British islands, they would excite the strongest possible feelings of horror, and stimulate our efforts to substitute a purer and more benign system in the place of this compound of cruelty and crime.[165]

But a still more intriguing analogue for the Pastor's vision can be found in the *Quarterly* article on the East India Company charter, which appeared in the same number as Southey's article on Malthus, popular education, and the poor laws. Defending the civilizing effects of an increased commercial intercourse with India, the *Quarterly* argued that the Hindus need not be irretrievably tainted by 'religious prejudices', since

> how do we know that our ancestors were less attracted to the dogmas of their Druids, than the Hindoos are to those of Bramah, Vishnoo, or Seva? One thing is quite certain, that no superstition can be more terrible, no conquest over the human mind more complete, no penalties against disobedience more dreadful, than those which the Druids exercised over the ancient Britons.[166]

Such reflections were perhaps inspired by a minor, but significant body of opinion amongst English orientalists that traced certain druidical, as well as Christian, religious forms back to a common origin in Hinduism. Southey himself had speculated whether 'we swear by a Sanscrit God, whose worship was imported into the Sacred Isles of the West when the Druids came from Hindostan?'[167]

Wordsworth, one suspects, would have admitted his attraction to such religious syncretism only if it was used, like the *Quarterly*

[165] [John Shore, Lord Teignmouth], *Considerations on the Practicability, Policy, and Obligation of Communicating to the Natives of India the Knowledge of Christianity* (1808), 92. See also Wilberforce, *Substance of the Speeches*, 49–50.

[166] [Barrow], 'Papers Respecting the E. I. Company's Charter', *Quarterly Review*, 8 (Dec. 1812), 260–1.

[167] [Robert Southey], 'Buchanan's Journey through Mysore, Canara, and Malabar', *Annual Review*, 6 (1808), 55. Southey's speculations derived from Francis Wilford's 'Essay on the Sacred Isles in the West', *Asiatick Researches*, 8 (1805), 245–367, which he noticed favourably in the same volume of the *Annual Review* (649–51). Cf. Nigel Leask, *British Romantic Writers and the East: Anxieties of Empire* (Cambridge, 1992), 107.

passage and the Pastor's vision, to enforce the lesson of Britain's providential elevation above the 'savage Nations'. Yet the imagery of sacrifice and pagan ritual formed one of the deepest wellsprings of Wordsworth's poetic imagination, and its climactic reappearance within *The Excursion*'s entwined historical narratives of Britain's national and imperial destiny is far from unambiguous. Certainly, the language of idolatry and immolation is a recurrent feature of Wordsworth's imagery in Books VIII and IX of *The Excursion*, playing a central role in the Wanderer's attacks on the false religion of the manufacturing system:

> Men, Maidens, Youths,
> Mother and little Children, Boys and Girls,
> Enter, and each the wonted task resumes
> Within this Temple—where is offered up
> To Gain—the Master Idol of the Realm,
> Perpetual sacrifice.
>
> (viii. 180–5)

> Our Life is turned
> Out of her course, wherever Man is made
> An offering, or a sacrifice, a tool
> Or implement . . .
>
> (ix. 113–16)

The Wanderer's imaginative identification of the nation's manufactures with the pagan idolatry of 'savage Nations' bears directly upon the Pastor's vision, which now appears suspended between a linear, providentialist historical narrative, and a more unsettling revelation in which we literally do 'see / The thing that hath been as the thing that is', as the Druids' sanguinary rituals evoke the contemporary horrors of both Hindu idolatry and the 'Perpetual sacrifice' offered by Britain's morally debased manufacturing 'philosophy' to 'Gain—the Master Idol of the Realm'.[168]

For much of the nineteenth century, British imperialism continued to be justified in terms of an alliance between 'commerce and Christianity', although a certain ideological contradiction also persisted between the secular forces of 'civilization', and the moral and religious

[168] Wordsworth's revisions to the *Prelude* reinforce the association of commercial philosophy and idolatry. See *The Fourteen Book* Prelude, xiii. 77–8: 'that idol proudly named / "The Wealth of Nations"'.

legitimacy offered by the church.[169] Such tensions are certainly apparent in the spiritualized alliance of Christianity, commerce, and the imperial state that *The Excursion* attempts to evoke in its final books. Although by 1814 Wordsworth had brought himself to endorse the nation's industrial and commercial resources, as vital contributors to its wartime power and guarantors of its post-war global ascendancy, he was ultimately unable to sustain his vision of Britain's imperial destiny in Books VIII and IX of *The Excursion*, just as he failed to resolve his doubts about the 'natural' capacity of the nation's 'savage Horde' for rational piety. Such doubts and misgivings perhaps help to explain why the poem's Victorian readers preferred for the most part to dwell on its more personal, spiritual consolations. Yet the irresolution of the poem's political and social vision remains pronounced enough to inform the sombre, uncertain mood of *The Excursion*'s conclusion.

The 1800 'Prospectus' to *The Recluse*, which was printed at the beginning of *The Excursion*, records Wordsworth's hope 'that my Song / With star-like virtue in its place may shine; / Shedding benignant influence' (88–90). By returning to this image at the very end of the poem, Wordsworth could implicitly figure the reception of *The Recluse* itself, as night falls at the end of Pastor's 'Vesper service', and

> inferior Lights appeared
> Faintly, too faint almost for sight; and some
> Above the darkened hills stood boldly forth
> In twinkling lustre
>
> (ix. 762–5)

Together, these two passages identify the starry 'Lights' of the poem's conclusion with the morally and socially transformative influence of Wordsworth's poetry, recalling in the process the Wanderer's insistence that the 'primal duties shine aloft—like stars' (ix. 238). But they also evoke, perhaps more insistently, the 'punctual stars' that the Wanderer describes in Book VIII, and which,

> While all things else are gathering to their homes,
> Advance, and in the firmament of heaven
> Glitter—but undisturbing, undisturbed
>
> (viii. 159–61)

[169] Brian Young, '"The Lust of Empire and Religious Hate": Christianity, History, and India, 1790–1820', in Stefan Collini *et al.* (eds.), *History, Religion, and Culture: British Intellectual History 1750–1950* (Cambridge, 2000), 106–7; Andrew Porter, '"Commerce and Christianity": The Rise and Fall of a Nineteenth-Century Missionary Slogan', *Historical Journal*, 28 (1985), 597–621.

This night falls, not over the 'darkened hills' of the Pastor's Lakeland idyll, but over factory workers entering 'a many-windowed Fabric huge', from which breaks 'an unnatural light / Prepared for never-resting Labour's eyes' (viii. 167–9). Wordsworth's stars remain otherworldy, 'undisturbed'; but also 'undisturbing', with the implicit suggestion of occluded ineffectuality. Their 'punctual' arrival even carries the hint that the heavens themselves have been assimilated to the strict temporal rhythms of industrial production. These lines might, then, be read as an allegory of the widening breach between the new economic order and Wordsworth's earlier vision of a 'Song / With star-like virtue . . . shedding benignant influence'. But they also convey the more subdued, elegiac hope that, if it can no longer expect to serve as a transfiguring vehicle of social renewal, *The Recluse* might at least take its place in a remote literary firmament, 'a silent company . . . charged / With peaceful admonitions for the heart / Of all-beholding Man, earth's thoughtful Lord' (viii. 159–68). This hope, however, *The Excursion*'s subsequent history has only fitfully realized.

CODA: THOMAS DE QUINCEY, LIBERAL TORYISM, AND LITERARY POWER

In stressing the extent to which Coleridge and Wordsworth attempted to reach some kind of ideological accommodation with the 'spirit of commerce', this chapter has suggested a degree of convergence between Lake school literary conservatism and the ideological origins of 'liberal Toryism' during the Napoleonic Wars. Such a conclusion is perhaps easier to draw than it might once have been, for it is now clear that the Liverpool government saw its programme of commercial liberalization not as a radical departure from, but rather as a return to pre-war economic conditions. The policies of the Tory government in the early 1820s, including modification of the Corn and Navigation Laws and the encouragement of entrepôt trade and joint stock ventures, far from constituting an intellectual surrender to the spirit of laissez-faire, were conceived as strategic interventions in the market that would, it was hoped, normalize and regulate those 'natural' forms of competition of most benefit to the country in the long term. There is perhaps something more than a superficial similarity between such attitudes and Coleridge's argument for the necessity of curbing only those unnatural excesses of the spirit of commerce (including the 1815 Corn

Law) that had left the country open to damaging 'periodical Revolutions of Credit'.[170]

While it would be wrong to construe the liberal Tory economic reforms of the post-war years as a unified legislative programme based on overtly theoretical premisses—and still less as the triumph of secular free trade philosophy—parliamentary debates on commercial policy both heightened the contemporary rage for political economy, and were in turn influenced to a significant extent by the ongoing ideological struggles for control of the new science. The evangelical political economy of Thomas Chalmers, for example, if not a significant influence on policy, was for many liberal Tories an important validation of the compatibility of economic science and Christian ethics.[171] Ricardian economists were not, however, completely without hope of making their voice heard within the government of this period. William Huskisson, the President of the Board of Trade, attended the first of McCulloch's Ricardo Memorial Lectures in 1824 and, despite Ricardo's strong links with philosophic radicalism and liberal Whiggism, McCulloch hoped that the presence of men such as Huskisson and Frederick Robinson at the lectures would 'remove any obstacle, on account of political opinions, to young Tories coming to my private prelections'.[172] One young Tory who had already fallen under the spell of Ricardian economics was Thomas De Quincey, whose writings for the *London Magazine* in the early 1820s suggest how, for a brief period, it might have seemed possible to reconcile the literary belletrism of the Lake school with the analytical rigour of the Ricardian economist.

In the *Confessions of an English Opium-Eater*, serialized in the *London* in 1821, De Quincey dated his infatuation with Ricardo from 1819, when a friend in Edinburgh had sent him a copy of the *Principles*. He was, apparently, amazed at the book's achievement. 'Mr. Ricardo had deduced, *à priori*, from the understanding itself, laws which first gave a ray of light into the unwieldy chaos of materials, and had constructed what had been but a collection of tentative discussions into a science of regular proportions, now first standing on an eternal basis.' De Quincey's expressions of admiration were at this point focused almost entirely upon the methodological innovations of the *Principles*. He understood Ricardo's deduc-

[170] Hilton, *Corn, Cash, Commerce*, 176–80; Coleridge, *Lay Sermons*, 203.

[171] Hilton, *Age of Atonement*, 57–9.

[172] *Selections from the Correspondence of the Late Macvey Napier*, ed. Macvey Napier (1879), 39, quoted in Hilton, *Age of Atonement*, 41.

tivism to have unleashed the analytical potential of a discipline that was already 'eminently an organic science (no part, that is to say, but what acts on the whole, as the whole again re-acts on each part), yet the several parts may be detached and contemplated singly'.[173]

A little over a year later, and just prior to his attempted exposition of Ricardian theory in the 'Dialogues of the Three Templars on Political Economy', De Quincey undertook another serialized piece for the *London*, 'Letters to a Young Man whose Education has been Neglected'. The 'Letters' are best known for their seminal redefinition of 'literature' as a vehicle of affective power, in opposition to the discourses of 'science' and 'knowledge', and have thus commonly been seen as an important symbolic moment in the progressive historical differentiation of the 'aesthetic' and 'instrumental' spheres.[174] Although at no point in the 'Letters' does De Quincey explicitly invoke the discipline of political economy, his discussion of the relationship between textualized knowledge and the growth of commercial civilization clearly intersects with his enthusiasm for Ricardian theory as the key to the wealth of nations, as well as informing his distinction between scientific knowledge and literary power.

Thus, although 'Letters' can certainly be regarded as a critical response to Coleridge's opinions on authorship and the nature of imaginative literature, De Quincey's discussion of the antithetical discourse of scientific knowledge may well also have been inspired by contemporaneous disagreements between Malthus and Ricardo over the inferential status of political economy—disagreements that centred upon Malthus's pointed remark that 'the science of political economy bears a nearer resemblance to the sciences of morals and politics than to that of mathematics'.[175] De Quincey's 'Letters', on the contrary, endorse a broadly Ricardian methodology, reclaiming the idea of mathematical analysis as the paradigmatic instance of the discourse of knowledge, and going on to celebrate the accretion of logically structured scientific knowledge as an essential condition of commercial prosperity.

[173] [Thomas De Quincey], 'Confessions of an English Opium-Eater', *London Magazine*, 4 (Oct. 1821), 370–1.

[174] Jonathan Bate, 'The Literature of Power: Coleridge and De Quincey', in Tim Fulford and Morton D. Paley (eds.), *Coleridge's Visionary Language* (Cambridge, 1993), 137–50; Nigel Leask, 'Toward a Universal Aesthetic: De Quincey on Murder as Carnival and Tragedy', in John Beer (ed.), *Questioning Romanticism* (Baltimore, 1995), 92–120.

[175] Thomas Robert Malthus, *Principles of Political Economy Considered with a View to their Practical Application* (1820), ed. John Pullen, 2 vols. (Cambridge, 1989), i. 2.

The 'Letters' introduce the idea of the 'literature of power' by rehearsing a familiar early nineteenth-century anxiety concerning the uncontrollable material proliferation of textual knowledge. Their author confesses how, as a youth, he

> never entered a great library . . . but my predominant feeling was one of pain and disturbance of mind . . . I found that, subtracting all merely professional books—books of reference (as dictionaries, &c. &c. &c.)—from the universal library of Europe, there would still remain a total of not less than twelve hundred thousand books over and above what the presses of Europe are still disemboguing into the ocean of literature; many of them immense folios or quartos.[176]

This dread of textual proliferation, and the accompanying 'craving for a multifarious mastery over books', is tempered, however, by an appreciation of the distinction between the acquisition of knowledge, and the communication of affective power, as legitimate objects of the reading process. Thus, in his celebrated formulation, De Quincey asserts that 'All, that is literature, seeks to communicate power; all, that is not literature, to communicate knowledge'.[177] We seem encouraged to conclude that the frenetic acts of textual consumption induced by the 'present enormous accumulation of books' can be assimilated to the sphere of 'knowledge', and contrasted with the 'leisurely and genial communication' appropriate to 'deep intimacy with . . . great artists'.[178] In contrast to the distempered intellectual activity of the voracious reader, De Quincey suggests that a 'sublime unity' of intellect is attainable through a mode of reading more appropriate to the literature of power, allowing us 'to feel vividly, and with a vital consciousness, emotions which ordinary life rarely or never supplies occasion for exciting, and which had previously lain unawakened, and hardly within the dawn of consciousness'.[179]

This much seems entirely consistent with a sublimated critique of the effects of commerce upon literature and learning, including the 'multiplication of books', the potential debasement of reading to mere 'consumption', and the resultant fragmentation and vitiation of schol-

[176] [Thomas De Quincey], 'Letters to a Young Man whose Education has been Neglected', no. III, *London Magazine*, 7 (Mar. 1823), 327.

[177] Ibid. 331–3.

[178] Ibid. 328–30. Cf. Josephine McDonagh, *De Quincey's Disciplines* (Oxford, 1994), 66–90.

[179] [De Quincey], 'Letters', no. III, *London Magazine*, 7 (Mar. 1823), 332–3.

arly endeavour. The literature of power might thus appear to represent an idealized sphere of literary appreciation resistant to the corruptions of modern letters. But the 'Letters to a Young Man' also suggest that the study of '*Belles Lettres*', or the literature of power, is by no means 'self-sufficing' and must be balanced by the 'masculine exercise' provided by 'the severer sciences', pre-eminent among which are logic and mathematics.[180] According to De Quincey, mental health requires the intellectual virtues of scientific understanding, and skills such as 'comparing, combining, distinguishing, generalizing, subdividing, acts of abstraction and evolution, of synthesis and analysis', which should be practised by the aspiring man of letters until 'the most torpid minds are ventilated, and healthily excited by this introversion of the faculties upon themselves'.[181] It is only in the fourth letter, however, in the context of a discussion of languages, that De Quincey suggests the positive relation between such 'masculine' intellectual exercise and the commercial wealth and power of the nation as a whole. The scientific discourse of 'knowledge', and the relentless multiplication of textual matter, no longer induce anxiety in the author, but are the cause for frank celebration. The 'bare amount of books annually published in the several countries of Europe' is identified as an index of English, German, and French superiority in 'the great commerce of thought and knowledge in the civilized world'. De Quincey goes on to argue that,

> for the cultivation of knowledge in a more comprehensive sense, and arrived at its present stage, large simultaneous efforts are of more importance than the longest successive efforts. Now, for such a purpose, it is self-evident that the means at the disposal of every state, must be in due proportion to its statistical rank. For not only must the scientific institutions, the purchasers of books, &c. keep pace with the general progress of the country; but commerce alone, and the arts of life, which are so much benefited by science, naturally react upon science, in a degree proportioned to the wealth of every state in their demand for the aid of chemistry, mechanics, engineering, &c., &c.[182]

De Quincey's recommendations concerning the intellectual 'cultivation' of his fictitious correspondent suddenly broaden at this point into an analysis of the productive intellectual economy appropriate to an entire nation. Just as his notional addressee's course of study should exhibit internal unity and external relations, to allow both coherence and

[180] Id., *Letters*, no. I, ibid. 7 (Jan. 1823), 86–7.
[181] Id., *Letters*, no. III, ibid. 7 (Mar. 1823), 326.
[182] Id., *Letters*, no. IV, ibid. 7 (May 1823), 557.

expansion, so a given country's textual 'accumulations of knowledge' should be 'here and there converged intensely enough for all useful purposes' in metropolitan centres, while simultaneously also being 'healthily diffused over the whole territory'.[183]

'Some empires . . . are built for growth,' De Quincey claims at the beginning of the 'Letters', 'others are essentially improgressive, but are built for duration, on some principle of strong internal cohesion. Systems of knowledge, however, and schemes of study, should propose both ends.' The reader only subsequently discovers that Britain, and by implication the British Empire, is fortunate enough to exhibit just such an ideal form of intellectual organization, since it is founded upon an aboriginal principle of unity in diversity, such that the spirit of emulation and competition between the 'three great divisions' of the nation (England, Scotland, and Ireland) stimulates 'the internal excitement of the national energies; whilst, in regard to any external enemy, or external rival, the three nations act with the unity of a single force'.[184] Anticipating later nineteenth-century attempts to employ nationalist rhetoric as a prop for the intellectual justification of a free trade empire, this passage is also notable for the way in which the ideal organization of the nation's productive intellectual energies corresponds to De Quincey's account of political economy in the *Confessions* as an 'organic science', in which 'part' and 'whole' act and react upon each other, much as Coleridge had stressed the mutual implication of the 'harmonious whole' and 'remaining parts' in great poetry.[185]

By the end of the 'Letters', De Quincey's definition of the literature of power no longer seems so self-evidently superior to the discourse of knowledge; and nor, perhaps, are the two categories so unambiguously antithetical. The communication of affective literary power by the poet is understood to occur through the productive organization of 'myriads of modes of feelings' pre-existent in the reader, while the materially productive power unleashed by the progressive accretion of knowledge at the macroscopic level of the British imperial intellect is facilitated by a structurally analogous organization of unity in diversity. The collective power and prosperity of the whole are guaranteed through the competitive intellectual commerce occurring between various provinces,

[183] [De Quincey], *Letters*, no. IV, 557–8.

[184] Id., *Letters*, no. II, ibid. 7 (Feb. 1823), 190; id., *Letters*, no. IV, ibid. 7 (May 1823), 558.

[185] Semmel, *Free Trade Imperialism*, 208–10; Coleridge, *Biographia*, ii. 15.

colonies, and client states. De Quincey understood Ricardian economics, in the words of Robert Maniquis, as 'the human mind discovering its own laws in societal form' and thus, along with mathematics and logic, as both an archetypal expression of the discourse of 'knowledge' and a vital structural counterpart to the 'literature of power'.[186]

The 'Letters to a Young Man' follow Coleridge in arguing for the necessity of a literary class devoted to preserving and promulgating the literature of power. Yet the 'Letters' also critically engage with Coleridge's strictures against the professionalization of the literary character, since according to De Quincey, the country should encourage the formation of a professional cadre of *littérateurs*, drawn from the 'overstocked trades and professions', and permanently devoted to 'the service of the highest purposes which grace and dignify our nature'.[187] His insistence on the interrelation of the literature of power and the discourse of knowledge, in the intellectual economy of both the individual and the nation, suggests that De Quincey intended his idealized national intelligentsia to reconcile the professionalized, scientific rigour of Ricardian economics with the organicist sensibilities of the Lake school, fusing Coleridgean literary conservatism with the commercial dynamism of post-war Britain.[188] But, if De Quincey harboured any real hopes of converting Coleridge himself to the Ricardian cause, they surely did not survive the mid-1820s, as the ideological fault line separating secular economic discourse from conservative literary culture became increasingly difficult to negotiate.

[186] [De Quincey], 'Letters', no. III, *London Magazine*, 7 (Mar. 1823), 333; Robert Maniquis, 'Lonely Empires: Personal and Public Visions of Thomas De Quincey', *Literary Monographs*, 8 (1976), 114.

[187] Coleridge, *Biographia*, i. 223–31; [De Quincey], 'Letters', no. I, *London Magazine*, 7 (Jan. 1823), 90.

[188] Cf. Leask, *British Romantic Writers*, 198–9.

CHAPTER FOUR

Radicals, Reformers, and Legislators of the World

In October 1817, an anonymous contributor to *Blackwood's Edinburgh Magazine* embarked upon one of the most notorious campaigns of critical abuse in British literary history. Its author's single most remarkable achievement, and one that has coloured the literary historiography of the Romantic period ever since, was to condense a whole panoply of prejudices, snobbery, and opprobrium into a single, inspired appellation:

> While the whole critical world is occupied with balancing the merits, whether in theory or execution, of what is commonly called THE LAKE SCHOOL, it is strange that no one seems to think it at all necessary to say a single word about another new school of poetry which has of late sprung up among us. This school has not, I believe, as yet received any name; but if I may be permitted to have the honour of christening it, it may henceforth be referred to by the designation of THE COCKNEY SCHOOL.

Beginning thus, the first of several *Blackwood's* articles 'On the Cockney School of Poetry' went on to target the writer and journalist Leigh Hunt as 'the ideal of a Cockney poet' and the leader of the new school, 'a man certainly of some talents, of extravagant pretensions both in wit, poetry, and politics, and withal of exquisitely bad taste, and extremely vulgar modes of thinking and manners in all respects'.[1] Subsequent issues of the magazine extended the attack to such members of Hunt's London acquaintance as William Hazlitt, Benjamin Haydon, and, most famously, John Keats. By 1819, the principal author of the 'Cockney School' articles, John Gibson Lockhart, could remark that the epithet

[1] [John Gibson Lockhart], 'On the Cockney School of Poetry. No 1', *Blackwood's Edinburgh Magazine* (hereafter *Blackwood's*), 2 (Oct. 1817), 38–9. Kim Wheatley, 'The *Blackwood's* Attacks on Leigh Hunt', *Nineteenth-Century Literature*, 47 (June 1992), 1–31.

'has already been adopted by the Quarterly, and almost all the minor Reviews, and the whole regiment of the Magazines—and from these it has been carried into the vocabulary of half the Newspaper editors in the united kingdom'. And a further two years later, one of Lockhart's victims, William Hazlitt, was still railing against the 'crew of mischievous critics at Edinburgh' for inventing the Cockney nickname, and the 'ignorant, stupid, and pigeon-livered' public for giving it credit.[2]

Lockhart, together with his occasional collaborator John Wilson, maintained that their 'hatred and contempt' for the 'Cockney calumniator' Hunt was inspired by the tasteless and licentious nature of his 'polluted muse', rather than the political radicalism of his *Examiner* newspaper (which had landed Hunt and his brother John in prison in 1813 for their criticisms of the Prince Regent).[3] Yet the *Blackwood's* criticisms of the poetry of Hunt, and later Keats, were nevertheless directly related to their political loyalties. As Lockhart put it, the 'Cockney School of Politics . . . is so intimately connected with the Cockney School of Poetry, that it is almost impossible to describe the one without using many expressions equally applicable to the other'.[4] The poets' gauche, lightly worn classicism, their affected libertinism and myopically suburban attitudes, were all repeatedly invoked in order to mark them as both culturally and socially *arriviste*, if not upstart. But *Blackwood's* heartily avowed class prejudices were in this respect inextricably linked with their equally undisguised distaste for the politically, as well as socially, levelling tendencies of Hunt and his circle.[5]

The Cockney epithet tended to obscure the actual social composition of the *Examiner* group, which included both the lower-middle-class Keats and the aristocrat Shelley (whom *Blackwood's* considered to be 'of the "COCKNEY SCHOOL", so far as his opinions are

[2] [John Gibson Lockhart], *Peter's Letters to his Kinfolk*, 2nd edn., 3 vols. (Edinburgh, 1819), ii. 222; William Hazlitt, *Table-Talk; or, Original Essays* (1821), 229–30.

[3] [Lockhart], 'On the Cockney School of Poetry. No III', *Blackwood's*, 3 (July 1818), 453; Carl Woodring, 'Leigh Hunt as Political Essayist', in Leigh Hunt, *Political and Occasional Essays*, ed. Lawrence Huston Houtchens and Carolyn Washburn Houtchens (New York, 1962), 10–26.

[4] [Lockhart], 'Cockney Poetry and Cockney Politics—Bristol Hunt and Hampstead Hunt', *Blackwood's*, 5 (Sept. 1819), 639.

[5] See Nicholas Roe, *John Keats and the Culture of Dissent* (Oxford, 1997), 10–26; Jeffrey N. Cox, *Poetry and Politics in the Cockney School: Keats, Shelley, Hunt and their Circle* (Cambridge, 1998), 18–37.

concerned').[6] But for Lockhart, the idea of the 'Cockney School' was invaluable. It not only allowed the collective denigration of the politically reformist group of writers and artists associated with the *Examiner*, but also served to dissociate the Cockneys from the 'Lake School' and, above all, from 'the sublime Wordsworth'. The Hunt circle's admiration for Wordsworth was a particular source of outrage to Lockhart, as it seemed provocatively intended to align the latter's 'dignified purity of thought', and hard-won conservative convictions, with the political and aesthetic precocity of the *Examiner* group.[7]

The very potency of the *Blackwood's* attacks has inspired several more recent attempts to reassert the political and cultural significance of the Hunt circle by inverting the original, negative valuation of 'Cockney' poetics. The same terms that Lockhart employed in his abuse of the *Examiner* group can also be used, in a far more sympathetic way, to illuminate an early nineteenth-century struggle between conservative literary culture and a politically progressive literary grouping subversive of the elitist and aristocratic associations of a polite, classically inflected literary style.[8] But that the critical rehabilitation of the Cockney school as a vigorous and effective vehicle for cultural radicalism should borrow its leading terms from the abuses of its opponents is also suggestive of the oppressive ideological climate facing post-war literary *liberales* such as Hazlitt, Shelley, and Keats. This period of British cultural history has often been described as peculiarly uncongenial to those of its literary representatives who were unambiguously opposed to a post-war European order that was marked 'on the one hand, by domestic and foreign events of the greatest moment and, on the other, by the manifest absence of moral or spiritual focus'.[9]

Although this interpretation has gained a particular resonance with those wishing to understand the 'Romantic ideology' in terms of the

[6] [John Gibson Lockhart], 'Observations on the Revolt of Islam', *Blackwood's*, 4 (Jan. 1819), 475–6.

[7] [Lockhart], 'On the Cockney School of Poetry. No I', *Blackwood's*, 2 (Oct. 1817), 40.

[8] In addition to Cox, *Poetry and Politics*, and Roe, *John Keats*, see also Richard Cronin, 'Peter Bell, Peterloo, and the Politics of Cockney Poetry', in Kelvin Everest (ed.), *Essays and Studies 1992. Percy Bysshe Shelley: Bicentenary Essays* (Cambridge, 1992), 63–87; William Keach, 'Cockney Couplets: Keats and the Politics of Style', *Studies in Romanticism*, 25 (1986), 182–96.

[9] Jerome McGann, *The Romantic Ideology: A Critical Investigation* (Chicago, 1983), 110; see also Marilyn Butler, *Romantics, Rebels and Reactionaries: English Literature and its Background 1760–1830* (Oxford, 1981), 125; Peter L. Thorslev, Jr., 'Post-Waterloo Liberalism: The Second Generation', *Studies in Romanticism*, 28 (1983), 437–61.

idealist supersession of historical process, it has actually enjoyed a much longer history within the rhetorical arsenal of Romantic literary historiography. Indeed, it has often been assumed that the 'second generation' of English Romantic authors found themselves besieged not just by the class-conscious Tories of *Blackwood's*, but also by the philistine and spiritually enervated ideology of the nineteenth-century bourgeoisie, instantiated above all in Benthamite utilitarianism and political economy. The 'meanness' against which writers within the Hunt circle reacted must, in this case, be understood principally by reference to 'the classical economists, the minds bound by a utilitarian psychology, the living practitioners of "one idea"'.[10]

The critical manifestos of writers such as Shelley and Hazlitt have long functioned as documents of the second-generation Romantic reaction to this latter, monolithic understanding of an impoverished bourgeois ideology—whether as imaginative protests at 'the aggressive individualism and the primarily economic relationships which the new society embodied' or, at a more sublimated level, as a defence of poetry and literature against the 'abstract', mechanizing tendencies of utilitarianism and empirical science.[11] In the most general terms, the literary historiography of this period has shown a continued willingness to organize its subject matter in opposition to some kind of unitary, oppressive, and intellectually myopic science of society, embracing both Malthusian economics and Benthamite utilitarianism, and expressive of the individualistic ethos of a philistine middle class. If such contrasts used to be employed as a way of defining, by opposition, the emancipatory creative fecundity of the literary imagination, then this is a creative resource that can now also be regarded as impotently aestheticized, if not ideologically suspect.

It is, however, only at the risk of considerable historical distortion that the political milieu of the Hunt circle can be reduced to a simple binary opposition, between the philistine, individualistic tendencies of utilitarianism and political economy, on the one hand, and the literary imagination, however defined, on the other. For one thing, in political and intellectual terms Malthus and Bentham can hardly be aligned except in terms so broad as to be largely uninformative. Although both Bentham and the Ricardian school accepted a secularized version of the

[10] Woodring, *Politics in English Romantic Poetry*, 4.

[11] Raymond Williams, *Culture and Society*, 42; Roy Park, *Hazlitt and the Spirit of the Age: Abstraction and Critical Theory* (Oxford, 1971), 9–76.

population principle, they were nevertheless generally recognized as friends to the reformist cause. Malthus, by contrast, was commonly regarded, within both popular and polite reformist circles, as a despicable agent of tyrannical government. The Hunt circle's relationship with the Benthamites was thus, for the most part, quite distinct from their hostility to Malthusian political apologetics. But, to complicate matters further, the selective employment of anti-economistic rhetoric by writers such as Shelley and Hazlitt took place against the background of a broader, popular radical reaction against Malthusian economic discourse that originated with the most important radical journalist of the era, William Cobbett. In order to assess the broader significance of 'Cockney school' radicalism within early nineteenth-century political culture, it will therefore be necessary, not only to clarify the nature of the Hunt circle's attitudes to Bentham and Malthus, but also to re-examine the relationship between Malthusian economics and the popular radicalism of Cobbett's *Political Register*.

COBBETT, HAZLITT, AND RADICAL ANTI-ECONOMISM

Of all the nineteenth-century critics of Malthusian ideas, William Cobbett was the most indefatigable, pugnacious, and perhaps also influential. While his objections to the 'check-population philosopher' could hardly be said to have involved a high level of theoretical engagement with the *Essay on Population*, they were nevertheless both rhetorically potent and politically acute. The principle of population, Cobbett maintained, ran counter both to the Christian injunction 'to increase and multiply', and to the true laws of nature, which bid the individual to '*love* and seek the gratification of that passion in a way that leads to the procreation of his species'. To discourage marriage, as 'Parson Malthus' proposed, was tantamount to blasphemy: 'Perhaps anything so directly *Atheistical* was never before openly avowed.'[12] But Cobbett's hostility to the *Essay on Population* also had a broadly class-based component. The idle rich 'would restrain the labourer from marrying, that they and the like of them might enjoy and revel in luxury by means of the further

[12] William Cobbett, 'To Parson Malthus', *Cobbett's Weekly Political Register*, 34 (8 May 1819), 1024–5 (hereafter *Political Register*); id., *Cobbett's Sermons* (1822), 242–4.

deductions that they would then make from his labour'. It was not surplus population, nor lack of moral restraint, but rather 'paper-money and taxes' that had produced the increase in pauperism noted by Malthus, and to prove his point, Cobbett embarked on a doggedly quixotic campaign to refute the 'great national lie' that the population of the country was increasing.[13] As late as 1834, as the Poor Law Amendment Bill made its way through Parliament, Cobbett was still attempting to turn public opinion against Malthus's ideas, even going so far as to publish a comic play on the subject.[14]

Although his anti-Malthusian polemic failed materially to influence the course of poor law reform, the powerful combination of 'sexual populism' and political denunciation which characterized Cobbett's attacks proved a strong influence upon extra-parliamentary resistance to the new law.[15] He continued to oppose what he regarded as the Malthusian provisions of the New Poor Law up until his death in 1835, inspiring a wide spectrum of opposition to the Act which included 'Tory Radicals' such as Richard Oastler as well as the Chartist leader Feargus O'Connor.[16] But perhaps just as importantly, Cobbett also played a vital part in popularizing a powerful rhetorical critique of economic discourse more generally, which portrayed the new science as the dismal product of obscurantist 'feelosophers'. The influence of Cobbett's anti-Malthusian rhetoric can be traced not just in British social critics such as Thomas Carlyle, but also in the writings of Karl Marx, who thought Cobbett's own economic views naive, but whose scathing attacks on

[13] Ibid. 259; id., 'To Parson Malthus. On the Population of England', *Political Register*, 46 (12 Apr. 1823), 66–7, 113. See Herman Ausubel, 'William Cobbett and Malthusianism', *Journal of the History of Ideas*, 13 (1952), 250–6; Charles H. Kegel, 'William Cobbett and Malthusianism', *Journal of the History of Ideas*, 19 (1958), 348–62; John W. Osborne, *William Cobbett: His Thought and his Times* (New Brunswick, 1966), ch. 7. The best short summary is to be found in George Spater, *William Cobbett: The Poor Man's Friend*, 2 vols. (Cambridge, 1982), ii. 551–3.

[14] William Cobbett, *Surplus Population: and Poor-Law Bill. A Comedy, in Three Acts* (n.d. [1834]); repr. from *Political Register*, 72 (28 May 1831), 493–511.

[15] G. D. H. Cole, *The Life of William Cobbett* (1924), 410–19; William Cobbett, *Cobbett's Legacy to Labourers* (1834), 5–42, 99–141; John Knott, *Popular Opposition to the 1834 Poor Law* (1986), 32–3. On Cobbett as a 'sexual populist', see Ian Dyck, *William Cobbett and Rural Popular Culture* (Cambridge, 1992), 103. This idea should, however, be qualified by reference to the profoundly masculinist perspective that Cobbett shared with much contemporary radical discourse; on which see Anna Clark, *The Struggle for the Breeches: Gender and the Making of the British Working Class* (1995), 141–57.

[16] Cecil Driver, *Tory Radical: The Life of Richard Oastler* (New York, 1946), 278–82; James Epstein, *The Lion of Freedom: Feargus O'Connor and the Chartist Movement* (1982), 18; G. D. H. Cole, *Chartist Portraits* (1941), 310.

'Parson Malthus' in *Capital* owe a clear debt to the polemical tone of the *Political Register*.[17]

It has long been acknowledged, though usually as a mere curiosity of intellectual biography, that Cobbett's initial disposition towards Malthusian economics was very far from the relentless animosity that he later came to feel, and for which he is much better known. There is, moreover, an appealingly simple explanation for his early and uncharacteristic admiration for the *Essay on Population*. Upon returning to England from America in 1800, Cobbett turned some of his considerable journalistic skills to anti-jacobin propaganda, an employment that culminated in the anonymous *Important Considerations for the People of this Kingdom*, an alarmist Francophobe broadside distributed to every parish in the country during the invasion scare of 1803. The first edition of Malthus's *Essay* (1798), while addressed to a considerably more educated readership than Cobbett's *Considerations*, can also be regarded as a counter-revolutionary document, in so far as its primary object was to refute the utopian philosophies of Godwin and Condorcet. Cobbett's original enthusiasm for Malthus's ideas might thus be explained in terms of their shared commitment to the politics of anti-jacobinism.[18]

The truth of the matter, however, is both more complex, and more revealing of the relationship between Malthusian doctrine and early nineteenth-century popular politics. For one thing, Cobbett's public approbation of Malthus's *Essay* only began during the period in which he was already well on his way to embracing the cause of political radicalism. His initial attraction to the *Essay* seems, moreover, to have had little to do with the anti-utopian polemic of the first edition, but rather to have been inspired by apparent congruities between the principle of population and political arguments with which Malthus himself could by no means have been expected to concur. Cobbett's subsequent denunciation of the *Essay* was, in turn, strongly influenced by the turbulent political situation of 1805–7 and, more specifically, the widening split between Foxite Whiggism and Burdettite popular radicalism. Cobbett's critique of Malthusian ideas was to take on a momentum and an intensity that were quite unparalleled in the post-war reform movement. The terms of that critique, however, were determined in large part by the shifting political

[17] S. S. Prawer, *Karl Marx and World Literature* (Oxford, 1978), 254, 317–18.

[18] Ausubel, 'William Cobbett', 250; Winch, *Riches and Poverty*, 292.

allegiances of popular radicalism in the period between the death of Pitt and the Peninsular War.

One of Malthus's earliest appearances in the pages of *Cobbett's Weekly Political Register*, in 1805–6, was as a valuable, but entirely unwitting, ally in the *Register*'s poisonous crusade against the anti-slavery movement, or the 'Friends of the Blacks', as Cobbett preferred to call them. The 'profound work of Mr. Malthus', the *Register* proclaimed, had exposed the 'erroneous or hypocritical humanity' of abolitionists such as Wilberforce, by implying not only that the continued depredation of the African population would not have a significant impact on living standards, but also that the enforced celibacy of Jamaican slaves could be justified on the grounds that '*checks to population*' were 'conducive to the *good* of mankind'. Malthus was stung to reply to Cobbett in an appendix to the 1806 edition of the *Essay on Population*, in which he made clear his opposition to a trade that he considered 'disgraceful to us as men and as Christians'.[19] But Cobbett's idiosyncratic endorsement of the population principle was by no means confined to the slavery issue, since he was also prepared to employ Malthusian rhetoric in the context of domestic politics, in his burgeoning campaign against the Pittite 'system' of taxation, public debt, and political corruption.

In September 1804, Cobbett began his celebrated series of public letters 'To the Rt. Hon. William Pitt, on the Causes of the Decline of Great Britain'. He was motivated in this personal campaign against the Prime Minister by a growing distaste for parliamentary corruption in general, but also by his disillusionment with the self-serving, factional character of the new government, which seemed to Cobbett to be no real improvement upon the incompetent peacemongering of the old Addington administration. However, his impatience with Pitt was also informed by a growing hostility to the latter's economic policies and, more specifically, the increasing dependence of public finances upon the national debt and the Sinking Fund, together with Pitt's apparent partiality to the commercial and manufacturing interests at the expense of both farmers and the rural poor.

Cobbett was neither ignorant of nor uninterested in the implications of contemporary economic argument for the conduct of government

[19] *Political Register* (18 Jan. 1806), 65, 76; ibid. (16 Feb. 1805), 231; Malthus, *Essay* (1803), ii. 230–2. For Cobbett's response, see *Political Register*, 11 (9 Mar. 1807), 361. On this episode, and Malthus's links with prominent abolitionists, see James, *Population Malthus*, 124–6, 81–2.

policy. His inclinations in such matters were influenced by a fundamental dissatisfaction with Adam Smith's *Wealth of Nations*, as well as his growing enthusiasm for Paine's *Decline and Fall of the English System of Finance*, which he appears to have encountered as early as 1797.[20] But Cobbett seems also to have been willing to apply the lessons of Malthus's *Essay on Population* to the economic condition of the country. In his fourth letter to Pitt (which appeared in December 1804), he declared that 'it is a proposition firmly established and universally admitted, that the multiplication of the human species is always in due proportion to the means of subsistence; nor will it be denied, that the tendency of the human species to multiply is much greater than the rapidity with which it is possible to increase the produce of the earth for their maintenance'. Malthus was certainly not the only writer to have made such claims, but this elucidation of the 'principle of population', as Cobbett went on to describe it, seems like a clear enough allusion to the *Essay on Population*. However, as in the case of his arguments on the slavery issue, Cobbett's letter to Pitt is remarkable for the way in which it employs the basic premisses of Malthusian doctrine to an end that runs directly counter to Malthus's own conclusions. Thus, while the *Essay* had argued for the advantages of a bounty on the exportation of corn, Cobbett chose to use the 'principle of population' to denounce just such a measure, on the grounds that population 'is frequently checked by the deficiencies of agriculture, but agriculture never can, except from very singular circumstances, be checked by the deficiencies of population; or, in other words, by the want of a demand for corn'. There was therefore no need to encourage production through an export bounty, as Addington and Pitt proposed, since domestic demand would always keep pace with agricultural growth. Cobbett seems to have been aware of the ironies of his position, since he went on to refer Pitt on this issue to 'the doctrine of your great master', Adam Smith, with whom Cobbett, for once, found himself in grudging agreement.[21]

While Cobbett's appropriation of Malthusian ideas was opportunistic, and on occasion deeply objectionable, it appears to have been neither cynical nor uninformed. Cobbett seems genuinely to have admired

[20] Cole, *Life of Cobbett*, 85–6; Dyck, *William Cobbett*, 30. Cobbett himself dated his acquaintance with Paine's economic work to 1803: see William Cobbett, *Paper against Gold and Glory against Prosperity*, 2 vols. (1815), i. 442.

[21] Cobbett continued to maintain that, 'wherever there is a subsistence, there will be *a proportionate population*', even after he had come to disagree with Malthus 'as to the *checking of population*' (*Political Register* (23 Apr. 1808), 646).

Malthus and, as late as December 1805, privately compared his intellectual authority to that of Newton.[22] That his respect for Malthus should endure this long is puzzling, particularly since the *Essay on Population* not only supported the maintenance of a corn bounty, but also included an argument of brutal frankness for the abolition of the poor laws. Cobbett's growing sympathy for the plight of rural workers had been deepened by his investigations, in autumn 1804, into the actual condition of agricultural labourers in Hampshire. These provided ample evidence that the distresses suffered by many such labourers and their families could not simply be explained as a result of idleness, moral decline, or sexual profligacy, as many opponents of public poor relief had previously argued (although Cobbett continued to berate the working people of England for their lack of independence).[23] His experiences in Hampshire did not, however, prompt him to any expression of dissatisfaction with Malthus's own, notorious arguments for the abolition of the poor laws, until two and a half years later.

Cobbett's apparent willingness to overlook Malthus's views on this issue can perhaps be explained in terms of certain underlying points of ideological agreement. The *Essay on Population* displayed a far stronger agrarian bias than many contemporary economic texts and, in common with Cobbett's writings of this period, expressed a corresponding dissatisfaction with definitions of national prosperity which, like that offered in Smith's *Wealth of Nations*, placed undue stress on the value of commercial and manufacturing wealth. Such wealth had, according to the *Essay*, increased quite disproportionately in recent decades, and in so doing had thrown a greater proportion of the 'lower classes of society' into 'unhealthy occupations, and . . . employments in which the wages of labour are exposed to much greater fluctuations than in agriculture . . .'.[24] Malthus's political sympathies were broadly Old Whig (like those of Cobbett's patron, William Windham), with the result that, as we have seen, the second *Essay* of 1803 did not

[22] Lewis Melville, *The Life and Letters of William Cobbett in England and America*, 2 vols. (1913), i. 293.

[23] Dyck, *William Cobbett*, 29–32.

[24] Malthus, *Essay* (1803), ii. 81. In a similar vein, Cobbett's third letter to Pitt argued against prevailing assumptions governing the assessment of 'the prosperity of nations'. He noted 'the numerous turnpike roads and canals, the amazing manufactories of Manchester and Birmingham, the immense extent and riches of London'. All of this, however, was proof merely of individual, rather than '*national* wealth', which latter Cobbett equated with 'national *power*', and a valiant collective martial spirit: *Political Register*, 6 (27 Oct. 1804), 610–18.

simply argue that popular education and the practice of moral restraint would obviate much of the need for public poor relief, but went on to state that a social reformation of this kind would also deliver the English people from the threat to their liberty presented by demagogues, despots, and mob politics. This was not so very far from Cobbett's realization, around the same time, of 'the need for independence at all levels of society, whether from the parish rates or from government funds'.[25] It would, of course, be foolish to deny that Cobbett had tacit, but very significant, differences of opinion with the *Essay*; but it seems equally clear that he had good reasons to overlook them for as long as he did. It would certainly be wrong to assume either that his initial reaction to Malthusian political economy was to regard it as the latest manifestation of a new science inherently inimical to a vanishing rural popular culture, or that the primary motivation for his subsequent opposition to the *Essay* was its incompatibility with some form of traditionary moral economy.[26] Cobbett's initial approbation of Malthusian ideas was both strategic and considered; his subsequent repudiation of the *Essay on Population* was correspondingly neither instinctive nor capricious.

When Cobbett did finally turn the *Register* against Malthus's *Essay*, it was in response to Whitbread's poor law reform bill of 1807. Whitbread's plan undoubtedly helped to focus Cobbett's attention upon the desirability of poor law amendment and the coercive attitudes of many would-be reformers. But, because of the prominent connection between Whitbread's bill and Malthus's *Essay*, which was noted by both supporters and opponents of the proposals, the Whitbread controversy also led Cobbett to question the validity of Malthus's own opinions on these issues. 'Damn them,' he wrote privately of the bill's supporters, 'they would put badges upon us all. The poor are yet *too free* for them.'[27] Whitbread's bill certainly sought to diminish the voting power of small ratepayers within parish vestries, a proposal that Cobbett later singled out for harsh attack, along with the national education plan which formed an integral part of Whitbread's proposals, and to which Malthus had publicly given his

[25] Malthus, *Essay* (1803), ii. 122–36; Dyck, *William Cobbett*, 24.

[26] On Cobbett and 'moral economy', see ibid. 79–81, 202–5; Roger Wells, 'The Moral Economy of the English Countryside', in Adrian Randall and Andrew Charlesworth (eds.), *Moral Economy and Popular Protest: Crowds, Conflict and Authority* (Basingstoke, 2000), 209–71.

[27] Melville, *Life and Letters*, ii. 5; Cole, *Life of Cobbett*, 137.

support.[28] But Cobbett's hostility to Whitbread's legislative proposals, and the contempt which he henceforth reserved for Malthusian doctrine, cannot be fully explained by reference to the bill's content alone, since it was also crucially influenced by the shifting political relationship between popular radicalism and reformist Whiggism after the death of Pitt in January 1806.

The Ministry of All the Talents, which rose rather unsteadily from the ashes of Pitt's government, was founded on a delicate alliance between William Grenville and Charles James Fox, a circumstance that quickly began to increase tensions between the Foxite party and its radical supporters.[29] Thus, when Fox himself died only a few months later, the way was already prepared for a divergence between the remnants of the Old Opposition, and a strenuously 'independent' form of popular radicalism centred upon the county of Middlesex and Fox's old constituency in the borough of Westminster.[30] Cobbett's reactions to this rapid train of events are indicative of his growing disillusionment with the state of parliamentary politics. He had initially been prepared to argue for Fox's inclusion in the Talents, but his old enmity for the Whig leader quickly resurfaced and in August 1806 he began a series of public letters in the *Register*, 'To the Electors of Westminster', in which he repeatedly attacked the Whigs for succumbing to the compromises and corruptions of high office.[31]

Fox's death in September necessitated an election in Westminster, and Cobbett's poor opinion of the Whigs seemed to have been further vindicated when one of Fox's oldest allies, Richard Brinsley Sheridan, made what looked like a secretly negotiated withdrawal from the Westminster contest in favour of Lord Percy, an aristocratic young Grenvillite.[32] Percy was duly elected, but the subsequent dissolution of Parliament necessitated a second Westminster contest in November.

[28] *Political Register* (28 Feb. 1807), 336; ibid. (29 Aug. 1807), 327–9; Eastwood, *Governing Rural England*, 126.

[29] Michael Roberts, *The Whig Party 1807–1812* (1939), 2nd edn. (1965), 172–83; James J. Sack, *The Grenvillites 1801–29: Party Politics and Factionalism in the Age of Pitt and Liverpool* (Urbana, Ill., 1979), 85–101, 130.

[30] A. D. Harvey, 'The Ministry of All the Talents: The Whigs in Office, February 1806 to March 1807', *Historical Journal*, 15 (1972), 645; Hone, *For the Cause of Truth*, 148–61; Peter Spence, *The Birth of Romantic Radicalism: War, Popular Politics and English Radical Reformism, 1800–1815* (Aldershot, 1996), 38–46.

[31] *Political Register* (19 Apr. 1806), 585–92; ibid. (10 May 1806), 673–86; ibid. (9 Aug. 1806), 193–200.

[32] Spater, *William Cobbett*, i. 178–9.

Sheridan stood once again, displaying further proof of his 'rather desperate ambition to step into Fox's shoes'.[33] This time, however, Sheridan found himself opposed by a young merchant named James Paull, who entered the contest with the blessing of the leading Middlesex radical, Sir Francis Burdett. Cobbett's involvement in Westminster politics was by this stage quite extensive: along with Burdett, he actively supported Paull's independent candidacy, and repeatedly appeared on the hustings during the election.[34] Although Paull was defeated, and Sheridan elected, the rapid collapse of the Talents ministry precipitated a further, decisive election in May 1807.

At this point, an influential and tightly organized committee of Westminster electors resolved to secure the election of Burdett himself, whose long-standing ambition to win a seat in Middlesex had recently been disappointed after acrimonious exchanges with his erstwhile friends in the Whig party. Because Burdett resolved to remain entirely uninvolved in the election both personally and financially, the committee's successful mobilization of the Westminster electors has come to be regarded as something of a turning point in the development of popular political organization more generally, in so far as it appeared to reverse completely the traditional balance of power between the political elite and an increasingly self-confident artisanal and middle-class electorate.[35] The confused and acrimonious circumstances in which Paull retired from this last contest saw Cobbett drawing progressively closer to the Westminster committee in their mutual support for Burdett, whose eventual election was greeted as an unexpected, but nevertheless resounding victory for the independent cause, which demonstrated both 'the spontaneous exertions of the people' and 'the progress of public opinion'.[36] The committee certainly felt vindicated in its hostility to Whig 'hypocrisy'. By electing Burdett in such a manner, the 'middle classes of society' had registered their conviction

[33] Hone, *For the Cause of Truth*, 152.

[34] *History of the Westminster and Middlesex Elections; in the Month of November, 1806* (1807), 18; Spater, *William Cobbett*, i. 181.

[35] J. M. Main, 'Radical Westminster, 1807–1820', *Historical Studies: Australia and New Zealand*, 12 (1965–7), 186; J. R. Dinwiddy, 'Sir Francis Burdett and Burdettite Radicalism', *History*, 65 (1980), 18; M. W. Patterson, *Sir Francis Burdett and his Times (1770–1844)*, 2 vols. (1931), ii. 192–218.

[36] [Francis Place and John Richter], *An Exposition of the Circumstances which Gave Rise to the Election of Sir Francis Burdett* (1807), 14. On the rift between Burdett and Paull, see John Horne Tooke, *A Warning to the Electors of Westminster* (1807); James Paull, *A Refutation of the Calumnies of John Horne Tooke* (1807); and Thompson, *Making*, 502–5.

that 'all public men were alike, and that with "country" in their mouths, their whole object was to share the spoil'.[37] Cobbett wholeheartedly endorsed these sentiments, and his vituperative attacks on Sheridan in the weeks before polling marked his final breach with the Whig opposition, and sealed the terms of an enduring alliance with the radical leaders Burdett and Cartwright.

It was this course of events that provided the political context for Cobbett's attacks on Samuel Whitbread's poor law reform bill. In the wake of his impeachment of Viscount Melville, Addington's first lord of the Admiralty, Whitbread had come to be regarded by many as, along with Sheridan, a possible future leader of the Foxite Whigs. His subsequent exclusion from the Talents ministry was a source of bitter resentment, but it did much to preserve his standing with radical opinion, at least in the short term. In September 1806 a group of Westminster electors approached Whitbread in the hope that he would become their candidate, and thus afford them 'an opportunity of once more evincing their spirit and independence and their resentment at being considered either the tools of Party or subservient vassals of any administration'.[38] Ominously, however, Whitbread declined and, like Sheridan, threw his support behind Lord Percy as the most desirable candidate. He nevertheless chose to involve himself closely in Westminster politics, and further confirmed his allegiance to the Foxite cause by giving his unqualified public support to Sheridan in the general election.[39] Indeed, a Gillray print depicting the Westminster hustings in November 1806 shows Whitbread standing with a supportive hand on Sheridan's shoulder, whilst the enraged Whig candidate is mocked by Paull, who in turn is flanked by Cobbett and Burdett.[40] Whitbread's standing with the radicals was further compromised when, the following month, he only narrowly avoided a duel with Burdett after the latter's attack on 'Mr. Whitbread' and the 'place-holding and place-hunting party' in a public address to the freeholders of Middlesex. Much to Cobbett's dismay,

[37] [Place and Richter], *Exposition*, 5–6.

[38] Letter to Whitbread, quoted in Fulford, *Samuel Whitbread*, 159–61; Spence, *Romantic Radicalism*, 39.

[39] *History of the Westminster and Middlesex Elections*, 135–6, 142–3, 201; Fulford, *Samuel Whitbread*, 164.

[40] Frederick George Stephens and Mary Dorothy George, *A Catalogue of Political and Personal Satires Preserved in the Department of Prints and Drawings in the British Museum*, 11 vols. (1870–1954), viii. 476–8. This print is attached to the frontispiece of the *History of the Westminster and Middlesex Elections*, and is reproduced in Spater, *William Cobbett*, i. 181.

Burdett was forced to make a humiliating public apology in a doomed attempt to preserve his connection with the Whigs, and realize his hopes of a seat for Middlesex.[41]

To a very large extent, therefore, the question of Whitbread's political loyalties stood at the very centre of the disintegrating alliance between popular radicalism and parliamentary Whiggism. This fact cannot have escaped Cobbett, who must also have realized that the most significant result of a successful attack on Whitbread's credibility as a true friend of the people would be to render the breach between the Old Opposition and the Burdettites irrevocable, thus ridding the radical cause once and for all of their subordinate, dependent relation to the Foxite party in Parliament. Whitbread's poor law reform bill, a legislative proposal of overreaching ambition, coercive intent, and perhaps also suspect motive, provided the perfect opportunity. Moreover, Malthus's Foxite credentials and strong association with Whitbread's bill suddenly made the *Essay on Population* both politically vulnerable, and strategically useful to Cobbett, particularly given the severity of many of Malthus's references to the profligate poor. An attack on Malthus was thus also, by implication, an attack on Whitbread, and hence upon the Whig–radical connection itself.

This certainly suggests a strong political motive for Cobbett's decision, in the months before the Westminster election of May 1807, to devote considerable space in the *Register* to a series of three anonymous letters on Malthus and the poor laws. In their author, he assured his readers, the 'check-population philosopher, Mr. Malthus, has met with a formidable opponent, who will, I confidently hope, continue on until he has completely put down the hard-hearted doctrines of this misanthropic economist'.[42] The letters themselves were composed by William Hazlitt, who could not have been ignorant of the broader strategic purpose served by his contributions to the *Register*. In fact, Hazlitt seems to have been particularly engaged by the fortunes of the Whig party during the period immediately preceding his attack on Malthus. After Pitt's death, and the formation of the Talents, he had published a pamphlet addressed to 'the Old Opposition', in which he sternly reminded the Foxites of their loyalty to an older and purer form of Whiggism. This document, together with his *Eloquence of the British Senate* (1807),

[41] *History of the Westminster and Middlesex Elections*, 441; Fulford, *Samuel Whitbread*, 166–70; *Political Register* (15 Nov. 1806), 764; ibid. (27 Dec. 1806), 993–1001.

[42] Ibid. (14 Mar. 1807), 397.

suggests that, up to this date, Hazlitt's political convictions were based upon an idealized vision of eighteenth-century parliamentary politics, rather than popular agitation 'out of doors'.[43] His pointed, if qualified, admiration for both Burke and Fox suggests, moreover, that Hazlitt's ideological inclinations before this date tended towards an essentially nostalgic form of oppositional Whiggism.[44] This apparent faith in a kind of ever-receding Rockinghamite golden age would undoubtedly have been severely tested by the compromises and failures of the Talents. At the very least, his sudden involvement in political writing between 1806 and 1807 indicates Hazlitt's keen awareness of how crucial this period was for the survival and regeneration of Foxite politics. He must, then, also have realized the significance of the deteriorating relationship between the Old Opposition and Burdettite radicalism, along with the central role in this relationship that was played by Whitbread.

It was no coincidence, therefore, that Hazlitt submitted his criticisms of Malthus to the *Political Register* just as Cobbett's own attacks on the Foxite Whigs were reaching a peak of intensity; nor that he used his first letter to the *Register* to launch a vituperative attack on Whitbread's poor law bill—legislation which, Hazlitt noted, had been presented to Parliament 'under the auspices' of Malthus's system.[45] His decision to align Whitbread and Malthus as enemies of the people and defenders of aristocratic self-interest quite accurately reflected the 'disappointment and disillusionment of many radicals' after the Whigs' return to power, and the growing rift between the popular reform movement and the Foxite party.[46] Hazlitt also had what might be described as a more purely intellectual interest in the refutation of Malthus's ideas, and his letters to the *Register* were soon expanded and published in book form. The resultant *Reply to the Essay on Population* constituted an extensive critique of Malthus's arguments on the grounds of their originality, logical consistency, empirical veracity, and philosophical foundations. But although Hazlitt's morally benevolist view of human nature was at odds with Malthus's faith in

[43] [William Hazlitt], *Free Thoughts on Public Affairs* (1806); id., *The Eloquence of the British Senate* (1807), 2nd edn., 2 vols. (1808). See id., *Complete Works*, ed. P. P. Howe, 21 vols. (1930–4), i. 138; P. P. Howe, *The Life of William Hazlitt* (1922), 92–5.

[44] Cf. John Kinnaird, *William Hazlitt: Critic of Power* (New York, 1978), 108–9; Tom Paulin, *The Day-Star of Liberty: William Hazlitt's Radical Style* (1998), 138–9.

[45] *Political Register* (14 Mar. 1807), 402.

[46] Hone, *For the Cause of Truth*, 151.

the psychological primacy of self-interest, his objections to the *Essay on Population* in this respect also had an important political dimension.[47] The Westminster electors' break with the Whigs was justified by Cobbett with reference to the arrogant *hauteur* and scarcely concealed self-interest of the existing parties, whom he identified with the 'united influence of the government, the aristocracy, and the dependent clergy, operating upon avarice, upon self-interest, and upon self-preservation'.[48] Such charges were clearly echoed in Hazlitt's attack on Whitbread's 'cold, philosophic indifference', and the reliance of his poor law reform bill upon Malthus's 'very convenient doctrine' that 'the ends of public virtue and benevolence are best answered by the meanness, pride, extravagance, and insensibility of individuals'.[49]

The *Essay on Population*, like Whitbread's poor law bill, seemed to Hazlitt completely inimical both to the true spirit of the Whig party, and to the benevolist philosophy which he had previously expounded in his *Essay on the Principles of Human Action* (1805). Equally, however, his attachment to 'principle' was too strong for him to remain entirely approving of Cobbett's vigorous but inconsistent brand of politics, and his Whig sympathies quickly (but never completely) reasserted themselves in the years after 1807.[50] His attack upon Whitbread's bill might then have been conceived not so much as an outright abandonment of the Whig tradition, as Hazlitt understood it, but as an implicit warning to the Foxites to rid themselves of principles and policies that would 'play the game into the hands of those whose views of government and civilisation are very different from . . . [Whitbread's] own'.[51] Nevertheless, Hazlitt's letters to the *Register* did nothing to contradict Cobbett's own view that the Old Opposition,

[47] [Hazlitt], *Reply to the Essay on Population*. For detailed analyses of Hazlitt's theoretical objections to Malthus, see William P. Albrecht, *William Hazlitt and the Malthusian Controversy* (Port Washington, 1969); Boner, *Hungry Generations*, 60–7; Kenneth Smith, *The Malthusian Controversy* (1951), 68–78. On Hazlitt and moral benevolism, see David Bromwich, *Hazlitt: The Mind of a Critic* (New York, 1983), 46–57; Kinnaird, *William Hazlitt*, 42–4.

[48] *Political Register* (29 Nov. 1806), 838.

[49] Ibid. (14 Mar. 1807), 402, 398.

[50] [Hazlitt], *Spirit of the Age*, 331–51. Hazlitt went on to write for both radical and Whig publications, and remained ambivalently poised between 'popular' and 'polite' journalistic forms. See Thompson, *Making*, 820–2; and John Whale, 'Hazlitt on Burke: The Ambivalent Position of a Radical Essayist', *Studies in Romanticism*, 25 (1986), 465–81.

[51] *Political Register* (14 Mar. 1807), 399.

including Whitbread, was irrevocably tainted by the corruptions of parliamentary office.

Hazlitt's declared hostility to the Whitbread bill was certainly quite as uncompromising as that of his editor. He even went so far as to damn the bill's proposals for a system of national schooling in terms surprisingly redolent of its conservative opponents, albeit inflected with a distinctly Cobbett-esque veneration for the manners of the rural poor. 'In the country,' Hazlitt's first letter declared,

> the people read moral or religious, or, at least, innocent books, and therefore, they are benefited by them; in towns, they as often meet with licentious and idle publications, which must do them harm. . . . Will those hot-beds of vice, the factories of Manchester, &c. be less fruitful for having the *farina* of knowledge sprinkled over them? Will not corruption quicken faster, and spread wider for having this new channel opened to it? Will a smattering in books, and the current pamphlets of the day tend to quench and smother the flame of the passions, or will it add fuel to them?[52]

Cobbett himself took up this theme in the *Register* in August. Contesting Whitbread's claim that literacy and heightened morality were necessarily linked, he pointed to the recent 'tenfold' increase in 'books, pamphlets, reviews, magazines, newspapers, reading-rooms, circulating libraries . . .', before going on to note the licentious nature of many of the productions issuing from 'Grub Street and the novel shops'. Whitbread's bill attributed much of the contemporary rise in pauperism to the vices of the people, Cobbett pointed out, yet the rapid growth of literacy and print culture amongst the poor had actually coincided with this alleged process of moral degeneration. However, in a typically provocative development of his argument, Cobbett went on to dismiss the political, as well as moral, benefits of popular literacy on the grounds that the majority of the British press was in the hands of writers 'hired . . . to deceive the people; to spread falsehood instead of truth, darkness instead of light'. Such uncompromising hostility to Whitbread's education proposals might be explained in terms of Cobbett's wish to defend traditional rural culture against the narrow and over-intellectualized definition of 'education' promoted by a metropolitan elite.[53] But it was also guided by a keen sense of political corruption, and of the need to

[52] Ibid. (14 Mar. 1807), cols. 400–1; see also Hazlitt, *Reply to the Essay on Population*, 136.

[53] *Political Register* (29 Aug. 1807), 329–33; Dyck, *William Cobbett*, 36–7; Osborne, *William Cobbett*, 228.

renew the culture of politics through the felt immediacy of the radical platform. The electors of Westminster, Cobbett maintained, did not gain their political enlightenment 'from the press, but from being upon the spot; from *hearing* and *seeing* and receiving conviction of, what the press disguises from other men . . .'.[54]

This last statement is quite revealing of the way in which Cobbett's developing understanding of the radical cause entailed a rejection not just of Whig politics, but also of the respectable and 'improving' political culture that went with it. He set himself in this respect against contemporary reformist publications such as Benjamin Flower's *Political Review*. The *Review* embodied an older tradition of middle-class dissenting radicalism, within which Hazlitt himself had also been raised. Its editor's political principles not only proved rather more conciliatory towards parliamentary Whiggism than those of the *Political Register*, they also placed a fundamental stress upon the spread of literacy and the diffusion of textualized knowledge as instruments of political emancipation. Flower's expressions of disappointment at Burdett's apparently indiscriminate attacks on parliamentary corruption were thus accompanied by firm declarations of support for those examples of Whig reform, such as Whitbread's education bill, which were conducive to the 'education of the lower classes', and popular 'knowledge of those truths which concern our political welfare, our rights and duties in society'.[55]

Hazlitt was in the end much closer to Flower than to Cobbett on this issue. He never repeated his 1807 attack upon popular education, and thereafter frequently declared his faith in the political and social benefits of popular literacy. By contrast, Cobbett's radicalized rejection of parliamentary politics was accompanied by a thoroughgoing denunciation of the literary and journalistic culture which surrounded and sustained it, a position which, given its medium, can appear absurdly self-contradictory in its extreme hostility to the self-improving culture of print.[56] However, it is important to bear in mind that such attitudes were closely connected to Cobbett's growing conviction that the corruption of contemporary political culture was reflected in the aloof, self-

[54] *Political Register* (29 Aug., 1807), 334; see also *History of the Westminster and Middlesex Elections*, 248.

[55] *Flower's Political Review*, 1 (Mar. 1807), pp. xciv–xcv; ibid. 1 (June 1807), pp. xcix, c; see also ibid. 1 (Jan. 1807), pp. i–xvi.

[56] Raymond Williams, *Cobbett* (Oxford, 1983), 44–53.

serving character of the public press.[57] And this, in turn, suggests how the growing influence of 'political economy', including Malthus's *Essay*, could strike Cobbett as a further symptom of the debased condition of contemporary political life. By dismissing economic discourse as a collection of etiolated, over-refined, and obfuscatory abstractions, Cobbett could implicitly identify it, along with the obnoxious productions of contemporary journalism, as the ideological avatars of a vicious and corrupt political system increasingly alienated from public feeling and the sense of the people.

From this point of view, it is of some significance that the first example of Cobbett's negative characterization of political economy, as intrinsically selfish and cold-hearted, should occur in the course of his criticisms of Pitt's political character. In his fifth letter to Pitt, in December 1804, Cobbett expressed his surprise that the Prime Minister should have refused to be guided by Adam Smith on the question of a corn bounty, 'when you have, in so many instances, followed him too closely in those matters where the warlike or diplomatic statesman should have soared above the cold political economist!'[58] The frigid abstractions of *The Wealth of Nations* were thus counterposed, not to the benefits of a cottage economy and the traditional economic practices of the rural poor, but rather to the virile, manly conception of political virtue which Pitt so conspicuously failed to embody.

As radical dissatisfaction with the conduct of the parliamentary Whigs became more acute, this rhetorical distinction provided Cobbett with a striking, visceral rhetoric in which to evoke the ideological differences between the existing parties and the friends of the people. In the wake of Whitbread's poor law bill, Malthusian doctrine could credibly be implicated as the ideological tool of political corruption, and this further allowed Cobbett to assimilate the *Essay on Population* to the damning critique of *The Wealth of Nations* that had begun to emerge in the course of his attacks upon the Pitt system. As a result, Malthus and Smith came to stand together as joint apologists for a haughty and corrupt political order which tainted all the existing parties. The economists' abstract speculations represented for Cobbett the most extreme example of that attenuated grip upon the actual which characterized the polite culture of traditional politics, while simultaneously offering a

[57] Cf. Kevin Gilmartin, *Print Politics: The Press and Radical Opposition in Early Nineteenth-Century England* (Cambridge, 1996), 173–5.

[58] *Political Register* (8 Dec. 1804), 883.

spuriously learned justification for the self-interested pursuit of place and patronage. Such convictions are clearly at work in his scathing denunciation of the debt that Whitbread's bill owed to 'the juvenile œconomists . . . drafted from the office of the Edinburgh Review, which is a sort of depot for speculators in politics, who go off, each in his turn, to write himself into place'.[59]

By this point, the economists' philosophical defence of *amour propre* had come to signify not just a Mandevillean vision of human society, but also the political venality which such theories both excused and occluded. In his letters to the electors of Westminster of September 1807, Cobbett attacked the Whig *Morning Chronicle* and *Edinburgh Review* as perfect examples of that degeneracy of the political press to which he had recently drawn attention in connection with Whitbread's education proposals. Neither of these publications, he complained,

> has any feeling at all, either for the people, or for the honour of the country; they are zealous only when the *particular interests* of their faction and themselves are at stake. But, what I like in them least of all, is that there never, even by accident, drops from their pen any sentiment whence we can reasonably conclude that they love this country better than another for any reason besides that of its being likely that they shall be able *to make more of it*. There is a coldness in their principles and opinions that I hate. Adam Smith seems to be their sole guide. The gain, the mere pecuniary, and even present, gain of the thing is all they appear to look at.

These remarks allowed Cobbett to note a pointed contrast with Sir Francis Burdett, who had 'upon no occasion sided against his country'.[60] The deficiencies of political economy, like those of the Whigs, were thus delineated by reference to an ideal of public character and political expression increasingly identified exclusively with the radical cause. The Whig press's growing enthusiasm for political economy was understood by Cobbett to have revealed a shameful disregard for the vigorous, disinterested, and patriotic spirit that should properly inform the language and conduct of politics, and that survived only in the virtuous independence of Burdettite popular radicalism.

This is not to say that Cobbett really did abandon all faith in the 'œconomists'—as his repeated citations from William Spence's *Britain*

[59] *Political Register* (29 Aug. 1807), 335.
[60] Ibid. (5 Sept. 1807), 364–5.

Independent of Commerce made clear only a few weeks later. But his critique of political economy—and Malthusian ideas in particular—nevertheless proved an exceptionally effective rhetorical weapon in Cobbett's successive campaigns against government measures such as the establishment of select vestries in 1819 and, of course, the Poor Law Amendment Act of 1834.[61] Beyond this, however, there is also an important sense in which the events of 1805–7 helped to condition what might be described as a 'radical anti-economism': an ingrained resistance to the pre-political analysis of economic exploitation which appears to have exerted a considerable influence on radical discourse in the first half of the nineteenth century.[62] The persistence of such attitudes certainly has some bearing on the emergence of radical political economy in the mid-1820s. It is only at this point, in the writings of William Thompson, Thomas Hodgskin, and John Gray, that one can discern 'the articulation of the theoretical foundations of a distinctively anti-capitalist and socialist political economy', a process which prepared the way for the piecemeal, qualified acceptance of political economy by the working-class press over the course of the 1830s.[63]

The precise relations between popular economic analysis, and older radical concepts of exploitation, corruption, and the just price, are still not entirely settled, but clearly have important implications for our broader understanding of both radicalism and socialism in nineteenth-century Britain.[64] By situating the development of Cobbett's anti-Malthusianism in the context of the Whig–radical split of 1805–7 and the emergence of a stridently 'independent' model of popular reformist organization, the developing tensions between radical politics and economic discourse can be thrown into somewhat sharper relief. The Westminster contests of these years were a decisive episode in the re-emergence of a popular reform movement self-consciously disaffiliated both from the political culture of parliamentary Whiggism, and from

[61] On the former, see Cole, *Life of Cobbett*, 410.

[62] See Gareth Stedman Jones, 'Rethinking Chartism', in id., *Languages of Class: Studies in English Working Class History 1832–1982* (Cambridge, 1983), 103–6; Patrick Joyce, *Visions of the People: Industrial England and the Question of Class, 1848–1914* (Cambridge, 1991), 64.

[63] Noel W. Thompson, *The People's Science: The Popular Political Economy of Exploitation and Crisis 1816–34* (Cambridge, 1984), 11, 219.

[64] On possible connections between a pre-classical 'moral economy' and early socialism, see Gregory Claeys, *Machinery, Money and the Millennium: From Moral Economy to Socialism, 1815–60* (Cambridge, 1987), 188–95.

its ideological apologists in the press. To the extent that Cobbett's critique of Malthusian political economy was shaped by these developments, it was also intimately bound up with his emergent conception of a truly independent form of radical political culture. If this explains why Cobbett's hatred of 'political economy' attained such a totemic status within his subsequent writings, then it might also help to account for the more general resistance, within certain sections of the popular reform movement, towards the idiom and insights of radical economists in the decades that followed.

'THE GENIUS OF A LEGISLATOR': SHELLEY, BENTHAM, AND THE HUNT CIRCLE

Only in the 1820s did reformist neo-Malthusians such as Francis Place and Richard Carlile have any success in rehabilitating the reputation of the *Essay on Population* amongst 'respectable' radical audiences. Hazlitt, however, continued to maintain his forthright opposition to Malthusian doctrine, and went on to republish a number of extracts from his *Reply* to Malthus between 1817 and 1819, presumably in response to the fifth edition of the *Essay* and the legislative changes in poor law administration of 1818–19.[65] His views on the population controversy would undoubtedly have recommended him to Percy Shelley when the two writers first met, sometime between 1812 and 1814. Shelley had already criticized Malthus as one of those philosophers who 'would tell me not to make people happy, for fear of overstocking the world, and to permit those who found dishes placed before them on the table of partial nature, to enjoy their superfluities in quietness, though millions of wretches crowded round but to pick a morsel . . .'.[66]

But while Hazlitt had never really been a convert to Godwin's political philosophy, Shelley's objections to the *Essay* were far more directly connected to its critique of Godwinian perfectibilism. As he complained to Godwin himself in 1812,

> Political Justice was first published in 1793; nearly twenty years have elapsed since the general diffusion of its doctrines. What has followed? . . . Out of the many who have read that inestimable book how many in short have

[65] William Hazlitt, *Political Essays* (1819), 401–39; id., *Works*, vii. 407–8; Eastwood, *Governing Rural England*, 130–1; William Godwin, *Of Population* (1820).

[66] Howe, *Life of Hazlitt*, 229; Percy Bysshe Shelley, *Proposals for an Association* (1812), in *Prose Works*, ed. E. B. Murray (Oxford, 1993–), i. 52–3.

taken it up to gratify an ephemeral vanity and when the hour of its novelty had passed threw it aside and yielded with fashion to the arguments of Mr. Malthus![67]

While Hazlitt's anti-Malthusianism was primarily conditioned by his involvement in the Whig–radical split in Westminster, Shelley's interest in the *Essay* was far more closely connected with the simmering Malthus–Godwin controversy. This explains why his most intensive period of anti-Malthusian writing also coincided with the composition and publication of Godwin's *Of Population* (1820), which Shelley later declared to be a 'victorious & decisive' reply to Malthus.[68] Inspired by Godwin, Shelley began studying the *Essay on Population* in October 1818. He later included an attack upon moral restraint in his *Philosophical View of Reform* (1819), and incorporated short allegorical critiques of Malthus in two poems published in 1820, *Oedipus Tyrannus* and *Prometheus Unbound*.[69]

Like Coleridge, Shelley does not seem to have objected to the principle of population *per se*, but rather to have been provoked by Malthus's apparent misuse of that principle in order to undermine Godwin's ideas, and thereby justify the oppressive, unequal condition of contemporary British society. 'Malthus is a very clever man,' he concluded after reading the *Essay* in 1818, '& the world would be a great gainer if it would seriously take his lessons into consideration . . . but what on earth does he mean by some of his inferences!'[70] These 'lessons' appear to have confirmed Shelley both in his vegetarianism, and his support for artificial methods of birth control, practices that it is certainly hard to imagine Malthus himself condoning. On the other hand, although he followed Cobbett's *Paper against Gold* in his violent opposition to paper money and the national debt, Shelley

[67] Percy Bysshe Shelley, *Letters*, ed. Frederick L. Jones, 2 vols. (Oxford, 1964), i. 267 (8 Mar. 1812); see also id., *Prose Works*, i. 277.

[68] Shelley, *Letters*, ii. 364 (22 Oct. 1821).

[69] Mary Shelley, *Journals*, ed. Paula R. Feldman and Diana Scott-Kilvert (Oxford, 1987), 228–9; C. E. Pulos, 'Shelley and Malthus', *Publications of the Modern Language Association of America*, 67 (1952), 113–24. Byron's poetic allusions to the *Essay on Population*, by contrast, were considerably less severe: he had met Malthus socially, and would have associated him with the Whig reformism of Holland House, rather than the sinister machinations of despotic government. See *Byron's Letters and Journals*, ed. Leslie A. Marchand, 12 vols. (1974–82), ix. 19; Frederick L. Beaty, 'Byron on Malthus and the Population Problem', *Keats–Shelley Journal*, 18 (1969), 17–26.

[70] Shelley, *Letters*, ii. 43 (8 Oct. 1818); P. M. S. Dawson, *The Unacknowledged Legislator: Shelley and Politics* (Oxford, 1980), 48–9.

failed to take issue on these matters with Malthus, despite their clear differences.[71] Indeed, Shelley repeatedly (and quite justifiably) associated Malthus's ideas with William Paley, rather than secular economists such as Smith, Ricardo, or Mill.[72] He read Malthus's *Essay* primarily as a political performance, 'calculated to lull the oppressors of mankind into a security of everlasting triumph', in the same vein as Paley's notorious *Reasons for Contentment* (1792). It only made matters worse, as far as the infidel Shelley was concerned, that both Malthus and Paley couched their arguments in the language of liberal Anglican theodicy. The author of the *Essay* was 'a priest of course, for his doctrines are those of a eunuch and a tyrant'.[73]

There is little justification, therefore, for linking Shelley's anti-Malthusianism with his famous critique of political economy in the *Defence of Poetry* (which was composed in 1821). This is a particularly important point, since the rhetoric of Shelley's *Defence* has done more, perhaps, than any other text of the period to establish the idea of a fundamental antithesis between the 'Romantic' aesthetic sensibility and economic science. The *Defence*'s central attack upon political economy is, for this reason, worth quoting at some length:

> We have more moral, political and historical wisdom than we know how to reduce into practise; we have more scientific and œconomical knowledge than can be accommodated to the just distribution of the produce which it multiplies. The poetry in these systems of thought, is concealed by the accumulation of facts and calculating processes. . . . The cultivation of those sciences which have enlarged the limits of the empire of man over the external world, has, for want of the poetical faculty, proportionally circumscribed those of the internal world; and man, having enslaved the elements, remains himself a slave. To what but a cultivation of the mechanical arts in a degree disproportioned to the presence of the creative faculty, which is the basis of all knowledge, is to be attributed the abuse of all invention for abridging and combining labour, to the exasperation of the inequality of mankind? From what other cause has it arisen that these discoveries which should have lightened, have added a weight to the curse imposed on Adam? Thus Poetry, and the principle of Self, of which money is the visible incarnation, are the God and Mammon of the world.[74]

[71] Shelley, *Prose Works*, i. 86; St Clair, *The Godwins and the Shelleys*, 464–5; Kenneth Neill Cameron, 'Shelley, Cobbett, and the National Debt', *Journal of English and Germanic Philology*, 42 (1943), 197–209.

[72] Shelley, *Prose Works*, i. 277; id., *Poetry and Prose*, ed. Donald H. Reiman and Sharon B. Powers (New York, 1977), 135.

[73] Percy Bysshe Shelley, *Complete Works*, ed. Roger Ingpen and Walter E. Peck, 10 vols. (1926–30), i. 242; ibid. vii. 32.

[74] Shelley, *Poetry and Prose*, 502–3.

This passage has very little in common with Shelley's earlier attacks on Malthus, none of which had mentioned either the division of labour, or the machinery question (and Shelley would certainly have been aware of Malthus's own reservations about the manufacturing system). The *Defence*'s case against 'scientific and economic knowledge' seems far more likely to have been directed at the alliance of utilitarian radicals, liberal Whigs and Ricardian economists, who together made up that broad political coalition that Hazlitt was later to describe as the 'new school of reform'.

It is well known that Shelley composed the *Defence of Poetry* in a 'sacred rage' against Thomas Love Peacock's sophisticated, semi-ironic defence of utilitarian values in *The Four Ages of Poetry*.[75] Although Peacock was a good friend of Shelley, he also enjoyed close links with the philosophic radicals: he dined regularly with Bentham, and was employed by the East India Company under James Mill.[76] *The Four Ages of Poetry* certainly exemplifies the kind of utilitarian suspicion of imaginative 'fiction' that was quite prevalent within the philosophic radical party at this time (although, as we have seen, the Benthamites were rather less concerned with poetic dissimulation than with the legalistic and political fictions which masked the oppressive practices of aristocratic government). In his private correspondence with Shelley, Peacock suggested that 'moral, political, and physical science' was gradually coming to dominate the attention of the most advanced minds of the age, at the expense of the audience for poetry, which now comprised 'the mere dregs of the intellectual community'.[77] This provocative contrast between poetry and 'useful' knowledge was further developed in the *Four Ages*, in which Peacock invited his reader to concede

> that the great and permanent interests of human society become more and more the main spring of intellectual pursuit; that in proportion as they become so, the subordinacy of the ornamental to the useful will be more and more seen and acknowledged; and that therefore the progress of useful art and science, and of moral and political knowledge, will continue more and more to withdraw attention from frivolous and unconducive, to solid and conducive studies . . .[78]

[75] Shelley, *Letters*, ii. 261 (15 Feb. 1821).

[76] Butler, *Peacock Displayed*, 172.

[77] Thomas Love Peacock to P. B. Shelley, in Thomas Love Peacock, *Works*, ed. H. F. B. Brett-Smith and C. E. Jones, 8 vols. (1924–34), viii. 219–20 (4 Dec. 1820).

[78] [Thomas Love Peacock], 'The Four Ages of Poetry', *Ollier's Literary Miscellany*, 1 (1820), 199.

Shelley's spirited riposte to Peacock eventually succeeded not only in answering the *Four Ages of Poetry*, but also in shaping the enduring myth of a fundamental breach between the philistine preoccupation with 'scientific and œconomical' knowledge, supposedly typical of the Benthamites, and the aestheticized sensibilities of post-war Romantic radicalism. This reading of the *Defence* has certainly helped to perpetuate an overly rigid opposition between 'Romantics' and 'utilitarians', in both politics and ethics, by distorting the more complex, and often congenial relationship that existed between Benthamite utilitarianism and the 'literary' radicalism of Shelley and the Hunt circle. The personal and ideological affiliations between these two groups were considerably more extensive than is commonly realized, and to understand the broader context in which Shelley composed the *Defence of Poetry*, it will be necessary to reconstruct some of these connections in a certain amount of detail.

As the circumstances of Peacock's personal and professional life suggest, there was a complex and extensive network of social relationships linking the philosophic radicals and the Hunt circle. Some of these connections, it must be admitted, were clearly sources of tension and resentment: Bentham was forced to resort to legal threats against his impecunious tenant, William Hazlitt; while Francis Place, who was Bentham's most important link with the world of London radicalism, seems to have taken an instant dislike to Shelley's aristocratic manners.[79] But there were also many more convivial encounters between Bentham's Westminster coterie and Hunt's circle of literary acquaintance. Walter Coulson, for example, who served at one time as Bentham's amanuensis, went on to become a frequent dining companion of Hunt, Lamb, and the Shelleys, as well as godfather to Hazlitt's son. Byron's close friend, John Cam Hobhouse, was also a leading philosophic radical, and an important mediator between Byron and the Benthamite Greek Committee (a draft of Bentham's *Constitutional Code* accompanied Stanhope and Byron on their ill-fated expedition to Greece).[80] Hazlitt was friendly with the young Benthamite Joseph Parkes; while Godwin, Hunt, and

[79] Jeremy Bentham, *Correspondence*, ed. Stephen Conway *et al.*, 11 vols. so far (London and Oxford, 1968–), ix. 113; Claire Clairmont *et al.*, *The Clairmont Correspondence: Letters of Claire Clairmont, Charles Clairmont, and Fanny Imlay Godwin*, ed. Marion Kingston Stocking, 2 vols. (Baltimore, 1995), i. 22 n.

[80] See F. Rosen, *Bentham, Byron, and Greece: Constitutionalism, Nationalism and Early Liberal Political Thought* (Oxford, 1992). Rosen decisively rejects the 'myth of the opposition between Bentham . . . and Byron' (p. 10).

Shelley all knew Bentham's friend, Basil Montagu, the lawyer and social reformer.

Most importantly, however, Hunt himself became an ardent supporter of the philosophic radical cause after Bentham visited him before his trial for libelling the Prince Regent in 1812, and then again during his subsequent imprisonment.[81] Bentham's concern at the government's open contempt for the freedom of the press had already inspired him to express his solidarity with the political victims of the libel laws in his *Elements of the Art of Packing*. But Bentham also had another motive for seeking Hunt's friendship. As he wrote in 1812, the *Examiner* was the newspaper that, 'especially among the high political men, is the most in vogue. It sells already between 7,000 and 8,000 . . . The editor . . . Hunt, has taken me under his protection, and trumpets me every now and then in his paper . . .'. These remarks should not, however, be taken to imply that Hunt had the upper hand in their relationship. Bentham was a figure of reputation and influence, even in 1812, and Hunt was equally anxious to secure his support, particularly after the *Examiner* gradually began to shed its readership (the paper's circulation fell by more than two-thirds in the decade leading up to 1821).[82] Within a few years of his conversion to the reformist cause, and his first meeting with Hunt, Bentham had established important links with London popular radicalism as well as the Whig party establishment. In 1817 his *Plan of Parliamentary Reform* was circulated to a number of Members of Parliament, and the following year he formed an alliance with Sir Francis Burdett, which led to the introduction of Bentham's *Resolutions on Parliamentary Reform* into the House of Commons itself.[83] The *Plan* was quickly reprinted in a popularized form by the radical journalist Thomas Wooler, and before long Bentham's *Radical Reform Bill* and censorial jurisprudence were being singled out for praise by leading popular reformist periodicals.[84] Meanwhile, despite a certain impatience with the obscurities of his style, the *Examiner* continued to 'trumpet' Bentham, 'this venerable philosopher and patriot, this friend of

[81] Bentham, *Correspondence*, viii. 256–9; Leigh Hunt, *Autobiography*, 3 vols. (1850), ii. 155.

[82] Bentham, *Correspondence*, viii. 252; Philip Harling, 'Leigh Hunt's *Examiner* and the Language of Patriotism', *Historical Journal*, 61 (1996), 1160.

[83] Elie Halévy, *The Growth of Philosophic Radicalism*, trans. Mary Morris (1928), 261–2; William Thomas, *The Philosophic Radicals: Nine Studies in Theory and Practice 1817–1841* (Oxford, 1979), 41–2.

[84] See, e.g. *Hone's Reformists' Register*, 1 (17 May 1817), 518; *Medusa; or, Penny Politician*, 1 (6 Mar. 1819), 22; *Black Dwarf*, 4 (24 May 1820), 706–7; ibid. (2 May 1820), 625.

the human race, this distinguished and pure and amiable member of society'.[85] The paper was certainly not troubled by the ideological tensions between its popular constitutionalism and Bentham's professed hostility to common law. Indeed, Hunt was no different in this respect from other leading reformers such as John Wade, Thomas Wooler, and John Cartwright, all of whom managed to reconcile their declared respect for Bentham with a commitment to constitutionalist discourse.[86]

Early in 1817, Shelley took a house in Marlow, near Windsor—a move that coincided with his publication of two political pamphlets, *A Proposal for Putting Reform to the Vote* and *An Address to the People on the Death of Princess Charlotte.* In both of these works Shelley adopted the pseudonym 'The Hermit of Marlow', a clear signal of his self-conscious desire to influence political events from an intellectual and geographical distance. 'I am undec[e]ived in the belief that I have powers deeply to interest, or substantially to improve, mankind,' he wrote to Hunt in December 1816. 'How far my conduct and my opinions have rendered the zeal & ardour with which I have engaged in the attempt, ineffectual, I know not. . . . But thus much I do not seek to conceal from myself, that I am an outcast from human society . . .'[87] It was this combination of self-importance, missionary zeal, and a keen sense of persecution that led Shelley to adopt the 'Hermit of Marlow' persona. In doing so, however, he also associated himself with an Enlightenment veneration for the isolated *philosophe* as a figure whose solitary lucubrations might contribute, in an indirect but profound manner, to the universal improvement of humanity. The exaltation of private intellection into a form of political activism seemed briefly to have been realized by Godwin in the 1790s, and it was an ideal to which Shelley himself increasingly aspired. His 1817 poem *Laon and Cythna* incorporated a 'Hermit old' who, addressing the poem's revolutionary hero, celebrates the inspirational political power of philosophical truth:

Yes, from the records of my youthful state,
  And from the lore of bards and sages old,
From whatso'er my wakened thoughts create
  Out of the hopes of thine aspirings bold,
  Have I collected language to unfold

[85] *Examiner* (6 Aug. 1820), 499. Modern commentators have often seemed a little apologetic about Hunt's veneration of Bentham. See e.g. Louis Landré, *Leigh Hunt (1784–1859): Contribution à l'histoire du Romantisme anglais*, 2 vols. (Paris, 1935–6), ii. 73–4.

[86] Gilmartin, *Print Politics*, 58–9.

[87] Shelley, *Letters*, i. 517 (8 Dec. 1816).

Truth to my countrymen; from shore to shore
Doctrines of human power my words have told,
They have been heard, and men aspire to more
Than they have ever gained or ever lost of yore.[88]

The *Quarterly Review* correctly identified the aged 'Hermit' of *Laon and Cythna* as an allusion to William Godwin's sympathies for the ideals of French Revolution.[89] However, in the changed political milieu of post-war England, it was Jeremy Bentham who most successfully embodied the type of radical intellectual that Godwin had once represented. Throughout this period, Bentham's writings and ideas were disseminated through a widening circle of devoted 'disciples' and influential admirers, recalling the manner in which Godwin's utopian philosophy had captured the imagination of the radical intelligentsia in the aftermath of the French Revolution.[90] And this might suggest a further significance to Shelley's decision to style himself 'The Hermit of Marlow' in his 1817 pamphlets, since the list of intended recipients for his *Proposal* included a number of Bentham's acquaintances and associates (including Place, Burdett, Lord Holland, Brougham, and Douglas Kinnaird).[91] All of these men would have recognized a parallel between the 'Hermit of Marlow' and Bentham's own, well-known sobriquet, the 'Hermit of Westminster'. Leigh Hunt, who received copies of both Shelley's *Proposal*, and Bentham's *Plan*, would certainly have been struck by this connection, having made much of his impending visit to Bentham's 'hermitage' in his correspondence of 1812.[92]

Shelley's growing respect for Bentham can only have been heightened by the latter's 'rabid anti-clericalism', a temperamental and intellectual disposition which closely conformed to Shelley's own tendencies on religious matters.[93] These affinities became much more significant two years later, in 1819, when the reform movement was dealt a severe blow by the trial and imprisonment for blasphemous libel of Richard Carlile, the leading radical freethinker in the country. The trial attracted the attention of both Bentham and Place, and followed hard on Bentham's publication of *Church-of-Englandism*, a strident attack on the Anglican Establishment which he insisted on distributing against the legal advice

[88] Shelley, *Complete Works*, i. 300.

[89] *Quarterly Review*, 21 (Apr. 1819), 468; Dawson, *Unacknowledged Legislator*, 71.

[90] S. E. Finer, 'The Transmission of Benthamite Ideas, 1820–50', in Gillian Sutherland (ed.), *Studies in the Growth of Nineteenth-Century Government* (1972), 11–32.

[91] Shelley, *Letters*, i. 532–4 (Feb. 1817).

[92] Hone, *For the Cause of Truth*, 275–6; Bentham, *Correspondence*, viii. 258.

[93] Halévy, *Philosophic Radicalism*, 295; see also Hunt, *Autobiography*, ii. 194.

of his friend Samuel Romilly.[94] A copy of the book certainly found its way to the *Examiner*, which was fulsome in its praise for this latest production of the 'venerable Reformist'. These circumstances give an additional importance to Shelley's championing of Bentham's religious opinions in a public letter to the *Examiner* on Carlile's trial. 'Is not Mr. Bentham a Deist?' he wrote approvingly to Hunt. 'What men of any rank in society from their talents are *not* Deists whose understandings have been unbiased by the allurements of worldly interest?'[95] Carlile certainly recognized the intellectual kinship between Shelley's free thought and Benthamite radicalism, since he went on to publish pirated editions of both *Queen Mab* (Shelley's youthful poetic attack on 'Kingcraft and Priestcraft'), and Bentham's *Analysis of the Influence of Natural Religion*.[96]

Six months after the Carlile trial, in May 1820, Shelley wrote to Hunt asking whether 'you know any bookseller who w[oul]d publish for me an octavo volume entitled "A philosophical View of Reform". It is boldly but temperately written—& I think readable—It is intended for a kind of standard book for the philosophical reformers politically considered, like Jeremy Bentham's something, but different & perhaps more systematic.' Shelley's 'volume', although unfinished, has long been recognized as the single most important statement of his political philosophy, and Bentham's *Plan of Parliamentary Reform* has generally been acknowledged as the 'something' upon which it was modelled. [97] But the extent of Bentham's influence upon the *Philosophical View of Reform* is still consis-

[94] Joel H. Wiener, *Radicalism and Freethought in Nineteenth Century Britain: The Life of Richard Carlile* (Westport, Lown., 1983), 45; James E. Crimmins, *Secular Utilitarianism: Social Science and the Critique of Religion in the Thought of Jeremy Bentham* (Oxford, 1990), 154, 163.

[95] *Examiner* (4 Apr. 1819), 210; Shelley, *Letters*, ii. 143 (3 Nov. 1819). Shelley also singled out Romilly as a 'professed Unitarian' (ii. 140), an observation that is made rather more piquant by the fact that, two years before, Romilly had been retained as legal counsel for John Westbrook (Shelley's first father-in-law) and instructed to argue that Percy should be denied guardianship of his children on the grounds of his Deistical principles. See also *Examiner* (2 Feb. 1817), 75.

[96] Richard Holmes, *Shelley: The Pursuit* (1974), 209; [Jeremy Bentham], *Analysis of the Influence of Natural Religion on the Temporal Happiness of Mankind*, ed. 'Philip Beauchamp' [George Grote] (1822). Carlile also published extracts from Bentham's *Church-of-Englandism* under the title *Mother Church Relieved by Bleeding* (1823), which was itself republished two years later by John and Leigh Hunt.

[97] Shelley, *Letters*, ii. 201 (26 May 1820); see Kenneth Neill Cameron, *Shelley: The Golden Years* (Cambridge, Mass., 1974), 149; James Chandler, *England in 1819: The Politics of Literary Culture and the Case of Romantic Historicism* (Chicago, 1998), 186–94, 231; Terence Allan Hoagwood, *Skepticism and Ideology: Shelley's Political Prose and its Philosophical Context from Bacon to Marx* (Iowa City, 1988), 167–209.

tently underestimated, largely because of the assumption that Shelley must have regarded Bentham as an 'anti-agrarian' proponent of industrial society, whose bourgeois class interests were fundamentally irreconcilable with Shelley's own, visionary brand of aristocratic agrarianism.[98] Yet, far from identifying philosophic radicalism with industrialization and the iniquities of capitalist society, the *Philosophical View* suggests that, at least in 1820, Shelley considered Bentham's philosophy to offer an important corrective to economic inequality and the spirit of commerce.

The first section of the *Philosophical View* contrasts the 'mechanical sciences', not with poetry but with 'the labours of the political philosophers'. It was the rapid rise of the former which, according to Shelley, had given a disproportionate influence to the commercial interest:

> Commerce was pursued with a perpetually increasing vigour, and the same area of the Earth was perpetually compelled to furnish more and more subsistence. The means and sources of knowledge were thus increased together with knowledge itself, and the instruments of knowledge. The benefit of this increase of the powers of man became, in consequence of the inartificial forms into which society came to be distributed, an instrument of his additional evil. . . . Modern society is thus a[n] engine assumed to be for useful purposes, whose force is by a system of subtle mechanism augmented to the highest pitch, but which, instead of grinding corn or raising water[,] acts against itself and is perpetually wearing away or breaking to pieces the wheels of which it is composed.

The novelty of this agrarian critique of commerce and manufacturing lies in the way in which Shelley transposes the deleterious consequences of unchecked mechanization to the higher, metaphorical level of society itself. The *Philosophical View* goes on, however, to suggest that the 'subtle mechanism' of modern society looks set to be restored to its true workings by the 'political philosophers', whose labours have resulted in

> the establishment of the principle of utility as the substance, and liberty and equality as the forms according to which the concerns of human life ought to be administered. By this test the various institutions regulating political society have been tried . . . And many new theories, more or less perfect, but all superior to the mass of evil which they would supplant, have been given to the world.[99]

[98] Michael Henry Scrivener, *Radical Shelley: The Philosophical Anarchism and Utopian Thought of Percy Bysshe Shelley* (Princeton, 1982), 131, 105; Donald H. Reiman, 'Shelley as Agrarian Reactionary', *Keats–Shelley Memorial Bulletin*, 30 (1979), 5–15.

[99] Shelley, *Complete Works*, vii. 10.

Shelley clearly considered the 'principle of utility' to offer an ideological corrective to economic inequality and commercial overbalance, and this suggests why he also chose to identify 'Godwin and Bentham' as the pre-eminent 'political philosophers of our own age'. Shelley regarded both men as utilitarians and political reformers in a high Enlightenment tradition, whose philosophical insights promised to correct the delicate 'mechanism' of society, restoring it to the cause of 'liberty and equality'. At this point, then, Shelley seems to have primarily regarded Bentham (with some justification) as a political radical, legal reformer, and religious freethinker, rather than an anti-agrarian apologist for commerce and manufactures; and it was therefore entirely unproblematic for him to link Godwin and Bentham together as the leading intellects of the age. There is certainly no suggestion in the *Philosophical View* that Shelley associates Bentham either with the French *philosophes* (whom he accuses of 'limitedness of view') or with the 'exact and intelligible but superficial school' of Locke.[100]

Shelley did have several clear points of difference from Bentham on the practical details of reform. Indeed, the third section of the *Philosophical View* explicitly takes issue with 'Mr. Bentham and other writers [who] have urged the admission of females to the right of suffrage', and goes on to argue against voting by ballot—a central proposal of Bentham's *Plan*.[101] Yet Shelley also clearly favoured a practical political collaboration between Bentham, Godwin, and the Hunt circle:

> The poets, philosophers and artists ought to remonstrate [to the government], and the memorials entitled their petitions might show the diversit[y] [of] convictions they entertain of the inevitable connection between national prosperity and freedom, and the cultivation of the imagination and the cultivation of scientific truth, and the profound development of moral and metaphysical enquiry. Suppose these memorials to be severally written by Godwin, Hazlitt, Bentham, and Hunt, they would be worthy of the age and of the cause; these, radiant and irresistible like the meridian sun would strike all but the eagles who dared to gaze upon its beams, with blindness and confusion.[102]

On basic questions of political philosophy there were also rather fewer manifest differences between Shelley and Bentham than is sometimes supposed, at least with reference to those of Bentham's works with which Shelley was familiar. Of course, Bentham was far more sceptical

[100] Shelley, *Complete Works*, vii. 8–9.
[101] Ibid. vii. 44.
[102] Ibid. vii. 52.

about the power of benevolent sympathy than either Godwin or Shelley. But, on the other hand, a cancelled passage in the *Philosophical View* does concede that,

According to the principles of human nature as modified by the existing opinions and institutions of society a man loves himself with an overweaning love. The generous emotions of disinterested affection which the records of human nature and our experience teach us that the human heart is highly susceptible of are confined within the narrow circle of our kindred and friends.[103]

Much the same point had been made in Bentham's *Traités de législation civile et pénale*, which Shelley had read in 1814, and which also stressed the need for the wise legislator to cultivate the faculty of sympathy amongst the people. Through the exercise of sympathy, Bentham remarked, the 'individual acquires more extension; he ceases to be solitary; he becomes collective. We see ourselves, so to speak, doubled in those we love.'[104]

There was, however, one fundamental issue upon which Bentham clearly diverged from both Shelley and Godwin, since as Michael Scrivener has pointed out, Bentham's principal perspective was that of the legislative reformer, while Godwin's philosophical anarchism sought to collapse all public law into a fluid and enlightened form of regulative 'opinion'.[105] As we have seen, Bentham did give a central place to the 'moral sanction' of public opinion as an important tool of the 'indirect legislator'. Nevertheless, the methodological focus of his work remained centred upon legislative codification and, to that extent, was irreconcilable with Godwinian anarchism. Manuscript fragments associated with the *Philosophical View* suggest that Shelley recognized the need to distinguish some sense of the 'Constitution', as a collection of 'written institutions or traditions', from the 'Law', considered as a set of quasi-Godwinian 'opinions or moral principles'.[106] Likewise, in the *Philosophical View* itself, Shelley attempted to reconcile his commitment to the cause of constitutional reform with a more strictly Godwinian identification of political amelioration with the progressive enlightenment of intellect and opinion. If the former aspiration aligned him with the concrete legislative proposals of Bentham's *Plan*, then the latter,

[103] Percy Bysshe Shelley *et al.*, *Shelley and his Circle, 1773–1822*, ed. Kenneth Neill Cameron and Donald H. Reiman, 8 vols. (Cambridge, Mass., 1961–86), vi. 994.

[104] Bentham, *Theory of Legislation*, 36; Shelley, *Letters*, i. 384.

[105] Scrivener, *Radical Shelley*, 15; Dawson, *Unacknowledged Legislator*, 104–5.

[106] Shelley, *Complete Works*, vi. 289.

Godwinian emphasis upon the historical progress of public opinion reflected the more gradualist component of Shelley's politics, and allowed him to give imaginative literature a central place in the reformist cause, by identifying 'poetry' as the most important vehicle for the enlightenment of opinion. It is this latter position that lies behind the most celebrated passage in the *Philosophical View*, a passage which Shelley later used (in a slightly modified form) to conclude the *Defence of Poetry*:

> For the most unfailing herald, or companion, or follower, of an universal employment of the sentiments of a nation to the production of beneficial change is poetry, meaning by poetry an intense and impassioned power of communicating intense and impassioned impressions respecting man and nature. . . . It is impossible to read the productions of our most celebrated writers, whatever may be their system relating to thought or expression, without being startled by the electric life which there is in their words. They measure the circumference or sound the depths of human nature with a comprehensive and all-penetrating spirit at which they are themselves perhaps most sincerely astonished, for it [is] less their own spirit than the spirit of their age. They are the priests of an unapprehended inspiration, the mirrors of gigantic shadows which futurity casts upon the present; the words which express what they conceive not; the trumpet which sings to battle and feels not what it inspires; the influence which is moved not but moves. Poets and philosophers are the unacknowledged legislators of the world.[107]

The famous final line of this quotation has been traced to analogous statements in Samuel Johnson's *Rasselas* and Godwin's *Life of Chaucer*.[108] But it actually has a far more immediate—and literal—reference to Shelley's attempts to reconcile his literary reformism with Benthamite jurisprudence in the *Philosophical View*.

In 1819 Bentham was well known not just for his *Plan of Parliamentary Reform*, but also for his *Traités* on civil and penal legislation, and his *Papers Relative to Codification and Public Instruction*, a collection of his correspondence with a number of American politicians, the Russian Emperor and Prince Adam Czartoryski of Poland, in which Bentham offered to draw up codes of law for their respective nations.[109] His legislative proposals had so far proved singularly unsuccessful. However,

[107] Shelley, *Complete Works*, vii. 19–20.

[108] Dawson, *Unacknowledged Legislator*, 218; Cameron, *Shelley*, 207.

[109] Jeremy Bentham, *Papers Relative to Codification and Public Instruction* (1817), in id., *'Legislator of the World': Writings on Codification, Law and Education*, ed. Philip Schofield and Jonathan Harris (Oxford, 1998). Bentham received 'el titulo glorioso de legislador

the *Codification Papers* clarified the extent of Bentham's ambitions as a constitutional and political philosopher, and publicly revealed his communications with reformist politicians around the world (including some of the same territories that Shelley went on to discuss in the first section of the *Philosophical View*, in his own global survey of the effects of the 'new philosophy' of utility). It is uncertain whether Shelley got a chance to study the *Codification Papers* before he left England in March 1818. But he is very likely to have seen not only Walter Coulson's two-part review in the *Examiner*, but also Samuel Romilly's discussion in the *Edinburgh*. Romilly expressed the usual reservations about Bentham's style, yet also noted that 'the present publication contains some of the most important views on the subject of Legislation . . . that have ever yet been laid before the public', identified Bentham as a 'citizen of the world in the purest sense', and claimed that, 'if not to his contemporaries, yet to remoter ages, and yet uncivilized nations, he will be a Teacher and a Legislator'.[110]

Shelley's *Philosophical View* should in fact be viewed as a contribution to a larger debate within the Hunt circle, sparked by Bentham's growing influence as a legislator and a radical, and centred on the relationship between the literary culture of poetry and the practicalities of political and constitutional reform. William Hazlitt had already expressed his views on this issue in Hunt's new periodical, the *Yellow Dwarf*, in January 1818. Beginning with a familiar, ritual scolding of the Lake school for abandoning their 'former well-timed enthusiasm against tyrants and conquerors', Hazlitt went on to observe that this 'sort of shuffling on the side of principle, and tenaciousness on the side of power, seems to be the peculiar privilege of the race of modern poets. The philosophers, if not much wiser, appear to be honester. Some of these had been taken in, but they want to be let out.' It soon becomes apparent that Hazlitt is referring to Bentham, whose *Codification Papers* had exposed his misguided assumption that an autocrat like Emperor Alexander might institute a programme of constitutional reform. Yet, in pointed contrast to the Lake poets, Bentham realized his mistake, and 'could not brook this league with detected hypocrisy and barefaced

del mundo' in 1826, from Jose del Valle, the Central American lawyer, economist, and politician (ibid. 370).

110 See *Examiner* (12 Oct. 1817); ibid. (19 Oct., 1817); Bentham, *Correspondence*, ix. 95; [Samuel Romilly], 'Bentham on Codification', *Edinburgh Review*, 29 (Nov. 1817), 217–37.

power. . . . That is, Mr. Bentham had not, like Messrs. Coleridge, Wordsworth, and Southey, been playing at fast and loose with fiction . . . .'[111] This sympathetic comparison of Bentham's political integrity with the treachery of the Lake school appeared in the same month as Hazlitt's *Lectures on the English Poets*, suggesting a pointed political subtext to his declaration, in the first lecture, that 'the progress of knowledge and refinement has a tendency to circumscribe the limits of the imagination, and to clip the wings of poetry'.[112] At this point, then, Hazlitt's defence of Bentham against the apostasies of the Lake poets seems to broaden out into a sceptical interrogation of the ideological burden of 'poetry' itself. 'The spirit of poetry is in itself favourable to humanity and liberty,' he wrote in the *Examiner* in December 1816, 'but, we suspect, not in times like these . . . Poetry dwells in a perpetual Utopia of its own, and is, for that reason, very ill calculated to make a Paradise upon earth . . . Poetry, like law, is a fiction; only a more agreeable one.'[113] Hazlitt's repeated references to 'fiction' in this context, and their association with the discourse of law, seem like a quite direct allusion to Bentham's devastating critique of the 'pestilential breath of fiction' pervading the English legal system, and suggest that, at least in the late 1810s, Hazlitt was prepared to concede both the political expediency of Bentham's jurisprudential radicalism, and the corresponding practical redundancy of 'poetic' utopianism.[114]

The *Examiner*'s 1820 review of *Bentham's Radical Reform Bill* also registered a certain anxiety concerning the relationship between political reform and poetic culture and, like Hazlitt, sought to justify rather than condemn Bentham's aversion to imaginative fiction:

Every successive publication of our venerable Author is an additional monument to his reputation,—a further display of that acuteness and grasp of intellect, which constitutes his excellence. . . . Mr. Bentham's, in short, is the genius of a legislator, whose greatest merit consists in the extent and completeness of his designs. Imagination and Fancy are not legislative qualities: they appear to be inconsistent with the more practical talents. Perhaps the same mind cannot

[111] [William Hazlitt], 'The Press—Coleridge, Southey, Wordsworth, and Bentham', *Yellow Dwarf*, 1 (3 Jan. 1818), 4–5.

[112] William Hazlitt, *Lectures on the English Poets* (1818), 18. In *Table-Talk* (p. 360) Hazlitt makes a similar contrast between the political consistency of Bentham and Godwin, and the apostasy of the Lakers.

[113] [Hazlitt], 'Illustrations of the Times Newspaper', *Examiner* (22 Dec. 1816), 802.

[114] Jeremy Bentham, *A Comment on the Commentaries* and *A Fragment on Government*, ed. J. H. Burns and H. L. A. Hart (1977), 411 n.

possess powers so distinct, to any great degree at least, and the combination might reduce each species of intellect into mediocrity.[115]

Bentham's growing influence clearly provoked the Hunt circle to some uneasy reflections on the 'practical', legislative efficacy of imaginative literature—an understandable anxiety, given the rapid penetration of Benthamite ideas into the popular reform movement, and the threatened marginalization of the Hunt circle's more literary orientation. Despite his apparent faith in the poet as an 'unacknowledged legislator', Shelley himself registered a very similar concern in his confession to Peacock that 'I consider Poetry very subordinate to moral & political science, & if I were well, certainly I should aspire to the latter . . .'.[116] Much, certainly, can be made of utilitarian 'philistinism' as a source of tension between the philosophic radicals and the *Examiner* group. But Bentham's notorious lack of interest in the literary preoccupations of Hunt's society seems only to have been problematic in this respect to the extent that it highlighted doubts within the Hunt circle itself concerning the adequacy of the poetic imagination as a vehicle of political reform.[117]

It was against this background that Peacock composed *The Four Ages of Poetry*, which can now be recognized as an attempt to force these issues into the open by representing some of the implications of the utilitarian distrust of imaginative 'fiction' in the most extreme terms. Peacock's argument seems to have been partly indebted to Robert Forsyth's *Principles of Moral Science* (1805), but a more topical point of reference was provided by James Mill's recently published *History of British India* (1817).[118] 'The first literature is poetry,' Mill had argued in the *History*. 'Poetry is the language of the passions, and men feel before they speculate.' He went on, as we have seen, to identify the poetic imagination with oral culture, in contrast to the textualized and analytical thought typical of more advanced nations. The bardic tradition, including 'the literature of the Hindus' as well as Homer and Ossian, thus represented the primordial point of departure for Mill's hierarchical history of literary civilization.[119]

115 *Examiner* (2 Jan. 1820), 12.

116 Shelley, *Letters*, ii. 71 (23–4 Jan. 1819).

117 Cf. Andrew Hemingway, 'Genius, Gender and Progress: Benthamism and the Arts in the 1820s', *Art History*, 16 (1992), 619–46.

118 Butler, *Peacock Displayed*, 286–7; Majeed, *Ungoverned Imaginings*, 165.

119 Mill, *History of British India*, i. 362–70.

Peacock's semi-parodic version of Mill's stadial historiography postulated four successive 'ages' of literary accomplishment and decline. Since mankind had now entered the final age, the contemporary eclipse of poetry by 'useful' knowledge was not just a temporary aberration, justified by the practical exigencies of political and social change, but rather a further, inevitable staging post in the progressive history of civilization itself. As 'the sciences of morals and of mind advance towards perfection,' Peacock argued, 'as they become more enlarged and comprehensive in their views, as reason gains the ascendancy in them over imagination and feeling, poetry can no longer accompany them in their progress, but drops into the background, and leaves them to advance alone'.[120]

It was this incisive and witty polemic that provoked Shelley to question his previous belief, announced in the *Philosophical View*, that Benthamite politics and philosophy was entirely compatible with the literary sensibilities of writers such as Godwin, Hazlitt, and Hunt. Although he discreetly avoided actually naming Bentham in the *Defence*, Shelley's reply to the *Four Ages of Poetry* clearly involves a tacit critique of the philosophic radical party quite as severe as Peacock's own implicit aspersions on the 'progressive' pretensions of the *Examiner* group's literary reformism. Shelley thereby departed not just from his own previous attempts to reconcile Benthamite jurisprudence with Godwinian gradualism, but also from the Hunt circle's broadly sympathetic attitude to the Benthamite political programme. Whereas in the *Philosophical View* Shelley had represented Godwin and Bentham as the enlightened proponents of a single 'principle of utility', in the *Defence of Poetry* he chose to stress the qualitative differences between higher and lower forms of utility, in a manner that anticipates J. S. Mill's subsequent, critical modification of Benthamite philosophy. In the former, higher sense, according to Shelley,

> whatever strengthens and purifies the affections, enlarges the imagination, and adds spirit to sense, is useful. But the meaning in which the Author of The Four Ages of Poetry seems to have employed the word utility is the narrower one of banishing the importunity of the wants of our animal nature, the surrounding men with security of life, the dispersing the grosser delusions of superstition, and the conciliating such a degree of mutual forbearance among men as may consist with the motives of personal advantage.[121]

120 [Peacock], 'Four Ages', *Ollier's Literary Miscellany*, 1 (1820), 190.

121 Shelley, *Poetry and Prose*, 500–1.

Romilly's review of the *Codification Papers* had declared that, for Bentham, 'Utility is the foundation of all Morals, and should be the object of all Legislation: Not . . . that selfishness, which some moralists affect to understand as meant, by what is useful,—but *general* utility,—an augmentation of the happiness, and the diminution of the misery of the great mass of individuals of which every community is composed'.[122] This was certainly Shelley's view when he composed the *Philosophical View of Reform*, a judgement that had been borne out by the radical recommendations of the *Plan of Parliamentary Reform*, and the approbation with which they had been greeted by the popular reform movement. In the *Defence of Poetry*, however, Shelley chose to identify the 'durable, universal, and permanent' form of utility exclusively with the selfless pleasures of the poetic imagination. In doing so, he avoided an overt attack upon the philosophic radical party, while implicitly identifying Benthamite philosophy with that 'transitory and particular' form of utility which is concerned solely with 'the motives of personal advantage' dictated by 'the selfish and calculating principle'.[123]

This shift of emphasis probably also inspired Shelley to modify the nature of his economic critique. In the *Philosophical View*, he had condemned an economic system that sought to 'increase the labours of the poor and those luxuries of the rich which they supply', and that had turned 'children into lifeless and bloodless machines at an age when otherwise they would be at play before the cottage doors of their parents . . . .'[124] At this point, Shelley may well have been drawing upon Wordsworth's observations on industrialization, and the demise of the 'short holiday of childhood' in Book VIII of *The Excursion*.[125] But his analysis of the country's economic situation was much more closely linked to a radical critique of the paper money system, 'one of those execrable contrivances of misrule which overbalance the materials of common advantage produced by the progress of civilization . . . .'[126] Although Shelley's bullionist attitudes seem at times like a dim echo of Ricardo, he was primarily indebted in this respect to Cobbett's persistent attacks on the national debt and paper money in the *Political*

[122] [Romilly], 'Bentham on Codification', *Edinburgh Review*, 29 (Nov. 1817), 217.

[123] Shelley, *Poetry and Prose*, 500–3.

[124] Shelley, *Complete Works*, vii. 27.

[125] Wordsworth, *Poetical Works*, v. 274.

[126] Shelley, *Complete Works*, vii. 25.

Register.[127] For Shelley, as for Cobbett, the critique of paper money and the national debt was closely associated with an attack on Malthus, who had sought to excuse the depredations of the ruling classes by arguing 'that the evils of the poor arise from an excess of population', rather than taxation, paper money, and the national debt.[128]

Such an attack could hardly be extended to the Ricardian school, who were not only well known for their links with the philosophical radicals, but were also fierce defenders of monetary convertibility. In both these respects the Ricardians escaped the brunt of the anti-Malthusian diatribe against aristocratic government and paper money, and this may help to explain why, in the *Defence of Poetry*, Shelley abandoned his earlier analysis in favour of a much more expansive identification between economic discourse as a whole and the 'selfish and calculating principle' of the vulgar utilitarian: 'Whilst the mechanist abridges, and the political œconomist combines, labour, let them beware that their speculations, for want of correspondence with those first principles which belong to the imagination, do not tend, as they have in modern England, to exasperate at once the extremes of luxury and want.'[129] It was the mere exercise of calculating 'speculation' that was now identified as the root cause of economic inequality, as Shelley sought to privilege the poetic imagination by opposing it to all forms of 'mechanical' and 'calculating' discourse, including by implication both Benthamite utilitarianism and Ricardian economics.

It is, however, still worth remembering that, while the *Defence of Poetry* undoubtedly incorporated an important critique of Benthamite utilitarianism, it was largely provoked by a desire to respond in kind to Peacock's overstated polemic in *The Four Ages of Poetry*. There is certainly little justification for regarding the *Defence* as a representative statement of Shelley's attitudes to the philosophic radicals, still less of second-generation 'Romantic' sensibilities in general. Indeed, Shelley's largely accommodatory attitude to Benthamite politics and jurisprudence exemplifies the fluidity of the ideological relationship between the Benthamites and the Hunt school in the years following Waterloo. Even Hazlitt, who tends to be thought of as an unqualified critic of Bentham, conspicuously avoided such an attack until the mid-1820s.

[127] Jerrold E. Hogle, *Shelley's Process: Radical Transference and the Development of his Major Works* (New York, 1988), 236–8; Cameron, 'Shelley, Cobbett, and the National Debt'.

[128] Shelley, *Complete Works*, vii. 32.

[129] Shelley, *Poetry and Prose*, 501.

By that point, of course, Shelley, Keats, and Byron were dead, and Hunt's hopes of forging a truly effective journalistic synthesis of poetry and politics, which had already received a severe blow with the failure of the collaborative journal *The Liberal*, must have seemed all but extinguished.

Meanwhile, however, the influence of the Benthamite party upon popular radicalism and liberal Whiggism continued to make itself felt in a variety of contexts, from the Society for the Diffusion of Useful Knowledge and the mechanics' institutes movement, to radical economics and 'zetetic' free thought—developments which threatened to leave the Hunt circle, or what was left of it, as an isolated literary rump of metropolitan middle-class reformism.[130] Nor does it seem entirely credible to argue for the ideological significance of the *Examiner* group's 'Cockney' classicism by identifying it as the legitimate successor to an eighteenth-century tradition of dissenting radicalism. The Hunt circle did include such ambivalent scions of dissenting culture as Hazlitt and Keats. But it was philosophic radicalism that served as the principal haven for unitarian reformers between the rapid decline of rational dissent in the 1790s and its renaissance in the 1830s, attracting such prominent figures as William Frend, W. J. Fox, and Thomas Southwood Smith.[131]

All of which perhaps helps to explain why a somewhat embittered Hazlitt chose to launch his celebrated campaign against utilitarian radicalism in January 1824, with his portrait of 'Bentham' for the *New Monthly Magazine*, a piece that was subsequently reprinted as the first essay in *The Spirit of the Age*.[132] Much has been made of the long-standing philosophical convictions informing Hazlitt's benevolist, neo-Burkean critique of Bentham—convictions that can be traced right back to his defence of the faculty of sympathetic imagination in 1805.[133] But it is just as significant that Hazlitt should have refrained from publicly applying those principles to the Benthamite party until the last few years of his life, a decision which can only be explained by reference to

[130] Cf. Dart, *Rousseau, Robespierre and English Romanticism*, 212; and Cookson, *Friends of Peace*, 106–7, who warns that the *Examiner*'s political significance should not be overstated.

[131] John Seed, 'The Role of Unitarianism in the Formation of Liberal Culture 1775–1851: A Social History', University of Hull Ph.D. (1981), 334–6. Hazlitt himself identified the 'new school of reform' with rational dissent. See his *Plain Speaker: Opinions on Books, Men, and Things*, 2 vols. (1826), ii. 450.

[132] *New Monthly Magazine*, 10 (Jan. 1824), 68–76.

[133] See Park, *Hazlitt*, 43–76; Kinnaird, *William Hazlitt*, 124.

the strong links between the Hunt circle and the philosophic radicals before the mid-1820s, along with the waning influence of the *Examiner* group's literary reformism after this point. Hazlitt's attacks on the 'Ultra-Radicalism' of the new school are both vigorous and sustained, but they nevertheless betray the same acute sense of ideological isolation which is also registered in many of his later, 'familiar' essays.[134] This certainly bears on the difference in tone between his largely sympathetic piece on Bentham's *Codification Papers* in 1818, and his subsequent accusation, in 1826, that the Benthamites had conspired 'to strip the cause of Reform (out of seeming affection to it) of every thing like a *mis-alliance* with elegance, taste, decency, common sense, or polite literature'.[135] Such claims were all too easy to vindicate by reference to Bentham's own prose, 'a barbarous philosophical jargon' that reproduced at a stylistic level the spirit of mechanistic abstraction informing the utilitarian philosophy. The 'retrograde reformers' of the Westminster school might have claimed to be 'legislators for the world, and stewards to the intellectual inheritance of nations', but they were in fact misguided slaves to 'abstract reason' who had forced polite literature into an exclusive alignment with the forces of conservatism. 'They proceed by the rule and compass, and with none but demonstrable conclusions, and leave all the taste, fancy, and sentiment of the thing to the admirers of Mr. Burke's Reflections on the French Revolution.'[136]

It was also at this point that Hazlitt chose to extend his charge of mechanistic philistinism to the 'classical' economics of Ricardo, Mill, and McCulloch.[137] His 'Hints on Political Economy', published in the *Examiner* in 1826, purported to expose the logical fallacies vitiating Ricardian economics, in much the same spirit as the *Reply* to Malthus of twenty years before. Hazlitt did offer some concise criticisms on the subject of value and rent, employing a conventional distinction between productive and unproductive labour.[138] His primary objection to the Ricardian school, however, presupposed the fundamental incompatibility of economic discourse with the reformist cause that it claimed to

134 [Hazlitt], 'The New School of Reform', in *Plain Speaker*, i. 440.

135 Ibid. i. 440.

136 William Hazlitt, *Spirit of the Age*, 23; [id.], 'On People of Sense', in *Plain Speaker*, ii. 132, 135, 126.

137 [Hazlitt], 'The New School of Reform', in ibid. i. 446.

138 [Hazlitt], 'Hints on Political Economy', *Examiner* (24 Dec. 1826), 817–18; see also [id.], 'Queries Addressed to Political Economists', *Examiner* (9 Apr. 1826), 225–6; id., 'On the Effects of War and Taxes', *The Champion and Sunday Review* (31 Aug. 1817), 273–4.

serve. 'If it were a science,' he claimed, political economy 'must proceed on fixed and unalterable principles, and could be of no use; for the same mechanical causes must in all cases produce the same mechanical effects, and the world would go on as it has done, in spite of them and their discoveries'—a typically succinct, and somewhat distorting identification of economic 'science' with panglossian determinism. Despite their political sympathies with the philosophic radicals, the language of the Ricardians had 'too much resemblance to Mr. Malthus's "grinding law of necessity"' to be entirely trustworthy. 'Indeed,' he went on, 'I see no other tendency in many of these speculations but to turn political abuses into *philosophical fixtures*'. Hazlitt was repelled by Ricardo's acceptance of the Malthusian relationship between wages and population. Nevertheless, while Malthus himself remained clearly identified with the forces of reaction, Hazlitt continued to view the Ricardian school rather differently, as misguided reformists who had played the radical cause into the hands of tyrannical, 'legitimist' government. Contrary to Ricardo, Hazlitt maintained that the 'condition of the poor will not be ameliorated by making a *science* of the caprice, insolence, luxury, prejudices, and insensibility of the rich!'[139]

Hazlitt's *Plain Speaker* (1826) includes a philosophical dialogue on 'The New School of Reform', at the end of which the author's imaginary utilitarian interlocutor remarks dismissively that 'The poets have spoiled you for all rational and sober views of society'. Reading Hazlitt's later essays, it is certainly tempting to see the literary reformism of the Hunt circle as a heroic last stand on the part of a cultured, literary radicalism, in the face of an aggressively philistine version of bourgeois ideology that was already well on its way to becoming 'the working creed of industrialisation, an inalienable part of the middle-class mind'.[140] Yet such a conclusion would misrepresent both the *Examiner* group, and the Benthamite 'new school of reform'. The former, as we have seen, was considerably more receptive to the philosophic radical cause than Hazlitt's later essays might suggest. Leigh Hunt certainly responded coolly to Hazlitt's attack on the 'eminent and venerable' Bentham, and persevered in his belief that the apparent estrangement of 'literature' and 'science' was a temporary

[139] *Examiner* (24 Dec. 1826), 817. See also *Examiner* (9 Apr. 1826), 225; Hazlitt, *Spirit of the Age*, 249; [id.], *Plain Speaker*, i. 461–2.

[140] Ibid. i. 465; Butler, *Peacock Displayed*, 187.

by-product of the ongoing reform crisis.[141] As he wrote in 1825, in a piece on 'Fiction and Matter-of-Fact',

> It is, in fact, remarkable, that the growth of science, and the reappearance of a more poetical kind of poetry, have accompanied one another. . . . How is it, that the poetical impulse has taken this turn in a generation described to be so mathematical? Whence has arisen among us this exceeding fondness for the fictions of the East, for solitary and fanciful reveries, for the wild taste of the Germans . . . and even for a new and more primitive use of the old Pagan Mythology . . . Politics may be thought a very unlikely cause of poetry, and it is so with Ministers and Gazeteers; yet politics, pushed further than common, have been the cause of the new and greater impetus given to the sympathies of the imagination . . .

According to Hunt, as politics had become more and more scientific, so, paradoxically, had it led to a complementary resurgence of the poetic imagination.[142] Hunt probably considered himself vindicated in this claim in the following years, as the *Westminster Review* opened its pages to literary reviewers such as F. D. Maurice and W. J. Fox, while a second generation of philosophic radicals, including Edward Lytton Bulwer and John Stuart Mill, reasserted the compatibility of utilitarian reform with the cause of imaginative literature.[143]

John and Leigh Hunt sold the *Examiner* in 1828, and editorial control passed to one of Leigh's protégés, Albany Fonblanque, who oversaw the paper's transformation into an openly avowed organ of the philosophic radicals. But Fonblanque also preserved the literary classicism of Hunt's *Examiner*, fused with his own healthy enthusiasm for eighteenth-century English prose.[144] John Stuart Mill observed that, as a result, his writing was 'intelligible, or at least impressive, only to persons of literary, one might say almost *classical* education, & most of *them* are not radicals'—a reproach that, a few years earlier, might easily have been directed at Hunt himself, along with rest of the 'Cockney school'.[145] Nevertheless, Fonblanque was one of the most important journalistic spokesmen for

[141] *Examiner* (9 Jan. 1825), 21; [Hunt], 'Mr. Hazlitt and the Utilitarians', *Tatler* (28 Sept. 1830), 81–2.

[142] Ibid. (2 Jan. 1825), 3.

[143] See James Mulvihill, 'The Poetics of Utility: Benthamite Literary Reviewing, 1824–1836', *English Studies in Canada*, 15 (1989), 149–61.

[144] Thomas, *Philosophic Radicals*, 312–13.

[145] J. S. Mill to Thomas Carlyle (22 Dec. 1833), in *Collected Works*, ed. J. M. Robson *et al.*, 33 vols. (Toronto and London, 1981–1991), xii. 201; quoted in Thomas, *Philosophic Radicals*, 313.

the philosophic radical cause, most notably on the controversial, and genuinely popular, issue of the newspaper stamp tax.[146] Indeed, Mill himself was happy to use Fonblanque's *Examiner* as a platform for his own attempts to introduce an aesthetic sensibility into utilitarian politics. His series of articles on 'The Spirit of the Age', which appeared in the paper during 1831, sought to moderate between the Lake school's veneration of the 'wisdom of ancestors' and a progressive, Benthamite faith in 'the march of intellect'—a project which would soon lead him to the distinctly Shelleyan claim that, 'in an age of revolutions in opinion, the contemporary poets, those at least who deserve the name . . . if they are not before their age, are almost sure to be behind it'.[147] Mill's early writings on literature did not succeed in defusing the increasingly influential rhetorical opposition between imaginative 'poetry' and the calculating, utilitarian tendencies of 'science' and 'political economy'. But they do suggest that the ambivalent relationship between the Hunt circle and philosophic radicalism did not so much mark a lasting breach between middle-class philistinism and the anti-bourgeois allegiances of English literary culture, as prefigure the internal contradictions of nineteenth-century liberal ideology as a whole.

146 Ibid. 324–6.

147 [John Stuart Mill], 'The Spirit of the Age. No. 1', *Examiner* (9 Jan 1831), 20; [id.], 'The Two Kinds of Poetry', *Monthly Repository*, NS 7 (Nov. 1833), 723–4.

CHAPTER FIVE

Robert Southey and the Infections of Commerce

With a certain amount of hindsight, it is possible to view the rejection of Burdett's Catholic emancipation bill by the Lords in 1825, and the financial crash of the following winter, as having inaugurated the extended political crisis that culminated in Britain's constitutional revolution of 1828–32. The 1826 depression provoked both renewed calls for economic protectionism, and a hardening of high Tory prejudices concerning the radical affiliations of political economy. Exacerbating the ongoing dissension over the Catholic question, the impact of economic failure began to polarize conservative opinion, with the result that, in Boyd Hilton's words, '"free trade" was erected into a false symbol of the differences between traditionalists and the "enthusiastick philosophers" of modernity'.[1] By the latter half of the 1820s it would be neither credible nor desirable to yoke a belletristic literary conservatism to the analytical rigours of Ricardian science in the manner attempted by De Quincey in 1821.[2] As mainstream literary periodicals such as the *Quarterly Review* and *Monthly Magazine* shifted towards an Ultra Tory position, the shibboleths of free trade and political economy joined infidel radicalism, parliamentary reform, and Catholic emancipation as the ideological anathemas of a newly militant conservatism.[3]

Within the ranks of the Tory press, *Blackwood's Edinburgh Magazine* stands out as the most striking example of the transformation in

[1] Hilton, *Corn, Cash, Commerce*, 200; Berg, *Machinery Question*, 254–68; Barry Gordon, *Economic Doctrine and Tory Liberalism 1824–1830* (Basingstoke, 1979), 96.

[2] It is significant in this respect that De Quincey's later economic writings expressed some alarm at the way in which Ricardo's theory of rent seemed to reveal the exploitative nature of landed wealth, thereby justifying the anarchistic politics of 'anti-social jacobins': Thomas De Quincey, *The Logic of Political Economy* (Edinburgh, 1844), 193.

[3] Sack, *Jacobite to Conservative*, 181–3, 236.

conservative cultural politics that took place during this period.[4] Almost from its inception, in 1817, *Blackwood's* seemed audaciously assured of its claims to political and journalistic pre-eminence. But, while 'Maga' soon became one of the most influential periodicals in Britain, its spectacular (and often scandalous) rise owed much to the magazine's provocative manipulation of the idea of Scottish cultural provincialism, a strategy that further reinforced its profound temperamental differences from the staid cosmopolitanism of the *Edinburgh Review*. The terms of its campaign against the 'Cockney School', for example, cannot be fully understood without appreciating the way in which the magazine's alternately proud and playful attitude to its own provincial identity consistently informed its representation of Hunt's metropolitan poetic coterie as eccentric, upstart suburbanites.

Blackwood's ascendancy as one of the most successful literary periodicals of the 1820s began with the magazine expressing a broad sympathy with evangelical liberal Toryism. Despite maintaining a consistent support for the Corn Laws, it nevertheless defended a providential view of the market as a site for the divine reconciliation of individual self-interest, and largely accepted the 'principle of that entire freedom which distinguishes the liberal commercial policy of modern times'.[5] After 1825, however, the magazine's sympathies shifted away from the anti-poor law pieties of Thomas Chalmers, and towards the protectionist political economy of David Robinson.[6] *Maga's* growing distaste for free trade was accompanied by regular attacks on the government for its alleged thraldom to the dogmas of 'political economy' and the 'New System' of liberal Toryism.[7]

[4] Useful studies of *Blackwood's* include J. M. Milne, 'The Politics of *Blackwood's*, 1817–1846: A Study of the Political, Economic and Social Articles in *Blackwood's Edinburgh Magazine*, and of Selected Contributors', Newcastle University Ph.D. (1984); Peter T. Murphy, 'Impersonation and Authorship in Romantic Britain', *English Literary History*, 59 (1992), 625–49; Jon P. Klancher, *The Making of English Reading Audiences, 1790–1832* (Madison, 1987), 52–60.

[5] 'Mr. Russell', 'Reflections on the Theory of Population', *Blackwood's Edinburgh Magazine* (hereafter *Blackwood's*), 4 (Nov. 1818), 209; see also ibid. 4 (Oct. 1818), 58–9; 5 (May 1819), 171; 15 (June 1824), 653.

[6] Salim Rashid, 'David Robinson and the Tory Macroeconomics of *Blackwood's Edinburgh Magazine*', *History of Political Economy*, 10 (1978), 258–70; Frank Whitson Fetter, 'The Economic Articles in *Blackwood's Edinburgh Magazine*, and their Authors, 1817–1853', *Scottish Journal of Political Economy*, 7 (1960), 85–107. Both Rashid and Fetter underplay the economic views of the magazine before 1825. On Chalmers and the Poor Laws, see *Blackwood's*, 4 (Nov. 1818), 207–9; ibid. 6 (Oct. 1819), 18–20; ibid. 8 (Nov. 1820), 178–9.

[7] [David Robinson], 'Mr. Huskisson's Speech in Defence of Free Trade', *Blackwood's*, 19 (Apr. 1826), 474–88; [id.], 'The Meeting of Parliament', ibid. 20 (Dec. 1826), 859.

Even more striking, however, is the way in which this shift in the magazine's economic and political views was accompanied by a corresponding reorientation in its more literary preoccupations.

Before 1825, *Blackwood's* laid a great deal of stress on imaginative literature, and especially poetry, as a moderating influence on the sceptical, rationalist tendencies of a highly civilized commercial society. The combination of Lockhart's Schellingian idealism and John Wilson's civic idealization of individual and national 'character' led both writers to the conclusion that literary history formed the purest expression of the 'spirit of nationality', allowing the magazine's critical apotheoses of Scott, Wordsworth, and Burns at once to define a distinctly Scottish literary tradition, and to suggest the sublimation of that tradition into the canons of an all-embracing British national identity.[8] Imaginative literature, and especially poetry, was reimagined by *Blackwood's* as an index of national character and religious feeling, and frequently assimilated to an idealist defence of traditional or 'popular' culture considered as an expression of national *Geist*.[9] The renascent spirit of 'ancient literature' was consistently represented by the magazine as an effective counterbalance to the sceptical, cosmopolitan taste and 'metaphysical restlessness' accompanying the advent of print capitalism and the 'diffusion of knowledge' in socially and economically advanced nations.[10] Overturning the dominant Scottish intellectual tradition of 'common sense' empiricism, this distinctive, idealist reconception of literary nationalism was intended, at least in the early years of the magazine, to moderate the culturally enervating implications of economic modernity diagnosed by a previous generation of Scottish intellectuals. Commercial society could, it seemed to the *Blackwood's* critics, successfully maintain traditional patterns of social cohesion and habitual deference through a reawakening of the 'ancient spirit' of national literature.[11]

[8] [John Gibson Lockhart], 'Letters on the Present State of Germany', *Blackwood's*, 3 (Apr. 1818), 26.

[9] [John Wilson], 'On Campbell's Specimens of English Poetry', *Blackwood's*, 4 (Mar. 1819), 697; [John Gibson Lockhart], 'A Few Thoughts on Public Feeling', ibid. 3 (June 1818), 297.

[10] [John Gibson Lockhart], 'Remarks on Schlegel's History of Literature', ibid. 3 (Aug. 1818), 511; [Henry Matthews], 'Thoughts on the Present Political Aspect of the Times', ibid. 8 (Feb. 1821), 487. See also [Lockhart], *Peter's Letters*, ii. 348–63.

[11] 'Mr. Russell', 'On the Decline of a Taste for Metaphysics', *Blackwood's*, 4 (Mar. 1819), 682–7; [John Wilson], 'On the Revival of a Taste for our Ancient Literature', ibid. 4 (Dec. 1818), 266.

After the mid-1820s, however, the magazine's critical discussions of such matters placed a new emphasis on the necessity for a paternalistic and dispensatory form of popular education, rather than one which relied upon the 'liberal diffusion of ideas' through the expansion of commercial markets.[12] Where *Blackwood's* had previously celebrated the '*intellectualization*' of the nation under the moderating influence of poetic genius, now it warned of the dire political consequences that would flow from the hubristic 'intellectual self-confidence' of the lower orders if the leisured and powerful members of society neglected to act together as a paternalistic 'priesthood of knowledge'.[13] Spurred on by Ultra Protestant contributors such as George Croly, and despite the magazine's continued publication of poetry and prose fiction, *Blackwood's* increasingly extolled the virtues of devotional over imaginative literature as an agency of right feeling. Wilson's previous, Wordsworthian assertion that 'poetry is religion' no longer seemed an adequate response to the blasphemous outrages of a new breed of radical infidels, whose growing prominence must have done much to crystallize his doubts concerning the orthodoxy of *The Excursion*.[14] In his review of Aird's *Religious Characteristics*, in 1827, Wilson complained that, 'If we turn our attention away from the Sacred Profession, we shall not find that, in the present age, the current of thought runs strongly with men of genius towards religion.'[15] The necessity for 'moral and religious' educational content in all forms of literature was repeatedly urged by *Blackwood's* writers as a defence against the impending social anarchy threatened by the commercial spirit, which was now increasingly understood as a kind of universal solvent for 'old relations . . . local attachments . . . the close, daily, familiar, loving bond between the higher and lower'.[16]

Determined intervention in the public mind was rendered even more imperative by the secularizing tendencies of liberal educational publishing ventures, and in 1829 *Blackwood's* hailed the appearance of John Murray's *Family Library* as the 'first *Tory* series of cheap books', congratulating the publisher upon its 'salutary principles, moral, political,

[12] 'The Muses Welcome to St. James', *Blackwood's*, 10 (Aug. 1821, pt. 2), 83.

[13] 'Vindex', 'Rise, Progress, Decline, and Fall of the Edinburgh Review', *Blackwood's*, 10 (Dec. 1821), 677; [John Wilson], 'Education of the People', ibid. 27 (Jan. 1830), 1, 6.

[14] [John Wilson], 'On Mr Campbell's Specimens of English Poetry', *Blackwood's*, 4 (Mar. 1819), 697.

[15] [John Wilson], 'Aird's Religious Characteristics', *Blackwood's*, 21 (June 1827), 677.

[16] [John Wilson], 'Education of the People', *Blackwood's*, 27 (Jan. 1830), 9, 14.

and religious', and contrasting it with the mass publications of the Society for the Diffusion of Useful Knowledge, which concealed radical sympathies behind the façade of 'useful knowledge'.[17] The vitriolic character of the magazine's attacks on Henry Brougham, and utilitarian educational schemes more generally, found its counterpart in a growing enthusiasm for the work of the Bible Society.[18] This was closely linked to what *Maga* described as the 'Irish Question' and the perceived necessity for a large-scale programme of religious re-education amongst Irish Catholics.[19] While in 1822 *Blackwood's* had linked the invention of printing with the demise of the oral culture of the minstrelsy and the vitiation of a truly imaginative (and hence national) literature, by 1829 the notional emergence of print culture in the sixteenth century had been subsumed into a pan-European narrative of harmonious economic development and Protestant Reformation, in opposition to both godless radicalism and the idolatrous corruptions of Rome.[20]

The ideological realignment effected by *Blackwood's Magazine* during the 1820s shows very clearly how, from the middle of the decade, the political and ecclesiastical establishment considered itself under attack, not just from O'Connell's Catholic Association, but also from the forces of radical infidelism symbolized in the conservative press by publishers such as Carlile and Hone. As one, typically concerned clergyman declared in 1826,

> Never was there a period, in which the authority of the divine revelation was more daringly impugned, than in the present times. Infidelity no longer confines itself to the high places of the earth, or to the disdainful solitudes of the arrogant in intellectual superiority. It is penetrating the mass of society: it is entering the cottages of the poor, where it mingles poison in their cup, and ashes with their bread.[21]

But the example of *Blackwood's* also demonstrates how anxiety about the possible dangers posed by the 'diffusion of knowledge' to the interests

[17] [John Gibson Lockhart], 'The Family Library', *Blackwood's*, 26 (Sept. 1829), 416, 413.

[18] [David Robinson], 'The Faction', *Blackwood's*, 22 (Oct. 1827), 426–7; [David Robinson], 'The Bible Societies', ibid. 18 (Nov. 1825), 624–32; Sack, *Jacobite to Conservative*, 214.

[19] [Samuel O'Sullivan], 'Modern Reformation in Ireland', *Blackwood's*, 26 (July 1829), 84–96.

[20] [Eyre Evans Crowe], 'On the Drama', *Blackwood's*, 11 (Apr. 1822), 443; [George Croly], 'Luther', ibid. 25 (Jan. 1829), 26–39.

[21] Caleb Evans Birt, *The Advantages Arising from the Combination of Learning with Piety* (1826), 13.

of church and state could be linked to concerns over the rate of socio-economic change and the rise of commerce and manufactures—a conjunction that was only reinforced by the increasingly high profile of a militantly secular philosophic radicalism and its well-known affiliations with liberal political economists such as Ricardo and McCulloch.

By 1828, however, the year of the repeal of the Test and Corporation Acts, Tory fears were clearly centred around the Catholic question. Not only did the prospect of emancipation seem to contradict the terms of the Revolution Settlement and the Coronation Oath, but, from the point of view of many High Churchmen, ultramontane spiritual allegiances could seem 'a natural concomitant of a claim to a right of rebellion'.[22] During 1828 and 1829 'Brunswick' clubs sprang up both in Ireland and England, joining other anti-Catholic societies such as the Orange Institution and Pitt clubs, demonstrating the existence of a widespread, if relatively unfocused, popular Protestant revival. Meanwhile, Ultra propagandists such as Henry Phillpotts and William Van Mildert embarked on an extensive press campaign against the impending capitulation of Parliament and Crown to the emancipationist cause.[23]

It is in this context that we must view the appearance of the two texts which, taken together, define the limits of 'Romantic conservatism' in this period, Coleridge's *Church and State* and Robert Southey's *Colloquies on the Progress and Prospects of Society*. Both were published in 1829, the year of the Emancipation Act, and both were informed in important ways by the Catholic question. Yet the ideological differences between the two works are pronounced, to the extent that while *Church and State*, in developing the themes of the *Lay Sermons* and *Aids to Reflection* (1825), was to prove a foundational text of the Broad Church movement, the *Colloquies* went on to become closely associated with Ultra Protestantism, the paternalistic Tory radicalism of Michael Thomas Sadler and Richard Oastler, and the nostalgic nationalism of the Young England movement.[24] In this respect, an examination of Southey's political

[22] J. C. D. Clark, *English Society 1688–1832: Ideology, Social Structure and Political Practice during the Ancien Regime* (Cambridge, 1985), 354. See also G. I. T. Machin, *The Catholic Question in English Politics 1820 to 1830* (Oxford, 1964), 16–17; G. F. A. Best, 'The Protestant Constitution and its Supporters, 1800–1829', *Transactions of the Royal Historical Society*, 5th ser., 8 (1958), 105–27.

[23] Machin, *Catholic Question*, 131–3; Sack, *Jacobite to Conservative*, 107.

[24] On Coleridge and liberal Anglicanism, see Richard Brent, *Liberal Anglican Politics: Whiggery, Religion, and Reform 1830–1841* (Oxford, 1987), 164, 181–2. On Southey's relation to Sadler and Lord Ashley, see Carnall, *Robert Southey*, 190–2.

thought, while rewarding in its own right, is also salutary in highlighting the progressive ideological bifurcation of Lake school conservatism in the course of the 1820s, thereby correcting that more reductive view of Romantic social criticism as a unified, linear tradition stretching from Burke through Coleridge and on to Carlyle, Ruskin, and Morris.

Like Wordsworth and Coleridge, Southey did make some significant concessions on the national benefits of commerce and manufactures during the war years.[25] He was, nevertheless, far more consistently and unequivocally critical of the 'commercial system' than his fellow Lakers.[26] It is something of an irony, given his later reputation as the most cynical of political turncoats, that Southey also found it more difficult than either Wordsworth or Coleridge to shake off the vestiges of his earlier, radical sympathies. He was, for example, still recommending economical reform and a reduction in taxation in 1807 (albeit for rather different reasons from those he had owned in the 1790s).[27] It was this stubborn hostility to economic modernity and the monied interest which, as his reactionary inclinations became progressively more egregious, helped to make Southey a kind of Ultra *avant la lettre*—a transformation that was further assisted by his growing reluctance to deviate publicly from a rigid attachment to Anglican orthodoxy, despite the manifestly eccentric religious beliefs which he continued to espouse in his private correspondence.[28]

We should not forget that it was Southey rather than Coleridge who was regarded by his contemporaries as the literary figurehead of the Tory establishment at this time. He relished the opportunity provided by the laureateship to champion the cause of church and state in verse, and to defend the 'moral purity' of English literature against interlopers such as Byron.[29] After the embarrassing publication of his youthful revolutionary drama *Wat Tyler* in 1817, Southey had little choice but to accept that he was now, for better or worse, the public face of Lake school apos-

[25] [Robert Southey], *Letters from England: By Don Manuel Alvarez Espriella* (1807), 2nd edn., 3 vols. (1808), ii. 93; [Robert Southey and John Wilson Croker], 'Capt. Pasley on the Military Policy of Gr. Britain', *Quarterly Review*, 5 (May 1811), 407–11. On Croker's selective revisions of the latter article, see Carnall, *Robert Southey*, 127.

[26] [Southey], *Letters from England*, iii. 83–94.

[27] Ibid. iii. 104–6.

[28] Philip Harling, 'Robert Southey and the Language of Social Discipline', *Albion*, 30 (1998), 640–1.

[29] Robert Southey, *A Vision of Judgement* (1821), pp. xx–xxi.

tasy and renascent cultural conservatism. However misguided it might have been to engage in a public battle of wits with Byron, he did so with as much verve as he could muster, and did much to define the terms of the acrimonious, politically charged dispute between the 'Lakist' and 'Satanic' schools of poetry. But Southey's greatest contemporary importance was undoubtedly as a political journalist and social critic, whose prolific writings in the *Quarterly Review* and the *Colloquies on Society* made a significant, and influential, contribution to political debate in the years leading up to Catholic emancipation.

REPRESENTING REFORMATION

The constitutional historiography of the emancipation crisis has tended to overshadow the literary–historical elements of the 'Catholic question', and indeed the wider relationship between particular constitutional positions on this issue and rival historical interpretations of the cultural and economic development of the English polity. The emancipation debate refocused old questions concerning the relationship between endowed learning and economic modernization, which typically found their historical focus in the religious confrontations of the Reformation. Burke's counter-revolutionary writings in the 1790s had been marked by a distinct tension between what might be described as the 'cultural' and 'constitutional' implications of the disendowment of the Roman Church by Henry VIII. Indeed, this ambivalence may well have contributed to the decline of Burke's posthumous reputation, amid growing distrust of his alleged Catholic sympathies on the part of many Pittite Tories.[30] The same kinds of equivocation, which went to the heart of what it meant to speak of a distinctively Protestant English history, were raised once more in the context of the emancipation crisis of the 1820s. Coleridge's *Church and State*, for example, traced the absence of a national 'clerisy', or learned class, to the Tudor failure to use the 'nationalty' appropriated from the Catholic Church to endow an intellectual order of this kind.[31] As a statement of his convictions on learning and education that its author had been developing for some years, *Church and State* nevertheless stood in a somewhat elliptical relation to mainstream debate on the Catholic question. It was Southey who achieved far greater visibility on this issue, as on others, as the

[30] Sack, 'Memory of Burke', 629.
[31] Coleridge, *Church and State*, 52–3.

leading spokesman for the Ultra cause in the pages of the *Quarterly*, in his ecclesiastical histories, and in the *Colloquies on Society* themselves. But the starting point for Southey's influential and distinctive conservative polemic was his interpretation of English history since the Reformation, the development of which was crucially informed by the context of the emancipation debate.

In his *Book of the Church* (1824), Southey offered a rather indulgent portrait of Henry VIII as, in spite of his faults, a benevolent and 'munificent patron of literature and the arts'. His accession to the throne had coincided with the expansion of trade, the discovery of printing, rapid advances in the 'liberal arts', and 'learning rising, as it were, from the dead', where it had previously languished under the influence of 'Romish fraud'. Although Southey expressed his regret that some of the country's monasteries were not reformed as 'seats of literature and religious retirement', *The Book of the Church* was unapologetic in its presentation of a determinedly Protestant version of English social, economic, and intellectual history.[32] In this respect, Southey was implicitly taking issue with an alternative vision of early modern European literature and learning that was simultaneously being promulgated by a resurgent English Catholic intelligentsia. Catholic historians, quite unsurprisingly, placed much greater stress upon the achievements of Renaissance scholarship and, in particular, the contribution of Catholic literary patrons such as Pope Nicholas V, in comparison to the efflorescence of intellectual activity in post-Reformation England (which latter period, perhaps uncoincidentally, was later to form the core of the institutionalized discipline of English Literature).[33]

Charles Butler, a cisalpine Catholic lawyer and leading campaigner for emancipation, was stung to reply to Southey's Anglican literary history in particularly aggrieved tones. 'The great advances,' Butler complained,

> which were made in every branch of literature, both on the Continent and in England, previously to the reformation, are kept in the background by yourself, and most other writers against the roman-catholic religion, so that the generality of readers think, that the revival of polite literature was entirely owing to the reformers; but justice should be done to our catholic ancestors.

[32] Robert Southey, *The Book of the Church* (1824), 5th edn. (1841), 295, 237, 267.

[33] See e.g. Joseph Berington, *A Literary History of the Middle Ages* (1814), 473–6, 495–507. Sheridan Gilley, 'Nationality and Liberty, Protestant and Catholic: Robert Southey's Book of the Church', *Studies in Church History*, 18 (1982), 409–32.

While Protestant Bible societies were busy urging the necessity of a 'New Reformation' in Ireland aided by the Stanhope printing process, Butler argued that the religious crisis of the sixteenth century had actually impeded the growth of manners and learning and that, contrary to Protestant hagiographies of figures such as Luther and Tyndale, the Catholic Church had been fully prepared to utilize the invention of printing to disseminate vernacular translations of the Bible.[34]

The rise of Reformation historiography as a politically charged subject was further fuelled by the emergence of radical and liberal interpretations of the period, which either focused upon its persecutory and repressive nature, as in Cobbett's *History of the Protestant 'Reformation'* (1824–6), or stressed its long-term efficacy as a harbinger of political liberty, rational Enlightenment, and the diffusion of knowledge in the printed medium of the English language. This latter tendency, which owed much to the presbyterian sympathies of Scottish Enlightenment historiography, united such temperamentally opposed figures as William Hazlitt and James Mill, the latter having published an extensively annotated translation of Charles Villers's *Essay on the Spirit and Influence of the Reformation* in 1805.[35] There was, clearly, a significant intersection between the Catholic question and early nineteenth-century historiographical debates on literature, education, and the progress of knowledge; and this in turn suggests that accounts of the constitutional revolution of 1828–32 which treat it as a crisis of the Anglican *ancien régime* while denying the importance of 'secular' forms of reformist discourse may overlook the many points of connection that bound the religious component of political argument to wider social issues.[36] The emergence of the Catholic question as a central concern of conservative writers in the later 1820s by no means precluded its links with other aspects of contemporary political debate, such as the 'commercial system', the constitutional function of the press, and the rise of 'public opinion'.

[34] Charles Butler, *The Book of the Roman-Catholic Church* (1825), 180–4. Southey replied in his *Vindiciæ Ecclesiæ Anglicanæ* (1826).

[35] William Cobbett, *A History of the Protestant 'Reformation'*, 2 vols. (1824–6); Charles Villers, *Essay on the Spirit and Influence of the Reformation of Luther*, trans. James Mill (1805); L. O. Frappell, 'The Reformation as Negative Revolution or Obscurantist Reaction: The Liberal Debate on the Reformation in Nineteenth-Century Britain', *Journal of Religious History*, 11 (1980), 289–307. For typical Anglican rejoinders, see the Oxford Professor of Poetry [Henry Hart Milman], 'The Reformation in England', *Quarterly Review*, 33 (Dec. 1825), 1–37; Sharon Turner, *The History of the Reign of Henry the Eighth*, 2nd edn., 2 vols. (1827).

[36] See e.g. J. C. D. Clark, *English Society*, 424.

Although his essays on Catholic emancipation strongly marked the *Quarterly* as an organ of the Ultras (against the more moderate inclinations of its editors), Southey's analysis of the Reformation in works less directly connected to the Catholic question is far more ambiguous regarding its long-term effects on English society, precisely because his understanding of the religious conflicts of this period were closely tied to a historical critique of the rise of commerce and manufactures.[37] Amplifying upon Burke's comments on endowed learning and the Reformation in his counter-revolutionary writings of the 1790s, Southey tended on the whole towards the view that, while the religious conflicts of the sixteenth century represented a necessary corrective to the corruptions of the church, their protracted influence on the development of learning and literature had been highly deleterious to the politics and culture of post-Elizabethan England. From the disendowment of monastic learning to the debauched Gallicism of Restoration culture, and on to the radicalized literary marketplace of his own day, English society continued to suffer the intellectual consequences of the Protestant Reformation.

Similar complaints had been an occasional theme of Anglican social thought in the post-war years, surfacing in discussions of the growth of popular infidelity and radicalism, and the perceived decline in respect for the clergy as a learned and endowed order.[38] Southey himself had been meditating these issues for some years prior to the emancipation crisis of 1825. But his attitude to the historical effects of the Reformation was also bound up with a range of other issues, including the rise of commerce and manufacturing, the expansion of reading audiences, and the increasing democratization of the printed media of political debate. To this extent, Southey's conviction of the constitutional and theological desirability of the Reformation remained in constant tension with his analysis of its disastrous long-term impact on politics, society, and learning.

Southey's *Quarterly* essay on the 'Rise and Progress of Popular Disaffection', published in January 1817, traced the contemporary spirit of radicalism back to the 'religious disputes under Henry VIII . . . [which]

[37] For militant Protestantism, see, in particular, Southey's essay in the *Quarterly Review*, 38 (Oct. 1828), 535–98. This essay decisively influenced the *Quarterly*'s stance on the Catholic question in the months preceding emancipation: Scott Bennett, 'Catholic Emancipation, the "Quarterly Review", and Britain's Constitutional Revolution', *Victorian Studies*, 12 (1969), 283–304.

[38] See e.g. George Edmund Shuttleworth, *The Church and the Clergy* (1820), 22–3, 33.

divided the nation . . . and produced a long train of consequences, which are acting at this hour, and the end of which no human foresight can discern'. Religious schism had thus fomented a spirit of faction in secular politics, as Catholics abandoned their loyalty to the Protestant state, and Puritans succumbed to the temptations of republican and democratic opinions.[39] Southey clearly believed himself to be providing a credible genealogy for English radicalism, stretching from the Tudor period, through to the Civil War, and on to the popular protest of his own day. But beyond this, the article on 'Popular Disaffection', together with Southey's other contributions to the *Quarterly* in this period, clearly reflect his desire to draw the broader patterns of social, intellectual, and economic development into one overarching historical narrative. The sixteenth century was, as a result, repeatedly portrayed as heralding the end of paternalistic, feudal society—'the patriarchal age' as Southey called it.[40] Enclosures, rising rents, the disappearance of small farms and church lands, and the growth of 'landlords, unconnected with . . . [their tenants] by any habits or hereditary feelings'; all were dated from this period, and understood to have resulted in the desuetude of charitable institutions, a drastic rise in pauperism and the emergence of a migratory, mendicant population sustained by the poor laws rather than by customary ties of charitable obligation. The rise of commercial society and the blight of manufacturing industry were thus exposed as the remote consequences of the dissolution of a feudal *Gemeinschaft* some time in the sixteenth century. It should not, however, be concluded that Southey was a wholly unreconstructed opponent of economic modernity. Like Wordsworth, he held manufacturing to be 'an evil only in its abuse: within certain bounds it is essential to the cultivation and improvement and prosperity of a nation; and . . . no nation can become either highly civilized or permanently powerful without manufactures'.[41]

The various social, political, and economic aspects of this particular narrative of 'the world we have lost' were brought together in Southey's account of the historical growth of the press: it is no coincidence that

[39] [Robert Southey], 'Rise and Progress of Popular Disaffection', *Quarterly Review*, 16 (Jan. 1817), 516. Much of Southey's work for the *Quarterly* was collected, with additions and corrections, in *Essays, Moral and Political*, 2 vols. (1832).

[40] [John Rickman and Robert Southey], 'On the Means of Improving the People', *Quarterly Review*, 19 (Apr. 1818), 81; for a discussion of authorship, see Orlo Williams, *Lamb's Friend*, 197.

[41] [Robert Southey], 'The Poor', *Quarterly Review*, 15 (Apr. 1816), 194; [id.], 'Emigration Report', *Quarterly Review*, 37 (Mar. 1828), 573. Eastwood, 'Intellectual Origins', 317.

he identified the introduction of steam power and the multiplication of newspapers as two of the most significant material advances in recent history.[42] The essay on 'Popular Disaffection' argued that the full effects of the dispossession of learning from 'colleges and convents' became apparent only in the eighteenth century. At this point, 'literary adventurers', loosed from the patronage of endowed institutions of learning, began to multiply: 'men of letters were not known in England as a distinct class in society till the beginning of the last century', Southey claimed, 'and during the present reign they have increased in number at least fifty-fold.'[43]

Their very existence as a disendowed and 'separate class' militated against the men of letters being sympathetic to the 'established order of things' and encouraged them to embrace the new, post-Reformation commercial ethos. George III should have enjoyed a reign of peace, prosperity, and consensus, but, as the spirit of commerce came increasingly to taint the profession of letters, the press drastically exacerbated the existing tendencies to political dissension inherent in the English polity:

> During the two preceding reigns the circulation of political writings had been comparatively trifling, and their effect not very great. We had not yet learned to talk of the reading public, or to call ourselves a thinking people. The pamphlets and flying squibs of the day were above the reach of the multitude, and beneath the notice of the learned . . . But a tremendous alteration was now to take place, and the art of popular writing was at the same time carried to perfection and directed to the most mischievous of all purposes.[44]

The progress of commerce, arts, and manufactures had produced a vibrant, commercialized culture of print, and this in turn fostered the dissemination of that 'superficial philosophy, which, deriving every thing from without, led the way for gross materialism with all its pernicious consequences'. This 'foul philosophy', partly French in origin, and partly a product of British empiricism and sceptical infidelity, affected to treat 'man as a mere material machine' and was in this respect equally culpable for the sceptical materialism of the French revolutionaries and the brutalizing ideology of the British manufacturing classes.[45]

42 [Southey], 'The Poor', 195; id., *Colloquies*, i. 201–2.

43 [Id.], 'Popular Disaffection', *Quarterly Review*, 16 (Jan. 1817), 538.

44 Ibid. 541, 530.

45 Ibid. 527; id., *History of the Peninsular War*, 3 vols. (1823–32), i. 46. See also id., *Colloquies*, i. 170.

The literary marketplace provided an ideal medium for the popularization of these ideas. Indeed, Southey went so far as to claim that 'Literature is, like every thing else, a trade in England,—I might almost call it a manufactory'.[46] The post-war renaissance of popular radical journalism was thus ironically exposed as a product of the very same economic forces to which it was increasingly finding itself opposed. Once stripped of the humanizing influences of religion, morality, and custom, and effectively reduced to the status of material machines, the inhabitants of the new manufacturing towns provided the seedbed for a radical press which was itself the remote product of the unchecked commercialization of literary culture.[47] The growth of commercial society could thus be seen to have necessitated the rise of a radical, and radically immoral press through the internal logic of its own historical development. The diseases of the 'body politic' seemed to Southey to resemble those of the corporeal body, and, 'of all the shocking diseases to which the human frame is liable, the most shocking and the most loathsome is that in which it is devoured by the vermin which its own diseased humours have generated'. This analysis goes some way to explaining Southey's enduring belief that 'All the other confluent causes of discontent are trifling in themselves and light in their consequences compared to the seditious press', a conviction which eventually led him beyond the anonymity of his *Quarterly* articles to the notorious *Letter to William Smith*, in which he openly demanded the strenuous, legally enforced suppression of 'seditious' journalistic activity.[48]

'THIS DISTEMPERED AGE': THE EPIDEMIOLOGY OF OPINION

Southey's vivid reference to the diseased condition of the body politic was far from incidental to the central preoccupations of his social and political criticism. Throughout his major articles for the *Quarterly*, he repeatedly alluded to political dissension, moral decay, and religious schism in the language of physical sickness and infection. His historical account of the Reformation and its consequences reads at times like a veritable pathogenesis of popular radicalism: the zealous sectarianism of the sixteenth century incubated the germs of civil war, 'as some

[46] [Id.], *Letters from England*, iii. 40.
[47] [Id.], 'Popular Disaffection', *Quarterly Review*, 16 (Jan. 1817), 542.
[48] Ibid. 513, 551; id., *A Letter to William Smith* (1817), 31–2.

diseases are known in a certain degree to be influenced by any endemic malady which happens to prevail', while the Restoration saw religious disputes and the bitter party spirit to which they gave rise 'settled into a chronic disease', and working to 'infect the whole moral and intellectual nature of man'. By Southey's day, the 'endemic moral malady of this distempered age' appeared serious enough to threaten the ultimate climacteric of revolution.[49] But this rhetorical obsession also extended well beyond his analysis of popular politics, as Southey employed similar imagery in his account of manufacturing industry and the commercial system, which he described as a cancerous 'wen' or 'tumour' on society.[50]

The suffusion of Southey's political and social criticism with the language of disease and infection tends to strike the modern reader as a lurid, but essentially figurative stylistic peculiarity. It would, however, have been interpreted somewhat differently by those of Southey's medical contemporaries who were themselves concerned with the implications of economic and social change for the nation's 'health', in a very literal sense. One of the most striking examples of this early nineteenth-century convergence between medical science and social criticism is provided by Thomas Beddoes, a Bristol physician and political reformist whose lectures Southey had attended in the 1790s.[51] In his *Hygëia: or Essays Moral and Medical* (1802–3), Beddoes argued both that the 'encouragement of manufactures . . . [entails] the creation of a miserable and sickly population', and that the credit-driven indulgences of consumer society were producing enervation and disease in the middle classes.[52] Such conclusions were very similar to those drawn by Southey himself, and Beddoes's work does, indeed, make a brief appearance in the *Colloquies*, in connection with the belief that the 'same causes operate upon the moral as upon the physical character'.[53]

Beddoes seems to have been convinced that there was some kind of causal link between the excesses of middle-class consumerism and the physiological and moral corruptions of his patients. Southey's *Quarterly*

[49] [Id.], 'Popular Disaffection', *Quarterly Review*, 16 (Jan. 1817), 513, 521–2, 552.
[50] Eastwood, 'Ruinous Prosperity', 74.
[51] Storey, *Robert Southey*, 113; Roy Porter, 'Reforming the Patient in the Age of Reform: Thomas Beddoes and Medical Practice', in Roger French and Andrew Wear (eds.), *British Medicine in the Age of Reform* (1991), 9–17.
[52] Thomas Beddoes, *Hygëia: or Essays Moral and Medical*, 3 vols. (Bristol, 1802–3), i. 84.
[53] Southey, *Colloquies*, i. 130.

essays combine this insight with an under-consumptionist sensitivity to the dangers of glut. The 'body politic may be plethoric like the body natural', he wrote: 'there is a state of prosperity which, like overfeeding, disposes the system for inflammatory diseases, or makes it break out in blains and blotches.'[54] The 'endemic moral maladies of . . . the middle classes' were intimately connected with the intellectual ethos of commercial society, which he identified with 'cosmopolitan *liberality*', and 'a false philosophy, sapping the very foundation of religion'.[55] Yet Southey was perhaps even more disturbed by the pathological effects of manufactures upon the labouring poor, an anxiety which he had first voiced in his *Letters from England* (1807). The 'health physical and moral' of industrial labourers had been comprehensively destroyed by their occupations, complained the *Letters*' pseudonymous Spanish narrator, Espriella; 'they die of diseases induced by unremitting task work, by confinement in the impure atmosphere of crowded rooms'.[56] But while Southey was clearly willing to adapt Beddoes's synthesis of moral and medical discourse to his own political ends, the master metaphor governing his pathological diagnosis of contemporary society was drawn from a different quarter of contemporary medical theory—the early nineteenth-century debate on the nature of contagious disease.

Descriptions of the spread of radical or impious opinion in terms of infectious disease had been a staple of conservative political rhetoric since at least the 1790s. Southey's use of such language, however, is remarkable for both its frequency and its connotative range. Throughout his political writings, pestilence, plague, viruses, and infection are invoked over and over again, in a variety of different contexts. Roman Catholicism, a species of 'religious madness', is identified as dangerously 'infectious'; while the 'moral pestilence' of American and French revolutionary politics is compared to the intercontinental spread of a deadly pandemic. Even Irish immigration is understood in terms of the insidious communication of the 'disease of pauperism'.[57] Above all, however, Southey applied the language of contagion to the 'moral plagues' generated and communicated by commerce, manufactures, and the press. This concern with what might be termed the 'moral

54 [Id.], 'The Poor', *Quarterly Review*, 15 (Apr. 1816), 190.

55 [Id.], 'Popular Disaffection', ibid., 16 (Jan. 1817), 541–2.

56 [Id.], *Letters from England*, ii. 88.

57 [Id.], 'The History of Europe, 1808', *Edinburgh Annual Register*, i (1808), 8; [id.], 'Popular Disaffection', *Quarterly Review*, 16 (Jan. 1817), 534; id., *Essays*, ii. 258.

epidemiology' of manufacturing towns was indebted in part to George III's surgeon, John Hunter, who, Southey noted, had

> predicted that our manufactories would engender new varieties of pestilence. New and specific diseases they have produced, but the only pestilence which has yet manifested itself is of a moral nature. Physical diseases are not more surely generated by crowding human beings together in a state of filth and wretchedness, than moral ones by herding them together in a state of ignorance.[58]

This association of 'moral' and 'physical' infections reflects Southey's broader interest in the early nineteenth-century controversy over the nature of contagious disease, which found one of its most important expressions in a debate between the *Quarterly* and *Westminster* reviews during the mid-1820s.

The origins of the upsurge in anti-contagionist theory in this period have generally been traced to Charles Maclean, a political pamphleteer and long-standing employee of the East India Company, whose strenuous arguments for the environmental, rather than the contagious, nature of epidemic diseases were closely linked to attacks on the quarantine laws as unnecessary barriers to international trade.[59] Although the long-term history of anti-contagionist discourse does not support the argument that it was a straightforward reflex of the laissez-faire instincts of mercantile and commercial interest groups, it does seem that, in this period at least, the issues of free trade and political economy were very near the forefront of scientific debate in this area, and tended to divide medical opinion on political grounds. Hostile contemporaries were certainly quite explicit in attributing anti-contagionist opinions to a commitment to commercial liberalization.[60]

In 1825 the *Westminster* entered the fray, publishing two anti-contagionist articles by Thomas Southwood Smith, the unitarian and

[58] [Robert Southey], 'Inquiry into the Poor Laws, &c.', *Quarterly Review*, 8 (Dec. 1812), 338; see also id., *Colloquies*, i. 50.

[59] See e.g. Charles Maclean, 'Summary of the Facts and Inferences', *Pamphleteer*, 16 (1820), 153–92.

[60] Id., 'Suggestions for the Prevention and Mitigation of Epidemic and Pestilential Diseases', *Pamphleteer*, 10 (1817), 452; id., 'Remarks on the British Quarantine Laws', *Pamphleteer*, 21 (1823), 443–4; William Macmichael, 'A Brief Sketch of the Progress of Opinion on the Subject of Contagion', *Pamphleteer*, 25 (1825), 530; Roger Cooter, 'Anticontagionism and History's Medical Record', in Peter Wright and Andrew Treacher (eds.), *The Problem of Medical Knowledge: Examining the Social Construction of Medicine* (Edinburgh, 1982), 87–108; Alan Bewell, *Romanticism and Colonial Disease* (Baltimore, 1999).

sanitary reformer who was later to enjoy the dubious honour of dissecting Bentham's corpse in the name of medical science and the Greatest Happiness Principle. Smith made it quite clear that the subject of contagion 'is interwoven with the commercial welfare of nations', and that the quarantine system was needlessly injurious to 'commerce in general', serving no other purpose than to further the 'mischievous influence and power' enjoyed by a meddlesome and 'despotic government'.[61] Smith was answered in the *Quarterly* by Robert Gooch, a close friend of Southey who was to go on to provide an appendix on nursing for the *Colloquies* and who probably also assisted its author with a note on 'Medical Police'.[62] Gooch had already written on plague and contagion for the *Quarterly* in 1822, and he was quick to condemn 'modern free-thinkers in medicine', such as Maclean and Smith, as self-willed epistemological iconoclasts—which was not so very far from the truth, given that anti-contagionists such as Smith saw themselves as 'revolutionary ideologues for the intellectual, and hence social, liberation of their class', struggling against the sinister, entrenched, and intertwined interests of the medical and political establishments.[63]

While the anti-contagionism debate began to gather momentum in the wake of Maclean's controversial investigations into the plague (published in 1817–18), Southey's political essays in the *Quarterly* consistently employed the imagery of pestilence and plague as a way of turning contagionist rhetoric against the proselytes of the commercial spirit who would deny its reference to real medical phenomena. The 'moral contagion' unleashed upon the manufacturing poor was thus exposed as a direct consequence of the commerical spirit and laissez-faire principles which obstructed the moral policing of industrial towns. But Southey seems to have been equally outraged by the way in which philosophic radicals and liberal Whigs used the tenets of economic liberalism to inform a normative model of the unrestricted flow of information and opinion facilitated by the press. His response was to employ contagionist rhetoric—with all its protectionist connotations—in an implicit critique of the liberal defence of print culture and public opinion, by describing the unregulated circulation of textualized opinion in terms of an uncontrollable discursive epidemic.

[61] [Southwood Smith], 'Contagion and Sanitary Laws', *Westminster Review*, 3 (Jan. 1825), 136; [id.], 'Plague—Typhus Fever—Quarantine', *Westminster Review*, 3 (Apr. 1825), 530.

[62] Southey, *Colloquies*, i. 318–20.

[63] Cooter, 'Anticontagionism', 95.

Contagionists strongly favoured the maintenance of quarantine laws, and the interventionist 'policing' of international trade. In attacking 'the anti-contagion philosophers', as he called them, Southey extended this principle to the moral policing of infectious opinion.[64] 'Great cities do not with more certainty generate foul air, and condense contagion, than they assist the propagation of moral diseases,' he wrote. 'And yet, under a good police, medical and moral, the means, both of prevention and remedy, might be applied.' The rapidity with which such 'pernicious principles' were being disseminated in large towns was, however, symptomatic of much wider socio-economic changes which had left the body politic peculiarly susceptible to infection.[65] Discussing the rise of sceptical irreligion in the early eighteenth century, Southey noted that, at this time,

> the circulation of opinions was slow because of the little intercourse between one part of the country and another . . . No provincial newspapers were extant; there were no circulating libraries, no book-clubs, no reviews, and the earliest magazines had but just been established. Every month now produces more books than were at that time published in a year, and the number of readers has multiplied in equal, or greater proportion.

Yet if, even in this earlier period, 'the pestilence of infidelity was but too widely disseminated', in the present state of society the germs of immorality, scepticism, and political disaffection appeared capable of surging through the body politic virtually unchecked.[66] The 'state is now more artificially and intimately combined,' he wrote in 1816; 'it resembles a spider's web, in which the slightest impact upon any one of the threads is felt throughout the whole . . . the rapid intercourse which commercial activity has created has given wings to fashion and folly, and the politics of Paris and of London are canvassed in every pot-house where the English language is spoken'.[67]

The growth of a 'public press', which followed the ascendancy of the commercial spirit and the intrusion of market principles into the intellectual sphere, seemed to have left the modern body politic with a constitutional susceptibility to the ravages of epistemic infection, and the consequent contamination of the public mind by immorality, infidelism,

[64] [Southey], 'Emigration Report', *Quarterly Review*, 37 (Mar. 1828), 567.

[65] [Rickman and Southey], 'Means of Improving the People', ibid., 19 (Apr. 1818), 92–3.

[66] [Southey], 'Popular Disaffection', ibid., 16 (Jan. 1817), 528.

[67] [Id.], 'The Poor', ibid., 15 (Apr. 1816), 191.

and political radicalism. The essay on 'Parliamentary Reform' described the freethinking 'smatterer in philosophy' as relatively harmless only when confined to 'private practice'. The sphere of private intellection was thus contrasted with a diseased act of textual communication in which the published page was impregnated with the unwholesome breath of the demagogue. When such a figure 'commences professor of moral and political philosophy for the benefit of the public,—the fables of old credulity are then verified—his very breath becomes venomous, and every page which he sends abroad carries with it poison to the unsuspicious reader'. The radical text thus becomes a '*virus*' with which freethinking philosophers 'inoculate' the unsuspecting public.[68] The contagious medium of the public press, Southey believed, had allowed the moral and intellectual diseases of the commercial spirit to jump the class barrier from Beddoes's corpulent middle-class patients to the industrial poor, disseminating radical and irreligious opinions through the public mind without hindrance or regulation. The only remedy seemed to lie with Bell's monitorial system and the National Society's proposals for popular education in the principles of the established church. The 'invention of printing', he suggested, 'did not come more opportunely for the restoration of letters, and for the blessed work of reformation, than Dr. Bell's discovery to vaccinate the next generation against the pestilence which has infected this'.[69]

The very ubiquity of contagionist rhetoric in Southey's prose is suggestive of the equally all-pervasive infections of the 'commercial spirit', which 'was never so universal . . . as it is in England, where it extends to every thing and poisons every thing:—literature, arts, religion, government are alike tainted, it is a *lues* [a plague or pestilence] which has got into the system of the country, and is rotting flesh and bone'.[70] Southey's overwrought epidemiological imagery attempted to institute and sustain a vituperative critical position defiantly immune to the infectious spread of the commercial spirit throughout the discursive order, a development that was signalled most clearly by the remorseless rise of the 'metapolitics' of political economy. The dehumanizing

[68] [Id.], 'Parliamentary Reform', *Quarterly Review*, 16 (Oct. 1816), 227; id., *Essays*, i. 330.

[69] [Id.], 'Inquiry into the Poor Laws', *Quarterly Review*, 8 (Dec. 1812), 353. See also id., *Colloquies*, ii. 75–6; id., *Letter to William Smith*, 35–6.

[70] [Id.], *Letters from England*, iii. 85–6.

abstractions of this new science appeared to have reached epidemic proportions of textual fecundity, spawning 'volumes upon volumes of metaphysical politics'.[71] In a confused synthesis of contemporary medical beliefs with the satirical scatology of Pope and Swift, the *Colloquies* describe this relentlessly proliferating new idiom of political argument as the product of an age in which 'the filth and refuse of an ill-ordered society have accumulated, and the waters of its broken conduits, and the contents of its sewers have met and stagnated, and all together has become rank, noxious, putrescent and pestilential. Their philosophy is the growth of such a compost!'[72] The growing enthusiasm in radical circles for the 'mechanical philosophy' over more humanizing, literary idioms was symptomatic of the way in which the putrescent abstractions of deluded 'meta-politicians' could suffer popularization at the hands of a commercialized and irresponsibly entrepreneurial public press, with the consequent intensification of their pestiferous, communicable nature.

Southey suggested in the *Colloquies* that 'freedom of trade, like freedom of the press, may require restrictions', and there is a clear connection between his call for government regulation in the case of commerce and manufactures, and that of radical journalism. Both served as conduits for an infectious 'moral pestilence', misguidedly encouraged by the liberalizing tenets of political economy.[73] It would, then, be quite wrong to approach Southey's social criticism with the aim of recuperating the humanitarian critic of industrial capitalism while ignoring the other, equally enduring image of the Romantic laureate as a literary apostate baying shrilly for the arrest of his fellow journalists. Southey was quite clear that 'state physicians' must intervene to regulate the press and contain the 'political contagion' of diseased opinion.[74] But the transportation of seditious libellers to the ideological lazaretto of New South Wales should be followed by government investment in the education and employment of the poor. 'The first duty of government is to stop the contagion; the next, as far as possible, to remove the causes which have pre-disposed so large a part of the populace for receiving it.'[75]

[71] Id., *Colloquies*, i. 124.

[72] Ibid. ii. 262; see also ibid. ii. 125.

[73] Ibid. ii. 250.

[74] Id., *Essays*, i. 368; [id.], 'Parliamentary Reform', *Quarterly Review*, 16 (Oct. 1816), 230. See also id., *Colloquies*, i. 111.

[75] [Id.], 'Inquiry into the Poor Laws', *Quarterly Review*, 8 (Dec. 1812), 351.

Despite Southey's undoubted prominence as a political journalist and social critic, many of his more extreme views on the constitutional function of public opinion and the press were considerably out of step with much anti-reform argument during this period. Conservative representations of the rise of public opinion during the 1810s and 1820s increasingly tended to stress its fluctuating and suggestible nature in order to argue that, precisely because of this mutability, the public mind could find legitimate expression only within the balance of powers already embodied in the existing constitution.[76] On this view public opinion, as the raw expression of new social formations and economic interests, was to take its rightful place in the unreformed constitution in order that its potential for misdirection and inconstancy could be tempered by the wisdom of representative government. Southey made an isolated, but significant, concession to this argument in his 1816 essay on parliamentary reform, in which he endorsed the rise of public opinion as a timely constitutional counterweight that supplemented the government's representative function without the need for legislative tampering:

> They who seek to lessen the influence of the crown, keep out of sight the increased power which has been given to public opinion by the publication of the parliamentary debates, and the prodigious activity of the press.—The first of these circumstances alone has introduced a greater change into our government than has ever been brought about by statute; and on the whole, that change is so beneficial as to be worth more than the additional expense which it entails upon us during war. This momentous alteration gives, even in ordinary times, a preponderance to the popular branch of the constitution . . .[77]

That the argument Southey employs here proved an important resource for Tory anti-reform rhetoric is confirmed by the critical attention it received from the Whig politician Lord John Russell, in his *Essay on the History of the English Government and Constitution*.[78] Russell's defensive tone reflected his party's perception that not only was the *language* of 'public opinion' being appropriated by its political opponents, but that public opinion itself (considered as the expression of an enfranchised 'political nation') could not be expected to fall in automatically with a

[76] Wahrman, *Imagining*, 190–9; J. A. W. Gunn, *Beyond Liberty and Property: The Process of Self-Recognition in Eighteenth-Century Political Thought* (Kingston, Ont., 1983), 289–99.

[77] [Southey], 'Parliamentary Reform', *Quarterly Review*, 16 (Oct. 1816), 272.

[78] Lord John Russell, *An Essay on the History of the English Government and Constitution*, 2nd edn. (1823), 429–30.

reforming Whig agenda. The result was an intensification of the gradualist emphasis in Whig rhetoric in the run-up to the Reform Act, and a greater stress upon the progressive nature of public opinion over the long term.[79]

By this time, however, certain elements of anti-reform rhetoric could be said to have developed a distinctly 'liberal Tory' complexion, most notably for our purposes in the case of Coleridge's *Church and State*. Coleridge represented the growth of public opinion and the press as important compensating powers redressing the inordinate influence of the landed over the 'personal' interest of 'manufacturing, mercantile, distributive, and professional classes'.[80] The election of 'great landowners' as borough representatives, combined with the lack of any mechanism for the periodical adjustment of borough rights to keep pace with the growth of their 'wealth and independence' had, according to Coleridge, shifted 'the very weights intended for the effectual counterpoise of the great land-holders . . . into the opposite scale'. Having apparently set up a reformist case, Coleridge went on to assert of these 'apparent defects and imperfections' in the realization of the idea of the constitution that 'we will neither regret nor set about amending [them], till we have seen whether an equivalent force had not arisen to supply the deficiency'. This new force was adumbrated as an additional and fortuitous counterbalance to the 'permanence' of the landed interest, thus vindicating the homeostatic poise of the constitution as an 'Idea' of reason progressively realized in history.

> Roads, canals, machinery, the press, the periodical and daily press, the might of public opinion, the consequent increasing desire of popularity among public men and functionaries of every description, and the increasing necessity of public character, as a means or condition of political influence—I need but mention these to stand acquitted of having started a vague and naked possibility in extenuation of an evident and palpable abuse.[81]

Coleridge seems at this point to have been following the argument of the Tory parliamentarian Alexander Mackinnon, whose treatise *On the Rise, Progress and Present State of Public Opinion* was published the year before *Church and State*. Mackinnon had linked the progress of 'civiliza-

[79] See e.g. the speeches by Jeffrey (1830) and Macaulay (1831) in *Parliamentary Debates*, 3rd ser., iii. 77–8, vii. 307; and John Cannon, *Parliamentary Reform 1640–1832* (Cambridge, 1973), 244.

[80] Coleridge, *Church and State*, 25.

[81] Ibid. 29.

tion' and 'proper religious feeling' with the growth of the 'middle class' and the capitalization of manufacturing, commerce, and the press.[82] The rise of the press and public opinion as expressions of the bourgeois–professional 'personal interest' were integrated by Coleridge into the unfolding providential history of the idea of the constitution, just as, in a slightly different idiom, Mackinnon had argued that the need for parliamentary reform had been obviated by the growth of 'roads, canals, harbours, ships, mail roads, [and] steam-vessels', which, as both the product and further stimulant of 'wealth and civilization', were indissolubly linked to 'the growth and strength of public opinion . . . [which] gains strength in proportion to facility of communication, either through the means of the press, or by intercourse between one place and another'.[83]

Coleridge was careful to distinguish (or, as he would prefer, 'desynonimize') Mackinnon's middle-class civilization from the national church's duty to 'cultivate' the nation: the imperative to 'form and train up the people of the country to obedient, free, useful, organizable subjects, citizens, and patriots' was incompatible with a definition of 'civilization' based on narrowly socio-economic criteria.[84] But Coleridge was nevertheless willing to appropriate Mackinnon's liberal analysis of the rise of public opinion and the press as an example of the progressive, providential manifestation of the quasi-Platonic 'Idea' of the common law constitution.[85] It is a measure of the widening ideological differences within Lake school conservatism that Southey could never have endorsed *Church and State*'s (albeit perhaps strategic) defence of the influence of the 'commercial system' upon the press and public opinion. The development of his own social and political opinions left Southey intensely resistant to the values of commercial humanism. Indeed, his startlingly profound disaffection with economic modernity inspired not only the rhetoric, but also the literary form of Southey's most important work of social criticism, the *Colloquies on the Progress and Prospects of Society*.

[82] Alexander Mackinnon, *On the Rise, Progress and Present State of Public Opinion* (1828).

[83] Ibid. 13 and n. See also Wahrman, *Imagining*, 299–302; Jonathan Parry, *The Rise and Fall of Liberal Government in Victorian Britain* (New Haven, 1993), 27.

[84] Coleridge, *Church and State*, 54. Coleridge had first made the distinction between 'cultivation' and 'civilization' in 1818; *Church and State* applied it for the first time along class lines, following Mackinnon's association of 'civilization' with the 'middle class'. See Coleridge, *Friend* (1818), i. 494; id., *Church and State*, 27–8.

[85] David Aram Kaiser, '"The Perfection of Reason": Coleridge and the Ancient Constitution', *Studies in Romanticism*, 32 (1993), 29–55.

THE *COLLOQUIES ON SOCIETY*: POLITICS, HISTORY, AND THE PUBLIC MIND

The 1828 edition of Isaac D'Israeli's popular essay on *The Literary Character* registered an acute sense of unease respecting the 'moral darkness and disorganization' afflicting contemporary Britain. The book's dedication to his friend, Robert Southey, stressed in particular the laureate's belief, which D'Israeli shared, that 'the revolutions of Society have operated on our literature, and that new classes of readers have called forth new classes of writers. The causes, and the consequences, of the present state of this fugitive literature, might form an inquiry which would include some of the most important topics which concern the PUBLIC MIND'.[86] This allusion to the forthcoming *Colloquies*, which Southey had been composing on and off since 1817, succinctly identified one of the book's central themes—the unprecedented mobility and social penetration of public opinion which had been effected by the commercialization of the printed word. 'All classes are now brought within the reach of . . . current literature,' Southey declared in the *Colloquies*, 'that literature which, like a moral atmosphere, is, as it were, the medium of intellectual life, and on the quality of which, according as it may be salubrious or noxious, the health of the public mind depends'.[87]

In comparison to Coleridge's *Church and State*, the *Colloquies* have on the whole been treated considerably less seriously as a piece of extended social and political analysis. A great deal of the responsibility for this state of affairs must be attached to Macaulay's 1830 review, which, as we saw in the Introduction, proved just as effective a demolition of Southey's intellectual credentials as Macaulay's earlier attack on Mill's 'Essay on Government', and left Southey with an enduring reputation as a muddled, reactionary aesthete, 'a man who regards politics, not as a matter of science, but as a matter of taste and feeling'.[88] What truth there is in such claims needs to be balanced against the fact that his reviews of Mill and Southey served to define, in a complementary fashion, the parameters of Macaulay's own developing sense of the appropriate province of political science, understood as an adjunct of his moderate, reformist Whig politics, just as much as they were concerned with

[86] Isaac D'Israeli, *The Literary Character*, 4th edn., 2 vols. (1828), i, pp. xxxiii, ix.

[87] Southey, *Colloquies*, ii. 362–3.

[88] [Macaulay], 'Southey's Colloquies on Society', *Edinburgh Review*, 50 (Jan. 1830), 533, 540; Eastwood, 'Intellectual Origins', 314; id., 'Ruinous Prosperity', 73–4.

a critical analysis of these two texts in their own rights.[89] In both reviews, Macaulay's interests were best served by a reductive and frankly derisory treatment of the methodological peculiarities of each work, and, in Southey's case in particular, the *Colloquies* have gained a lasting reputation as an impressionistic, ill-informed and ultimately vacuous piece of writing that offered little serious challenge to the liberal evangelists of the nineteenth-century industrial order. Yet the *Colloquies* continue to deserve our attention, not just as the fullest exposition of their author's political and social opinions, but also as the first, and in some ways most extreme example of that nostalgic, neo-feudalist variety of conservative historicism which, from Young England to the Gothic revival, played a significant part in the politics and culture of mid-nineteenth-century Britain.

Constructed as a series of Lakeland dialogues between Southey (whose thinly disguised persona is given the name 'Montesinos') and the ghost of Thomas More, the *Colloquies* explore at more length, and with greater dramatic force, the same historical schema which Southey had previously developed in his work for the *Quarterly*. His immensely successful patriotic biographies, such as the *Lives of the British Admirals*, represented the heroic character as an expression of its age and nation; and while Thomas More was of course a much more ambiguously heroic figure as far as Southey was concerned, he could, nevertheless, give a similarly embodied expression to the age of the Reformation.[90] But Sir Thomas's morbid, spectral commentaries on nineteenth-century England also seem intended to reinforce a sense of the relation, both causal and analogical, between the age of the Reformation and the emergent industrial society of Southey's day. The sixteenth and the early nineteenth centuries are thus described as two 'grand climacterics' in human history, and approached in dialogic fashion by 'comparing the great operating causes in the age of the Reformation, and in this age of revolutions'.[91] For Southey, the dialogue form allowed the *Colloquies* to function as a kind of dialectical conversation between remote historical periods, in which past and present mutually informed each other.

[89] On Macaulay and James Mill, see Donald Winch, 'The Cause of Good Government: Philosophic Whigs versus Philosophic Radicals', in Collini *et al.*, *That Noble Science*, 100.

[90] David Eastwood, 'Robert Southey and the Meanings of Patriotism', *Journal of British Studies*, 21 (1992), 279–87.

[91] Southey, *Colloquies*, i. 18–19; Mendilow, *Romantic Tradition*, 67.

By establishing a sense of connection between the revolutionary turmoil of his contemporary experience and the 'great revolution' of the Reformation, 'the most momentous by which civilized society had ever, till then, been convulsed', the *Colloquies*' representation of the past could also function as a kind of normalizing activity, in which the historical imagination played a redemptive, sense-making role. As Southey's friend Sharon Turner put it in the preface to his *History of England*,

> Time is every day passing before us such extensive scenes of action, and such stupendous revolutions, that it seems to have become necessary to drop much of the detail in which former historians have properly indulged, in order to bring events together more in their connected masses; and to exhibit them in those great operations and results which have most influenced the succeeding periods.[92]

The *Colloquies*' ongoing comparison between the European world's two greatest 'revolutions' was thus also, in part, an attempt to re-establish a sense of historical continuity between pre- and post-revolutionary epochs. In this respect the reanimation of More can be understood as an elaborately realized literalization of a particularly pervasive trope of nineteenth-century historicism—the idea of historical enquiry as a type of palingenesis or resurrection, 'the pious reconstruction of the past in its integrity'.[93]

The *Colloquies*' historical narrative begins, familiarly enough, with the decline of feudal villeinage and the subsequent emergence of 'free labourers', a class which, according to Sir Thomas, soon splintered into an embryonic bourgeoisie and a destitute and largely criminal underclass.[94] Early forms of agrarian capitalism merely foreshadowed 'the rapid growth of commerce and . . . the great influx of wealth from the new found world . . . A trading spirit thus gradually superseded the rude but kindlier principle of the feudal system: profit and loss became the rule of conduct; in came calculation, and out went feeling.' The decline of 'clerical influence' on morals and learning, and the increasing wretchedness and ignorance of the lower classes, signalled the final ascendancy of the commercial spirit and mechanical philosophy, some

92 Sharon Turner, *History of England*, 3 vols. (1814–23), i, p. v.

93 Hayden White, *Metahistory: The Historical Imagination in Nineteenth-Century Europe* (Baltimore, 1973), 146.

94 Southey, *Colloquies*, i. 72–3; Alice Chandler, *A Dream of Order: The Medieval Ideal in Nineteenth-Century English Literature* (1971), 102–13.

time in the eighteenth century.[95] However, the evils of vagabondage and pauperism continued to keep pace with the rise of commerce and manufactures, so as to become, by the early nineteenth century, 'more intimately connected with the constitution of society, like a chronic and organic disease'. Montesinos does attempt to offer a slight qualification of More's gloomy prognoses by suggesting that 'the manufacturing system is a necessary stage in the progress of society', and by arguing that without its resources the British economy would have proved unable to sustain the war effort against Napoleon. The 'ordinary and natural consequences of commerce are every way beneficial,' Southey claimed; 'they are humanizing, civilizing, liberalizing . . .'. Nevertheless, 'the immediate and home effect of the manufacturing system, carried on as it now is upon the grand scale, is to produce physical and moral evil, in proportion to the wealth which it creates'.[96]

But the *Colloquies* are also centrally concerned, like Southey's *Quarterly* essays, with the effects of these momentous socio-economic changes upon literature, learning, and the press; and, above all, with the increasing democratization of political life through the rise of a 'Government of Public Opinion'.[97] According to Southey, the gradual ascendancy of the commercial spirit had tainted first scholarship, then the 'public press', and finally the 'public opinion' of the nation as a whole; while, at the same time, the growth of a middle class had produced greater competition for clerical livings and a large class of disillusioned literary 'adventurers'. The press had replaced the pulpit as the organ of public opinion, just as the cash nexus had replaced religion as the primary incentive to scholarship and literary endeavour. In contrast to the contemporary Anglican Church's apparent ineffectuality as a guardian of the social order, the press was more difficult to control; 'it acts more continuously as well as more widely', making it the obvious instrument of the apostles of infidelity and sedition.[98]

Macaulay recognized the significance of Southey's attack on the growing strength of public opinion, and strenuously defended an unregulated free market in opinion as the only legitimate arbiter of political good. 'A government can interfere in discussion', he maintained in his review of the *Colloquies*, 'only by making it less free than

[95] Southey, *Colloquies*, i. 79, 100–10.
[96] Ibid. i. 93, 158, 197.
[97] Ibid. ii. 202.
[98] Ibid. ii. 131, 205–6; see also ibid. ii. 50, 106–7.

it would otherwise be'.[99] Southey, on the contrary, linked the abstract dogmas of economic liberalization with the dangerously unregulated diffusion of political knowledge, and consequently with moral and physical disease: 'such are the notions of liberty in England, that evils of every kind, physical, moral, and political, are allowed their free range.' The 'plague of diseased opinions' afflicting the country, unleashed by a class of speculative literary adventurers and threatening the institution of 'ochlocracy', constituted the retributive final stage of the epochal ascendancy of the commercial spirit, or what E. P. Thompson was to describe, from a somewhat different perspective, as the 'great arch' of English bourgeois revolution.[100]

Southey's mounting concern at the political and moral 'infections' of the press and public opinion inspired a profound reassessment of his duties as poet laureate, a post that he had held since 1813. The claim that his 'prominence as a political writer and his reputation as a poet gave the laureateship renewed public eminence' might seem like a rather facetious suggestion. Yet Southey's contemporary political and literary reputation should not be underestimated: it was clearly far more substantial than many more unfortunate occupants of the post, before or since.[101] Moreover, Southey did much to redefine the laureateship, for better or worse, as an appointment which conferred certain broader responsibilities for moral reflection and commentary upon the state of the nation. It is particularly significant in this respect that the *Colloquies* were originally intended as an educational text, a 'Book of the State' to be taught alongside *The Book of the Church* under a monitorial system of national schooling.[102]

Southey was clearly very eager to use his official position as the literary mouthpiece of the political establishment to pursue the moral reformation of British society. He remained equally determined, however, to cultivate an authorial persona which would remain studiously aloof from the corrupting degradations of the 'trade' of literature. The conceit of More's ghostly reanimation was more than just a claim to 'conscious continuity with the first phase of the humanist challenge', as Raymond Williams has suggested, for it also allowed Southey

99 [Macaulay], 'Southey's Colloquies', *Edinburgh Review*, 50 (Jan. 1830), 549–51.

100 Southey, *Colloquies*, i. 56; E. P. Thompson, 'Peculiarities of the English', in id., *The Poverty of Theory and Other Essays* (1978), 47.

101 Eastwood, 'Meanings of Patriotism', 274.

102 See Eastwood, 'Intellectual Origins', 284; Robert Southey, *Selected Letters*, ed. John Wood Warter, 4 vols. (1856), iii. 416.

to present the *Colloquies* as the product of his scholarly communion with a historical period immediately anterior to the pathological corruptions of the republic of letters by the spirit of commerce, and thus to distinguish his own interventions in the public mind from the intellectual contagions of venal literary 'adventurers'.[103] The framing device of More's reanimation established an implicit distinction between an ideal of respectful didactic colloquy appropriate to the nation's moral re-education, and the speculative trading in infectious opinion characteristic of the diseased 'public mind' of Southey's age. By abstracting the *Colloquies*' didactic function into the private sphere of genial, gentlemanly conversation, Southey symbolically distanced his own social critique from the infectious encroachments of the 'public press', while simultaneously legitimating his self-styled role as a kind of patriotic laureate seer.[104]

The *Colloquies* repeatedly contrast the golden age of monastic learning with the increasing incompatibility between a 'trading people' and 'Sound learning'.[105] Speaking of the period immediately prior to the Reformation, More remarks that

> All men of learning in those days were, with very few exceptions, either monks or clergy; and they were not so many but that the Church and the Monasteries could provide for all. You have a numerous and rapidly increasing class of literary men, and a still more numerous one of persons, who take their opinions from them with as implicit a faith, and as much prostration of intellect, as the simplest peasant exhibits to the wiliest priest. That a little learning is dangerous, is true enough to have past into a proverb; it is not less true that a very little suffices for the stock in trade, upon which the scribes and scriveners of literature, who take upon themselves to direct the public, set up.[106]

The genial conversation of More and Montesinos allegorizes a readerly intimacy evocative of that earlier historical period in which the 'press . . . wrought only for a small part of the community', in contrast to its contemporary productions which appear to reach 'all classes, disseminating good and evil with a rapidity and effect inconceivable in former ages, as it would have been impossible'.[107]

[103] Raymond Williams, *Culture and Society*, 24.
[104] Southey, *Colloquies*, i. 152–3.
[105] Ibid. i. 282; see also ibid. ii. 36.
[106] Ibid. ii. 90–1.
[107] Ibid. i. 235.

This imaginative determination to recuperate a sense of scholarly Renaissance dialogue is expedited through the rhetorical conventions of literary antiquarianism. Sir Thomas's famous work of political theory evokes Southey's own disillusioned pantisocratic idealism; but More's ghostly presence also figures the text of *Utopia* itself (as well as the indeterminate ontology of its ideal commonwealth). Indeed, for Montesinos, it is the study of the textual document, considered as the expression of a singular consciousness embedded within a particular historical milieu, which offers the closest approximation to the literal 'resurrection' of the past. The dialogue with More's ghost also operates, therefore, as a sophisticated allegory of Southey's bibliophilic antiquarian historiography. Montesinos's library becomes a 'speaking remembrancer', in which he learns 'from the living minds of other ages'—the genial literary representatives of their times whose 'minds are in their works'.[108] Drawing on Isaac D'Israeli's sociological taxonomy of the literary character, the *Colloquies* represent Montesinos (and thus also Southey, of course) as an archetypal 'man of letters', an 'inheritor of whatever has been discovered by persevering labour, or created by inventive genius', and hence as the preserver and transmitter of a vital literary inheritance which might serve as a moral and intellectual counterweight to the forces of commerce and irreligion.[109]

Because of the profound historical equivalence of the Reformation and the present 'age of revolutions', the imaginative resurrection of Sir Thomas represents an affirmation of cultural consanguinity resistant to the historical schism dividing pre- and post-revolutionary epochs. That Southey's symbolic recuperation of the spirit of sixteenth-century scholarship is, indeed, intended to stave off the encroachments of a turbulent political present is suggested by the fact that the dispersion and concentration of the 'living minds' of Montesinos's library run in tandem with the ebb and flow of the forces of revolution. 'Not a few of these volumes', Montesinos remarks of his collection, 'have been cast up from the wreck of the family or convent libraries during the late Revolution'.[110] The reconstruction of bibliographical provenance—and the analogous idea of 'literary tradition' itself—act as metaphors for the reconstitution of a political legitimacy shattered by the forces of revolution. Thus, at one point in the *Colloquies* Montesinos relates how

[108] Id., *Colloquies*, ii. 345, 341, 339.
[109] Ibid. ii. 344.
[110] Ibid. ii. 337.

'About a score of the more out-of-the-way works in my possession belonged to some unknown person, who seems carefully to have gleaned the bookstores a little before or after the year 1790. He marked them with certain ciphers, always at the end of the volume . . . I have endeavoured without success to discover the name of their former possessor'.[111] The measure of the old regime's resistance to restoration (historiographical or otherwise) is suggested in the indecipherability of these ciphers, which, like the hieroglyphs More imagines engraved upon Keswick's prehistoric Lakeland monoliths, simultaneously invite and deny an interpretive act recuperative of an occulted past. The *Colloquies*' reanimation of the past offers the pleasures of identification, repetition, and mastery, but also the anxieties of alienation, disconnection, and estrangement. As such, the conceit of the haunting of the present by the past seems particularly appropriate to a literary form that is forced by its own internal logic into an experience of history as pre-eminently uncanny.[112]

SOUTHEY, MALTHUS, AND CULTURAL GLUT

The dialogue between More and Montesinos figures the conservative hermeneutics of literary antiquarianism, the imaginative recuperation of the 'living minds' of the past through a textual medium allegorized by Sir Thomas's ghostly presence. But, while Southey was irresistibly drawn to the solitary consolations of literary and historical research, he felt equally compelled to address himself to the country at large, to fulfil his obligations as laureate by communicating the *Colloquies*' 'wholesome truths' to a wayward nation. The dialogue form allowed the author to assert a nominal rhetorical distance from the unregulated marketplace of diseased ideas and corrupted language, in which 'what are called liberal opinions' were used to justify teaching 'the whole of the lower classes to read the incentives to vice, impiety and rebellion, which are prepared for them by an unlicensed press'.[113] Yet, precisely because of its unchecked corruption, the instruction of the popular mind in its 'moral and religious duties' was an imperative duty, forcing Southey to

[111] Ibid. ii. 338.

[112] Ibid. i. 43–4; cf. Stephen Bann, 'The Sense of the Past: Image, Text, and Object in the Formation of Historical Consciousness in Nineteenth-Century Britain', in *The New Historicism*, ed. H. Aram Veeser (New York, 1989), 113, 106.

[113] Southey, *Colloquies*, i. 35.

regard the *Colloquies*, like the *Book of the Church* and his patriotic biographies, as a redressive intervention in public opinion in the cause of church and state.[114] The *Colloquies* are thus oriented both inwards, towards a Renaissance humanist ideal of dialogue in retirement, arbitrated by august standards of deference and civility; and outwards, towards a 'public mind' perceived quite distinctly from this ideal, and indeed defined in opposition to it. In this case, however, dialogic 'communion' has as its corollary public 'communication', with its recurrent connotation of diseased, infectious opinion. Montesinos's reverential antiquarian accumulation of the literature and history of the past, described by More as an act of physical consumption or 'foliophagy', thus finds its contemporary equivalent in the discursive fecundity of 'Political Economy' and 'the New Science of Population', which Southey describes elsewhere as the intellectual equivalent of intestinal infection.[115]

The eccentricities of the *Colloquies'* literary form suggest the extent of Southey's anxiety that his public persona should in some sense transcend an 'intellectual atmosphere' contaminated by the forces of commerce, literary 'speculation', and the new sciences of society. Yet, despite the quite extraordinary vehemence of his attacks on the contagious abstractions of the new 'metapolitics', the *Colloquies'* diagnosis of the progress and prospects of society are themselves deeply infected with the arguments and assumptions of Malthusian economic thought. Malthus's mediate influence upon Southey's later writings is most obviously apparent in the latter's conversion to an abolitionist stance on the issue of the Poor Laws—a *volte face* which probably owed much to the urgings of his friend John Rickman, and which Southey managed to sustain only by an elaborate pattern of overt denunciation and the selective, covert appropriation of Malthusian argument.[116] Although scathing in his attacks on Malthus's recommendation of 'moral restraint' in the 1803 *Essay*, for example, Southey went on to condone an identical solution to the population problem. He was certainly willing to put his name to John Rickman's declaration, in 1818, that the 'one thing needful is to give the lower classes that knowledge and those principles which shall make them

114 Eastwood, 'Intellectual Origins', 279–80; Southey, *Selected Letters*, iii. 43.

115 Id., *Colloquies*, ii. 353; [id.], 'The Poor', *Quarterly Review*, 15 (Apr. 1816), 235.

116 Eastwood, 'Ruinous Prosperity', 75; Winch, *Riches and Poverty*, 312; Orlo Williams, *Lamb's Friend*, 151–2, 237.

understand that moral restraint is a duty, and that their duty and their interest are the same'.[117]

During the late 1810s, the *Quarterly* moved towards a position of support for the *Essay on the Principle of Population*, and in 1823 Malthus himself was persuaded to contribute to the review. His attacks on Ricardo certainly did much to consolidate an emergent rapprochement between the Tory press and Malthusian economics.[118] Despite his old antipathies, Southey must have been aware of the ideological support that the *Essay's* measured defence of agricultural protectionism could provide for Tory political argument, while Malthus's own attacks on Ricardo's 'abstract' and deductive methodology in the *Quarterly* may well have proved surprisingly compatible with Southey's own view of the intellectual absurdities of the new science of society. Nevertheless, Southey remained stubbornly unwilling to alter his view of Malthus's system as a spurious 'pseudo-science', which, by contravening 'the order of nature and of Providence', played the debate on population into the hands of those more godless, radicalized exponents of economic theory.[119]

After 1817 Malthus seems to have acquired a heightened sensitivity to the danger of periodic gluts of capital and goods. In the *Principles of Political Economy* (1820) he praised the economic effects of national debt and taxation, and recommended an increase in government expenditure, such as public works, as a means of overcoming capital glut.[120] This position was broadly compatible with Coleridge's *Lay Sermons*, which likewise placed considerable emphasis on the cyclical nature of economic growth; but it also suggests certain parallels with Southey's post-war critique of the country's commercial system. Such similarities do not so much imply the capitulation of 'Romantic' critique to a hegemonic new science of society, as suggest that the economic instincts of the Lake school formed part of a broader, under-consumptionist opposition to 'classical' macroeconomic orthodoxy, which had a considerable presence in the conservative press of the period, and which could draw on the

117 [Rickman and Southey], 'Means of Improving the People', *Quarterly Review*, 19 (Apr. 1818), 96–7.

118 [John Bird Sumner], 'Malthus on Population', *Quarterly Review*, 17 (July 1817), 369–403; [George Taylor], 'Godwin and Malthus on Population', ibid. 26 (Oct. 1821), 148–68. Malthus's contributions to the periodical can be found in vols. 29 (Apr. 1823), 214–39; and 30 (Jan. 1824), 297–334. See Semmel, *Free Trade Imperialism*, 73–5.

119 [Southey], 'Emigration Report', *Quarterly Review*, 37 (Mar. 1828), 572.

120 Semmel, *Free Trade Imperialism*, 66; Malthus, *Principles*, i. 353–4; ibid. i. 511–12.

arguments of a range of economic writers, from Spence, Malthus, and Chalmers through to a later generation of Tory political economists led by William Whewell and Richard Jones.[121]

Southey was adamant that selfishness and competition dominated the conduct of trade; and that, so long as this was the case, 'so long will a manufacturing country be liable to the distress that arises from having overstocked its markets'.[122] The post-war depression was in large part caused by the 'avidity with which immediate gain has been pursued' by the manufacturing and commercial interests. The iron trade, for example, 'was literally ruined by its prosperity, as overfeeding brings on disease in the animal body and death'. Cyclical economic distress would continue to afflict the body politic like a chronic and recurring infection, as machinery replaced human labour: 'we shall consequently suffer at intervals, more or less frequent, under that disease, which, in its hot fit, is mistaken for a symptom of public health, and in its cold one, shakes the body of the nation like an ague.'[123]

Because it was 'the tendency of the commercial, and more especially of the manufacturing system, to collect wealth rather than to diffuse it', Southey recommended that a 'liberal expenditure in peace upon public works' would have the same beneficial effect as war-time taxation and provisioning: 'Money thus expended will flow like chyle into the veins of the state, and nourish and invigorate it.' Macaulay's predictable response was to remark that, for Southey, the 'calamities arising from the collection of wealth in the hands of a few capitalists are to be remedied by collecting it in the hands of one great capitalist, . . . the all-devouring state'.[124] But Southey also proposed that colonization abroad, and the improvement of waste land at home, might provide solutions to the country's redundant population. 'The seas are ours,' he declared, 'and to every part of the uninhabited or uncivilized world our laws, our language, our institutions, and our Bible may be communicated'. Colonial emigration could thus function as the restorative 'bleeding' of a plethoric and apoplectic body politic.[125]

[121] See Gambles, *Protection and Politics*, 50–1; Hilton, *Age of Atonement*, 52; Waterman, *Revolution*, 245.

[122] [Southey], 'Emigration Report', *Quarterly Review*, 37 (Mar. 1828), 573.

[123] [Id.], 'Works on England', ibid., 15 (July 1816), 568; [id.], 'Emigration Report', ibid., 37 (Mar. 1828), 573.

[124] Southey, *Colloquies*, i. 193; id., *Letter to William Smith*, 40; [Macaulay], 'Southey's Colloquies', 562.

[125] [Southey], 'Inquiry into the Poor Laws', *Quarterly Review*, 8 (Dec. 1812), 356; [id.], 'Emigration Report', ibid., 37 (Mar. 1828), 577.

Malthus had conceded in 1817 that emigration might provide only a 'temporary relief' to Britain's distresses. It was left to Henry Brougham, and latterly Edward Gibbon Wakefield, to use the presumption of capital glut to justify a policy of 'free trade imperialism' in which the colonies would provide the destination for 'superabundant' capital as well as population.[126] Despite his ingrained imperialist sensibilities, Southey was far from viewing Britain's colonial economy in such terms, and followed other conservative writers, such as John Galt, in regarding colonial trade and emigration as potential correctives to an overcapitalized domestic economy.[127] The commercial system was corrupt, and needed to be restrained, rather than further encouraged through the aggressive expansion of colonial markets and a free trade empire. Moreover, despite his support for colonial emigration, Southey also acknowledged that, much like the manufacturing system, emigration tended to disrupt the 'natural ties' and 'domestic affections' essential for social order.[128]

Instead, Southey suggested that the excesses of the commercial system in England might be cured by a retributive process of capital flight to rival nations. Investment in foreign funds would permit 'redundant wealth' to flow abroad, allowing the 'benefits of commerce' to be multiplied, and its evils mitigated, through the global diffusion of wealth. In the *Colloquies*, Montesinos predicts that

> No sense of patriotism will check this [capital flight]; no laws can prevent it . . . This would be the euthanasy of the system, a gradual and easy decay without a shock; and, perhaps . . . were time allowed . . . we might then hope for a palingenesia, a restoration of national sanity and strength, a second birth . . . perhaps, I say . . . and were time allowed . . . for I say this doubtfully, and that ghostly shake of the head with which it is received does not lessen the melancholy distrust wherewith it is expressed.[129]

Montesinos's anxious hope is that the higher, providential laws of the market will ultimately bring about the restoration of 'natural' socio-economic relations, much as Southey's imaginative resurrection of Sir Thomas sought to effect a palingenetic restoration of the genteel scholarly mores of Renaissance literary culture. Throughout the

[126] Malthus, *Essay* (1803), i. 347; Henry Brougham, *An Inquiry into the Colonial Policy of the European Powers*, 2 vols. (Edinburgh, 1803); Semmel, *Free Trade Imperialism*, 45–7, 82–91.

[127] Gambles, *Protection and Politics*, 165–75.

[128] Southey, *Colloquies*, ii. 259.

[129] Ibid. i. 190; ibid. ii. 245.

Colloquies, Montesinos and his ghostly interlocutor take more or less opposed views on such fundamental questions of historical destiny, allowing the dialogue form itself to stage the dialectical reconciliation of divine providence and human freedom. In the case of the 'distempered' commercial system, that dialectic touches on certain early nineteenth-century assumptions concerning the providential and retributive nature of the laws of political economy. What is more remarkable, however, is that although Southey retained deep uncertainties concerning the self-immolating tendency of the commercial system, he was nevertheless prepared to extend the theory of glut and the 'euthanasy' of commerce to the sphere of literary production and consumption.

Southey's 1817 essay on 'Popular Disaffection' identified the eighteenth-century emergence of 'men of letters', and their subsequent corruption, with the growth of commerce and manufactures. While financial entrepreneurs, 'in the eagerness of speculation, seemed to think it impossible that the markets which were open to them should ever be overstocked', the literary profession was castigated for having succumbed to an identical impulse of intellectual 'speculation'.[130] In the *Colloquies*, Southey further developed this analogy with the suggestion that literary capital, like its pecuniary counterpart, could generate market returns out of all proportion to initial investment. Literary speculators established their reputation with 'slender' intellectual 'capital . . . upon the strength of which they claim credit, and obtain it as easily as their fellow adventurers in trade'. The relentless drive to expand the literary, like the commercial, market had produced a glut of legitimate intellectual goods and consequently also an increase in morally corrupting texts that 'deal in scandal, sedition, obscenity, or blasphemy, whichever article may be most in demand, according to the disease of the age'.[131]

In his final, climactic speech in the *Colloquies*, Montesinos defends the positive aspects of the 'diffusion of literature', while noting that this process 'has rendered the acquirement of general knowledge impossible, [and] tends inevitably to diminish the number of sound scholars, while it increases the multitude of sciolists'.[132] The circulation of 'cheap pub-

[130] [Id.], 'Popular Disaffection', *Quarterly Review*, 16 (Jan. 1817), 538, 544.

[131] Id., *Colloquies*, ii. 350; [id.], 'Popular Disaffection', *Quarterly Review*, 16 (Jan. 1817), 539.

[132] Id., *Colloquies*, ii. 420.

lications for a wide public' suggests to Montesinos that 'in proportion as the common people are supplied with wholesome entertainment . . . they will be less liable to be acted upon by fanaticism and sedition'. But he goes on to predict that

> [the] very diffusion of cheap books and cheap prints may, in its natural consequences, operate rather to diminish than to increase the number of adventurers in the arts. . . . More pictures will be painted, but fewer exhibited, more poetry written but less published, and in both arts talents which might else have been carried to an overstocked and unprofitable market, will be cultivated for their own sakes, and for the gratification of private circles, becoming thus a source of sure enjoyment and indirectly of moral good.

In an extension of under-consumptionist expectations to the sphere of literature and the arts, Montesinos predicts that the glut of commodified 'imitative talent' sapping the moral energies of the nation will annihilate itself in an analogous fashion to the projected 'euthanasy' of the commercial system as a whole.[133] The country's excess cultural capital will not, like superfluous economic capital, spill over into foreign and colonial markets, but instead will circumvent the corrupting influence of commerce (which generated the literary speculators of the radical press) by dissipating itself in the libraries, drawing rooms, and parlours of the nineteenth-century middle class. Just as emigration, the diffusion of religious principles, and the encouragement of moral restraint promise to eradicate the country's redundant labouring population, so the domestication of disendowed literary talent will operate as a check on that 'multiplication of books, which in its proportionate increase marvellously exceeds that of your growing population'.[134] For Montesinos, then, the 'health of the public mind' is to be safeguarded by the restrictive identification of the 'medium of intellectual life' with 'individual and domestic enjoyment', and the progressive displacement of middle-class cultural production and consumption into the private sphere.[135]

The conclusion to the *Colloquies* thus suggests a certain refinement of the Lake school ideal of humanistic, literary education that is lacking in comparable texts such as Coleridge's *Church and State*. On the one hand, Southey discriminated a primarily religious form of what he called 'moral culture' which, derived (via Rickman) from the Malthusian

[133] Ibid. ii. 421–4.
[134] Ibid. ii. 365.
[135] Ibid. ii. 423.

concept of moral restraint, was principally invoked in relation to the labouring classes, and which required, as far as Southey was concerned, a national, publicly funded system of parochial education in order to produce a 'people properly instructed in their duty, and trained up in habits of industry and hope'.[136] Yet Southey also gestured towards a specifically aesthetic sense of intellectual culture, which he identified above all with the middling orders of society. He noted with regret that the cost of a scholarly education had gradually risen, owing to 'the great increase of the middle ranks, by the higher degree of civilization which exists in those ranks', and by the monopolization of the few lucrative educational endowments that still existed by 'the sons of the wealthy' rather than poor scholars.[137] Nevertheless, this disendowed middle rank had, by the late 1820s, reached such a state of fevered intellectual activity that Southey began to entertain the hope that a cyclical, retributive cultural glut might finally legitimize its socio-economic identity. While in 1807 he had noted that the 'commercial system has long been undermining the distinction of ranks in society', by the time of the *Colloquies* he could claim, with considerably more confidence, that the 'growth of commercial wealth, the increase of our naval and military establishments, and the progress of education among the middle orders, have shaded the gradations of rank so imperceptibly into each other, that in this respect the social order has never been more happily constituted'. This shift of emphasis reflects Southey's realization that the conservative 'miscibility' of the English class system (famously celebrated in Burke's *Reflections*) might be reinvigorated by the creation of an aristocracy of spirit, a 'nobility . . . producible by culture'.[138]

Southey thus went rather further than his contemporaries in distinguishing the necessity for a national system of religious education—as a defence against popular infidelism, political disorder, and demographic crisis—from the secular, middle-class culture of 'imitative talent'. He did so, moreover, by employing the same under-consumptionist principles that informed Malthusian economic doctrine, and that we are more used to regarding as the intellectual anathema of aesthetic culture and its literary practitioners. Possessed of a more urgent intimation of the protracted post-1828 crisis of the Anglican establishment than Coleridge's plans for an endowed clerisy would suggest,

136 Id., *Colloquies*, ii. 104; [id.], 'The Poor', *Quarterly Review*, 15 (Apr. 1816), 235.

137 Id., *Colloquies*, ii. 131.

138 [Id.], *Letters from England*, iii. 83; id., *Colloquies*, ii. 216–18.

Southey moved towards the conclusion that the disendowed middle classes must take their place in Coleridge's 'progressive interest' of professional and commercial classes while pursuing the morally ennobling practice of aesthetic cultivation in a private environment of domestic independence.

This increasingly secular, privatized idea of culture would be opposed to 'philistine' forms of commercial society in the first instance, and religious heterodoxy (in the guise of middle-class dissent) only subordinately, and even then primarily on the grounds of spiritual and aesthetic impoverishment—the 'dissidence of dissent' rather than doctrinal error. Yet, in the same way that this privatized and largely domesticated practice retained an enduring attachment to the idea of endowed state education (archetypally centred on the ancient universities), it never quite abandoned its affinity with the notion of plebeian 'moral culture', to the extent that it too was forced to assume the contradictory form of an essentially 'inward' and individualistic process of spiritual growth which simultaneously commanded recognition of, and deferral to, the public institutions of church and state.

Conclusion: The Politics of Romanticism

From around the mid-1820s, political economy began the long slow process of intellectual consolidation that would eventually see Peacock's 'science of the sciences' transformed into a professionalized, academic discipline. The Drummond Chair of Political Economy was founded at Oxford in 1825, closely followed by the creation of similar posts at London University and Cambridge.[1] Nevertheless, the professionalization of economic science over the course of the nineteenth century was both intermittent and piecemeal. The ideological identity of political economy also remained remarkably diffuse, as a distinctive variety of 'Tory' economics emerged to challenge the radical and liberal–Whig affiliations of Ricardo and McCulloch. By the early 1830s, leaders of 'advanced' conservative thought, such as William Whewell and Adam Sedgwick, found it quite possible to attack Lockean empiricism and Paleyite utilitarianism, while simultaneously promoting a new conception of economic science as an inductive social theodicy admirably adapted to the task of re-establishing the intellectual credibility of the ancient universities.[2] Whatever tacit concessions the Lake school were willing to make to the growing respectability of political economy, their overt expressions of antipathy were, from this perspective at least, increasingly out of step with the intellectual temper of the pre-Victorian period. The anti-economism of Ultras and 'Tory radicals' such as Robert Southey and Michael Thomas Sadler, while influential enough in the late 1820s and early 1830s, could thereafter often seem somewhat marginalized, while the aged Coleridge's bilious attacks on political economy as 'the most horrible perversion of humanity and

[1] S. G. Checkland, 'The Advent of Academic Economics in England', *The Manchester School of Economic and Social Studies*, 19 (1951), 50–1.

[2] J. B. Schneewind, *Sidgwick's Ethics and Victorian Moral Philosophy* (Oxford, 1977), 89; Checkland, 'Academic Economics', 49–50; Hilton, *Age of Atonement*, 42–55.

moral justice' proved all too easy to characterize as crude, reactionary, and misinformed.[3]

But the early nineteenth-century controversies surrounding economic science did not, by any means, simply disappear without trace, and nor could its practitioners be expected to pursue influence and respectability for their discipline by retreating at once into ever more obscure and specialized researches. The intellectual hegemony of political economy within the nascent social sciences, together with the relatively late date at which it became fully professionalized, only intensified the question of its status and value within the broader intellectual history of the Victorian period. And, of course, some version of the Lake school's attack on economic science did survive. From Carlyle to Ruskin and beyond, the 'literary critique of political economy was handed down to the twentieth century, and continues to haunt the historiography of, and cultural debate on, the consequences to British society of the industrial revolution'.[4] Part of the explanation for this, perhaps rather curious afterlife lies in the fact that the Lake poets' critique of political economy included, almost from its inception, a significant element of hostility to utilitarianism, both theological and secular. Largely as a result, the writings of the Lake school continued to exert a considerable influence upon the subsequent Victorian debate on the legitimacy of utilitarian ethics. Political economy was implicated in these developments, in the first instance, because of the intellectual links between Paleyite theological utilitarianism and Malthusian economics, but latterly also through the complex political and philosophical affiliations between Benthamism and the Ricardian school.

The historical influence of Lake school social criticism has, nevertheless, typically been represented in terms of a relatively homogenous Romantic tradition, a 'literary' or 'cultural' critique of industrial capitalism and its apologists, tenaciously preserving an embattled social conscience in defiance of an individualistic, spiritually impoverished nineteenth-century middle class. The persistence of this kind of perspective, which has had considerable consequences for our

[3] Samuel Taylor Coleridge, *Table Talk*, ed. Carl Woodring, 2 vols. (London and Princeton, 1990), i. 352.

[4] Winch, *Riches and Poverty*, 290; see also William D. Grampp, 'Classical Economics and its Moral Critics', *History of Political Economy*, 5 (1973), 359–74; Cheyney C. Ryan, 'The Fiends of Commerce: Romantic and Marxist Criticisms of Classical Political Economy', *History of Political Economy*, 13 (1981), 80–94.

understanding of nineteenth-century intellectual life, appears doubly curious given the notoriously unstable scholarly consensus on the ideological identity of 'British Romanticism' itself. The concept of the 'Romantic', considered as a descriptive category applicable both to a group of early nineteenth-century writers and texts, and to their subsequent influence on literary culture more generally, enjoyed a complex and sometimes confused history in Victorian journalism and belles lettres.[5] As an integral constituent of literary critical vocabulary, it has continued to trouble scholars and critics up until the present day. This is not the place to undertake a detailed study of the nineteenth-century construction, and contestation, of what might now be described as a 'Romantic ideology'. Something of the character of this process can, however, be suggested through a brief examination of the crucial early stages in the struggle over the ideological legacy of the Lake school, during the late 1820s and 1830s. But it also seems necessary to offer some concluding remarks on the equally complex history of Romantic social criticism in the more recent literary and intellectual historiography of the Victorian period.

THE RISE AND FALL OF ROMANTIC CRITIQUE

The enduringly problematic identity of British literary Romanticism can no doubt be related, in large part, to the relative historical instability of its poetic canon. Yet, despite its strong historical association with literature in verse, one of the most significant departures in the ongoing history of 'Romanticism', as an element of literary-historical discourse, has been its identification with a nineteenth-century tradition of social criticism in prose, a tradition that has often been understood to include some of the most trenchant Victorian critics of capitalist modernity. Literary studies of Victorian 'non-fiction prose' began to appear in the Anglo-American academy only around the 1930s, a development that can most obviously be explained as a function of ongoing disciplinary specialization.[6] From the very start, however, this new subcategory of Victorian literary studies often tended to be associated with some kind

[5] A history explored in some detail by George Whalley, 'England: Romantic—Romanticism', in Hans Eichner (ed.), *'Romantic' and its Cognates: The European History of a Word* (Manchester, 1972), 157–262. For an influential recent discussion, see McGann, *Romantic Ideology*, *passim*.

[6] Carol T. Christ, '"The Hero as Man of Letters": Masculinity and Victorian Nonfiction Prose', in Thaïs E. Morgan (ed.), *Victorian Sages and Cultural Discourse: Renegotiating*

of 'Romantic' sensibility. Émile Legouis, writing in 1934, claimed of nineteenth-century literary culture that the 'prophetic spirit of the great Romantics still survived; but it had passed from the poets to the prose writers. The guides to whom men turned when uncertain of their path were, apart from the scholars proper and the philosophers, such thinkers as Carlyle or Ruskin, and later, for a more limited public, Matthew Arnold.'[7] This attempt to recuperate a specifically Romantic tradition within non-fiction prose writing of the Victorian period might, then, be explained not just as a product of disciplinary expansion and specialization, together with the related, perennial desire to provide a historical genealogy for the academic critic's sense of social mission, but also as a defensive reaction to the modernist revolution in critical attitudes and, in particular, to the assault on Romantic sensibilities led by T. S. Eliot and (more ambivalently) F. R. Leavis.

From these early innovations within English literary studies, it is possible to trace the developments in scholarly and critical practice that would make some version of a Romantic ideological inheritance central to the literary-historical representation of Victorian social criticism. But this process was further encouraged by a presumption that the dominant contours of nineteenth-century intellectual life were constituted in the dynamic tension between two antithetical sensibilities: Romantic, conservative, idealist, and 'cultured', on the one hand; utilitarian, progressive, materialist, and 'philistine', on the other. Leavis's reinterpretation of John Stuart Mill's essays on 'Bentham' and 'Coleridge', while not the earliest, was nevertheless one of the most influential examples of this tendency to regard Romanticism and utilitarianism as the completing counterparts of a Victorian *Weltanschauung*.

The Leavisite project entailed a cautious and partial reappropriation of those 'Romantic' attitudes that were, superficially at least, compatible with the *Scrutiny* circle's nostalgic defence of 'organic society' against the 'technologico-Benthamite' encroachments of modern, mass civilization.[8] At the same time, his deference to the 'disciplined' quality of Bentham's thought, and praise for Mill's synthesis of the two thinkers,

Gender and Power (New Brunswick, 1990), 27; Stefan Collini, 'From "Non-fiction" Prose to "Cultural Criticism": Genre and Disciplinarity in Victorian Studies', in Juliet John and Alice Jenkins (eds.), *Rethinking Victorian Culture* (Basingstoke, 2000), 15.

[7] Émile Legouis, *A Short History of English Literature* (Oxford, 1934), 311, quoted in Christ, 'The Hero as Man of Letters', 27.

[8] See Mulhern, *Moment of 'Scrutiny'*; Donald Winch, 'Mr Gradgrind and Jerusalem', in Collini *et al.* (eds.), *Economy, Polity, and Society*, 243–66; and on the persistence of a

served to ground Leavis's own arguments for a 'more athletic conception of criticism as a discipline of intelligence' in the modern 'English School'. To that extent, Leavis's essay on Mill, Bentham, and Coleridge can also be regarded as an implicit response to T. S. Eliot's more patrician vision of post-war cultural retrenchment, as well as to I. A. Richard's supposedly 'unathletic' capitulation to utilitarian ideas.[9] But Leavis also claimed that the creative tension between Coleridgean and Benthamite intellectual currents formed a kind of master trope for understanding nineteenth-century culture as a whole. Bentham and Coleridge thus became the 'key and complementary powers by reference to which we can organize into significance so much of the field to be charted'.[10]

This argument has had a long and significant life of its own in literary and intellectual histories of the nineteenth century; but it has also had a considerable influence on subsequent literary approaches to Victorian social criticism. The latter field was first delineated, somewhat inexactly, by John Holloway's *The Victorian Sage* (1953), a work of New Critical formalization which embraced a startlingly diverse range of writers, including Carlyle, Disraeli, Eliot, Newman, Arnold, and Hardy. These 'sages' were drawn together by reference to their 'outlook' and mode of argument, an affinity that was reliant in the last analysis upon a kind of fideistic intuitionism. Yet, despite his wilful lack of historical perspective, Holloway was clear that the genealogy of the Victorian sage could be traced back to Coleridge, who 'might almost be called the founder in modern England of this kind of thought'. The intellectual sensibility peculiar to the sage was in turn implicitly counterposed to the shallow and dissociative mental habits associated with utilitarianism and positivism.[11] The sage was, moreover, described as having sought solutions to the most fundamental 'problems, both social and speculative',

distorting Leavisite hostility to Benthamism in studies of the nineteenth-century novel, see Kathleen Blake, '*Bleak House*, Political Economy, Victorian Studies', *Victorian Literature and Culture*, 25 (1997), 1–21.

[9] F. R. Leavis, 'Introduction' to J. S. Mill, *Mill on Bentham and Coleridge* (1950), 3rd edn. (1962), 2; T. S. Eliot, *Notes towards the Definition of Culture* (1948).

[10] Leavis, 'Introduction', 7.

[11] John Holloway, *The Victorian Sage: Studies in Argument* (1953), 4. The 'Positivist–Utilitarian attack on imaginative literature' would later be blamed for stifling recognition of the expressive possibilities of prose style being explored by Arnold, Ruskin, Carlyle, and Newman, which had first been suggested in the critical writings of the English Romantics: see Travis R. Merritt, 'Taste, Opinion, and Theory in the Rise

of the Victorian period (although these were rarely discussed within any determinate historical framework).

This formalist reluctance to deal explicitly with questions of historical context and intellectual influence severely limited Holloway's thesis, and it was only with Raymond Williams's *Culture and Society* (1958) that the idea of a discrete 'tradition' of nineteenth-century social criticism found its fullest, and most influential, expression. Where Holloway had treated the 'sage' through a series of largely synchronic case studies, Williams historicized—and politicized—his field of interest, resulting in an eclectic canon of novelists, poets, and social critics shaped by, and responsive to, the intellectual and material impact of the Industrial Revolution, stretching from Burke and the English Romantics through to Pugin, Ruskin, and Morris. Williams's strong emphasis on the Romantic component of this tradition discovered in the early nineteenth-century literary sensibility a distinctive reaction against mechanization and industrialization, and a corresponding imaginative defence of humanistic 'culture'. Williams's argument bore the distinct imprint of Leavis's discussion of John Stuart Mill, although Mill's essays on Bentham and Coleridge were now presented as a crucial turning point in a utilitarian sequestration—and consequent impoverishment—of the Coleridgean ideal of 'cultivation'.[12] This latter claim is, in fact, quite representative of the way in which many members of the British New Left came to identify with some version of the Romantic temper as part of a broader stress on the humanistic and indigenous sources of British radicalism after 1956. The result was the retrospective construction of a nineteenth-century 'culture and society tradition' of social critics, stretching from Coleridge and the other Romantic poets to Carlyle, Arnold, Ruskin, and Morris.

This development was, in turn, closely connected to a historical interpretation of the idea of 'culture' which situated the British origins of this concept firmly within a Romantic literary tradition. From the late 1950s, Williams's writings proved central, along with those of E. P. Thompson and Richard Hoggart, to the academic consolidation of what Alan Sinfield has termed British 'left-culturalism', a body of work that was to play a formative role in the subsequent emergence of Cultural

of Victorian Prose Stylism', in George Levine and William Madden (eds.), *The Art of Victorian Prose* (New York, 1986), 9–13.

[12] Raymond Williams, *Culture and Society*, 49–70.

Studies.[13] Both left-culturalism and the academic innovations which it inspired involved, to a greater or lesser extent, 'the critique of a certain reductionism and economism' identified within Marxism.[14] In this case, a Germano-Cumbrian genealogy for the idea of culture, which located it clearly within the terms of a nineteenth-century Romantic humanist assault upon utilitarianism, political economy, and the Mammonistic excesses of capitalist society, provided an exemplary way of mediating the problematic relationship between British left-culturalism and classical Marxist analysis. Indeed, this move could, with certain qualifications, be seen to be sanctioned by Marx himself, who had after all identified the 'romantic viewpoint' as the 'legitimate antithesis' of bourgeois ideology—albeit in the context of a critique of nostalgic primitivism which explained how, in pre-capitalist societies, 'the single individual seems to be developed more fully, [only] because he has not yet worked out his relationships in their fullness, or erected them as independent social powers and relations opposite himself'.[15]

The persistence of a capacious, ill-defined Romantic sensibility in the literary and intellectual historiography of the nineteenth century was subsequently encouraged by an influential account of Britain's long-term economic decline which stressed the role of certain 'cultural' factors in precipitating the nation's fall from international pre-eminence. These included the aristocratic and anti-business orientation of the public school system; the social and intellectual currency enjoyed by nostalgic forms of pastoralism and historicism; and a generalist, amateurist, and 'gentlemanly' ethical and professional ideal which stifled the growth of an entrepreneurial economy as well as inhibiting the emergence of a dynamic indigenous intelligentsia. The influence of this cultural model of national decline has been very wide, and can certainly be linked to a significant modulation in the representation of both Romanticism and utilitarianism in the intellectual historiography of the nineteenth century.

It appeared at one time quite unproblematic to depict the survival of a Romantic sensibility in Victorian Britain as an embattled response to a powerful and monolithic liberal consensus, comprising, in the words

[13] Alan Sinfield, *Literature Politics and Culture in Postwar Britain*, rev. edn. (1997), 241–5.

[14] Stuart Hall, 'Cultural Studies and its Theoretical Legacies', in Lawrence Grossberg *et al.* (eds.), *Cultural Studies* (New York, 1992), 279.

[15] Karl Marx, *Grundrisse*, trans. Martin Nicolaus (Harmondsworth, 1973), 162; Raymond Williams, *Politics and Letters: Interviews with* New Left Review (1979), 116.

of one critic, 'Benthamite ideology, with its unhistorical and analytic view of society, individualism and utilitarianism in ethics, laissez-faire in economics—the whole outlook of a progressive, increasingly industrial country'.[16] Reversing the ideological balance of power implied by this account, Gramscian historiography of the 1960s and 1970s now attributed the alleged failure of the English middle class to consolidate its commanding economic position in nineteenth-century society to the fact that the industrial bourgeoisie's preferred ideology—identified with Benthamite utilitarianism—was a 'fanatically bleak materialism . . . ill-suited to creating that cultural and value system which is the mark of a hegemonic ideology'.[17] A philistine, intellectually impoverished, and historically ineffectual bourgeois ideology now appeared to have capitulated before a dominant, reactionary, and anti-capitalist ethos sustained by 'a rather insouciant, romantic traditionalism'.[18] Meanwhile, from a rather different perspective, Martin Wiener's *English Culture and the Decline of the Industrial Spirit* set out to document a 'movement of reaction to the industrial revolution that traced back to the Romantic poets', and once again invoked J. S. Mill to show how 'even that exemplar of liberal thought' had recoiled from the values of 'commercial-industrial society'.[19]

Neo-liberal economic and educational 'modernizers' quickly seized upon these potential indictments of the anti-business attitudes supposedly lurking at the heart of the British national character. Indeed, the concern shown by scholars of the nineteenth century to counter the Thatcherite invocation of 'Victorian values' only latterly extended to a critical and coherent analysis of the crudely 'anti-entrepreneurial' interpretation of British culture that frequently

[16] Graham Hough, 'Coleridge and the Victorians', in Hugh Sykes Davies and George Watson (eds.), *The English Mind: Studies in the English Moralists Presented to Basil Willey* (Cambridge, 1964), 182.

[17] Perry Anderson, 'The Origins of the Present Crisis' (1964), repr. in id., *English Questions* (1992), 32. This aspect of the 'Nairn–Anderson thesis' was in turn challenged by E. P. Thompson, in 'The Peculiarities of the English' (1965), repr. in id., *Poverty of Theory*, 56–64.

[18] Tom Nairn, 'The Future of Britain's Crisis: A Political Analysis', in Isaac Kramnick (ed.), *Is Britain Dying? Perspectives on the Current Crisis* (Ithaca, NY, 1979), 245. This narrative has also influenced studies of nineteenth-century fiction. See e.g. Gallagher, *Industrial Reformation*, 267; and the discussion in McKendrick, '"Gentlemen and Players" Revisited'.

[19] Martin Wiener, *English Culture and the Decline of the Industrial Spirit, 1850–1980* (Cambridge, 1981), 29, 31–2; see also T. W. Heyck, *The Transformation of Intellectual Life in Victorian England* (1982), 190–4, 227.

went with it.[20] But, if the broader weaknesses vitiating many cultural explanations for national decline are now pretty apparent, their influence on our understanding of the Romantic movement, and its ideological legacy in British intellectual and literary life, has passed relatively unexamined.[21]

A heightened sensitivity to the supposedly anti-bourgeois attitudes pervading nineteenth-century literary culture certainly stimulated a new generation of literary historians and critics to challenge the Romantic identifications of the 'old' New Left. The 'Romantic humanist heritage . . . transmitted by the later Coleridge to Carlyle, Disraeli, Arnold and Ruskin' was now consistently attacked as the vehicle of a deceptively oppositional form of conservatism, a shift in perspective that would eventually converge with 'New Historicist' and 'cultural materialist' suspicions of the Romantic ideology as—at its crudest—a form of reactionary mystification. According to Terry Eagleton, for example, the 'impoverished empiricism' of utilitarian philosophy found itself

> driven to exploit the fertile symbolic resources of Romantic humanism, drawing on its metaphysical sanctions and quasi-feudalist social models to ratify bourgeois property relations. The 'Culture and Society' tradition is the literary record of this ideological conjuncture; John Stuart Mill, mechanistically harnessing Coleridge to Bentham in the late eighteen-thirties, provides one of its more palpable instances.[22]

Eagleton would later reimagine the rise of the Victorian 'sage', via Habermas, as a symptom of 'mounting class struggle' and the fragmentation of 'the bourgeois public sphere'. But the familiar, Romantically derived tradition of Victorian social critics remained firmly in

[20] See James Raven's commentary in 'British History and the Enterprise Culture', *Past and Present*, 123 (1989), 178–204; and, on Victorian values, Eric M. Sigsworth (ed.), *In Search of Victorian Values: Aspects of Nineteenth-Century Thought and Society* (Manchester, 1988); T. C. Smout (ed.), *Victorian Values* (Proceedings of the British Academy, 78, Oxford, 1992).

[21] In addition to Raven, 'British History', see W. D. Rubinstein, *Capitalism, Culture, and Decline in Britain 1750–1990* (1993); Bruce Collins and Keith Robbins (eds.), *British Culture and Economic Decline* (1990). For correctives to the idea of the middle class's nineteenth-century 'failure', see Janet Wolff and John Seed (eds.), *The Culture of Capital: Art, Power and the Nineteenth-Century Middle Class* (Manchester, 1988); R. J. Morris, *Class, Sect and Party: The Making of the British Middle Class, Leeds 1820–1850* (Manchester, 1990), 9–10.

[22] Terry Eagleton, *Criticism and Ideology: A Study in Marxist Literary Theory* (1976), 102–3. For a more recent attempt to identify a Romantic 'culture and society tradition' as a hegemonic instrument of the nineteenth-century state, see Lloyd and Thomas, *Culture and the State*.

place. The sage was once again identified with Coleridge, Carlyle, Kingsley, Ruskin, and Arnold. Amateurist, idealist, 'aloofly authoritarian', he (the title has only rarely been conferred on women) found himself temperamentally alienated from the growing professionalization of journalistic and literary culture.[23]

Such analyses helped to consolidate a yet more ambitious identification of Romantic values with the nineteenth-century 'literary intelligentsia' as a whole, a class whose governing ethos could now be depicted as nostalgic, pastoral, anti-capitalist, and suspiciously preoccupied with the paternalistic dissemination of 'culture'. The enduring ideological legacy of a 'moralized Romanticism' thus explained the 'crucial' fact that, in striking contrast to the Modernist generation, 'the Victorian intellectual . . . was not alienated'.[24] The hegemonic status of this conservative, and vestigially Romanticized literary intelligentsia could claim additional confirmation from its apparent development within the ideological vacuum created by the 'defective' nature of 'the rationalist philosophy of the new industrial-bourgeois order'.[25] The supposed values and attitudes of the Romantic movement could thus suggest the essential conservatism of nineteenth-century literary life as a whole, while simultaneously marginalizing the broader cultural significance of a notionally ineffectual and philistine bourgeois ideology.

More qualified studies of nineteenth-century intellectual life have done much to complicate this picture of the Victorian intelligentsia, often through detailed examination of the social and institutional contexts of cultural production and consumption, from metropolitan periodicals to the provincial voluntary society.[26] Yet the nature of the 'Romantic' legacy in Victorian Britain continues to seem rather obscure, despite our growing appreciation of the complex relationship between literary canon formation and Victorian cultural politics. The Romantic component of nineteenth-century social criticism, as well as Victorian

[23] Terry Eagleton, *The Function of Criticism: From the* Spectator *to Post-Structuralism* (1984), 37, 39, 47.

[24] Malcolm Bradbury, *The Social Context of Modern English Literature* (Oxford, 1971), 37–8. Cf. the related claim that the Coleridgean 'clerisy' provided 'an ideology for the intelligentsia' (Ben Knights, *The Idea of the Clerisy in the Nineteenth Century* (Cambridge, 1978), 7).

[25] Tom Nairn, 'The English Literary Intelligentsia', *Bananas*, ed. Emma Tennant (1977), 69. See also Terry Eagleton, *The Idea of Culture* (Oxford, 2000), 67.

[26] See e.g. Collini, *Public Moralists*, 37–57; Morris, *Class, Sect and Party*, 228–63.

middle-class values, is still described in terms of an anti-industrial 'culture and society tradition', which has in turn often been reliant upon a reductive opposition between Romanticism, on the one hand, and the impoverished, 'bourgeois' ideologies of utilitarianism and political economy, on the other.

TORIES, HIGH CHURCHMEN, AND APOSTLES: THE IDEOLOGICAL LEGACY OF THE LAKE SCHOOL

The preceding brief remarks go some way towards explaining why John Stuart Mill's essays on 'Bentham' and 'Coleridge' have assumed such a paradigmatic status within literary-historical discussions of English Romanticism's nineteenth-century afterlife. Taken together, Mill's essays portray a titanic struggle of ideas and feeling; 'the revolt of the human mind against the philosophy of the eighteenth century'.[27] But, particularly in the essay on Coleridge, such rhetoric often results from the way in which Mill appropriates, and situates his own intellectual development within, a particular historical narrative that was in large part derived from Coleridge himself—namely, the long-term material and intellectual influence of Lockean empiricism and the 'commercial spirit' upon English society. To interpret the essays on these, their own terms involves acceding to the same sorts of assumptions respecting the internal logic of intellectual history that Mill was developing through his appreciation, not just of Coleridge, but also of Comte and the Saint-Simonian idea of 'critical' and 'organic' historical periods. This fact alone might be sufficient to cast doubt on the apparent compatibility between Mill's essays and F. R. Leavis's subsequent representations of nineteenth-century intellectual and cultural history as delicately suspended between 'technologico-Benthamite' progress, and Romantic reaction.

But the enduring appeal of Mill's essays also has a great deal to do with his *Autobiography*, and its celebrated account of the role played by Lake school Romanticism (and, more specifically, Wordsworth's poetry) in rescuing him from the barren abstractions of Benthamite pedagogy. The assumption that Bentham and Coleridge, and Mill's essays upon them, represent the dominant, oppositional components of early nineteenth-century intellectual life has thus been encouraged by their supposed appropriateness as metonyms for Mill's own mental develop-

[27] [John Stuart Mill], 'Coleridge', *London and Westminster Review*, 33 (Mar. 1840), 263.

ment, and the resultant implicit elevation of their author into a kind of intellectual everyman for his age. Mill's mental crisis, and redemptive discovery of Wordsworth's conservative humanism, can thus be understood as a psycho-biographical vindication both of the 'revolt' of the nineteenth century against the eighteenth, and of the rather different, but clearly related claim that, 'Somewhere in the nineteenth century . . . the English middle class lost its nerve'.[28]

The continuing strength of such claims has often relied upon the assumption that, by 1840, the ideological associations of Wordsworth's poetry, and Lake school Romanticism more generally, were overwhelmingly nostalgic, conservative, and anti-industrial. In fact, however, the political and religious affiliations of the Lake school continued to be vigorously contested throughout the late 1820s and 1830s. One mid-Victorian writer, looking back to the period following Coleridge's death in 1834, noted the proliferation of competing 'attempts to claim his authority for various movements of the day', while a more recent commentator has remarked upon the 'striking' fact that 'Wordsworth could be of use to such opposed figures' as John Stuart Mill and William Whewell.[29] This was not, however, simply a function of the personal, 'spiritual' resources that Romanticism offered to a secularizing age; it also reflected the deeply contentious political dimension of the Lake school's critical reception in this period.[30] It is true that the extent of Wordsworth's early radicalism was little appreciated at this time, while the youthful jacobinism of Coleridge and Southey had largely been neutralized by teleological biographical narratives which led by a seemingly inexorable logic to the Lake poets' 'mature' political conservatism. Southey in particular, whose political apostasy was in certain respects far more dramatic than that of his fellow poets, found his reputation largely confined to the pantheon of the Tory literary establishment. But, in the case of Wordsworth and Coleridge at least, the years leading up to Mill's Wordsworthian 'conversion' also witnessed a new generation of liberal Anglicans and middle-class radicals attempting to wrest the

[28] Raymond Williams, *The Long Revolution* (1961), 319; Alfred Cobban, *Edmund Burke and the Revolt against the Eighteenth Century: A Study of the Political and Social Thinking of Burke, Wordsworth, Coleridge and Southey* (1929); Lepenies, *Between Literature and Science*, 104. The most balanced discussion of Mill's breakdown, together with its wider implications and connotations, is probably Thomas, *Philosophic Radicals*, 147–205.

[29] [F. J. A. Hort], 'Coleridge', *Cambridge Essays* (1856), 293; Gill, *Wordsworth and the Victorians*, 58.

[30] Ibid. 41.

ideological identity of the Lake school away from its Tory and High Church heirs-apparent.

As political consensus within the Tory party fragmented in the late 1820s, the Lake school critique of political economy and 'mechanical philosophy' attained a new degree of influence within Ultra opinion in the wake of the first Reform Act. By 1840, *Fraser's Magazine* was defending a Tory canon comprising Scott, Coleridge, Wordsworth, and Southey against the insidious influence of Bentham, McCulloch, the Mills, and Ricardo—the purveyors of 'useful knowledge', secular education, and political economy.[31] Over the course of the 1830s, the nostalgic, paternalistic politics exemplified by Southey's *Colloquies* became a hallmark of both 'Tory radicalism' and the Young England movement. Factory reformers such as Shaftesbury, Sadler, and Oastler, for example, all seem to have drawn on the Lake poets' denunciations of political economy in their own attacks on the manufacturing system.[32] Sadler's *Law of Population* is perhaps the best known Tory radical riposte to Malthusian ideas; but it was Robert Benton Seeley, an evangelical publisher and dedicated supporter of Shaftesbury, whose political writings displayed the most obvious debt to the Lake school critique of political economy.[33]

The influence of Lake school rhetoric was, however, even more pronounced in ecclesiological debate. Newman and Keble are merely the most familiar examples of the intellectual and spiritual debt owed by many early Victorian high Anglicans and tractarians to Wordsworth and Coleridge.[34] A number of other High Church controversialists of this period, including Christopher Wordsworth (the poet's nephew) and the young William Gladstone, clearly recognized the potential for reapplying the Lake poets' social and educational arguments to the secularizing forces at work in the ongoing 'diffusion of knowledge', which they

[31] [William Maginn], 'Useful Knowledge', *Fraser's Magazine*, 21 (Feb. 1840), 160, quoted in David Roberts, *Paternalism in Early Victorian England* (1979), 68.

[32] For evidence of Southey's influence on Young England, see [Lord John Manners] 'Anglo-Catholicus', *Monastic and Manufacturing Systems* (1843). Edwin Hodder, *The Life and Work of the Seventh Earl of Shaftesbury, K. G.*, 3 vols. (1886), i. 259; Richard Oastler, *Brougham versus Brougham, on the New Poor Law* (1847), pp. viii–xi; id., *Eight Letters to the Duke of Wellington* (1835), 41, 150 n.; Mendilow, *Romantic Tradition*, 150–70.

[33] Michael Thomas Sadler, *The Law of Population: A Treatise*, 2 vols. (1830); [Robert Benton Seeley], *The Perils of the Nation* (1843), p. xv; [id.], *Remedies Suggested, for Some of the Evils which Constitute 'The Perils of the Nation'* (1844), 43–52, 392–8.

[34] [John Henry Newman], 'State of Religious Parties', *British Critic*, 25 (Apr. 1825), 400. Prickett, *Romanticism and Religion*, 91–119, 152–210.

continued to regard as a serious challenge to popular instruction under the aegis of the established church. As early as the mid-1820s, the Cambridge divine Hugh James Rose was leaning heavily upon Coleridgean rhetoric in order to sharpen the terms of his opposition between a devotional understanding of 'pure Literature' and the secular debasement of learning that had accompanied the rise of the commercial spirit and the tyranny of 'public opinion'. Locke was condemned by Rose as the intellectual 'master' of the modern, Benthamite utilitarians and political economists, a breed of thinkers who, he claimed, reflected the predominance of a 'low and mechanical philosophy' of individualism and material greed. In an ethical atmosphere such as this, 'the leading publications . . . unquestionably speak of intellect, its improvement, and its progress, in the same language which they apply to any other commodity within the sphere of political economy'.[35] In 1836, Rose became the principal of King's College, London, and began to promote the idea of 'literature as a signifying vehicle for the promotion of traditional religious and nationalistic ideals', defined very much in opposition to the supposedly 'utilitarian' understanding of literary study emerging from the rival London University (henceforth University College).[36]

The Lake school element in High Church politics continued to find a focus in the educational debates of the 1830s leading up to the Whig national education bill of 1839.[37] Gladstone's *The State in its Relation with the Church* (1838) is perhaps the most obvious example of this tendency, a work that is explicitly indebted to Coleridge's 'beautiful and profound' ecclesiology in *Church and State*. Following Coleridge, Gladstone identified the Established Church with the 'soul, underlying and animating' the body politic, and hence with the responsibility for 'a *cultivation* of the inward man, which is the root, the corrective, and the safeguard of *civilisation*'.[38] Gladstone would go on in his *Church Principles* (1840) to make an explicit analogy between the 'revival of poetry' and 'what is termed, somewhat hazardously and loosely, a *revival* of religion'. He was thus able to invoke Coleridge's

[35] Hugh James Rose, *The Tendency of Prevalent Opinions about Knowledge* (Cambridge, 1826), 5–13; id., *Christianity Always Progressive* (1829), 19.

[36] Court, *Institutionalizing English Literature*, 88.

[37] On educational debate in this period, see Brent, *Liberal Anglican Politics*, 218–51.

[38] William Ewart Gladstone, *The State in its Relation with the Church* (1838), 2nd edn. (1839), 17. See also Christopher Wordsworth, 'On Secular Education' and 'The Office of Holy Spirit in Education', in id., *Occasional Sermons, Preached in Westminster Abbey*, 3rd ser. (1852).

moderating critique of Wordsworth's primitivist poetry of nature as an inspirational example of the need to balance affective, reforming vigour with the claims of tradition, precedent, and established forms—both ecclesiological and aesthetic.[39] That Gladstone's High Church politics could accommodate this kind of discussion with such apparent ease is particularly significant, given its parallels with John Stuart Mill's contemporaneous attempts, from within the philosophic radical party, to reconcile the reforming urge of Benthamism with Lake school conservativism. The politics of the Lake poets clearly formed an important, and apparently unproblematic, point of reference for a variety of reactionary positions in this period, from Ultra Tories to high Anglicans.

Yet, as Mill's example suggests, from around the mid-1820s the exclusively conservative religious and political affiliations of Wordsworth and Coleridge were progressively challenged by an eclectic alliance of scholars and journalists including Julius Hare, F. D. Maurice, John Sterling, and Thomas Carlyle. Strenuously intellectual, defiantly elitist, and ostentatiously preoccupied with the defence of spiritual and aesthetic values, the ideological programme which united this group was centred around its hostility to the godless, materialistic tendencies of Benthamite utilitarianism. Like the middle-class reform movement of the 1790s, the centres of this 'higher radicalism' were Cambridge and London. But unlike the radical dissenting culture of the eighteenth century, its religious constituency was primarily liberal Anglican rather than unitarian (whilst remaining intellectually receptive to such extreme representatives of nonconformist belief as Carlyle). For this group of young writers and journalists, the defence of imaginative literature, and a selective identification with the values and attitudes of the Lake school, became an important means of dissociating its intellectual and professional identity from the demotic purveyors of 'useful knowledge' associated with philosophic radicalism and the highly capitalized mass-publishing ventures of liberal Whigs such as Henry Brougham and Charles Knight.

The higher radicalism had its origins in the Cambridge 'Apostles' society of the 1820s; its guiding spirit was provided by F. D. Maurice, a lapsed unitarian with radical political sympathies who, like Coleridge,

[39] William Ewart Gladstone, *Church Principles Considered in their True Results* (1840), 17–18.

was to return to the Anglican fold in 1831.[40] In retrospect, Maurice recorded how, at Cambridge in the 1820s, Benthamism had been the 'prevalent faith' among the 'younger and cleverer undergraduates of the day'.[41] But this was also the period in which Cambridge philosophy began a decisive reaction against the utilitarian ethics of Paley and Bentham, a development which united both High and Broad Church tendencies within the university. The struggle between utilitarian and intuitionist moral systems was central to the intellectual life of Victorian Cambridge and, as a result, the spiritualized conservatism of Coleridge and Wordsworth presented itself as an important, if rather unorthodox, resource for a new generation of Cambridge-educated, politically reformist critics of Benthamite philosophy.[42] In this respect, the Apostles' interest in the Lake school was undoubtedly stimulated by Julius Hare, a liberal Anglican scholar of the higher criticism and an ardent disciple of Wordsworth and Coleridge, who was also particularly disparaging of 'Mr. Bentham' and the 'selfish philosophers' of utility.[43]

Maurice himself later claimed to have used the Apostles society as a forum for the defence of 'Coleridge's metaphysics and Wordsworth's poetry against the Utilitarian teaching', and his contributions to the short-lived *Metropolitan Quarterly Magazine* during the mid-1820s are certainly suggestive of an attempt to find a new medium for middle-class literary reformism along the lines suggested by Hare. Maurice mercilessly satirized the obscurantist prolixity of Benthamism, its intellectual servility to political economy and the pedantic science of utility; but he was equally disparaging of the more marginalized, belletristic radicalism of the Hunt circle, who had failed in their own, earlier attempts to reclaim the Lake poets for the cause of

[40] Peter Allen, *The Cambridge Apostles: The Early Years* (Cambridge, 1978), 73–86; W. C. Lubenow, *The Cambridge Apostles, 1820–1914: Liberalism, Imagination and Friendship in British Intellectual Life* (Cambridge, 1998), 110–11; Olive J. Brose, *Frederick Denison Maurice: Rebellious Conformist* (Athens, Oh., 1971).

[41] John Frederick Maurice, *The Life of Maurice, Chiefly Told in his own Letters*, 2nd edn., 2 vols. (1884), i. 176.

[42] Schneewind, *Sidgwick's Ethics*, 89–101. The remote influence of this debate upon twentieth-century 'Cambridge English' also helps to explain the central importance that F. R. Leavis accorded to Mill's essays on Bentham and Coleridge. Both the Leavises were attracted to the mid- to late-Victorian, 'Old Cambridge', world of Henry Sidgwick and Leslie Stephen, through whom they derived much of their understanding of Halévy's *Philosophic Radicalism*. See Ian MacKillop, *F. R. Leavis: A Life in Criticism* (Harmondsworth, 1995), 228–30, 276–8.

[43] [Julius and Augustus Hare], *Guesses at Truth: By Two Brothers*, 2 vols. (1827), ii. 280; i. 127–8; Gill, *Wordsworth and the Victorians*, 56–7.

reform.[44] Expanding upon the *Blackwood's* depictions of Hunt's 'Cockney School' as a vulgar sect of suburban radicals, Maurice offered a more capacious definition of Cockneyism, as a mixture of sentimentalism, immaturity, and, above all, 'egotism'. At this point, the 'Cockney' epithet could be applied not only to the 'disgusting' Hunt and 'intolerable' Hazlitt, but also to their supercilious detractors in the Tory press. What was required instead was a journalistic literary culture based, in Coleridgean terms, on principles rather than personalities—an intellectually strenuous mode of critical endeavour rather than dry ratiocination, mawkish sentiment, or sensationalist, self-glorifying hack work.[45] Although the rather juvenile satirical tone of the *Metropolitan* hardly lived up to such ideals, Maurice was already beginning to envision a principled, spiritually enlightened, and socially responsible form of journalism whose practitioners would be answerable to a far higher set of intellectual standards.

Maurice came closest to realizing these aspirations in the *Athenaeum*, which he and Sterling helped to establish in 1828, and which went on to become one of the most influential periodicals of the Victorian period. Indeed, the *Athenaeum* circle provides one of the earliest examples of the intellectual and institutional interpenetration of the universities and metropolitan journalism that was to prove so important in legitimizing the gentlemanly profession of the 'higher journalist'.[46] It is thus quite unsurprising that the paper should have evinced such hostility to commercial 'speculators' in the literary marketplace, who were consistently blamed for the contemporary degradation of literary taste. As a self-styled organ of educated, middle-class opinion, the *Athenaeum* blended philosophical pretension, spiritualized politics, and self-confident literary critical authority. It appealed to refined sensibilities capable of spiritual and imaginative 'feeling' and repelled by the levelling of intellectual distinctions implied by the 'march of mind'. The temper of Lake school literary conservatism was broadly compatible with much of this programme, a fact that has on occasion led to the *Athenaeum*

[44] Maurice, *Life of Maurice*, i. 176; [Frederick Denison Maurice], 'A Supplementary Sheet to Bentham's Book of Fallacies', *Metropolitan Quarterly Magazine*, 1 (1826), 353–77.

[45] [Id.], 'The New School of Cockneyism', ibid. 2 (1826), 37–8; [id.], 'The Age of Folly. No. II', ibid. 1 (1826), 257–79.

[46] Leslie A. Marchand, *The Athenaeum: A Mirror of Victorian Culture* (New York, 1971); Collini, *Public Moralists*, 39–42; Christopher Kent, 'Higher Journalism and the Mid-Victorian Clerisy', *Victorian Studies*, 13 (1969), 181–98.

circle's identification with a Romanticized strain of 'Tory' politics.[47] It would, however, be fairer to say that Wordsworth and Coleridge found themselves marshalled in support of an attempt to supplant Benthamism as the vehicle for 'progressive' middle-class opinion, and thus to build on the Apostles' growing reputation as what Mill later called 'a second Liberal and even Radical party'.[48] Maurice would certainly have been embarrassed by the reactionary excesses of the Lake poets' senescence; at least during this period, his political sensibility was far closer to what Matthew Arnold had in mind when he called himself a 'liberal of the future'.

In an 1828 article in the *Athenaeum* on 'The State of Society in England', Sterling portrayed utilitarianism as the peculiar vice of the 'modern englishman', and the philosophical equivalent of the 'general principles of profit and loss' described by political economy. More importantly, however, Sterling went on to identify utilitarian mammonism with aesthetic vulgarity and a superficial, fashion-conscious taste for literary amusement. This was one of the earliest, and most explicit attempts (after Hazlitt) to enforce the culturally and socially *declassé* connotations of Benthamite philosophy, which Sterling seems to have found conclusively substantiated by his observation that, in an intellectual climate dominated by utilitarianism, 'novels, and works on political economy, are the only books that now find favour'.[49] Sterling's tacitly class-conscious defence of higher literary pursuits echoed Maurice's previous declaration that 'In literature we are aristocrats to the core'.[50] However, this brazen defence of an aesthetic oligarchy in the republic of letters, and concomitant association of Benthamism with the vulgar novel reader, by no means implied the capitulation of the *Athenaeum* circle to reactionary or gentry values. On the contrary, it served to deny the more demotic radical associations of the Benthamite party (including its strategic alliances with the popular reform movement), while establishing in its place the educated middle-class critical authority exemplified by the *Athenaeum* itself. The stultified intellects and complacent indolence of the aristocracy were consistently viewed with sardonic disdain by

47 See e.g. Thomas, *Philosophic Radicals*, 169.

48 John Stuart Mill, *Autobiography* (1873), in id., *Collected Works*, i. 133.

49 [John Sterling], 'State of Society in England', *Athenaeum*, 1 (28 May 1828), 487; repr. in id., *Essays and Tales*, ed. J. C. Hare, 2 vols. (1848).

50 [Maurice], 'The Age of Folly. No. II', *Metropolitan Quarterly Magazine*, 1 (1826), 278.

Maurice and his peers, particularly in the context of university reform.[51]

Nor, perhaps, can the journal's ideological sympathies be exclusively identified with the professional middle class. The aim of the universities, according to Maurice, should be 'neither to make education more *professional*, nor a great deal more *general*; but solely to make it a better instrument for cultivating all the mental faculties'.[52] Moreover, as Robert Gray has pointed out, during the 1830s and 1840s the *Athenaeum*'s reviewers were happy to provide their readers with 'liberal defences of the factory system', and stringent criticisms of 'aristocratic and popular prejudices' against industrial manufactures.[53] The *Athenaeum* also expressed its admiration for Jean Baptiste Say's economic writings, and embraced the cause of trade liberalization on the grounds that 'the most useful lesson wisdom ever read to the world, is that of non-interference in the constitution and course of nature'.[54] Despite his association of aesthetic vulgarity with a narrow fascination for political economy, Sterling was quite capable of linking the moral and educational thought of the Lake poets with the spirtualized capitalism of Thomas Chalmers. The 'reform of thought and feeling' necessary in England would be accomplished, he claimed, only once its people had 'learnt to listen to the voices of the teachers, of such men as Wordsworth and Coleridge, and, in another way, Chalmers'.[55] Maurice even allowed himself, with some reluctance, to be proposed for the Oxford Chair in Political Economy in 1836, 'finding that there was no one else ready to come forward on this ground, that political economy is not the foundation of morals and politics, but must have them for its foundation or be worth nothing'.[56] Four years later, however, he secured a rather more congenial position as Professor of English Literature and History at King's College, London, replacing the Coleridgean High Churchman Hugh James Rose.

[51] See e.g. [id.], 'The Universities of Europe and America. Cambridge.—No. I', *Athenaeum*, 1 (3 Dec. 1828), 911.

[52] [Id.], 'The Universities of Europe and America. Cambridge.—No. II', ibid. 1 (17 Dec. 1828), 943.

[53] Robert Gray, *The Factory Question and Industrial England, 1830–1860* (Cambridge, 1996), 146.

[54] 'Practical Political Economy', *Athenaeum*, 1 (29 Aug. 1828), 675; see also ibid. 756.

[55] [Sterling], 'State of Society in England', ibid., 1 (28 May 1828), 487.

[56] Maurice, *Life of Maurice*, i. 210.

In place of the intellectually impoverished, utilitarian character of the age, the *Athenaeum* urged the primacy of spiritual values, of 'inward' truth as opposed to the empiricist philosophy of sensation. In this respect it was strongly influenced by the liberal Anglican ideas taking root in Cambridge and elsewhere at this time—a theological movement of which Coleridge was usually regarded as a genial but flawed precursor. Liberal Anglican philology certainly provided an important inspiration for the critical discussion of imaginative literature in the *Athenaeum*; and Julius Hare's Platonized version of the German higher criticism was particularly significant in this respect. Hare adopted a profoundly historicized attitude to language and literature, and sought to divine the workings of providence within the evolving literary culture of a people.[57] Languages thus became 'the barometer of national thought and character', and poetry a species of philosophy which could provide 'the key to the hieroglyphics of Nature'.[58] In his 'Sketches of Contemporary Authors', Maurice applied Hare's visionary philology to contemporary British literary culture, implicitly identifying the literary critic as a hierophantic interpreter of the spirit of the age. By 'studying the minds and works of great writers,' Maurice claimed,

> we arrive at a deeper and more living knowledge of the epoch to which we belong, than if we looked, however widely, over its surface, or mined, however long and darkly, in its inmost caves. It is, moreover, in the writings of such men, that we arrive at the most precise acquaintance with the general and permanent causes which, even around our daily paths, are moulding and inspiring the whole mass of that society, whereof ourselves are portions.[59]

On this basis, Maurice began to reassess contemporary literary culture in ways that eventually proved highly influential in the long-term development of the Romantic literary canon. For both Hare and Maurice, Wordsworth's poetry formed the pre-eminent example of the spiritual and intellectual influences governing the contemporary epoch.[60] But the 'higher radical' Maurice could also find a place in his poetic canon for Thomas Moore and, perhaps more surprisingly (given his contemporary reputation), Percy Shelley; not because of his political beliefs—which

[57] Duncan Forbes, *The Liberal Anglican Idea of History* (Cambridge, 1952), 6–7, 136–8.

[58] [Hare and Hare], *Guesses at Truth*, i. 134, 243.

[59] [Frederick Denison Maurice], 'Sketches of Contemporary Authors. No. I', *Athenaeum*, 1 (16 Jan. 1828), 33.

[60] [Id.], 'Sketches of Contemporary Authors. No. V.—Mr. Wordsworth', *Athenaeum*, 1 (19 Feb. 1828), 113–15.

Maurice considered impetuous and immature—but because of his natural piety and Platonic concern with the inner life of things. Maurice's attitudes in this respect reflect a broader, selective appreciation of Shelley's poetry that was slowly gaining ground within the *Athenaeum* circle.[61] Nevertheless, it was Wordsworth the poet, and Coleridge the philosopher, who remained central to the periodical's overriding opposition to the vulgar, empirical philosophies of utilitarianism and political economy.[62]

Thus, at the same time that the Lake school critique of political economy and the 'mechanical philosophy' was helping to shape a large section of Ultra Tory and High Church opinion, an alternative, embryonic Romantic canon, centred around Wordsworth and Coleridge, but also extending tentatively to Shelley, was simultaneously being defended by the higher radicals of the *Athenaeum* in their ongoing campaign against Benthamite utilitarianism. If the former development was quite obviously reactionary, the latter represented part of a more complex attempt to isolate and purify progressive middle-class opinion from the more extreme, universalist tendencies within utilitarian political discourse. John Stuart Mill's friendship with Sterling and Carlyle, and his exposure to the ideas of the *Athenaeum* circle in the London Debating Society, are well known, and touched on briefly in Mill's *Autobiography*. But the influence of the higher radicalism on the Benthamite party has usually been seen only in the rather circumscribed terms of Mill's personal intellectual development, and its influence upon the wider cultural politics of the early Victorian period proportionately diminished. Maurice himself began reviewing for the *Westminster* in the late 1820s, suggesting that the attitudes and ideas of the *Athenaeum* circle began to penetrate philosophic radical circles quite independently of Mill's relationship with Sterling.

Edward Lytton Bulwer's *England and the English* (1833) is a case in point, a work usually associated with the literary 'fringe' of philosophic radicalism but which also displays the clear influence of the Apostolic literary and political milieu of liberal Cambridge, most obviously in its attacks on the university's excessively empiricist and utilitarian cur-

[61] Neil Fraistat, 'Illegitimate Shelley: Radical Piracy and the Textual Edition as Cultural Performance', *Publications of the Modern Language Association of America*, 109 (1994), 410.

[62] On the 'middle-class' appropriation of Wordsworth's verse during the Victorian period, see Harrison, *Wordsworth's Vagrant Muse*, 173–93.

riculum. Bulwer's aristocratic affectations perhaps led him to single out Shelley for more praise than he was accustomed to at this time, even from the Apostles. Indeed, in *England and the English* it is Wordsworth and Shelley, rather than Wordsworth and Coleridge, who embody the 'deep undercurrent' of the age's 'intellectual spirit'. His qualified, but profoundly respectful appreciation of the 'refined and *refining* toryism' of Wordsworth is thus balanced by Bulwer's account of Shelley as 'the spiritualizer of all who forsake the past and the present, and, with lofty hopes and a bold philanthropy, rush forward into the future . . . '.[63] This was a very similar position to that of Mill, who not only appended an anonymous critique of Benthamism to *England and the English*, but also adapted Bulwer's two-handed canonization of Wordsworth and Shelley in a November 1833 essay on 'The Two Kinds of Poetry'. For Mill, Wordsworth exemplified the 'poetry of culture', a bounded, didactic style in which 'poetry is almost always the mere setting of a thought'; while Shelley emerged as a 'naturally poetical mind', which 'merely pours forth the overflowing of his feelings' in an admirable but undisciplined fashion.[64]

Hence already by 1833, the 'spiritual Toryism' of the Lake school could find itself comfortably integrated into a broadly reformist, anti-utilitarian strain of belletristic literary appreciation, which also gave a prominent place to Shelley—a known radical and freethinker. From this perspective, it becomes very difficult to see Mill's burgeoning interest in the politics and poetry of the Lake school as a capitulation to an inherently conservative value system. The Coleridgean element in Mill's intellectual development may indeed be rather slighter than has sometimes been claimed.[65] But, more importantly, the intellectual milieu within which Mill's exposure to Wordsworth and Coleridge took place was one in which the influence of the two principal Lake poets—in political, religious, and literary terms—appears to have been remarkably heterogeneous. This must have important consequences for our understanding of the ideological affiliations of the Romantic poetic canon as it developed in the course of the nineteenth and twentieth centuries. But it also warns against the reductive representation of the broader 'Romantic' presence within British culture and society as a unitary intellectual tradition, and still less as a stable and enduring

[63] Edward Lytton Bulwer, *England and the English*, 2 vols. (1833), ii. 96–9.

[64] [John Stuart Mill], 'The Two Kinds of Poetry', *Monthly Repository*, NS 7 (1833), 717.

[65] Thomas, *Philosophic Radicals*, 169.

refuge for conservative or anti-capitalist values. If the Lake poets' canonical status emerged directly from the early, and unresolved, struggle over their ideological legacy, then this might begin to explain why the issue of British Romanticism's broader role within nineteenth-century political and literary life continues to prove such a resonant, and contentious, subject.

Select Bibliography

Place of publication for non-periodical texts is London unless otherwise indicated.

PRIMARY TEXTS

Periodicals

Annual Review

The Anti-Jacobin; or, Weekly Examiner

Asiatick Researches

Athenaeum

Black Dwarf

Blackwood's Edinburgh Magazine

British Critic

Cambridge Essays

Champion and Sunday Review

Cobbett's Weekly Political Register

Critical Review

Eclectic Review

Edinburgh Annual Register

Edinburgh Review

Evangelical Magazine and Missionary Chronicle

Examiner

Flower's Political Review

Fraser's Magazine

The Friend

Hone's Reformists' Register

London Magazine

London Review

London and Westminster Review

Medusa; or, Penny Politician

Metropolitan Quarterly Magazine

Monthly Magazine

Monthly Repository

Monthly Review

New Monthly Magazine

Ollier's Literary Miscellany
Pamphleteer
Quarterly Review
Republican
The Tribune
The Watchman
Westminster Review
Yellow Dwarf

Letters, Notebooks, Journals, and Marginalia

Austen, Jane, *Letters*, ed. Deirdre Le Faye, 3rd edn. (Oxford, 1995).

Bentham, Jeremy, *Correspondence*, ed. Stephen Conway *et al.*, 11 vols. so far (London and Oxford, 1968–).

Byron, George Gordon, Lord, *Byron's Letters and Journals*, ed. Leslie A. Marchand, 12 vols. (1974–82).

Clairmont, Claire, *et al.*, *The Clairmont Correspondence: Letters of Claire Clairmont, Charles Clairmont, and Fanny Imlay Godwin*, ed. Marion Kingston Stocking, 2 vols. (Baltimore, 1995).

Coleridge, Samuel Taylor, *Collected Letters*, ed. Earl Leslie Griggs, 6 vols. (Oxford, 1956–71).

——*Marginalia*, ed. H. J. Jackson and George Whalley, 6 vols. (London and Princeton, 1980–).

——*Notebooks*, ed. Kathleen Coburn and Merton Christensen, 5 vols. (New York and London, 1957–).

Lamb, Charles, and Lamb, Mary, *Letters*, ed. E. V. Lucas, 3 vols. (1935).

Maurice, John Frederick, *The Life of Maurice, Chiefly Told in his own Letters*, 2nd edn., 2 vols. (1884).

Melville, Lewis, *The Life and Letters of William Cobbett in England and America*, 2 vols. (1913).

Ruskin, John, *Letters from Venice*, ed. John Lewis Bradley (New Haven, 1955).

Shelley, Mary, *Journals*, ed. Paula R. Feldman and Diana Scott-Kilvert (Oxford, 1987).

Shelley, Percy Bysshe, *Letters*, ed. Frederick L. Jones, 2 vols. (Oxford, 1964).

——*et al.*, *Shelley and his Circle, 1773–1822*, ed. Kenneth Neill Cameron and Donald H. Reiman, 8 vols. (Cambridge, Mass., 1961–86).

Southey, Robert, *Life and Correspondence of the Late Robert Southey*, ed. Charles Cuthbert Southey, 6 vols. (1849–50).

——*Selected Letters*, ed. John Wood Warter, 4 vols. (1856).

——*New Letters*, ed. Kenneth Curry, 2 vols. (New York, 1965).

Wilberforce, William, *Correspondence*, ed. Robert Isaac Wilberforce and Samuel Wilberforce, 2 vols. (1840).

Wordsworth, Dorothy, and Wordsworth, William, *Letters*, ed. Ernest de Selincourt, 2nd edn., rev. and ed. Chester L. Shaver *et al.* (Oxford, 1967–88).
Wordsworth, William, *The Fenwick Notes*, ed. Jared Curtis (1993).

Books and Pamphlets

Arnold, Matthew, 'Preface' to id. (ed.), *Poems of Wordsworth* (1879).
Bagehot, Walter, *Economic Studies*, ed. Richard Holt Hutton (1880).
[Bailey, Samuel], *A Critical Dissertation on the Nature, Measure, and Causes of Value* (1825).
[——] *Essays on the Formation and Publication of Opinions* (1821).
[——] *Essays on the Pursuit of Truth* (1829).
[——] *Questions in Political Economy, Politics, Morals, Metaphysics, Polite Literature, and other Branches of Knowledge; for Discussion in Literary Societies, or for Private Study* (1823).
[——] *The Rationale of Political Representation* (1835).
Barbauld, Anna Lætitia, *Eighteen Hundred and Eleven, a Poem* (1812).
Bayley, Peter, *Poems* (1803).
Beddoes, Thomas, *Hygëia: or Essays Moral and Medical*, 3 vols. (Bristol, 1802–3).
Bell, Andrew, *An Analysis of the Experiment in Education, made at Egmore, near Madras* (1797), 3rd edn. (1807).
——*Elements of Tuition, Part II. The English School* (1814).
[Bentham, Jeremy], *Analysis of the Influence of Natural Religion on the Temporal Happiness of Mankind*, ed. 'Philip Beauchamp' [George Grote] (1822).
——*Chrestomathia* (1815–17), ed. M. J. Smith and W. H. Burston (Oxford, 1983).
——*Church-of-Englandism and its Catechism Examined* (1818).
——*A Comment on the Commentaries* and *A Fragment on Government*, ed. J. H. Burns and H. L. A. Hart (1977).
——*An Introduction to the Principles of Morals and Legislation* (1781), ed. J. H. Burns and H. L. A. Hart (Oxford, 1996).
——*'Legislator of the World': Writings on Codification, Law and Education*, ed. Philip Schofield and Jonathan Harris (Oxford, 1998).
——*On the Liberty of the Press and Public Discussion* (1821).
——*Plan of Parliamentary Reform* (1817).
——*Traités de Législation civile et pénale* (1802), ed. Étienne Dumont, trans. Robert Hildreth as *The Theory of Legislation* (1931).
Berington, Joseph, *An Essay on the Depravity of the Nation, with a View to the Promotion of Sunday Schools* (Birmingham, 1788).
——*A Literary History of the Middle Ages* (1814).
Birt, Caleb Evans, *The Advantages Arising from the Combination of Learning with Piety* (1826).

Bone, John, *The Wants of the People, and the Means of Government* (1807).
Bowles, John, *A Letter to Samuel Whitbread*, 2nd edn. (1808).
——*Reflections on the Political and Moral State of Society, at the Close of the Eighteenth Century* (1800).
——*The Education of the Lower Orders* (1808).
Brougham, Henry, *A Discourse of the Objects, Advantages, and Pleasures of Science*, 2nd edn. (1827).
——*An Inquiry into the Colonial Policy of the European Powers*, 2 vols. (Edinburgh, 1803).
——*Practical Observations on the Education of the People* (1825).
——*Works*, 11 vols. (1855–61).
[Brown, John], *An Estimate of the Manners and Principles of the Times* (1757).
Buchanan, Claudius, *Colonial Ecclesiastical Establishment* (1813).
Bulwer, Edward Lytton, *England and the English*, 2 vols. (1833).
Burdon, William, *Three Letters Addressed to the Bishop of Llandaff* (Cambridge, 1795).
——*Unanimity Recommended* (Newcastle upon Tyne, 1803).
Burke, Edmund, *Writings and Speeches*, ed. Paul Langford, vol. viii, *The French Revolution 1790–94*, ed. L. G. Mitchell (Oxford, 1989).
Butler, Charles, *The Book of the Roman-Catholic Church* (1825).
Byron, George Gordon, Lord, *Complete Poetical Works*, ed. Jerome McGann, 7 vols. (Oxford, 1980–93).
Campbell, Augustus, *A Reply to the Article on Church Establishments in . . . the Edinburgh Review* (1823).
Campbell, Thomas, *Reprint of Mr. Campbell's Letter to Mr. Brougham* (1825).
Carlyle, Thomas, *The Life of John Sterling* (1851).
——*On Heroes, Hero-Worship, & the Heroic in History. Six Lectures* (1841).
——*Past and Present* (1843).
[Carpenter, Daniel], *Reflections Suggested by Mr. Whitbread's Bill* (1808).
Chalmers, Thomas, *The Application of Christianity to the Commercial and Ordinary Affairs of Life, in a series of Discourses*, 2nd edn. (Glasgow, 1820).
——*The Christian and Civic Economy of Large Towns*, 3 vols. (Glasgow, 1821–6).
——*Considerations on the System of Parochial Schools in Scotland* (Glasgow, 1819).
——*An Enquiry into the Extent and Stability of National Resources* (Edinburgh, 1808).
——*The Influence of Bible Societies, on the Temporal Necessities of the Poor* (1814), 4th edn. (Edinburgh, 1818).
——*On the Use and Abuse of Literary and Ecclesiastical Endowments* (Glasgow, 1827).
——*Works*, 25 vols. (Glasgow, 1836–42).
Cobbett, William, *Cobbett's Legacy to Labourers* (1834).
——*Cobbett's Sermons* (1822).

——*A History of the Protestant 'Reformation'*, 2 vols. (1824–6).

——*Paper against Gold and Glory against Prosperity*, 2 vols. (1815).

——*Surplus Population: and Poor-Law Bill. A Comedy, in Three Acts* (n.d. [1834]).

Coleridge, Samuel Taylor, *Biographia Literaria* (1817), ed. James Engell and W. Jackson Bate, 2 vols. (London and Princeton, 1983).

——*Essays on his Times in* The Morning Post *and* The Courier *(1798–1817)*, ed. David V. Erdman, 3 vols. (London and Princeton, 1978).

——*The Friend* (1809–10, 1818), ed. Barbara E. Rooke, 2 vols. (London and Princeton, 1969).

——*Lay Sermons* (1816–17), ed. R. J. White (London and Princeton, 1972).

——*Lectures 1808–1819 On Literature*, ed. R. A. Foakes, 2 vols. (London and Princeton, 1987).

——*Lectures 1795 on Politics and Religion*, ed. Lewis Patton and Peter Mann (London and Princeton, 1971).

——*On the Constitution of Church and State* (1829), ed. John Colmer (London and Princeton, 1976).

——*Table Talk*, ed. Carl Woodring, 2 vols. (London and Princeton, 1990).

——*The Watchman* (1796), ed. Lewis Patton (London and Princeton, 1970).

Colquhoun, Patrick, *A New and Appropriate System of Education for the Labouring People* (1806).

——*A Treatise on Indigence* (1806).

De Quincey, Thomas, *The Logic of Political Economy* (Edinburgh, 1844).

D'Israeli, Isaac, *The Literary Character*, 4th edn., 2 vols. (1828).

Dyer, George, *A Dissertation on the Theory and Practice of Benevolence* (1795).

Eden, Frederic Morton, *The State of the Poor*, 3 vols. (1797).

Ferguson, Adam, *An Essay on the History of Civil Society* (Edinburgh, 1767).

Flower, Benjamin, *National Sins Considered* (Cambridge, 1796).

Fox, Joseph, *A Comparative View of the Plans of Education, as Detailed in the Publications of Dr. Bell and Mr. Lancaster* (n.d. [1808]).

Frend, William, *Patriotism; or, The Love of our Country* (1804).

Gladstone, William Ewart, *Church Principles Considered in their True Results* (1840).

——*The State in its Relation with the Church* (1838), 2nd edn. (1839).

Godwin, William, *The Enquirer. Reflections on Education, Manners, and Literature* (1797).

——*An Enquiry Concerning Political Justice, and its Influence on General Virtue and Happiness*, 2 vols. (1793).

——*Of Population* (1820).

——*Thoughts Occasioned by the Perusal of Dr. Parr's Spital Sermon* (1801).

Goldsmith, Oliver, *An Enquiry into the Present State of Polite Learning in Europe* (1759).

Gordon, John, *The Causes and Consequences of Evil Speaking against Government* (1771).

[Hare, Julius, and Hare, Augustus], *Guesses at Truth: By Two Brothers*, 2 vols. (1827).

[Hazlitt, William], *An Essay on the Principles of Human Action* (1805).

——*Complete Works*, ed. P. P. Howe, 21 vols. (1930–4).

——*The Eloquence of the British Senate* (1807), 2nd edn., 2 vols. (1808).

[——] *Free Thoughts on Public Affairs* (1806).

——*Lectures on the English Poets* (1818).

[——] *The Plain Speaker: Opinions on Books, Men, and Things*, 2 vols. (1826).

——*Political Essays* (1819).

[——] *A Reply to the Essay on Population, by the Rev. T. R. Malthus* (1807).

——*The Spirit of the Age: or Contemporary Portraits*, 2nd edn. (1825).

——*Table-Talk; or, Original Essays* (1821).

History of the Westminster and Middlesex Elections; in the Month of November, 1806 (1807).

Hume, David, *Essays, Moral and Political*, 2 vols. (Edinburgh, 1742).

Hunt, Leigh, *Autobiography*, 3 vols. (1850).

Huskisson, William, *The Question Concerning the Depreciation of our Currency* (1810).

[Irving, Washington], *The Sketch Book of Geoffrey Crayon, Gent.* (1820).

Jarrold, Thomas, *A Letter to Samuel Whitbread* (n.d. [1807]).

Knox, Vicesimus, *Essays Moral and Literary*, new edn., enlarged, 2 vols. (1782).

——*Liberal Education* (Dublin, 1781).

Lancaster, Joseph, *Improvements in Education, as it respects the Industrious Classes of the Community* (1803).

Leckie, Gould Francis, *An Historical Survey of the Foreign Affairs of Great Britain*, 2 pts. (1808).

[Leslie, John], *A Summons of Wakening* (Hawick, 1807).

[Lockhart, John Gibson], *Peter's Letters to his Kinfolk*, 2nd edn., 3 vols. (Edinburgh, 1819).

[Long, Charles], *A Temperate Discussion of the Causes which have Led to the Present High Price of Bread* (1800).

Macaulay, Thomas Babington, *Critical and Historical Essays, Contributed to the Edinburgh Review*, 3 vols. (1843).

McCulloch, J. R., *A Discourse on the Rise, Progress, Peculiar Objects, and Importance of Political Economy* (Edinburgh, 1824).

——*The Principles of Political Economy* (1825).

Mackinnon, Alexander, *On the Rise, Progress and Present State of Public Opinion* (1828).

Mackintosh, James, *Vindiciæ Gallicæ* (1791).

[Malthus, Thomas Robert], *An Essay on the Principle of Population, as it Affects the Future Improvement of Society, with Remarks on the Speculations of Mr. Godwin, M. Condorcet, and Other Writers* (1798), repr. for the Royal Economic Society (1926).

——*An Essay on the Principle of Population; or a View of its Past and Present Effects on Human Happiness; with an Inquiry into our Prospects respecting the Future Removal or Mitigation of the Evils which it Occasions*, ed. Patricia James, 2 vols. (Cambridge, 1989).

[——]*An Investigation of the Cause of the Present High Price of Provisions* (1800).

——*A Letter to Samuel Whitbread* (1807).

——*Principles of Political Economy Considered with a View to their Practical Application* (1820), ed. John Pullen, 2 vols. (Cambridge, 1989).

[Manners, John, Lord], 'Anglo-Catholicus', *Monastic and Manufacturing Systems* (1843).

Marcet, Jane, *Conversations in Political Economy* (1816).

Martineau, Harriet, *Illustrations of Political Economy*, 9 vols. (1832–4).

Marx, Karl, *Grundrisse*, trans. Martin Nicolaus (Harmondsworth, 1973).

Mill, James, *Analysis of the Phenomena of the Human Mind*, 2 vols. (1829).

——*Commerce Defended* (1808).

——*Elements of Political Economy* (1821), 3rd edn., rev. (1826).

——*Essays* (1823), 2nd edn. (n.d. [1828]).

——*The History of British India*, 3 vols. (1817).

Mill, John Stuart, *Collected Works*, ed. J. M. Robson *et al.*, 33 vols. (Toronto and London, 1981–91).

Monck, John Berkeley, *General Reflections on the System of the Poor Laws* (n.d. [1807]).

Moore, John, *A View of the Causes and Progress of the French Revolution*, 2 vols. (1795).

Myers, F. W. H., *Wordsworth* (1881).

Oastler, Richard, *Brougham versus Brougham, on the New Poor Law* (1847).

——*Eight Letters to the Duke of Wellington* (1835).

Otter, William, *Reasons for the Education of the Poor at the Present Crisis* (1802).

Paine, Thomas, *Rights of Man* (1791).

Paley, William, *Natural Theology* (1802).

——*The Principles of Moral and Political Philosophy* (1785).

——*Reasons for Contentment* (Carlisle, 1792).

——*A View of the Evidences of Christianity*, 2nd edn., 2 vols. (1794).

Parr, Samuel, *A Spital Sermon* (1801).

Pasley, Charles William, *An Essay on the Military Policy and Institutions of the British Empire* (1810), 2nd edn. (1811).

Paull, James, *A Refutation of the Calumnies of John Horne Tooke* (1807).

[Peacock, Thomas Love], *Crotchet Castle* (1831).

——*Works*, ed. H. F. B. Brett-Smith and C. E. Jones, 8 vols. (1924–34).

Phillpotts, Henry, *A Letter to Francis Jeffrey* (Durham, 1823).

[Place, Francis, and Richter, John], *An Exposition of the Circumstances which Gave Rise to the Election of Sir Francis Burdett* (1807).

Pugin, Augustus Welby, *Contrasts; or, a Parallel Between the Noble Edifices of the Fourteenth and Fifteenth Centuries, and Similar Buildings of the Present Day; Shewing the Present Decay of Taste* (1836).

Purkiss, William, *Influence of the Present Pursuits in Learning as they Affect Religion* (Cambridge, 1786).

Raikes, Richard, *Considerations on the Alliance between Christianity and Commerce* (1806).

[Randall, W.], *The Warning Voice* (1807).

Remarks on a Late Publication, entitled, 'An Essay on the Principle of Population . . .' (1803 [1804]).

Remarks Upon 'A Bill . . . for Promoting and Encouraging of Industry amongst the Labouring Classes of the Community' (1807).

Ricardo, David, *On the Principles of Political Economy and Taxation* (1817), ed. Piero Sraffa and M. H. Dobb (Cambridge, 1951).

Roscoe, Henry, *Life of William Roscoe*, 2 vols. (1833).

Roscoe, William, *Considerations on the Causes, Objects and Consequences of the Present War* (1808).

——*On the Origins and Vicissitudes of Literature, Science, and Art, and their Influence on the Present State of Society* (Liverpool, 1817), repr. in *The Pamphleteer*, 11 (1818).

Rose, Hugh James, *Christianity Always Progressive* (1829).

——*The Tendency of Prevalent Opinions about Knowledge* (Cambridge, 1826).

Ruskin, John, *Fors Clavigera*, 5 vols. (London and Kent, 1871–7).

Russell, John, Lord, *An Essay on the History of the English Government and Constitution*, 2nd edn. (1823).

Sadler, Michael Thomas, *The Law of Population: A Treatise*, 2 vols. (1830).

[Seeley, Robert Benton], *The Perils of the Nation* (1843).

[——] *Remedies Suggested, for Some of the Evils which Constitute 'The Perils of the Nation'* (1844).

Shelley, Percy Bysshe, *Complete Works*, ed. Roger Ingpen and Walter E. Peck, 10 vols. (1926–30).

——*Poetry and Prose*, ed. Donald H. Reiman and Sharon B. Powers (New York, 1977).

——*Prose Works*, ed. E. B. Murray (Oxford, 1993–).

Shuttleworth, George Edmund, *The Church and the Clergy* (1820).

Smith, Adam, *An Inquiry into the Nature and Causes of the Wealth of Nations* (1776), ed. R. H. Campbell *et al.*, 2 vols. (Oxford, 1976).

——*Lectures on Jurisprudence*, ed. R. L. Meek *et al.* (Oxford, 1978).
——*The Theory of Moral Sentiments* (1759), ed. D. D. Raphael and A. L. Macfie (Oxford, 1976).
Southey, Robert, *The Book of the Church* (1824), 5th edn. (1841).
——*Essays, Moral and Political*, 2 vols. (1832).
——*History of the Peninsular War*, 3 vols. (1823–32).
——*A Letter to William Smith* (1817).
[——] *Letters from England: by Don Manuel Alvarez Espriella* (1807), 2nd edn., 3 vols. (1808).
——*Sir Thomas More: or, Colloquies on the Progress and Prospects of Society*, 2 vols. (1829).
——*Vindiciæ Ecclesiæ Anglicanæ* (1826).
——*A Vision of Judgement* (1821).
——and Southey, Charles Cuthbert, *Life of the Rev. Andrew Bell* (1844).
Spence, William, *Britain Independent of Commerce* (1807), 4th edn. (1808).
Stephen, Leslie, *Hours in a Library*, 3rd ser. (1879).
Sterling, John, *Essays and Tales*, ed. J. C. Hare, 2 vols. (1848).
Stewart, Dugald, *Collected Works*, ed. William Hamilton, 11 vols. (Edinburgh, 1854–60).
——*Elements of the Philosophy of the Human Mind*, 3 vols. (1792–1827).
——*Outlines of Moral Philosophy* (Edinburgh, 1793).
——*Philosophical Essays* (Edinburgh, 1810).
Sumner, John Bird, *A Treatise on the Records of the Creation*, 2 vols. (1816).
Supplement to the Fourth, Fifth and Sixth Editions of the Encyclopædia Britannica, 6 vols. (Edinburgh, 1816–24).
[Teignmouth, John Shore, Lord], *Considerations on the Practicability, Policy, and Obligation of Communicating to the Natives of India the Knowledge of Christianity* (1808).
Thelwall, John, *Poems Chiefly Written in Retirement* (1801).
——*A Letter to Francis Jeffray* [*sic*] (Edinburgh, 1804).
——*The Peripatetic; or, Sketches of the Heart, of Nature and Society*, 3 vols. (Southwark, 1793).
Tinney, John Pern, *Reflections on Some Questions Relative to the Present State of the Nation* (Salisbury, n.d. [1808]).
Tooke, John Horne, *A Warning to the Electors of Westminster* (1807).
[Townsend, Joseph]. *A Dissertation on the Poor Laws* (1786).
Trimmer, Sarah, *A Comparative View of the New Plan of Education* (1805).
Turner, Sharon, *History of England*, 3 vols. (1814–23).
——*The History of the Reign of Henry the Eighth*, 2nd edn., 2 vols. (1827).
Villers, Charles, *Esquisse de l'histoire de l'église depuis son fondateur jusqu'à la Réformation*, trans. James Mill as *Essay on the Spirit and Influence of the Reformation of Luther* (1805).

Waithman, Robert, *War Proved to be the Cause of the Present Scarcity* (1800).
Watson, Richard (Lord Bishop of Llandaff), *A Sermon Preached before the Stewards of the Westminster Dispensary* (1793).
Weyland, John, *A Letter to a Country Gentleman on the Education of the Lower Orders* (1808).
[Wharton, Richard], *Remarks on the Jacobinical Tendency of the Edinburgh Review* (1809).
Whitbread, Samuel, *Substance of a Speech on the Poor Laws* (1807).
Wilberforce, William, *Substance of the Speeches . . . on the Clause in the East-India Bill for Promoting the Religious Instruction and Moral Improvement of the Natives of India* (1813).
Wordsworth, Christopher (Bishop of Lincoln), *Occasional Sermons, Preached in Westminster Abbey*, 3rd ser. (1852).
Wordsworth, William, *The Excursion, Being a Portion of the Recluse, a Poem* (1814).
——*The Fourteen Book* Prelude, ed. W. J. B. Owen (Ithaca, NY, 1985).
——*Home at Grasmere: Part First, Book First, of* The Recluse, ed. Beth Darlington (Ithaca, NY, 1977).
——Lyrical Ballads *and Other Poems, 1797–1800*, ed. James Butler and Karen Green (Ithaca, NY, 1992).
——*Poems, Chiefly of Early and Late Years* (1842).
——*Poetical Works*, ed. E. de Selincourt and Helen Darbishire, 5 vols. (Oxford, 1940–9).
——*The Prelude: 1799, 1805, 1850*, ed. Jonathan Wordsworth *et al.* (New York, 1979).
——*Prose Works*, ed. W. J. B. Owen and J. W. Smyser, 3 vols. (Oxford, 1974).
——*The Thirteen Book* Prelude, ed. Mark L. Reed, 2 vols. (Ithaca, NY, 1991).
Wrangham, Francis, *A Dissertation upon the Best Means of Civilizing the Subjects of the British Empire in India* (1805).
——*Sermons, Practical and Occasional*, 3 vols. (1816).
Yates, Richard, *Patronage of the Church of England* (1823).
Young, Arthur, *The Question of Scarcity Plainly Stated* (1800).

SECONDARY TEXTS

Books and Articles

Albrecht, William P., *William Hazlitt and the Malthusian Controversy* (Port Washington, 1969).
Allan, David, *Virtue, Learning and the Scottish Enlightenment: Ideas of Scholarship in Early Modern History* (Edinburgh, 1993).

Allen, Peter, *The Cambridge Apostles: The Early Years* (Cambridge, 1978).

Altick, Richard D., *The English Common Reader: A Social History of the Mass Reading Public 1800–1900* (Chicago, 1957).

Anderson, Perry, *English Questions* (1992).

Ausubel, Herman, 'William Cobbett and Malthusianism', *Journal of the History of Ideas*, 13 (1952), 250–6.

Averill, James H., *Wordsworth and the Poetry of Human Suffering* (Ithaca, NY, 1980).

Bacon, Alan, 'English Literature Becomes a University Subject: King's College, London as Pioneer', *Victorian Studies*, 29 (1986), 591–612.

Bann, Stephen, 'The Sense of the Past: Image, Text, and Object in the Formation of Historical Consciousness in Nineteenth-Century Britain', in H. Aram Veeser (ed.), *The New Historicism* (New York, 1989), 102–15.

Bate, Jonathan, 'The Literature of Power: Coleridge and De Quincey', in Tim Fulford and Morton D. Paley (eds.), *Coleridge's Visionary Language* (Cambridge, 1993), 137–50.

——*Romantic Ecology: Wordsworth and the Environmental Tradition* (1991).

Bayley, C. A., *Imperial Meridian: The British Empire and the World 1780–1830* (1989).

Beaty, Frederick L., 'Byron on Malthus and the Population Problem', *Keats–Shelley Journal*, 18 (1969), 17–26.

Belchem, John, 'Introduction: The Peculiarities of Liverpool', in id. (ed.), *Popular Politics, Riot and Labour: Essays in Liverpool History 1790–1840* (Liverpool, 1992), 1–20.

——and Handy, Nick, 'Second Metropolis: The Middle Class in Early Victorian Liverpool', in Alan Kidd and David Nicholls (eds.), *The Making of the British Middle Class? Studies of Regional and Cultural Diversity since the Eighteenth Century* (Stroud, 1998), 58–71.

Bennett, Scott, 'Catholic Emancipation, the "Quarterly Review", and Britain's Constitutional Revolution', *Victorian Studies*, 12 (1969), 283–304.

Berg, Maxine, *The Machinery Question and the Making of Political Economy 1815–1848* (Cambridge, 1980).

——'Progress and Providence in Early Nineteenth-Century Political Economy', *Social History*, 15 (1990), 365–75.

Best, G. F. A., 'The Protestant Constitution and its Supporters, 1800–1829', *Transactions of the Royal Historical Society*, 5th ser., 8 (1958), 105–27.

——*Temporal Pillars: Queen Anne's Bounty, the Ecclesiastical Commissioners, and the Church of England* (Cambridge, 1964).

Bewell, Alan, *Romanticism and Colonial Disease* (Baltimore, 1999).

——*Wordsworth and the Enlightenment: Nature, Man, and Society in the Experimental Poetry* (New Haven, 1989).

Blake, Kathleen, '*Bleak House*, Political Economy, Victorian Studies', *Victorian Literature and Culture*, 25 (1997), 1–21.

Bonar, James, *Malthus and his Work* (1885), 2nd edn. (1924).

Boner, Harold A., *Hungry Generations: The Nineteenth-Century Case against Malthusianism* (New York, 1955).

Bradbury, Malcolm, *The Social Context of Modern English Literature* (Oxford, 1971).

Brantley, Richard E., *Wordsworth's 'Natural Methodism'* (New Haven, 1975).

Brent, Richard, *Liberal Anglican Politics: Whiggery, Religion, and Reform 1830–1841* (Oxford, 1987).

Brewer, John, *The Pleasures of the Imagination: English Culture in the Eighteenth Century* (1997).

——*The Sinews of Power: War, Money and the English State, 1688–1783* (1989).

Bromwich, David, *Disowned by Memory: Wordsworth's Poetry of the 1790s* (Chicago, 1998).

——*Hazlitt: The Mind of a Critic* (New York, 1983).

Brose, Olive J., *Frederick Denison Maurice: Rebellious Conformist* (Athens, Oh., 1971).

Brown, Ford K., *Fathers of the Victorians: The Age of Wilberforce* (Cambridge, 1961).

Brown, Stewart J., *Thomas Chalmers and the Godly Commonwealth in Scotland* (Oxford, 1982).

Burrow, J. W., *Whigs and Liberals: Continuity and Change in English Political Thought* (Oxford, 1988).

Butler, Marilyn, *Peacock Displayed: A Satirist in his Context* (1969).

——*Romantics, Rebels, and Reactionaries: English Literature and its Background 1760–1830* (Oxford, 1981).

Cameron, Kenneth Neill, 'Shelley, Cobbett, and the National Debt', *Journal of English and Germanic Philology*, 42 (1943), 197–209.

——*Shelley: The Golden Years* (Cambridge, Mass., 1974).

Cannon, John, *Parliamentary Reform 1640–1832* (Cambridge, 1973).

Carnall, Geoffrey, *Robert Southey and his Age: The Development of a Conservative Mind* (Oxford, 1960).

Chandler, Alice, *A Dream of Order: The Medieval Ideal in Nineteenth-Century English Literature* (1971).

Chandler, James, *England in 1819: The Politics of Literary Culture and the Case of Romantic Historicism* (Chicago, 1998).

——*Wordsworth's Second Nature: A Study of the Poetry and Politics* (Chicago, 1984).

Checkland, S. G., 'The Advent of Academic Economics in England', *The Manchester School of Economic and Social Studies*, 19 (1951), 43–70.

——'Economic Attitudes in Liverpool, 1793–1807', *Economic History Review*, NS 5 (1952–3), 58–75.

Christ, Carol T., '"The Hero as Man of Letters": Masculinity and Victorian Nonfiction Prose', in Thaïs E. Morgan (ed.), *Victorian Sages and Cultural Discourse: Renegotiating Gender and Power* (New Brunswick, 1990), 19–31.

Claeys, Gregory, *Machinery, Money and the Millennium: From Moral Economy to Socialism, 1815–60* (Cambridge, 1987).

Clark, Anna, *The Struggle for the Breeches: Gender and the Making of the British Working Class* (1995).

Clark, J. C. D., *English Society 1688–1832: Ideology, Social Structure and Political Practice during the Ancien Regime* (Cambridge, 1985).

Cobban, Alfred, *Edmund Burke and the Revolt against the Eighteenth Century: A Study of the Political and Social Thinking of Burke, Wordsworth, Coleridge and Southey* (1929).

Cole, G. D. H., *Chartist Portraits* (1941).

—— *The Life of William Cobbett* (1924).

Coleman, Dierdre, *Coleridge and* The Friend *(1809–1810)* (Oxford, 1988).

—— 'Re-Living Jacobinism: Wordsworth and the Convention of Cintra', *Yearbook of English Studies*, 19 (1989), 144–61.

Colley, Linda, *Britons: Forging the Nation 1707–1837* (New Haven, 1992).

Collini, Stefan, *Public Moralists: Political Thought and Intellectual Life in Britain 1850–1930* (Oxford, 1991).

—— 'From "Non-fiction Prose" to "Cultural Criticism": Genre and Disciplinarity in Victorian Studies', in Juliet John and Alice Jenkins (eds.), *Rethinking Victorian Culture* (Basingstoke, 2000), 13–28.

—— Whatmore, Richard, and Young, Brian (eds.), *Economy, Polity, and Society: British Intellectual History 1750–1950* (Cambridge, 2000).

—— —— —— (eds.), *History, Religion, and Culture: British Intellectual History 1750–1950* (Cambridge, 2000).

—— Winch, Donald, and Burrow, John, *That Noble Science of Politics: A Study in Nineteenth-Century Intellectual History* (Cambridge, 1983).

Collins, Bruce, and Robbins, Keith (eds.), *British Culture and Economic Decline* (1990).

Colmer, John, *Coleridge: Critic of Society* (Oxford, 1959).

Cook, Peter A., 'Chronology of the "Lake School" Argument: Some Revisions', *Review of English Studies*, NS 28 (1977), 175–81.

Cookson, J. E., *The British Armed Nation 1793–1815* (Oxford, 1997).

—— 'British Society and the French Wars, 1793–1815', *Australian Journal of Politics and History*, 31 (1985), 192–203.

—— *The Friends of Peace: Anti-War Liberalism in England, 1793–1815* (Cambridge, 1982).

—— 'Political Arithmetic and War in Britain, 1793–1815', *War and Society*, 1 (1983), 37–60.

Cooter, Roger, 'Anticontagionism and History's Medical Record', in Peter Wright and Andrew Treacher (eds.), *The Problem of Medical Knowledge: Examining the Social Construction of Medicine* (Edinburgh, 1982), 87–108.

Copley, Stephen, 'The "Natural" Economy: A Note on Some Rhetorical Strategies in Political Economy—Adam Smith and Malthus', in Francis Barker *et al.* (eds.), *1789: Reading Writing Revolution* (Essex, 1982), 160–9.

Cottrell, Stella, 'The Devil on Two Sticks: Franco-Phobia in 1803', in Raphael Samuel (ed.), *Patriotism: The Making and Unmaking of National Identity, i. History and Politics* (1989), 259–74.

Court, Franklin E., *Institutionalizing English Literature: The Culture and Politics of Literary Study, 1750–1900* (Stanford, Calif., 1992).

Cox, Jeffrey N., *Poetry and Politics in the Cockney School: Keats, Shelley, Hunt and their Circle* (Cambridge, 1998).

Crawford, Robert (ed.), *The Scottish Invention of English Literature* (Cambridge, 1998).

Crimmins, James E., *Secular Utilitarianism: Social Science and the Critique of Religion in the Thought of Jeremy Bentham* (Oxford, 1990).

Cronin, Richard, 'Peter Bell, Peterloo, and the Politics of Cockney Poetry', in Kelvin Everest (ed.), *Essays and Studies 1992. Percy Bysshe Shelley: Bicentenary Essays* (Cambridge, 1992), 63–87.

Cullen, M. J., *The Statistical Movement in Early Victorian Britain: The Foundations of Empirical Social Research* (Hassocks, 1975).

Dart, Gregory, *Rousseau, Robespierre and English Romanticism* (Cambridge, 1999).

Davidoff, Leonore, and Hall, Catherine, *Family Fortunes: Men and Women of the English Middle Class, 1780–1850* (1987), new edn. (1992).

Davie, George E., *The Social Significance of the Scottish Philosophy of Common Sense* (Dundee, 1973).

Dawson, P. M. S., *The Unacknowledged Legislator: Shelley and Politics* (Oxford, 1980).

de Marchi, Neil, 'The Case for James Mill', in A. W. Coats (ed.), *Methodological Controversy in Economics: Historical Essays in Honor of T. W. Hutchison* (Greenwich, Conn., 1983), 155–84.

Dinwiddy, J. R., 'Sir Francis Burdett and Burdettite Radicalism', *History*, 65 (1980), 17–31.

Ditchfield, G. M., 'English Rational Dissent and Philanthropy', in Hugh Cunningham and Joanna Innes (eds.), *Charity, Philanthropy and Reform: From the 1690s to 1850* (Basingstoke, 1998), 193–207.

Dobb, Maurice, *Theories of Value and Distribution since Adam Smith: Ideology and Economic Theory* (Cambridge, 1973).

Dobbs, A. E., *Education and Social Movements 1700–1850* (1919).

Driver, Cecil, *Tory Radical: The Life of Richard Oastler* (New York, 1946).

Dyck, Ian, *William Cobbett and Rural Popular Culture* (Cambridge, 1992).

Eagleton, Terry, *Criticism and Ideology: A Study in Marxist Literary Theory* (1976).
——*The Function of Criticism: From the* Spectator *to Post-Structuralism* (1984).
——*The Idea of Culture* (Oxford, 2000).
Eastwood, David, *Governing Rural England: Tradition and Transformation in Local Government 1780–1840* (Oxford, 1994).
——'Robert Southey and the Intellectual Origins of Romantic Conservatism', *English Historical Review*, 104 (1989), 308–31.
——'Robert Southey and the Meanings of Patriotism', *Journal of British Studies*, 21 (1992), 279–87.
——'Rethinking the Debates on the Poor Law in Early Nineteenth-Century England', *Utilitas*, 6 (1994), 97–116.
——'Ruinous Prosperity: Robert Southey's Critique of the Commercial System', *Wordsworth Circle*, 25 (1994), 72–6.
Eliot, T. S., *Notes towards the Definition of Culture* (1948).
Emsley, Clive, *British Society and the French Wars 1793–1815* (1979).
Epstein, James, *The Lion of Freedom: Feargus O'Connor and the Chartist Movement* (1982).
Fenn, Robert A., *James Mill's Political Thought* (New York, 1987).
Ferguson, Frances, *Solitude and the Sublime: Romanticism and the Aesthetics of Individuation* (New York, 1992).
Fetter, Frank Whitson, 'The Economic Articles in *Blackwood's Edinburgh Magazine*, and their Authors, 1817–1853', *Scottish Journal of Political Economy*, 7 (1960), 85–107.
Finer, S. E., 'The Transmission of Benthamite Ideas, 1820–50', in Gillian Sutherland (ed.), *Studies in the Growth of Nineteenth-Century Government* (1972), 11–32.
Fitzgibbons, Athol, *Adam Smith's System of Liberty, Wealth, and Virtue: The Moral and Political Foundations of* The Wealth of Nations (Oxford, 1995).
Foakes, R. A., '"Thriving Prisoners": Coleridge, Wordsworth and the Child at School', *Studies in Romanticism*, 28 (1989), 187–206.
Fontana, Biancamaria, *Rethinking the Politics of Commercial Society: The* Edinburgh Review *1802–1832* (Cambridge, 1985).
Forbes, Duncan, 'James Mill and India', *Cambridge Journal*, 5 (1951), 19–33.
——*The Liberal Anglican Idea of History* (Cambridge, 1952).
Fraistat, Neil, 'Illegitimate Shelley: Radical Piracy and the Textual Edition as Cultural Performance', *Publications of the Modern Language Association of America*, 109 (1994), 409–23.
Frappell, L. O., 'The Reformation as Negative Revolution or Obscurantist Reaction: The Liberal Debate on the Reformation in Nineteenth-Century Britain', *Journal of Religious History*, 11 (1980), 289–307.

Friedman, Michael H., *The Making of a Tory Humanist: William Wordsworth and the Idea of Community* (New York, 1979).

Fry, Michael, *The Dundas Despotism* (Edinburgh, 1992).

Fulford, Roger, *Samuel Whitbread 1764–1815: A Study in Opposition* (1967).

Fyfe, Aileen, 'The Reception of William Paley's *Natural Theology* in the University of Cambridge', *British Journal for the History of Science*, 30 (1997), 321–35.

Gallagher, Catharine, *The Industrial Reformation of English Fiction 1832–1867* (Chicago, 1985).

Gambles, Anna, *Protection and Politics: Conservative Economic Discourse, 1815–1852* (Woodbridge, 1999).

Gascoigne, John, *Cambridge in the Age of Enlightenment: Science, Religion and Politics from the Restoration to the French Revolution* (Cambridge, 1989).

Gaull, Marilyn, 'Malthus on the Road to Excess', in Richard Cronin (ed.), *1798: The Year of the* Lyrical Ballads (Basingstoke, 1998), 93–107.

Gill, Stephen, *William Wordsworth: A Life* (Oxford, 1989).

—— *Wordsworth and the Victorians* (Oxford, 1998).

—— 'Wordsworth's Breeches Pocket: Attitudes to the Didactic Poet', *Essays in Criticism*, 19 (1969), 385–401.

Gilley, Sheridan, 'Nationality and Liberty, Protestant and Catholic: Robert Southey's Book of the Church', *Studies in Church History*, 18 (1982), 409–32.

Gilmartin, Kevin, *Print Politics: The Press and Radical Opposition in Early Nineteenth-Century England* (Cambridge, 1996).

Glen, Heather, *Vision and Disenchantment: Blake's* Songs *and Wordsworth's* Lyrical Ballads (Cambridge, 1983).

Goldman, Lawrence, 'A Peculiarity of the English? The Social Science Association and the Absence of Sociology in Nineteenth-Century Britain', *Past and Present*, 114 (1987), 133–71.

Goldstrum, Max, 'Popular Political Economy for the British Working Class Reader in the Nineteenth Century', in Terry Shinn and Richard Whitley (eds.), *Expository Science: Forms and Functions of Popularization* (Dordrecht, 1985), 259–73.

Gordon, Barry, *Economic Doctrine and Tory Liberalism 1824–1830* (Basingstoke, 1979).

Gorman, Frank, 'Pitt and the "Tory" Reaction to the French Revolution 1789–1815', in H. T. Dickinson (ed.), *Britain and the French Revolution 1789–1815* (Basingstoke, 1989), 21–37.

Grampp, William D., 'Classical Economics and its Moral Critics', *History of Political Economy*, 5 (1973), 359–74.

Gray, Robert, *The Factory Question and Industrial England, 1830–1860* (Cambridge, 1996).

Gunn, J. A. W., *Beyond Liberty and Property: The Process of Self-Recognition in Eighteenth-Century Political Thought* (Kingston, Ont., 1983).

Haakonssen, Knud, 'From Moral Philosophy to Political Economy: The Contribution of Dugald Stewart', in V. Hope (ed.), *Philosophers of the Scottish Enlightenment* (Edinburgh, 1984), 211–32.

Halévy, Elie, *The Growth of Philosophic Radicalism*, trans. Mary Morris (1928).

Hall, Stuart, 'Cultural Studies and its Theoretical Legacies', in Lawrence Grossberg *et al.* (eds.), *Cultural Studies* (New York, 1992), 277–86.

Hamburger, Joseph, *James Mill and the Art of Revolution* (New Haven, 1963).

Hamilton, Paul, *Wordsworth* (Brighton, 1986).

Harling, Philip, 'Leigh Hunt's *Examiner* and the Language of Patriotism', *Historical Journal*, 61 (1996), 1159–81.

—— 'Robert Southey and the Language of Social Discipline', *Albion*, 30 (1998), 630–55.

—— *The Waning of 'Old Corruption': The Politics of Economical Reform in Britain, 1779–1846* (Oxford, 1996).

Harris, Wendell V., 'Interpretive Historicism: "Signs of the Times" and *Culture and Anarchy* in their Contexts', *Nineteenth-Century Literature*, 44 (1990), 441–64.

Harrison, Gary, *Wordsworth's Vagrant Muse: Poetry, Poverty and Power* (Detroit, 1994).

Harvey, A. D., 'The Ministry of All the Talents: The Whigs in Office, February 1806 to March 1807', *Historical Journal*, 15 (1972), 619–48.

Heavner, Eric K., 'Malthus and the Secularization of Political Ideology', *History of Political Thought*, 27 (1996), 408–30.

Heinzelman, Kurt, *The Economics of the Imagination* (Amherst, 1980).

Hemingway, Andrew, 'Genius, Gender and Progress: Benthamism and the Arts in the 1820s', *Art History*, 16 (1992), 619–46.

Heyck, T. W., *The Transformation of Intellectual Life in Victorian England* (1982).

Hickey, Alison, *Impure Conceits: Rhetoric and Ideology in Wordsworth's 'Excursion'* (Stanford, Calif., 1997).

Hilton, Boyd, *The Age of Atonement: The Influence of Evangelicalism on Social and Economic Thought 1785–1865*, 2nd edn. (Oxford, 1991).

—— 'Chalmers as Political Economist', in A. C. Cheyne (ed.), *The Practical and the Pious: Essays on Thomas Chalmers* (Edinburgh, 1985), 141–56.

—— *Corn, Cash, Commerce: The Economic Policies of the Tory Governments 1815–1830* (Oxford, 1977).

Himmelfarb, Gertrude, *The Idea of Poverty: England in the Early Industrial Age* (1984).

Hind, Robert J., 'Working People and Sunday Schools: England, 1780–1850', *Journal of Religious History*, 15 (1988), 199–218.

Hoagwood, Terence Allan, *Skepticism and Ideology: Shelley's Political Prose and its Philosophical Context from Bacon to Marx* (Iowa City, 1988).

Hodder, Edwin, *The Life and Work of the Seventh Earl of Shaftesbury, K.G.*, 3 vols. (1886).

Hogle, Jerrold E., *Shelley's Process: Radical Transference and the Development of his Major Works* (New York, 1988).

Hole, Robert, *Pulpits, Politics and Public Order in England 1760–1832* (Cambridge, 1989).

Holloway, John, *The Victorian Sage: Studies in Argument* (1953).

Holmes, Richard, *Shelley: The Pursuit* (1974).

Hone, J. Ann, *For the Cause of Truth: Radicalism in London 1796–1821* (Oxford, 1982).

Hont, Istvan, and Ignatieff, Michael (eds.), *Wealth and Virtue: The Shaping of Political Economy in the Scottish Enlightenment* (Cambridge, 1985).

Hough, Graham, 'Coleridge and the Victorians', in Hugh Sykes Davies and George Watson (eds.), *The English Mind: Studies in the English Moralists Presented to Basil Willey* (Cambridge, 1964), 175–92.

Howe, P. P., *The Life of William Hazlitt* (1922).

Howse, Ernest Marshall, *Saints in Politics: The 'Clapham Sect' and the Growth of Freedom* (1952), new edn. (1971).

Hutchison, T. W., *On Revolutions and Progress in Economic Knowledge* (Cambridge, 1978).

Innes, Joanna, 'Politics and Morals: The Reformation of Manners Movement in Later Eighteenth-Century England', in Eckhart Hellmuth (ed.), *The Transformation of Political Culture: England and Germany in the Late Eighteenth Century* (Oxford, 1990), 57–118.

Jacobus, Mary, *Tradition and Experiment in Wordsworth's* Lyrical Ballads *(1798)* (Oxford, 1976).

James, Patricia, *Population Malthus: His Life and Times* (1979).

Jarvis, Robin, *Romantic Writing and Pedestrian Travel* (Basingstoke, 1997).

—— 'Wordsworth and the Uses of Charity', in Stephen Copley and John Whale (eds.), *Beyond Romanticism: New Approaches to Texts and Contexts 1780–1832* (1992), 200–17.

Johnson, Richard, 'Educational Policy and Social Control in Early Victorian England', *Past and Present*, 49 (1970), 96–119.

Johnston, Kenneth, *The Hidden Wordsworth: Poet, Lover, Rebel, Spy* (New York, 1998).

—— *Wordsworth and* The Recluse (New Haven, 1984).

Joyce, Patrick, *Visions of the People: Industrial England and the Question of Class, 1848–1914* (Cambridge, 1991).

Kaiser, David Aram, '"The Perfection of Reason": Coleridge and the Ancient Constitution', *Studies in Romanticism*, 32 (1993), 29–55.

Keach, William, 'Cockney Couplets: Keats and the Politics of Style', *Studies in Romanticism*, 25 (1986), 182–96.

Kegel, Charles H., 'William Cobbett and Malthusianism', *Journal of the History of Ideas*, 19 (1958), 348–62.

Kennedy, William F., *Humanist versus Economist: The Economic Thought of Samuel Taylor Coleridge* (1958), new edn. (Westport, Conn., 1978).

Kent, Christopher, 'Higher Journalism and the Mid-Victorian Clerisy', *Victorian Studies*, 13 (1969), 181–98.

Kinnaird, John, *William Hazlitt: Critic of Power* (New York, 1978).

Klancher, Jon P., *The Making of English Reading Audiences, 1790–1832* (Madison, 1987).

Klein, Lawrence E., *Shaftesbury and the Culture of Politeness: Moral Discourse and Cultural Politics in Early Eighteenth-Century England* (Cambridge, 1994).

Knight, Frida, *University Rebel: The Life of William Frend (1757–1841)* (1971).

Knights, Ben, *The Idea of the Clerisy in the Nineteenth Century* (Cambridge, 1978).

Knott, John, *Popular Opposition to the 1834 Poor Law* (1986).

Koch, Mark, 'Utilitarian and Reactionary Arguments for Almsgiving in Wordsworth's "The Old Cumberland Beggar"', *Eighteenth-Century Life*, NS 13 (1989), 18–33.

Kopf, David, *British Orientalism and the Bengal Renaissance: The Dynamics of Indian Modernization 1773–1835* (Berkeley, Calif., 1969).

Landré, Louis, *Leigh Hunt (1784–1859): Contribution à l'histoire du Romantisme anglais*, 2 vols. (Paris, 1935–6).

Langan, Celeste, *Romantic Vagrancy: Wordsworth and the Simulation of Freedom* (Cambridge, 1995).

Laqueur, Thomas Walter, *Religion and Respectability: Sunday Schools and Working Class Culture 1780–1850* (New Haven, 1976).

Leask, Nigel, *British Romantic Writers and the East: Anxieties of Empire* (Cambridge, 1992).

——*The Politics of Imagination in Coleridge's Critical Thought* (Basingstoke, 1988).

——'Toward a Universal Aesthetic: De Quincey on Murder as Carnival and Tragedy', in John Beer (ed.), *Questioning Romanticism* (Baltimore, 1995), 92–120.

Leavis, F. R., 'Introduction' to J. S. Mill, *Mill on Bentham and Coleridge* (1950), 3rd edn. (1962).

LeMahieu, D. L., 'Malthus and the Theology of Scarcity', *Journal of the History of Ideas*, 40 (1979), 467–74.

——*The Mind of William Paley: A Philosopher and his Age* (Lincoln, Neb., 1976).

Lepenies, Wolf, *Die Drei Kulturen* (1985), trans. R. J. Hollingdale as *Between Literature and Science: The Rise of Sociology* (Cambridge, 1988).

Liu, Alan, *Wordsworth: The Sense of History* (Stanford, Calif., 1989).
Lloyd, David, and Thomas, Paul, *Culture and the State* (New York, 1998).
Lubenow, W. C., *The Cambridge Apostles, 1820–1914: Liberalism, Imagination and Friendship in British Intellectual Life* (Cambridge, 1998).
Lyons, Judson Stanley, *The Excursion: A Study* (New Haven, 1950).
McDonagh, Josephine, *De Quincey's Disciplines* (Oxford, 1994).
McGann, Jerome, *The Romantic Ideology: A Critical Investigation* (Chicago, 1983).
Machin, G. I. T., *The Catholic Question in English Politics 1820 to 1830* (Oxford, 1964).
McKendrick, Neil, '"Gentlemen and Players" Revisited: The Gentlemanly Ideal, the Business Ideal and the Professional Ideal in English Literary Culture', in id. and R. B. Outhwaite (eds.), *Business Life and Public Policy: Essays in Honour of D. C. Coleman* (Cambridge, 1986), 98–136.
——*et al.*, *The Birth of a Consumer Society: The Commercialization of Eighteenth-Century Society* (1982).
MacKillop, Ian, *F. R. Leavis: A Life in Criticism* (Harmondsworth, 1995).
MacLean, Kenneth, *Agrarian Age: A Background for Wordsworth* (New Haven, 1950).
Majeed, Javed, *Ungoverned Imaginings: James Mill's* The History of British India *and Orientalism* (Oxford, 1992).
Main, J. M., 'Radical Westminster, 1807–1820', *Historical Studies: Australia and New Zealand*, 12 (1965–7), 186–204.
Mandler, Peter, 'The Making of the New Poor Law Redivivus', *Past and Present*, 117 (1987), 131–57.
Maniquis, Robert, 'Lonely Empires: Personal and Public Visions of Thomas De Quincey', *Literary Monographs*, 8 (1976), 47–127.
Marchand, Leslie A., *The Athenaeum: A Mirror of Victorian Culture* (New York, 1971).
Mayo, Robert, 'The Contemporaneity of the *Lyrical Ballads*', *Publications of the Modern Language Association of America*, 69 (1954), 486–522.
Meek, Ronald L., *The Economics of Physiocracy: Essays and Translations* (1962).
Mendilow, Jonathan, *The Romantic Tradition in British Political Thought* (1986).
Merritt, Travis R., 'Taste, Opinion, and Theory in the Rise of Victorian Prose Stylism', in George Levine and William Madden (eds.), *The Art of Victorian Prose* (New York, 1986), 3–38.
Morris, R. J., *Class, Sect and Party: The Making of the British Middle Class, Leeds 1820–1850* (Manchester, 1990).
Morrow, John, 'Coleridge and the National Church', in Gordon J. Schochet (ed.), *Empire and Revolutions* (Washington, 1993), 333–45.
——*Coleridge's Political Thought: Property, Morality and the Limits of Traditional Discourse* (Basingstoke, 1990).

Mulhern, Francis, *The Moment of 'Scrutiny'* (1979).

Mulvihill, James, 'The Poetics of Utility: Benthamite Literary Reviewing, 1824–1836', *English Studies in Canada*, 15 (1989), 149–61.

Murphy, Peter T., 'Impersonation and Authorship in Romantic Britain', *English Literary History*, 59 (1992), 625–49.

Nairn, Tom, 'The English Literary Intelligentsia', in *Bananas*, ed. Emma Tennant (1977), 57–83.

—— 'The Future of Britain's Crisis: A Political Analysis', in Isaac Kramnick (ed.), *Is Britain Dying? Perspectives on the Current Crisis* (Ithaca, NY, 1979), 233–68.

Osborne, John W., *William Cobbett: His Thought and his Times* (New Brunswick, 1966).

Palmer, D. J., *The Rise of English Studies: An Account of the Study of English Language and Literature from its Origins to the Making of the Oxford English School* (1965).

Park, Roy, *Hazlitt and the Spirit of the Age: Abstraction and Critical Theory* (Oxford, 1971).

Parry, Jonathan, *The Rise and Fall of Liberal Government in Victorian Britain* (New Haven, 1993).

Patterson, M. W., *Sir Francis Burdett and his Times (1770–1844)*, 2 vols. (1931).

Paulin, Tom, *The Day-Star of Liberty: William Hazlitt's Radical Style* (1998).

Petersen, William, *Malthus* (1971).

Pfau, Thomas, *Wordsworth's Profession: Form, Class, and the Logic of Early Romantic Cultural Production* (Stanford, Calif., 1997).

Phillipson, Nicholas, 'The Pursuit of Virtue in Scottish University Education: Dugald Stewart and Scottish Moral Philosophy in the Enlightenment', in id. (ed.), *Universities, Society, and the Future* (Edinburgh, 1983), 82–101.

—— 'The Scottish Enlightenment', in Roy Porter and Mikulàs Teich (eds.), *The Enlightenment in National Context* (Cambridge, 1981), 19–40.

Pocock, J. G. A., 'Clergy and Commerce: The Conservative Enlightenment in England', in R. Ajello *et al.* (eds.), *L'Età dei Lumi: Studi Storici sul Settecento Europeo in Onore di Franco Venturi*, 2 vols. (Naples, 1985), i. 525–62.

—— 'Empire, Revolution and the End of Early Modernity', in id. *et al.* (eds.), *The Varieties of British Political Thought, 1500–1800* (Cambridge, 1993), 283–317.

—— *Virtue, Commerce, and History: Essays on Political Thought and History, Chiefly in the Eighteenth Century* (Cambridge, 1985).

Porter, Andrew, '"Commerce and Christianity": The Rise and Fall of a Nineteenth-Century Missionary Slogan', *Historical Journal*, 28 (1985), 597–621.

Porter, Roy, 'Reforming the Patient in the Age of Reform: Thomas Beddoes and Medical Practice', in Roger French and Andrew Wear (eds.), *British Medicine in the Age of Reform* (1991), 9–17.

Poynter, J. R., *Society and Pauperism: English Ideas on Poor Relief, 1795–1834* (1969).

Prawer, S. S., *Karl Marx and World Literature* (Oxford, 1978).

Prickett, Stephen, *Romanticism and Religion: The Tradition of Wordsworth and Coleridge in the Victorian Church* (Cambridge, 1976).

Pullen, J. M., 'Malthus's Theological Ideas and their Influence on his Principle of Population', *History of Political Economy*, 13 (1981), 39–54.

Pulos, C. E., 'Shelley and Malthus', *Publications of the Modern Language Association of America*, 67 (1952), 113–24.

Rashid, Salim, 'David Robinson and the Tory Macroeconomics of *Blackwood's Edinburgh Magazine*', *History of Political Economy*, 10 (1978), 258–70.

—— 'Economists and the Age of Chivalry: Notes on a Passage in Burke's *Reflections*', *Eighteenth-Century Studies*, 20 (1986), 56–61.

—— 'Political Economy as Moral Philosophy: Dugald Stewart of Edinburgh', *Australian Economic Papers*, 26 (1987), 145–56.

Raven, James, 'British History and the Enterprise Culture', *Past and Present*, 123 (1989), 178–204.

Redman, Deborah A., *The Rise of Political Economy as a Science: Methodology and the Classical Economists* (Cambridge, Mass., 1997).

Reiman, Donald H., 'Shelley as Agrarian Reactionary', *Keats–Shelley Memorial Bulletin*, 30 (1979), 5–15.

Richardson, Alan, *Literature, Education, and Romanticism: Reading as Social Practice, 1780–1832* (Cambridge, 1994).

Rieder, John, *Wordsworth's Counterrevolutionary Turn: Community, Virtue, and Vision in the 1790s* (1997).

Roberts, Daniel Sanjiv, *Revisionary Gleam: De Quincey, Coleridge, and the High Romantic Argument* (Liverpool, 2000).

Roberts, David, *Paternalism in Early Victorian England* (1979).

Roberts, Michael, *The Whig Party 1807–1812* (1939), 2nd edn. (1965).

Roberts, Michael J. D., 'Head versus Heart? Voluntary Associations and Charity Organizations in England, *c.*1700–1850', in Hugh Cunningham and Joanna Innes (eds.), *Charity, Philanthropy and Reform: From the 1690s to 1850* (Basingstoke, 1998), 66–86.

Roe, Nicholas, *John Keats and the Culture of Dissent* (Oxford, 1997).

—— *Wordsworth and Coleridge: The Radical Years* (Oxford, 1988).

Rosen, F., *Bentham, Byron, and Greece: Constitutionalism, Nationalism and Early Liberal Political Thought* (Oxford, 1992).

Rothschild, Emma, 'Adam Smith and Conservative Economics', *Economic History Review*, 2nd ser., 45 (1992), 74–96.

Rubinstein, W. D., *Capitalism, Culture, and Decline in Britain 1750–1990* (1993).

Ryan, Cheyney C., 'The Fiends of Commerce: Romantic and Marxist Criticisms of Classical Political Economy', *History of Political Economy*, 13 (1981), 80–94.

Sack, James J., *From Jacobite to Conservative: Reaction and Orthodoxy in Britain, c.1760–1832* (Cambridge, 1993).

—— *The Grenvillites 1801–29: Party Politics and Factionalism in the Age of Pitt and Liverpool* (Urbana, Ill., 1979).

—— 'The Memory of Burke and the Memory of Pitt: English Conservatism Confronts its Past, 1806–1829', *Historical Journal*, 30 (1987), 623–40.

St Clair, William, *The Godwins and the Shelleys: The Biography of a Family* (1989).

Salmon, David, *Joseph Lancaster* (1904).

Sampson, David, 'Wordsworth and the Poor: The Poetry of Survival', *Studies in Romanticism*, 23 (1984), 31–59.

Santurri, Edmund N., 'Theodicy and Social Policy in Malthus's Thought', *Journal of the History of Ideas*, 63 (1982), 315–30.

Scheffer, John D., 'The Idea of Decline in Literature and the Fine Arts in Eighteenth-Century England', *Modern Philology*, 34 (1936–7), 155–78.

Schneewind, J. B., *Sidgwick's Ethics and Victorian Moral Philosophy* (Oxford, 1977).

Schneider, Ben Ross, *Wordsworth's Cambridge Education* (Cambridge, 1957).

Schoenfield, Mark, *The Professional Wordsworth: Law, Labor and the Poet's Contract* (Athens, Ga., 1996).

Schofield, Thomas Philip, 'Conservative Political Thought in Britain in Response to the French Revolution', *Historical Journal*, 29 (1986), 601–22.

Scrivener, Michael Henry, *Radical Shelley: The Philosophical Anarchism and Utopian Thought of Percy Bysshe Shelley* (Princeton, 1982).

Searle, G. R., *Morality and the Market in Victorian Britain* (Oxford, 1998).

Seed, John, 'Unitarianism, Political Economy and the Antinomies of Liberal Culture in Manchester, 1830–50', *Social History*, 7 (1982), 1–25.

Semmel, Bernard, *The Rise of Free Trade Imperialism: Classical Political Economy and the Empire of Free Trade Imperialism 1750–1850* (Cambridge, 1970).

Shaffer, E. S., *'Kubla Khan' and the Fall of Jerusalem: The Mythological School in Biblical Criticism and Secular Literature 1770–1880* (Cambridge, 1975).

Sher, Richard B., *Church and University in the Scottish Enlightenment: The Moderate Literati of Edinburgh* (Princeton, 1985).

Sigsworth, Eric M. (ed.), *In Search of Victorian Values: Aspects of Nineteenth-Century Thought and Society* (Manchester, 1988).

Silverberg, Norman J., 'Financial and Monetary Policy of Great Britain during the Napoleonic Wars', *Quarterly Journal of Economics*, 38 (1924), 214–33.

Simon, Brian, *The Two Nations and the Educational Structure 1780–1870* (1960), new edn. (1974).

Simpson, David, *Romanticism, Nationalism, and the Revolt against Theory* (Chicago, 1993).

——*Wordsworth's Historical Imagination: The Poetry of Displacement* (New York, 1987).

Sinfield, Alan, *Literature Politics and Culture in Postwar Britain*, rev. edn. (1997).

Smith, Kenneth, *The Malthusian Controversy* (1951).

Smout, T. C. (ed.), *Victorian Values* (Proceedings of the British Academy, 78; Oxford, 1992).

Snow, C. P., *The Two Cultures* (1959), ed. Stefan Collini (Cambridge, 1993).

Soloway, R. A., *Prelates and People: Ecclesiastical Social Thought in England 1783–1852* (1969).

Spater, George, *William Cobbett: The Poor Man's Friend*, 2 vols. (1982).

Spence, Peter, *The Birth of Romantic Radicalism: War, Popular Politics and English Radical Reformism, 1800–1815* (Aldershot, 1996).

Spivak, Gayatri Chakravorty, 'Sex and History in *The Prelude* (1805): Books Nine to Thirteen', *Texas Studies in Language and Literature*, 23 (1981), 324–60.

Stedman Jones, Gareth, *Languages of Class: Studies in English Working Class History 1832–1982* (Cambridge, 1983).

Stewart-Robinson, Charles, 'The Pneumatics and Georgics of the Scottish Mind', *Eighteenth-Century Studies*, 20 (1987), 296–312.

Stokes, Eric, *The English Utilitarians and India* (Oxford, 1959).

Stone, Lawrence (ed.), *An Imperial State at War: Britain from 1689 to 1815* (1994).

Storey, Mark, *Robert Southey: A Life* (Oxford, 1997).

Thomas, Gordon Kent, *Wordsworth's Dirge and Promise: Napoleon, Wellington, and the Convention of Cintra* (Lincoln, Neb., 1971).

Thomas, William, *The Philosophic Radicals: Nine Studies in Theory and Practice 1817–1841* (Oxford, 1979).

Thompson, E. P., *Customs in Common* (1991).

——*The Making of the English Working Class* (1963).

——*The Poverty of Theory and Other Essays* (1978).

——*The Romantics: England in a Revolutionary Age* (Woodbridge, 1997).

Thompson, Noel W., *The People's Science: The Popular Political Economy of Exploitation and Crisis 1816–34* (Cambridge, 1984).

Thorslev, Peter L., Jr., 'Post-Waterloo Liberalism: The Second Generation', *Studies in Romanticism*, 28 (1983), 437–61.

Trott, Nicola, 'The Coleridge Circle and "The Answer to Godwin"', *Review of English Studies*, NS 41 (1990), 212–29.

Turner, Frank M., *Contesting Cultural Authority: Essays in Victorian Intellectual Life* (Cambridge, 1993).

Tyson, Gerald P., *Joseph Johnson: A Liberal Publisher* (Iowa City, 1979).

Uphaus, Robert W., 'Vicesimus Knox and the Canon of Eighteenth-Century Literature', *The Age of Johnson*, 4 (1991), 345–61.

Vincent, Emma, '"The Real Grounds of the Present War": John Bowles and the French Revolutionary Wars, 1792–1802', *History*, 78 (1993), 393–420.

Viswanathan, Gauri, *Masks of Conquest: Literary Study and British Rule in India* (1990).

Wach, Howard M., 'Culture and the Middle Classes: Popular Knowledge in Industrial Manchester', *Journal of British Studies*, 27 (1988), 375–404.

Wahrman, Dror, *Imagining the Middle Class: The Political Representation of Class in Britain,* c.*1780–1840* (Cambridge, 1995).

Wallace, Anne D., *Walking, Literature, and English Culture: The Origins and Uses of Peripatetic in the Nineteenth Century* (Oxford, 1993).

Waterman, A. M. C., *Revolution, Economics and Religion: Christian Political Economy, 1798–1833* (Cambridge, 1991).

Webster, Anthony, 'The Political Economy of Trade Liberalization: The East India Company Charter Act of 1813', *Economic History Review*, 2nd ser., 43 (1990), 404–19.

Wedd, Mary, 'Industrialization and the Moral Law in Books VIII and IX of *The Excursion*', *Charles Lamb Bulletin*, NS 81 (1993), 5–25.

Wells, Roger, 'The Moral Economy of the English Countryside', in Adrian Randall and Andrew Charlesworth (eds.), *Moral Economy and Popular Protest: Crowds, Conflict and Authority* (Basingstoke, 2000), 209–71.

Whale, John, 'Hazlitt on Burke: The Ambivalent Position of a Radical Essayist', *Studies in Romanticism*, 25 (1986), 465–81.

Whalley, George, 'England: Romantic—Romanticism', in Hans Eichner (ed.), *'Romantic' and its Cognates: The European History of a Word* (Manchester, 1972), 157–262.

Wheatley, Kim, 'The *Blackwood's* Attacks on Leigh Hunt', *Nineteenth-Century Literature*, 47 (1992), 1–31.

White, Hayden, *Metahistory: The Historical Imagination in Nineteenth-Century Europe* (Baltimore, 1973).

Wiener, Joel H., *Radicalism and Freethought in Nineteenth Century Britain: The Life of Richard Carlile* (Westport, Conn., 1983).

Wiener, Martin, *English Culture and the Decline of the Industrial Spirit 1850–1980* (Cambridge, 1981).

Williams, John, *Wordsworth: Romantic Poetry and Revolution Politics* (Manchester, 1989).

Williams, Orlo, *Lamb's Friend the Census-Taker: Life and Letters of John Rickman* (1912).

Williams, Raymond, *Cobbett* (Oxford, 1983).
——*Culture and Society 1790–1950* (1958).
——*The Long Revolution* (1961).
——*Politics and Letters: Interviews with* New Left Review (1979).
Wilson, Kathleen, *The Sense of the People: Politics, Culture and Imperialism in England, 1715–1785* (Cambridge, 1995).
Winch, Donald, *Adam Smith's Politics: An Essay in Historiographic Revision* (Cambridge, 1978).
——*Riches and Poverty: An Intellectual History of Political Economy in Britain, 1750–1834* (Cambridge, 1996).
Witherington, Donald J., 'Education and Society in the Eighteenth Century', in N. T. Phillipson and Rosalind Mitchison (eds.), *Scotland in the Age of Improvement: Essays in Scottish History in the Eighteenth Century*, new edn. (Edinburgh, 1996), 169–99.
Wolfson, Susan, *The Questioning Presence: Wordsworth, Keats, and the Interrogative Method in Romantic Poetry* (Ithaca, NY, 1986).
Wolff, Janet, and Seed, John (eds.), *The Culture of Capital: Art, Power and the Nineteenth-Century Middle Class* (Manchester, 1988).
Woodring, Carl, 'Leigh Hunt as Political Essayist', in Leigh Hunt, *Political and Occasional Essays*, ed. Lawrence Huston Houtchens and Carolyn Washburn Houtchens (New York, 1962), 3–71.
——*Politics in English Romantic Poetry* (Cambridge, Mass., 1970).
Wordsworth, Jonathan, 'On Man, on Nature, and on Human Life', *Review of English Studies*, NS 31 (1980), 2–29.
——'Revision as Making: *The Prelude* and its Peers', in Robert Brinkley and Keith Hanley (eds.), *Romantic Revisions* (Cambridge, 1992), 18–42.
——*William Wordsworth: The Borders of Vision* (Oxford, 1982).

Unpublished Dissertations

Craig, David, 'Republicanism Becoming Conservative: Robert Southey and Political Argument in Britain, *c.*1790–1817', University of Cambridge doctoral dissertation, in progress.
McCalman, Iain, 'Popular Radicalism and Freethought in Early Nineteenth-Century England: A Study of Richard Carlile and his Followers, 1815–32', Australian National University MA (1975).
Milne, J. M., 'The Politics of *Blackwood's*, 1817–1846: A Study of the Political, Economic and Social Articles in *Blackwood's Edinburgh Magazine*, and of Selected Contributors', Newcastle University Ph.D. (1984).
Seed, John, 'The Role of Unitarianism in the Formation of Liberal Culture 1775–1851: A Social History', University of Hull Ph.D. (1981).

OFFICIAL PUBLICATIONS AND WORKS OF REFERENCE

Dictionary of National Biography

Hansard's Parliamentary Debates

Houghton, Walter E., *et al.* (eds.), *The Wellesley Index to Victorian Periodicals*, 5 vols. (Toronto, 1966–89).

Public General Statutes

Reed, Mark L., *Wordsworth: The Chronology of the Early Years 1770–1799* (Cambridge, Mass., 1967).

——*Wordsworth: The Chronology of the Middle Years 1800–1815* (Cambridge, Mass., 1975).

Shine, Hill, and Shine, Helen Chadwick, *The Quarterly Review under Gifford: Identification of Contributors 1809–1824* (Chapel Hill, NY, 1949).

Stephens, Frederick George, and George, Mary Dorothy, *A Catalogue of Political and Personal Satires Preserved in the Department of Prints and Drawings in the British Museum*, 11 vols. (1870–1954).

Strout, A. L., *A Bibliography of Articles in Blackwood's Magazine, 1817–1825* (Lubbock, Tex., 1959).

Wu, Duncan, *Wordsworth's Reading 1770–1799* (Cambridge, 1993).

——*Wordsworth's Reading 1800–1815* (Cambridge, 1995).

Index